Fighting for Honor

The Carolina Lowcountry and the Atlantic World

Sponsored by the Carolina Lowcountry and Atlantic World Program of the College of Charleston

Money, Trade, and Power
Edited by Jack P. Greene, Rosemary Brana-Shute, and Randy J. Sparks

The Impact of the Haitian Revolution in the Atlantic World
Edited by David P. Geggus

London Booksellers and American Customers
James Raven

Memory and Identity
Edited by Bertrand Van Ruymbeke and Randy J. Sparks

This Remote Part of the World
Bradford J. Wood

The Final Victims
James A. McMillin

The Atlantic Economy during the Seventeenth and Eighteenth Centuries
Edited by Peter A. Coclanis

From New Babylon to Eden
Bertrand Van Ruymbeke

Saints and Their Cults in the Atlantic World
Edited by Margaret Cormack

Who Shall Rule at Home?
Jonathan Mercantini

To Make This Land Our Own
Arlin C. Migliazzo

Votaries of Apollo
Nicholas Michael Butler

Fighting for Honor
T. J. Desch-Obi

Fighting for Honor

The History of African Martial Art Traditions in the Atlantic World

T. J. Desch-Obi

THE UNIVERSITY OF
SOUTH CAROLINA PRESS

Cloth edition published by the University of South Carolina Press, 2008
Paperback and ebook editions published in Columbia, South Carolina,
by the University of South Carolina Press, 2021

www.uscpress.com

Manufactured in the United States of America

30 29 28 27 26 25 24 23 22 21
10 9 8 7 6 5 4 3 2 1

The Library of Congress has cataloged the cloth edition as follows:

Desch-Obi, M. Thomas J.
Fighting for honor : the history of African martial art traditions in the Atlantic world / T.J. Desch Obi.
p. cm. — (Carolina lowcountry and the Atlantic world)
Includes bibliographical references and index.
ISBN-13: 978-1-57003-718-4 (cloth : alk. paper)
ISBN-10: 1-57003-718-3 (cloth : alk. paper)
1. Martial arts—Africa. 2. Martial arts—North America. 3. Martial arts—South America. 4. Martial arts—History. 5. Martial arts—Anthropological aspects. I. Title.
GV1100.82D47 2008
796.81—dc22

2007043186

ISBN 978-1-64336-192-5 (paperback)
ISBN 978-1-64336-193-2 (ebook)

For my father

Contents

Illustrations

Figures

Maps

Acknowledgments

This book has been well over a decade in the making, and in that time I have accumulated unpayable debts and invaluable friendships. Several institutions contributed research funding: the Social Science Research Council, the Fulbright Fellowship Program, the University of California's Presidential Fellowship Program, the Ford Foundation, the City University of New York's PSC CUNY Program, the Eugene M. Lang Research Fellowship, and the National Endowment for the Humanities. My sincere appreciation goes to Herman Henning for seeing the value in this project. I am grateful to the staffs at Penn Center; the National Archives of Namibia; Arquivo Historico in Luanda Angola; Archives Generales Congregation du Saint-Esprit, Chivilly-Larue, France; Archive Coloniales, Paris; Arquivo Nacional, Rio de Janeiro; and Arquivo Publico Do Estado, Rio de Janeiro. A special thanks to Louisa Moy and the rest of the interlibrary loan department at Baruch College.

Beyond the people who helped me with earlier phases of research, I have had the support of numerous mentors, colleagues, and friends. Edward A. Alpers has continued to be a great source of insight and support. Christopher Ehret has been a patient mentor in historical linguistics and a constant resource. The insights of Michael Gomez, whose work has been an inspiration to me, have been a great help in the revisions of this text. I am exceedingly grateful to these three mentors for their unwavering guidance and support. While all mistakes in this book are my own, the credit for many insights belong to these mentors and various other scholars whose thoughtful scholarship and feedback I can only hope to emulate: John K. Thornton, Mary Karesch, Linda Heywood, Maria Conceção Neto, Christopher Kouri, Robert F. Thompson, Fu-Kiau kia Bunseki, Dominique Cyrille, Laurent Dubois, Kesha Fikes, Patrick Bellegarde-Smith, Victor Manfredi, Ivor Miller, Ras Michael Brown, and James Sweet. The latter three and David Geggus were kind enough to share unpublished materials with me. A special thanks to the late John Gwaltney, who brought me to an entirely unknown world, and to C. Daniel Dawson, who continues to introduce me to new worlds and ideas. I am grateful to my editor, Alex Moore, for his continued patience and support.

That I have been able to write a history of martial art traditions is due to the people who have guided me to the real experts and the openness of these masters to share their wisdom with me. I would like to pay tribute to my family members in Nigeria, the late Professor Boniface Obichere, and the various *di-mgba* who taught me. In the lowcountry and in Surry County, Virginia, I was blessed to be counted as part of the family of Flowers Jefferson, and I learned from Deacon Johnson, Deacon Robinson Ezekiel Mack, Mike Cohen, Herman Cunningham, and numerous others. In my more recent trips to the Caribbean, I have been warmly welcomed and guided by Maria Vicente, David Alexandre, Association Mi Mes Manmay Matnik (AM4), Pierre Dru, Daniel Georges Bardury, the Bausivoir family, Luc-Wans Duvalsaint, Modesto Cepeda, Tato Conrad, Jaques Komorn, and various martial art teachers, including Masters Yeye, Fronfrons, Rapsode, Dantes, Venture, Harpan Ti-Jean, and Petit Jolibois. Although the material was not overtly integrated into the manuscript, I gained much of my understanding of the other martial arts of the Central Africa and the Indian Ocean through the help of Katuku Wa Yemba, Jean-René Dreinaza, T'Keyah Crystal Keymah, Col. Charles Mambwe, Lubangi Muniania, David Togba, and Coloniel Muniania *et famille*. In Cuba and Venezuela I was taught by Lizette Carrion, Osvaldo Hernandez, Marcos Elizarde, Ignaco Piñero, Hector Ramos, Eduardo Sanoja, and Master Mercedes Perez. *O meu profundo reconhecimento à Paula Webba e familia, Governador Mutinde, Nando Walter, Justo Pedro, Frederico José de Abreu, Mestre Cobrinha e meu mestre, João Grande. Os meus eternos agradecimentos ao Gabriel Mangumbala e aos mestres de engolo, particularmente onongo wengolo Angelino.*

Special mention should be made of some of the many people who helped me through the process leading to this book. All translation errors are my own, but I am grateful to Arminda Lima, Joana Mendes, Aurora Maixim Tartare, and Dominique Cyrille for their help with translations and orthography. How can I begin to thank Johnita Due and Chris and Andrea Almeida-Mack for virtually managing my life while I was out of the country? Thanks to Carolyn Vieira-Martinez and Hileni Josephat for their moral support and help through the methodological process of historical linguistics. Mark Feijão Milligan was kind enough to lend his fabulous artistic skills to all the maps and illustrations. Many careful readers have shared their keen eyes, insights, and support, including Kathryn Pense, Andrea Almeida-Mac, Kathryn Dentinger, Dina Paul-Parks, Steve Faison, Yuko Miki, Antonio Tomás, Deolinda da Fonseca, Stella Auala, Imani Johnson, Edwina Ashie-Nikoi, Thomas Bartylla, Bernadette Atuahene, Salim Rollins, James Stanford, Malissa Masala, Michael Desharnes, Stephen Jackowicz, Brenton Wynn, and of course Sifu Mark Cheng. I would be remiss if I did not extend a special acknowledgment to those who were deepest in the trenches with me, not only adding their wisdom to the analysis but also doing things that only great friends would do—for example, hanging off the back of a truck to get to a research site or standing in for me during a machete sparring drill so that I could double-check that it was being filmed correctly. Olayinka

Fadahunsi, Andrea Queeley, Joana Mendes, and Hendrik Wangushu, I cannot thank you enough for all you have done.

It would take a manuscript in itself to acknowledge by name everyone who assisted me in the various stages of this adventure. I will have to thank collectively all my family and friends for their endless support and patience. Above all, I thank God for carrying me safely through shoot-outs, land mines, and civil wars, and for placing such wonderful people in my life.

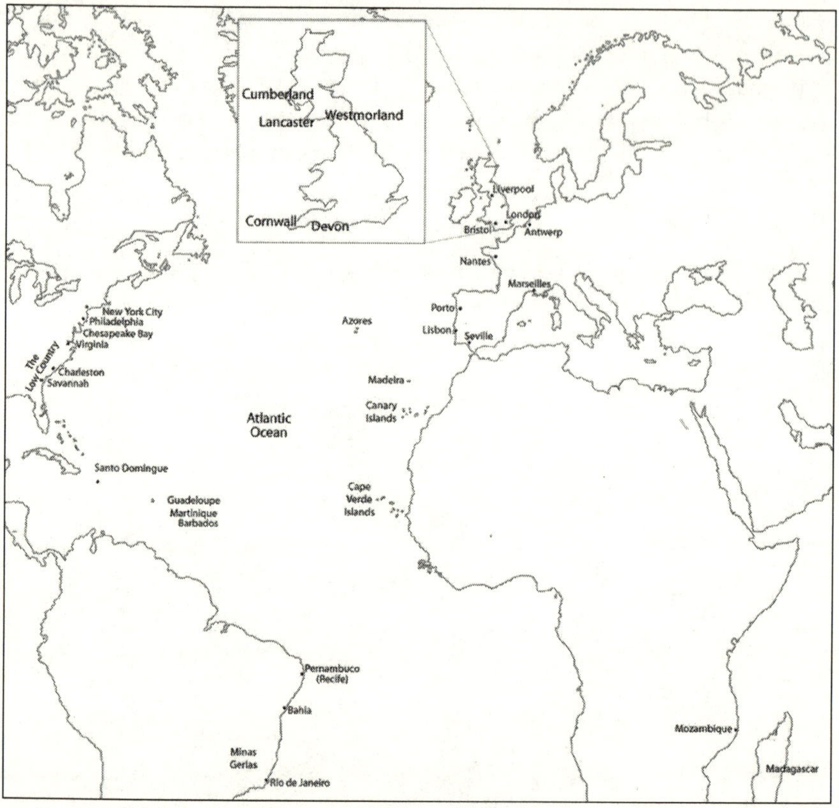

The eighteenth-century Atlantic world. Drawn by Soul Indigo

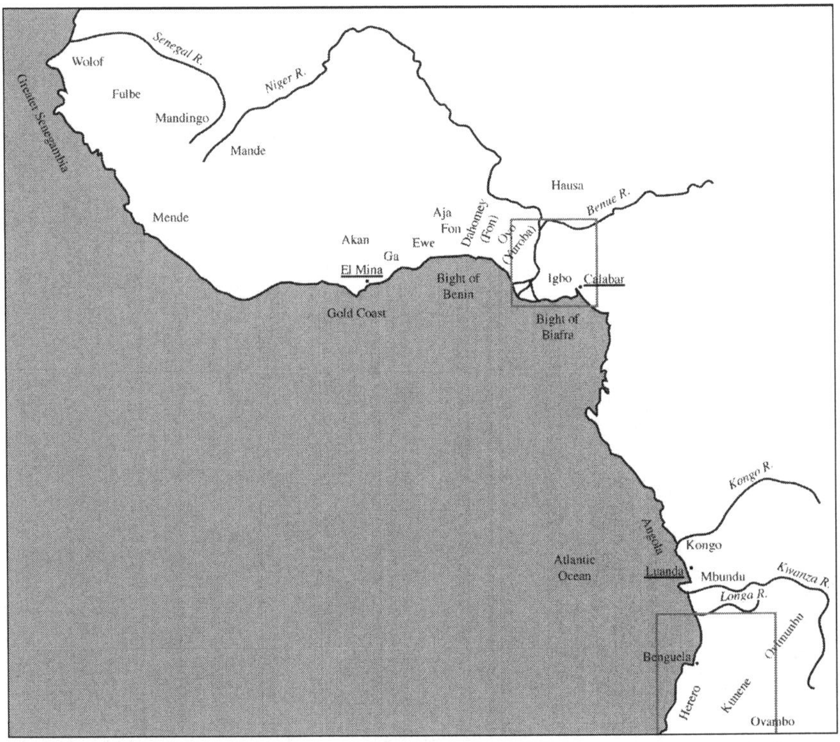

Eighteenth-century western Africa. Drawn by Soul Indigo

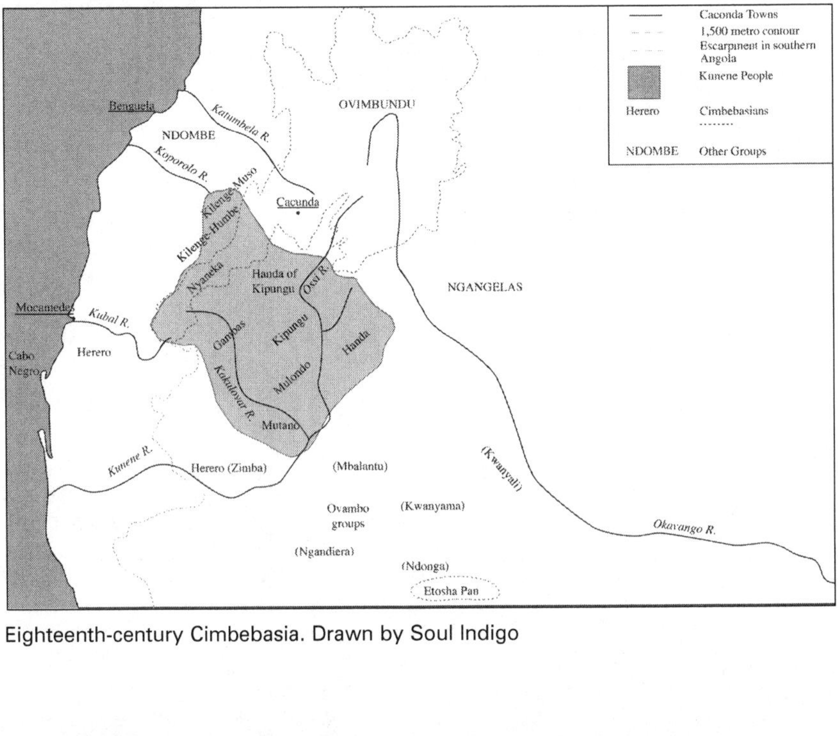

Eighteenth-century Cimbebasia. Drawn by Soul Indigo

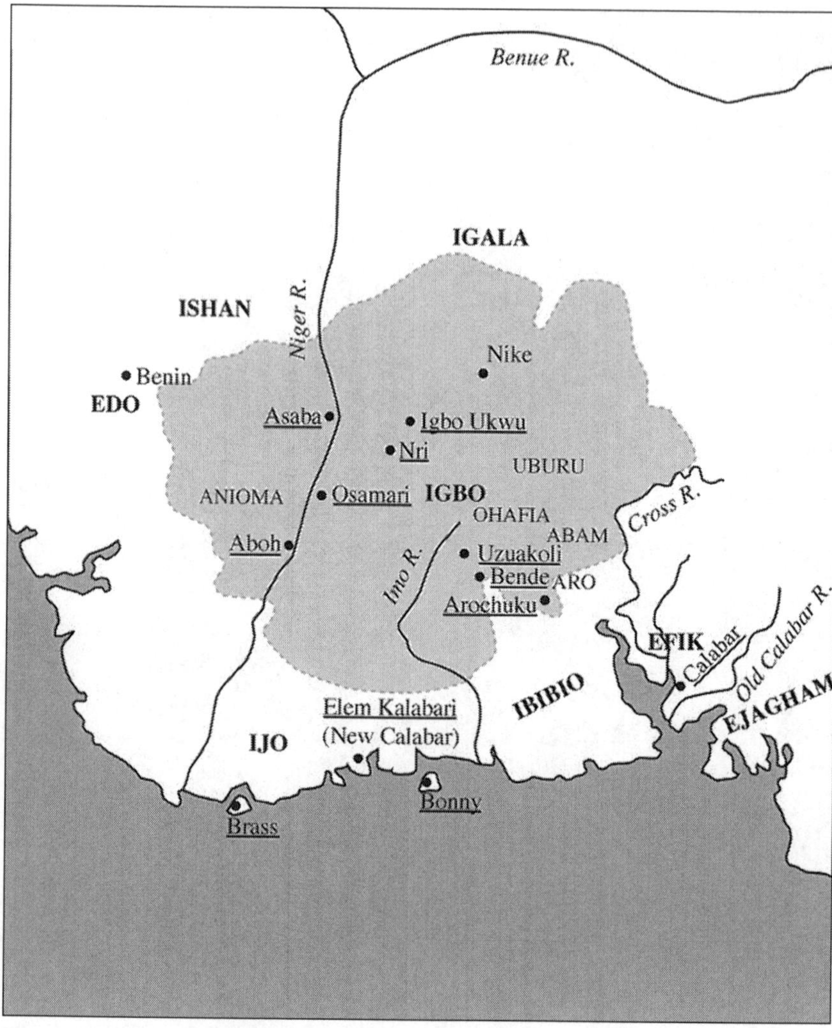

Eighteenth-century Bight of Biafra. Drawn by Soul Indigo

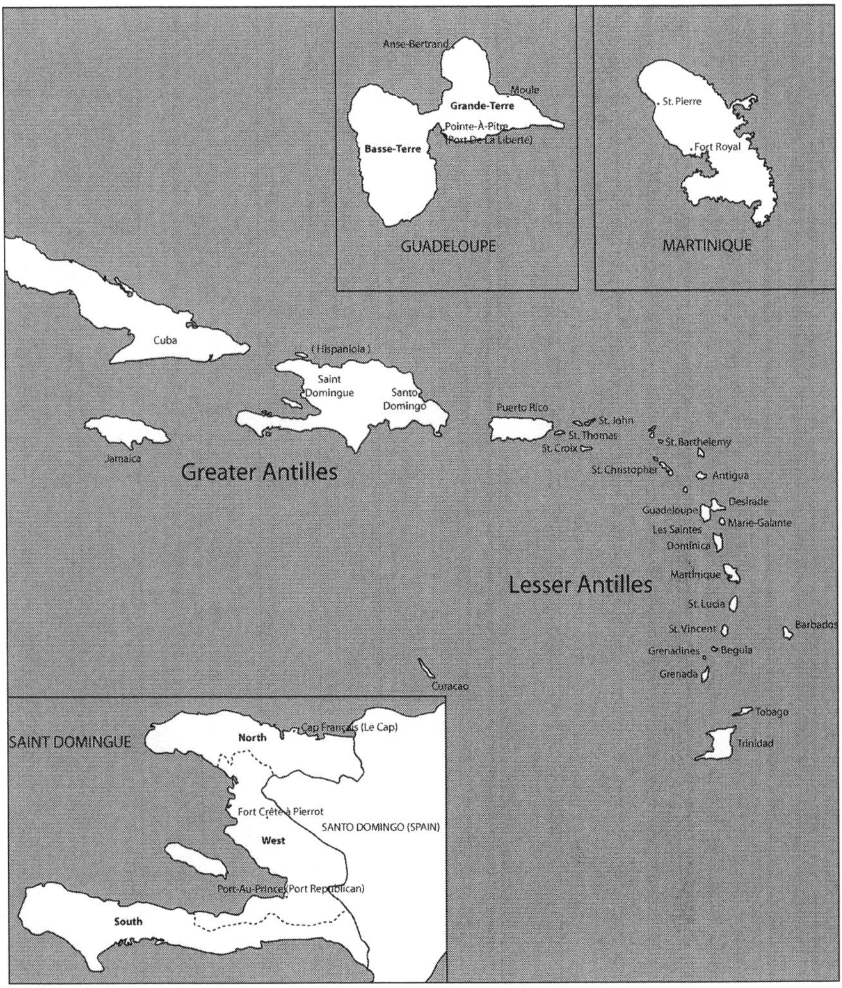

Eighteenth-century Caribbean Islands. Drawn by Soul Indigo

Fighting for Honor

Introduction

Divining an Approach

I spent the first summer after graduating from college in the coastal area of South Carolina researching the history of African martial art traditions in North America.[1] A friend from college was one of the few people I had met who knew about a martial art known as "knocking and kicking," or *yuna onse*. He directed me to a quiet Gullah community on the islands off the coast of Charleston, where the owner of the general store knew the art. When I arrived and asked Jack about the art, his face contorted, suggesting that he had no idea what I was talking about. I was crushed. My entire plan of research hinged on this one man who knew nothing of this art. As I had already made plans to spend almost two months in the area, I decided to keep trying to find someone in the community who could help me. Jack generously allowed me to hang out at his store and speak to his customers as they left. Although everyone I met was polite, I could tell that the question somehow made people feel uncomfortable; I would soon find out why. After weeks of this, Jack called me into the store and said that he remembered "that head-butting thing" being used by wrestlers and suggested I start with them.

Off I went in search of wrestlers. People told me there was not much wrestling anymore but that there were still plenty of elders around who used to be great wrestlers. I gradually made my way to two elders—Mary Duce and Deacon Johnson. They traded stories of how Duce had thrown Johnson in many bouts in their youth, some forty or fifty years ago. Deacon Johnson was kind and generous and invited me to his house to talk more. Although I had come to research the foot- and head-fighting art, I was quickly distracted by the wrestling form that he showed me. It involved two people embracing each other shoulder to shoulder while facing the same direction. One of the wrestlers would then wrap his/her leg around the other's, and they would try to throw each other from this side position.

This wrestling style was technically like the form of Igbo wrestling that I had learned in eastern Nigeria. In my village of Nnewi this particular form of wrestling was called *mgba*. When I explained to Johnson about my family in Nigeria and our form of wrestling, he asked me to demonstrate *mgba*. We were both struck by the similarity of the two arts and began to ponder together whether or not his "side-hold" wrestling was part of an African or Igbo legacy in the community. In our discussions he told me stories of another fighting art from Africa, one using head butting (knocking) and dynamic kicks. When I inquired about them, he showed me some techniques. He then told me that the art used to be a secret and that if I wanted to know more I should talk to someone whose father was a master of the art; to my surprise he led me back to Jack.

Jack now explained the art in even more detail and directed me to the local masters, including Deacon Johnson, who became my teacher. Although surprising to me at first, Jack's reversal is understandable considering the secrecy surrounding African cultural forms in general among blacks in "the lowcountry," the coastal plains and islands of South Carolina and Georgia. The folklorist Lydia Parish found this secrecy to be a central component of lowcountry black culture: "There are survivals of African songs on the coast of Georgia. But let no outsider imagine they can be heard for the asking. From experience I know this to be true. It took me three winters on St. Simon's to hear a single slave song, three times as many winters to see the religious dance called the ring-shout, still more winters to unearth the Buzzard Lope and similar solo dances. . . . The secretiveness of the Negro is, I believe, the fundamental reason for our ignorance of the race and its background, and this trait is in itself probably an African survival."[2] Knocking and kicking are surrounded by an even greater wall of secrecy because of their relationship with closed societies. It was my own African martial arts heritage that allowed me access into the closed circles. I later asked Jack why he had held information back when I first approached him. He replied that I had not asked him in the proper way and explained that the art had always been somewhat secret. He taught me the proper way to ask questions in order to make progress in my quest. I learned first to understand the world through the eyes of the people who would become my teachers and to ask questions from the perspective of their worldview.

This reorientation allowed me to break through another wall of silence when my research led me back to Africa for further fieldwork. I was heading not to my homeland of Nigeria but to the central and southern highlands of Angola, which was being ravaged by civil war.[3] In the mountainous region of Kilengues (between Benguela and the Mwila highlands) I encountered the foot-fighting art of *engolo;* this art was spread into the Americas under the name "knocking and kicking" in North America, *jogo de capoeira* in Brazil, and *danmyé* in Martinique. Like these daughter arts, *engolo* is based on inverted kicks[4] for attacks and acrobatics for defense. I was able to use archival sources to trace some aspects of the region's fighting systems back to the 1840s, but this was as early as written sources would allow me to delve. Whenever, wherever, and however I tried to engage my *engolo* teachers about the origins and development of the art, the answer was always "*engolo* comes from the ancestors."

This answer haunted me. How could I interview the ancestors? I had no written sources I could consult for any time periods earlier than the seventeenth century. When an African wants to find answers to a question that eludes explanation through direct observation, one option is to consult a diviner, who can present these questions directly to the ancestors. Of the many forms of divination in West Central Africa, the most potent and esteemed is human divination, through which ancestors are called back through ritual processes to enter mediums and speak directly to the seekers of answers. I was fortunate to work with Mupolo Kahavila, a *kimbanda,* or ritual specialist. *Kimbandas* were linked to the *engolo* during special initiation ceremonies, but more importantly, they oversaw general rites of human divination that would lead mediums (often the *kimbandas* themselves) through a ritual process that allowed ancestors' spirits to enter them. Once seated in a medium's head, an ancestor could then literally speak through the medium and answer questions posed by the *kimbanda*'s living clients. Although I learned much during my time with Kahavila, the ancestors also answered many of my pressing historical questions through historical linguistics.

Historical linguistics is not completely unlike human divination. Between trips to Angola, I went to a specialist, my professor Christopher Ehret. He initiated me into this still somewhat "mystical" process that would lead me directly to the thoughts and historical experiences of an ancestral community through the vocabulary of their descendants. I came with questions about where, when, and why this martial art developed; the questions could not be explained through ordinary means since the events clearly occurred long before written sources began describing the region and much farther back than oral history could directly lead me. At the end of this "ritual" process I found that I could now, in a way, "interview the ancestors" by understanding the cognitive underpinnings of ancestral terms. The term *kalunga* proved to be one of the central paradigms of the West Central African worldview and related to the evolution of *engolo.*[5]

This work is the story of *engolo,* a martial art that began in ancient Angola.[6] The study adopts an Angolan perspective to explore the origins of this unique martial art and its spread to the Americas. Furthermore, it uses Biafran traditions of martial art as a counterpoint to *engolo* and to explore the interactions between African martial art traditions in the Americas.[7]

As with Asian martial art traditions, African martial arts often reflected specific philosophies and worldviews. In the case of *engolo,* this worldview emanated out of the *kalunga* paradigm. While living in Angola, I came to understand that the term *kalunga* was used to identify aspects of the natural world (ocean, rivers, lakes, caves) and the supernatural world (ancestors, God, and the land of the dead). These seemingly disparate terms were brought together by an entire cosmological system that understood bodies of water to be bridges connecting the lands of the living and the realm of the dead. In reference to the spiritual realm linked to these bodies of water, *kalunga* invokes an inverted world where the ancestors walk with their feet up. This gave birth to a martial art that relied on supporting one's body with the hands and kicking while upside down. Masters of the art who were forced to endure the Middle Passage spread this aesthetic tradition of inverted kicks throughout the Americas.

In conceptualizing the ocean as a bridge, the *kalunga* paradigm influenced many Africans' perceptions of the Atlantic crossing. Indeed, although the Angolan and Biafran philosophical traditions were quite distinct and gave birth to radically different martial art forms, individuals from both traditions shared similar conceptions of the ocean as a bridge linking worlds together—most specifically, a bridge linking the lands of the living and the realm of the dead that would effect fears of Middle Passage but also give them hopes of return. For Angolans whites were perceived as coming from the sea and thus from the spirit world inhabited by both benevolent ancestors and harmful beings.[8] Europeans' blood-red skin and their insatiable appetite for captives identified them as the people of *Mwene Puto,* the Lord of the Dead, whose minions took captive Africans back across the sea and ate them.[9] Biafrans held a parallel belief, as evidenced in the narrative of Olaudah Equiano. He was enslaved as a youth from the Igbo hinterland of the Bight of Biafra and remembered that when taken aboard a slave ship, "I was persuaded that I had gotten into a world of bad spirits, and that they were going to kill me. . . . I asked them if we were not to be eaten by those white men with horrible looks, red faces, and long hair."[10]

Yet, the same paradigm that caused initial fear of passage also gave hope of return home across the bridge of the Atlantic once in the Americas. Like many other African groups, both Angolans and Biafrans shared the belief that the ocean could take them back across the Atlantic. Not far from where my research began in South Carolina was a spot called Igbo Landing, where a shipful of Biafrans were believed to have departed and walked back across the Atlantic to Igboland.[11] While Biafrans and other African groups carried shared ideas linking the sea and the spirit world, it is important to note that the enduring conception that would be passed on even to American-born bondsmen drew predominantly from the cognitive traditions of Angolans. This is reflected in the fact that the term *kalunga* was retained in African American vernaculars.[12] Walking through cemeteries in the lowcountry also highlighted the vibrancy of the *kalunga* paradigm among blacks in North America; their grave markings reveal their belief that if properly buried they would be able to cross the ocean back to Africa and the spiritual world of their ancestors.[13]

Similarly, the Central Africans who constituted the largest pool of forced immigrants to Brazil held the hope of return via the Atlantic *kalunga.* In Brazil some ritual specialists were at times believed to hold themselves on their hands upside down, revealing the continued association between physical inversion and access to the ancestral power. In the Caribbean, and indeed throughout the Americas, Africans who gained the proper spiritual force were believed to be able to fly back to Africa. However, those Africans and their descendants who remained in the Americas were not left behind unarmed. They continued to seek power through the Angolan martial art of inverted kicks and used it to seek honor, even under the social and physical oppression of racial slavery in the Americas.

African Diaspora Scholarship

This book adopts the Angolan cultural understanding of the ocean as a bridge linking two fundamentally connected worlds. In particular it aspires to explore the diaspora of martial art traditions emanating from southern Angola and the Bight of Biafra, two regions not often studied in terms of their influence on Atlantic world cultures.[14] Given that Biafrans constituted a large percentage of Africans brought to the Anglophone colonies, it is surprising that the study of their influence in the Americas is just beginning.[15] Similarly, the study of Central African influence across the Americas is only now beginning to take its proper place in African diaspora studies. Despite the recent push in this direction by texts such as *Central African and Cultural Transformations in the American Diaspora,* the overwhelming majority of this new scholarship focuses on the KiKongo and Kimbundu speakers of northern Angola.[16] Beyond the pioneering work of the ethnomusicologist Gerhard Kubik, I am not aware of another study that has investigated the cultural impact of southern Angolans in the Americas.[17]

This current project is rooted in the combative and philosophical traditions of Angola and the Bight of Biafra and then looks outward to North America, Brazil, and the Caribbean to track specific combative techniques. This geographic scope is necessarily broad because focusing on the specific cultural practice of Angolan combat traditions as the center of the study allows us to view the Central African tradition in a transnational context. While the geographical scope here is broad, the study is narrowed by descending from the nebulous level of "culture" to specific combat technologies.[18] The sacrifice that has to be made for such an analysis is that space will not allow for a detailed historical evolution of bondage and the bonded cultures of each particular location in the Americas. Luckily, however, this work has been done, and readers needing such a background are directed to such texts in the footnotes. Thus, while I attempt to provide a contextual background for the arts and people who practiced them, particularly in these less well-known areas of Africa, this study does not center on issues of identity or the creation of community-culture in the Americas beyond the extent to which these provided a backdrop for the martial arts. As such, this study is rooted around the vocabulary of "traditions" rather than "retentions," "creoles," or demographic-based "continuities."[19]

This focus on traditions is intended to bring together elements of both the prevalent "creolization" paradigm and the demographics-driven approaches that dominate the current literature under a common vocabulary. Although it would be unwise to extrapolate uncritically from martial arts to other cultural forms, this study may help illuminate some of the historical nuances of cultural interactions in the Americas that are not usually highlighted by these two approaches. The "creolization" model has contributed to understandings of culture by adopting linguistic theories, suggesting that the first generation of Africans who arrived speaking different languages had to create, using elements of their African languages and borrowing from European languages, a mixed pidgin language that would be inherited by the second generation as "creole." While the necessity for developing a spoken pidgin or lingua franca is quite clear and may have been paralleled by other elements of culture, in the case of martial arts there was no equivalent need to create a hybrid form that incorporated elements of various African and European systems. Bonded communities in the Americas more often utilized various distinct martial art traditions than they created hybridized combinations.

Understanding martial arts as living traditions will also help highlight their existence in areas where people from their specific African heartland were not present in dominating numbers. Tables showing percentages of Africans from different cultures brought into a certain region have become ubiquitous in the works of African diaspora scholars, this present study included. While these demographics are quite useful, their use at times equates demographic and cultural legacies. This study aims to move beyond gross figures by exploring martial arts as living traditions that could easily thrive outside of their original narrow demographics. Thus, while Douglas Chambers has persuasively argued that peoples from the Bight of Biafra constituted a dominant plurality in many areas of Virginia, the fact that the Angolan-derived kicking arts thrived in Virginia communities suggests that such demographic factors play an important but not always dominant role in cultural legacies.[20] My study thus reaffirms that these martial arts were not vague residues of demographic clustering but living traditions that could be spread by even a few knowledgeable exponents to other Africans and even to Europeans.

African "Martial Arts"

Exploring this largely overlooked dimension of life under bondage requires excavating knowledge systems and social practices not usually thought of as legitimate topics of historical inquiry.[21] The histories of martial arts, especially martial art traditions emerging from Africa, have not yet been systematically studied directly or in relation to their legacy among enslaved populations in the Americas. While "historians are more likely to study people thinking, governing, worshiping, or working," Elliott Gorn has demonstrated in his work on European American combat sports that how people fight "reveals much about past cultures and societies."[22] In this case, one of the new insights that may be revealed by examining combat traditions is a new perspective on the concept of honor among enslaved peoples. One limitation of emphasizing physical combat is that, in most of the cases we will explore, the participants were overwhelmingly male, making this largely a study of male-dominated subcultures. Although these various subcultures were quite distinct on both sides of the Atlantic, some of their martial techniques were shared and can serve as traceable data for historians, even in a transatlantic social history such as this one.

Martial arts are dynamic and open to variation; yet, at the same time they contain fundamentals that can, at times, be relatively stable across time. The Japanese term for this continuity is *kata,* which refers to the ideal form of an art, as opposed to the personal variation developed by each unique individual in free practice.[23] Thus, while the student in application may adopt variations on techniques more suited to his/her body, aesthetic sense, or experience, there is often a theoretically immutable point of reference that will be passed on to students. The African martial arts are not as regimented as the Japanese styles, but the same principle holds true. Martial art styles can be "invented," transformed, and taken in new directions. More often, however, individual practitioners will stress particular aspects of the style and develop their own variations on techniques, but without jeopardizing the fundamental paradigms of the tradition. Possibly the best example of this continuity in change is Egyptian stick fighting. Using hieroglyphics, detailed descriptions in the Ramesseum Papyrus (circa 1991 B.C.) of the techniques of the stick-fighting priests of Osiris, the observations of Herodotus, all the way through to modern ethnographies, Poliakoff demonstrates that while the religious and social contexts had changed radically, the art of stick fighting was a constant in Egyptian culture.[24] Similar studies have shown continuities in Nubian wrestling over two thousand years.[25] Given this potential stability of fundamental concepts in the midst of adaptations of detail, meaning, and social context, I refer to martial arts as "traditions." This term has been negatively associated with notions of an immutable element in a fixed ahistorical past. Yet, the idea of tradition is quite useful when employed, as suggested by Jan Vansina, as self-regulating processes emanating from an ancestral core paradigm.[26] Before embarking on this investigation, we must begin with an examination of some terms relating to martial arts.

I use the term "martial arts" here to refer specifically to the combative technologies that I trace across time and space. While these combative technologies are by-products of the historical contexts that gave rise to them, as living traditions each could also take on a life of its own that was not limited to any one social context. For example, the Angolan kicking art of *engolo* emerged from the ancestral paradigm of *kalunga*. Yet, in social practice the art was often performed in the context of festivals or rites of passage to the accompaniment of percussion and song. At other times it could be used as a silent form of dueling or self-defense, a form of recreation for young boys, or a sacred ritual of an initiation organization. On the other side of the Atlantic this kicking system was often practiced in communal dances or closed societies of bondsmen. Acknowledging the discontinuities and unique nature of the social conditions of bondage in the Americas is essential to address the complexity of these social practices. Therefore, these new contexts will be addressed as much as available data allow. However, the constant that I am tracing through these varied contexts is the shared technical approach to combat.

While a similar study could be done on the musical or other elements of these arts, it is specifically this technology of combat that I am referring to when I use the term "martial arts."[27] In its North American usage, the term generally signifies Asian unarmed combative practices such as Okinawan karate, Japanese judo, Chinese kung fu, or Korean tae kwon do. The Western world's failure to widely recognize African martial arts warrants a brief concluding discussion about the meaning of African "martial arts" and related terms and their relevance to the culture of the enslaved. In purely etymological terms, "martial arts" does not distinguish the various types of activities that can be described by this term. For clarity I will at times distinguish between war dances and three subcategories of martial arts: combat sports, fighting skills, and martial ways.[28]

Although they are not considered martial arts in the vernacular usage of the term as a self-defense art, war dances are in the more literal sense art forms relating to warlike activity. War dances involve set or improvised choreographies, usually by armed participants. These can be individual dances that develop or display the fighting ability of individual warriors through solo or paired dances. However, war dances are more often collective movements that develop or exhibit the polish and power of an entire army of warriors/dancers. War dances can serve as tools to meet a wide variety of needs: to historically document and reenact prior conflicts for nonparticipants and later generations; to celebrate after a victory; to encourage combatants before a conflict; to fulfill ritual protocols; or simply to allow a leader to review the state of his/her troops. An example from the ancient world would be the Greek pyrrhic, in which Greek soldiers perfected their combat skills through armed dance routines to the sound of the flute.[29] A contemporary practice somewhat analogous to war dancing is found in the United States Army's use of European American marching drills to drums or chants, which no longer serve any direct combative utility but are used to create unity.[30]

"Combat sports" or "combat games" are those forms of simulated combat that have as their objective to win in a contest with a fixed set of rules. Contemporary examples of combat sports include Olympic tae kwon do, Olympic wrestling, boxing, and sport fencing. Many unarmed African wrestling styles fall primarily under the genre of combat sport, although this can vary depending on the context.

"Fighting skills" can be loosely defined as those combat systems that prioritize the killing or incapacitating of an opponent by any means available in a real combat situation. Western examples could include the U.S. Marine Special Forces unarmed combat system; African examples could include Zulu spear and shield work.[31]

"Martial ways" will be defined here as those systems that develop self-defense skills but in which philosophical and stylistic considerations outweigh the importance of defeating an opponent. That is, they are conceived of as ways of self-perfection through martial technique, discipline, and spiritual code. The Japanese concept of martial art as *budo,* or martial way, is relatively recent with the twentieth-century development of karate-do, judo, and aikido, although perhaps an older Asian example can be found in the case of Chinese tai chi chuan.[32] For those initiated into masterhood, both the *engolo* and *mgba* fit squarely into this category. I will use the terms "martial arts," "martial traditions," "combat arts," or "combat forms" when not distinguishing among these more specifically defined categories.

A further distinction among various combat arts should be made regarding how these arts attempt to arrive at their objectives. While there are martial arts that deeply integrate both approaches, the arts being discussed here can theoretically be divided into grappling styles and percussive styles. Grappling styles are those combat forms that specialize in seizing and throwing an opponent to the ground, and they sometimes involve overcoming the opponent with joint locks, pins, and chokes or strangles. Percussive (or pugilistic) styles are those combat forms that specialize in striking an opponent with blows of the feet, knees, hands, elbows, head, or other body part. Although a few exceptional existing arts fundamentally combine these two approaches to combat, in most cases they remain practical distinctions that will be important to this analysis.

There were many styles of unarmed African combat arts, many of which may have also been spread into the Americas.[33] While there were exceptions to the rule, for the purposes of this study it is possible to think of wide areas in which particular approaches to combat predominated. The first is West African–style grappling, in which the practitioner's objective is to grab an opponent and throw him to the ground. Although the specific aspects of each ethnic group's wrestling style are unique, most of coastal West Africa from the Senegal River as far south as the Kwanza River forms a grappling zone in which wrestling dominated ritual combat.[34] To my knowledge, wrestling existed as a formal pastime in the precolonial societies of all the ethnic groups of this region, and in the vast majority of forms the contest is won or lost when an opponent is forced off balance.[35]

The Nigerian author Chinua Achebe describes a characteristic context for grappling in *Things Fall Apart:*

> The whole village turned out on the *ilo,* men, women and children. They stood round in a huge circle leaving the center of the playground free. . . . The wrestlers were not there yet and the drummers held the field. They too sat just in front of the huge circle of spectators, facing the elders. Behind them was the big and ancient silk-cotton tree, which was sacred. Spirits of good children lived in that tree waiting to be born. On ordinary days young women who desired children came to sit under its shade.
>
> There were seven drums arranged according to their sizes in a long wooden basket. Three men beat them with sticks, working feverishly from one drum to another. They were possessed by the spirit of the drums.
>
> The young men who kept order on these occasions dashed about, consulting among themselves and with the leaders of the two wrestling teams, who were still outside the circle, behind the crowd. Once in a while two young men carrying palm fronds ran round the circle and kept the crowd back by beating the ground in front of them or, if they were stubborn, their legs and feet.
>
> At last the two teams danced into the circle and the crowd roared and clapped. The drums rose to a frenzy. The people surged forward. The young men who kept order flew around, waving their palm fronds. Old men nodded to the beat of the drums and remembered the days when they wrestled to its intoxicating rhythm. . . .
>
> The last match was between the leaders of the teams. They were among the best wrestlers in all the nine villages. . . . Ikezue held out his right hand. Okafo seized it, and they closed in. It was a fierce contest. Ikezue strove to dig in his right heel behind Okafo so as to pitch him backwards in the clever *ege* style. But the one knew what the other was thinking. . . . The two wrestlers were now almost still in each other's grip. . . . The two judges were already moving forward to separate them when Ikezue, now desperate, went down quickly on one knee in an attempt to fling his man backwards over his head. It was a sad miscalculation. Quick as the lighting of Amadiora, Okafo raised his right leg and swung it over his rival's head. The crowd burst into a thunderous roar. Okafo was swept off his feet by his supporters and carried home shoulder high. They sang his praise and the young women clapped their hands: "Who will wrestle for our village? Okafo will wrestle for our village."[36]

This fictional account set in Igboland at the dawn of colonialism contains many elements typical of the "sportive" wrestling contests found throughout West Africa (for example, the ritual setting, drumming, improvised praise songs, and community participation). The wrestling of the Wolof, Fula, Mande, and other Senegambians, which was and continues to be a central pillar of Senegambian society, certainly must have made an impact on the wrestling practices of many enslaved communities in the Americas. However, the similarity of many West African styles to each other and to European styles makes it hard to trace them in the diaspora. This book will focus on a leg-wrapping style from Biafra to coastal Bantu-speaking areas, which might be distinct enough to be recognizable when it does appear in the Americas.[37]

The second and more central group of styles that we will follow emanates from the southern region of West Central Africa and is based on pugilism. While a few scattered groups practice pugilistic arts in the Kasai and "Greater Loango Coast" regions, these represent enclaves within a larger grappling area, with the exclusively pugilistic area being south of the Kwanza River.[38] In particular, the region that is currently southern Angola and northern Namibia is marked by a percussive style of fighting. Although Herero and Kunene boys may wrestle informally like all children, wrestling as a social institution does not exist for them. Rather, this niche is filled by the striking arts such as the *engolo* and *kandeka*.

The principal aim of these arts is to overcome an opponent by subduing him with strikes—in the case of the *engolo* this is predominantly kicks—but also to train one's defenses, which in the case of *kandeka* is accomplished by exchanging strikes with the open hand or sticks. The unarmed percussive arts must be understood in relation to the percussive use of stick fighting, which provided a larger context both in the Angolan highlands and in the Caribbean. From within these two broadly spread areas of related martial traditions, this study focuses on the side-hold grappling art from Biafra and the Kunene pugilistic tradition of Central Africa.

Although the Biafran grappling and the Angolan percussive arts were stylistically very different, both fulfilled similar social roles. Both were used as a form of entertainment when practiced to music, a form of dueling to settle personal scores, a ritualized form of conflict resolution, or a form of battlefield training for young soldiers. Central to all contexts is the concept of honor for the practitioner and often for the community through the honored practitioner.

Mastery in either art could bring a skilled practitioner respect for his graceful execution, the admiration of potential wives, and economic advancement. Each art provided a path of spiritual development that could take an exceptional adept to one of the highest forms of honor in Africa, the status of a transcendent hero. Someone who was initiated into full mastery of *engolo* could become a special kind of ancestor, one who could physically manifest in the bodies of his descendants. Similarly the Biafran art of *mgba* (and its cognates) could serve as a tool to achieve the highest of honors. A master of the martial art (*di-mgba*) who remained true to the accompanying moral code could become a transcendent hero, the most honored of ancestors, who could be called upon for guidance in important matters and could reincarnate among the living while retaining a position among the dead ancestors. In this sense both *engolo* and *mgba* can be understood as martial arts and more specifically as martial ways in the strict sense.

The importance of following these African martial arts into the Americas becomes clear when one considers that while it was economic in its objective, the slave system was ultimately held together by physical and symbolic (real or threatened) violence. Therefore, it should not be surprising that at times African combat traditions were used in the Americas as forms of self-defense against this violence. Many of the bondsmen who rose up in the Haitian Revolution may have relied on previous military experience and their stick- and machete-fighting arts. While such skills were at times used as forms of direct resistance, martial arts were more often used as means to fight for honor within the confines of bondage. These fights for honor in urban Brazil were often just as sanguine as the armed revolts more emphasized by many historians. For example, the Muslim uprising of 1835 in Bahia left only nine people dead. Despite the possession of firearms by the participants, all the dead victims were wounded by swords, knives, and lances, showing that "the few firearms the rebels were able to gather did nothing more than weigh them down."[39] In contrast, this number could have been equally the result of one week of activity by groups of bondsmen in Rio practicing the martial art of *capoeiragem*. As a police official reported of *capoeira* experts in the 1850s, "In only one afternoon of the month of February they committed seven murders in the parish . . . of Santa Anna."[40] Certainly, many more whites were killed during the 1828 uprising of German and Irish mercenaries, who were mowed down in large numbers by the *capoeira* experts.[41]

With this in mind, I do not want to stress the art's counter-hegemonic use to an extent that overshadows its use in gaining positions in service to the power structure or its creative roles in community performance and the enforcement of codes of honor. The continued use of martial arts in community performance rituals, conflict resolution, courting, and honor in the Americas was equally important to enslaved Africans. This cultural aspect acted as a form of social and psychological defense against the symbolic violence of racial slavery. The ideology of racism that underpinned the slave system presented a dominant image of Africans as without culture, history, or honor. By using these martial arts to reaffirm their self-worth, they were engaging in an equally important struggle against the symbolic violence that still plagues their descendants in the Americas.

The ancestral traditions of the African groups under consideration are the focus of part 1. First, historical, ethnographic, and linguistic methodologies are employed to explore the origin of the martial art of *engolo* in southern Angola before the twelfth century. The region was settled by Bantu-speaking pastoralists, who developed a form of dueling with strikes that imitated their prized cattle and their cosmological paradigm of *kalunga*. This ancient paradigm, which conceptualized inversion as a bridge between the land of the living and an inverted land of the dead, gave rise to the martial art of *engolo,* which utilized unique inverted kicking techniques. Discussion of the eighteenth- and nineteenth-century social disruptions, caused by frequent wars and Portuguese slave raiding, that brought mastery of this martial art are considered as an essential component of military training.

Next, the Biafran grappling tradition is introduced, with particular focus on the leg-wrapping-style *mgba* wrestling of the Igbo people. The Biafran region was not marked by rule of monarchs; rather, in this democratic society people were ruled by religious custom. The widespread concept of *omenani,* or proper custom, portrayed the shedding of blood as a serious taboo, and thus the martial art developed somewhat distinct from other combat forms. The various roles that wrestling played in Biafran societies are explored, followed by an outline of the trading systems through which more than a million and a half women and men from the Bight of Biafra were enslaved and shipped to the Americas.

Part 2 follows the developments of the African combat traditions in the Americas, where martial arts continued to play a key role in the society of enslaved Africans, albeit in radically new ways. This section explores why and how these martial arts were perpetuated by Africans and their descendants in North America in the eighteenth and nineteenth centuries. The use of combat arts as class and racial markers is explained. Examples from North America establish the contexts in which these arts would be centered throughout the Americas: maroon communities, performance circles, service to plantation owners, closed societies, and self-defense. Next, the discussion turns to the link between martial arts and the codes of honor of the enslaved community.

An investigation of the percussive and grappling arts of the French-speaking Caribbean follows. In particular the discussion highlights their use in the performance circles called here *bamboulas*. A return to the concept of *kalunga* shows the role that these arts played in easing the path to the ancestral world. In addition, an investigation of the importance of stick-fighting traditions in the Caribbean highlights the potential role of these arts in large-scale revolts.

The discussion next turns to the *jogo de capoeira,* the derivative form of *engolo* found in Brazil. It begins by considering the perpetuation of the Angolan foot-fighting tradition in urban centers of Brazil until the end of the nineteenth century. The available primary sources are used to investigate in more detail the inner workings of the *capoeira* societies that formed the primary social context for the art form. A transnational view of these African martial arts as living traditions in the Americas concludes the study.

One

Birth of Traditions

One From across the *Kalunga*

Pastoral Pugilism in Southern Angola to 1860

Most studies on slavery in West Central Africa focus on the interactions among the Portuguese and the kingdoms of Kongo and Ndongo. Yet, the region south of the Kuanza River contained some of the highest population densities in the region, and numbers of enslaved Africans extracted from the region were "possibly the highest in West Central Africa."[1] Among various other population clusters drawn into this southern Atlantic slaving system were Cimbebasian societies of southern Angola.[2] Cimbebasians developed a unique martial culture long before the arrival of Europeans and the waves of social conflict that followed in the wake of their influence.[3] While elements of this combative culture could be found among Cimbebasians and many of their neighbors, we will often focus here on the Kunene people, a Cimbebasian subgroup around the curve of the Kunene River, who developed a martial art complex involving archery, rock throwing, stick fighting, head butting, slap-boxing, and foot fighting.[4] This martial complex was used along with other tactics to resist Portuguese encroachment in the area from the seventeenth through the nineteenth centuries. Captives taken in these conflicts simultaneously carried these weapons into the Americas, sparking parallel evolutions of Kunene martial arts on both sides of the Atlantic. Our focus here will be on stick fighting, head butting, and particularly *engolo*—an unarmed martial art of this region that utilized inverted kicks—which because of its unique form is clearly traced over centuries in the Americas.

Engolo emerged out of shared ancestral concepts of religion, combat, and body mapping that appear to have coalesced in somewhat similar forms in the Kasai and Greater Loango regions farther to the north.[5] However, the art developed unique properties during the course of its social history in southern Angola, driven both by the process of individual inspiration and by external forces. From the emic or insider's view, the inheritors of *engolo* viewed the art as a gift from the ancestors from across the *kalunga*. From this perspective, the evolution of *engolo* was advanced by numerous individuals whose extreme prowess gradually raised the standard of combative excellence. Some of these martial art masters were socially acknowledged not only in their lifetimes but also even after their physical death. Death for Angolans represented rebirth into the land of the ancestors, where benevolent progenitors continued to watch over their living descendants. For most ancestors the care and intercession on the part of their progeny took place on the spiritual plane. Yet, in the Cimbebasian region, martial art masters, like some other transcendent ancestors, were believed to come back physically to the community from across the *kalunga* by "possessing" the bodies of their descendants. In doing so, they were understood to fuel their progeny with the power to transcend their normal physical limitations. In this way the ancestors were understood to return continually to the community to inspire later generations to new levels of mastery in the marital arts.

While ancestral inspiration from across the *kalunga* was one cause for the evolution of engolo, three transformations in the social history of the Cimbebasian region may have also been driving forces in the development and social import of the *engolo* and the entire martial complex of the society. The first was the gradual adoption of cattle as the basis of wealth, which led to an increased militarism that placed martial expertise at a premium. The second was a rapid social and military revolution brought on by the Imbangala *kilombo,* a radical reorientation of society away from family relations to initiation-based military communities. The region experienced a third revolution during European slave trading and military conquests.[6] This resulted in the forced migration of thousands of Cimbebasian peoples into the Americas, and along with them their unique marital art complex.

Ancestral Settlements along the Kunene River

Linguistic evidence suggests that the earliest identifiable settlers of Cimbebasia were Khoisan-speaking gatherer-hunters present from the first millennium B.C.E. Two other groups entered the region in the period of the last few centuries B.C.E. Emanating from what is now northeastern Botswana, new Khoisan groups speaking the proto-Kwadi language entered the area and were associated with raising small livestock in addition to gathering and hunting.[7]

Over the course of the first millennium, the Njila branch of Bantu languages entered the region from the north and began to spread throughout the area following the course of rivers.[8] Some of the communities that spoke or adopted Njila languages raised goats and cultivated black-eyed peas, groundnuts, and gourds in the wetlands along the region's rivers. Many Khoisan and possibly other groups were assimilated into these newly forming Njila Bantu-speaking communities, but some Khoisan communities remained distinct in more remote pockets. In the early centuries of the new era, many communities adopted cattle raising, sorghum cultivating, and iron working, which were introduced to the region from the east. Njila speakers were the first to adopt these new technologies and in turn introduced them to Khoisan-speaking herders. This may have increased the prestige and influence of Bantu languages, further inspiring others to learn them. The southernmost of these Bantu languages would later evolve into the Cimbebasian subgroup of Njila. Before their dispersal throughout the region, some proto-Cimbebasian language communities were clustered along the lower Kunene River: the ancestral Kunene speakers to the west of the river; proto-Herero-Themba-Hakoana just north of the river but west of the first group; and the proto-Kwanyama-Ambo just to the east of the river.[9] These three major clusters then spread out—via both migration and language acquisition by other communities—and began their gradual divergence likely between the second and sixth centuries C.E. The Herero-Themba-Hakoana cluster adopted nomadic pastoralism, spreading widely in drier coastal lands west of the escarpment and to the south. Proto-Kwanyama and other Ambo languages spread south into the Kuvelai basin. The ancestors of the Kunene group of languages dispersed along the Kunene, Kakulovar, and Ossi rivers. By the thirteenth century, when a brief period of increased rainfall was introduced, these groups had spread widely. With the desiccation that followed by 1300, these languages had already begun diverging into their respective languages and dialects.

Gradual political centralization was under way before 1300 along the Kunene River, where a large population of Kunene speakers clustered. Although the details of this process will remain obscure until archaeological work is done in the region, it is possible that the process evolved from the necessity of coordinated labor for the maximization of agriculture and pastoralism. The annual flooding of the rivers would have given the settlers a relatively secure water source for their sorghum and millet crops, and this led to greater population densities that would only later be surpassed by the agricultural communities in the highlands. Competition for the best-watered lands may have led in time to early political elaborations. The population density may have encouraged more central coordination than in the outlying savanna since the complexities of the flooding patterns required more controlled methods of land allocation.[10] The labor involved in maximizing the lands on the main rivers and channels may have helped elevate the chiefs into more powerful rulers in the same pattern as in the first Luba kingdom, via public works.[11] Certainly in later centuries territorial chiefs were in charge of organizing labor to create and maintain water reservoirs to be used during the dry season. These man-made lakes required large amounts of labor, and the soil extracted from them had to be moved to mounds around them, where fruit trees were planted.[12] Along with the growth of chiefs into lords in charge of public labor eventually came their ability to conscript labor for the "royal" fields on their own homesteads.[13]

This lordly influence over public labor would have been limited to the most densely populated area of the polity's heartland, the floodplains. Outlying areas may have been brought into the king's influence through a widespread system of political and military clientship via cattle redistribution.[14] With the centralization of political power, the earlier political system based on matrilineal kinship was matched by a network of client-patron relations linking kings, chiefs, other wealthy men (such as the ritual specialists known as *kimbandas*), and skilled soldiers. While the king with the help of conscripted labor kept a portion of his cattle, the majority was lent to subordinate chiefs in outlying areas. This linked them to the central authority, bolstered their own claims of legitimacy, and allowed them to lend cattle to ward headmen and other subordinates. Equally important, it enabled them to draw talented soldiers into their service. Cattle raiding was a constant reality in these regions, both as rituals of power and fertility in times of prosperity and as actual raids in times of drought.[15]

The constant reality of potential raids from other areas encouraged the development of militaristic strategies and values, and valorous soldiers were rewarded with cattle, clients, and wives.[16] Thus, the king, chiefs, and other wealthy men would have wanted to attract into their service the most skilled soldiers in the society. These soldiers would then be used in raids or to repel the raids of others. The distribution of cattle to clients also spaced out the king's herds over a wide area, thus expanding his influence while protecting him from total losses from raids outside the kingdom. Outlying chiefs and wealthy men could then redistribute royal cattle to their subordinates, thus linking chiefs, headmen, and fighters to the central political authority.[17] Cattle thus became central to notions of political legitimacy, a fact reflected in the eventual belief in sacred cattle, which came to represent the health of the kingdom.[18]

Through control over the best-watered land, public works, and political networks of client-patron ties, one polity along the Kunene expanded by the 1500s into a large and influential state. Although the details are sketchy, the awareness of a Cimbebasian kingdom referred to as Matama had reached northern Angola by late in the century. In 1591 Filippo Pigafetta wrote, "Beyond the Kingdom of Congo we may remember, is the country of the king of Angola, and farther towards the Cape of Good Hope that of King Matama, and the provinces ruled over by him, called Climbebe [Cimbebasia]."[19] Until archaeological work is done on the huge stone structures at the confluence of the Kunene and Ossi rivers, we can only speculate that these monumental walls may have been built by the lords of Matama.[20] These lords of the Kunene may have even had tributary states in the central highlands in the sixteenth century.[21] However, by the mid-seventeenth century a revolutionary social group would emerge initially from Cimbebasia and eventually replace Cimbebasian polities with military overlords: the Imbangala.

Imbangala Military Culture

The Imbangala were individuals initiated into bands known as *kilombos* and who radically altered the political face of the area of West Central Africa and introduced a new wave of military intensification. While cattle raiding was a normal response to the recurring droughts, this new variety of *kilombo* was a permanent rather than temporary adoption of militaristic subsistence methods. The *kilombos* represented a complete rejection of the agropastoral and lineage-based lifestyle.[22] The *kilombo* members, who were called Imbangala, lived in an initiation-based society that subsisted on military conquests. These people emanated from Cimbebasia,[23] spread north following the corridor between the coast and the escarpment where Andrew Battell encountered them in 1600, and then spread out over a vast area and steadily conquered new areas from Cimbebasia to Ndongo with their superior military capabilities.

These powerful Imbangala *kilombos* swept across West Central Africa and militarily dominated the previous inhabitants in much the same way that the Ngoni *amabutho* system later altered the face of southeastern Africa in the early nineteenth century. The Imbangala army shaped the tactical division of its forces into three prongs: the right horn (*mutanda*); the left horn (*muya*); and the vanguard (*muta ita*), which was used when fighting away from their fortifications.[24] Unlike the Zulu with their *ixwa*-stabbing spear, however, the Imbangala were not equipped with radically superior weapons. Most Imbangala used the same weapons as their enemies: bows, knives, and swords, while their primary weapon was possibly the war club/hatchet.[25] Occasionally certain individual Imbangala groups developed special techniques using particular weapons. António Oliveira de Cadornega noted one group that introduced a longbow so powerful that one end had to be planted in the ground to draw the string, and he mentioned another group that had especially effective techniques for using war hatchets.[26] However, these individual martial innovations were not the central factors that led to the numerous Imbangala military victories. Rather, the Imbangala success was based on their martial culture, which included disciplined military training and their adherence to the *yijila,* strict and sometimes brutal codes of behavior including the ritual practice of infanticide and cannibalism, which had revolutionary military repercussions.

Imbangala military training took place on both individual and regimental levels. Warfare in Angola was generally fought by specialists well trained in hand-to-hand combat. While most Angolan men would be somewhat proficient with bows and arrows because of their hunting experience, the close-quarters melee that followed brief missile weapon exchanges required special skills. Thus, many Angolan societies developed fighters with specialized combat skills who would act as soldiers for the rest.[27] Yet, these local champions could not claim the high degree of military preparation that was attained by the Imbangala, who were fully professional fighters living in a constant state of martial preparedness. The data does not indicate if elements of the martial arts of *kandeka* or *engolo* spread out of Cimbebasia along with the early Imbangala and as part of the training regimen of individuals. Only group training exercises have been documented among Imbangala groups.

Collective military preparation in West Central Africa often came in the form of mock battles and armed war dances called *nsanga* in northern Angola. European observers used various Portuguese derivations of the term to refer to an individual's defensive agility, training exercises, and war dances to demonstrate individual skills as well as the army's collective abilities before a ruler. Father Lorenzo, a Capuchin missionary in Central Africa in the early eighteenth century, notes that "then some of them commenced to 'sangare' that is, to make contortions to demonstrate their force and their dexterity."[28] Father Cavazzi recorded a training *nsanga* involving the Imbangala Queen Nzinga in her late seventies and her captains: "The captains were covered with furs, armed with bows, swords, and hatchets. In the middle of them, Nzinga herself, with swords and spears, made spectacular demonstrations of her ability, and when the priest complimented her on this, she responded modestly, 'sorry father because I am already old. But when I was young I yielded nothing to any Jaga in agility and in the ability to wound, such that I was not afraid to confront even a group of twenty-five armed soldiers, except if they had muskets, against which nothing will stop the destruction. But when against other weapons, that is where one can demonstrate one's courage, agility, and valor.'"[29]

Cavazzi describes collective *nsanga*, which he calls *sangamento*, as military reviews that allowed rulers to evaluate and reward their troops. Yet, these were not formally ordered processionals implied by the term "military review." While participation was a demonstration of group loyalty to the officiating ruler, individuals also exhibited their dexterity in their own solo movements against imaginary foes in attempts to outshine their rivals for the praise of the ruler.[30]

Although the Imbangala may have had the most frequent training of this type, *sangamento* was not exclusive to this group. Collective maneuvers involving the dancing out of large-scale encounters took place in Imbangala initiation ceremonies and also in other societies during ritual contexts, such as the feast day of Saint James—patron saint of the Kongo kingdom—and prior to most wars by West Central Africans.[31] While their relationship to spiritual power took on local expressions, all West Central Africans saw such dances as an essential part of the ritual preparation for battle.[32] Thus, West Central African armies would always dance before they left on a campaign.

Unique to the Imbangala was their form of military preparation on a regimental level, which was inseparable from the *kilombos*' political and strategic architectural formation. The bulk of most of the armies that faced the Imbangala consisted of a loose amalgam of fighters drawn from the lineage groups that served whichever leader had called up the army. The leaders directing such groups may have had no particular military skill or experience in carrying out tactical orders.[33] In contrast, a militarily skilled king led the *kilombos* along with a set of subchiefs who could be appointed and removed at the king's will. The rest of the fighting men (*gonzo/ngunza*) were divided into twelve squadrons, each led by a captain, or *musungo*.[34] The *kilombo* camp took the form of a fortified town surrounded by wooden palisades with twelve gates, one for each *musungo*, who held his position by virtue of demonstrated tactical ability and skill. Imbangala soldiers were all trained in group warfare as part of their "secluded" circumcision initiation phase prior to being fully initiated and allowed into the *kilombo*.[35] Indeed, once initiated, each young man still had to wear a degrading collar until he had killed a man in battle.[36] Even after this initiation-training phase, regimental drilling and exercises were everyday realties for the Imbangala soldiers. Thus, the Imbangala could field able commanders with well-prepared, experienced men who could move with a degree of coordination and expertise unattainable by most other armies they faced.[37]

The Imbangala also reaped military advantages deriving from their adherence to their ritual *yijila* codes. The *kilombo* was bound by a martial cult that centered on an ointment called *maji a samba*. Young boys who were to become Imbangala underwent martial training and an initiation ritual that culminated in their bodies being covered with the *maji a samba*.[38] This ointment was believed to confer invulnerability as long as the soldier strictly followed a set of *yijila*, which included forms of infanticide and cannibalism. Miller suggests that the Imbangala's killing of their children was a metaphor for the ceremonial elimination of matrilineal kinship ties and their replacement by the rules of the *kilombo*.[39] While children born in the *kilombo* would be killed, a woman was free to leave the confines of the *kilombo* and return with the child after giving birth, although the child would not be considered Imbangala until initiated. Thus, what was actually prohibited was the matrilineal link within the *kilombo* that could challenge the concept of a society based on initiation rather than kinship. Because they were based solely on initiation, Imbangala bands had the ability to assimilate an unlimited number of new soldiers. Losing an initial battle rarely destroyed a *kilombo*'s ability to win a war since a *kilombo* could quickly regenerate its forces by capturing, initiating, and training as many new recruits as were needed.[40]

As with infanticide, the *yijila* also included symbolic forms of cannibalism.[41] The concept of cannibalism may have resolved the ideological negative consequences stemming from the abolition of lineages and from the wanderings of the Imbangala bands. Many West Central Africans believed that the spirit of a person not buried in the lineage lands would return to torment those responsible. Thus, the Imbangala symbolically "ate" the bodies of their fallen comrades to keep their spirits from returning to cause them harm. In military terms the ritualized concept of cannibalism served a twofold purpose. First, it fostered bravery since cowardice in battle meant instant death and the disgrace of being "eaten." Because they believed the *maji a samba* protected those faithful to the *yijila,* cowards and fallen soldiers were seen as traitors to the law.[42] This intolerance of cowardice or any signs of weakness could be decisive as wars were usually decided when the first small unit gave way. In such cases the army of the defeated unit often fled in disorder since they believed the combat to be supernaturally predetermined. Once their comrades fell, they saw it as supernaturally futile to continue battle.[43] Second, the symbolic practices of infanticide and cannibalism made the Imbangala appear as nonhumans or superhumans in the eyes of their opponents, at times allowing the Imbangala to frighten their opponents into submission without serious opposition.[44]

The cumulative effect of all these aspects of the Imbangala martial culture was that the Imbangala had the military power to overcome even large centralized states. That the Imbangala had achieved a revolutionary military institution was confirmed by the fact that the mere rumor of their presence was enough to send large armies fleeing in complete disarray.[45] The price the Imbangala paid, however, was that they were constantly in need of new areas to conquer. They lived by raiding and warfare as a rejection of agriculture and the settled life. Andrew Battell, who lived among an Imbangala group in 1601–2, describes this predatory existence: "These Gagas [Jaga, that is, Imbangala] delight in no country, but where there is great stores of Palmares, or groves of palms. For they delight greatly in the wine and in the fruit of the palm, which serveth to eat and make oil. . . . When they settle themselves in any country, they cut down as many palms as will serve them wine for a month: and then as many more, so that in a little time they spoil the country. They stay no longer in a place than it will afford them maintenance. And then in harvest-time they arise, and settle themselves in the fruitfullest place they can find; and do reap their enemy's corn, and take their cattle. For they will not sow, nor plant, nor bring up any cattle, more than they take by wars."[46] Thus, the Imbangala settled only long enough to exhaust an area's resources before wandering in search of new areas to plunder.

This pillaging lifestyle spread Imbangala *kilombos* throughout West Central Africa. After destroying most of the major powers that existed before their arrival, individual *kilombos* eventually settled down and left the wandering life to found a series of major new states in the interior. These included the Mbundu kingdoms of Matamba, Kassange, and Holo and many of the major Ovimbundu kingdoms, such as Bie, Wambu, and Bailundu.

The southernmost extent of this expansion was in Cimbebasia, where they left the kingdoms of Mwila and Humbe Inene, which blended together elements of the earlier cattle culture with that of Imbangala overlords. Writing about the Imbangala, whom he called "Jaga," Avelot sketches the basis of this major transformation: "We may conjecture that the kingdom of Mataman, in the basin of the Kunene, was annihilated at the end of the sixteenth century under the attacks of the Jaga. It is in fact in this epoch that the Cimbemba or Damara, expelled from their country by invaders from the north, crossed the Kunene to take refuge in the Kaoko, whence the Vaherero came at a later time. . . . The conquerors formed from the pieces of the old empire two new kingdoms, that of Huila [Mwila] and that of Lunkumbi, the latter governed by the Humbi-inene, an authentically jaga title."[47] Humbe Inene was established with its capital at Mutano, and the kingdom of Mwila (known as Huila in the European sources) was to the north of it in the southern highlands.[48]

These kingdoms incorporated the local agropastoralists of the region with their Imbangala overlords and some gather-hunters. This process was paralleled further north in the central highlands, where the Imbangala destroyed the old central highlands polities and set up new kingdoms with themselves as overlords. Initially the division between the conquerors and conquered was very apparent, as seen in Pilheiro de Lacerda's 1797 description of the highlands people, "who are divided into two groups, those of one are called 'Quimbundos' (those who do not eat human flesh); the others are called 'Quimbangalas,' who eat it."[49] However, these two elements of society, the Imbangala and their vassaled peoples, eventually merged into the Ovimbundu people in the central highlands. A similar process was taking place in the Kunene region with the gradual political amalgamation of agropastoralists and their Imbangala military overlords. Additionally the Kunene kingdoms included gathering-hunting peoples who may have been vassaled politically but often retained a separate identity.[50] These three elements, then, were brought together in the Kunene societies of Humbe Inene and Mwila.

The new kingdoms of Mwila and Humbe Inene were extensive and also held at least nominal political influence over a wide area beyond their national boundaries. According to Avelot, "The kingdom of the 'great Humbe' embraced at that time the whole basin of the Upper Cunene as far as its confluence with the Caculuvar. The Huila, Muila, or Hila [Mwila], farther to the west, occupied the plateaus between the Kunene and the ocean."[51]

The *ombala* (kingdom) of Mwila directly controlled its heartland areas. Subordinate kingdoms such as the Gambos (Ngambwe) or Njau were ruled via subordinates, while some pastoralist groups to the east of the highlands were at least nominally vassals. The political complex of Humbe Inene spread out from the capital at Eholo Lya Kana in Mutano. It was composed of four subsidiary regions of Mulondo, Handa, and Kamba, with their own subordinate capitals; and Mutano, where the central lands were ruled directly under the king. In addition, Mutano lords extended at least symbolic political influence over some outlying Ambo kingdoms and Zimba pastoral chiefdoms.[52]

Kunene Social Systems

By the time there were detailed reports on Mwila and Humbe Inene in the nineteenth century, the Imbangala overlords and their agropastoral subjects had long since merged into a single people, known by their southern neighbors as the Ovambangala, or for our purposes, Kunenes. In order to understand the social context of their martial arts, we must first explore the Kunene social systems of the familial homestead, the clan and ward groupings, and the political hierarchy of the *ohamba* (king).[53]

Homesteads

The basic social unit of the Kunene was the *eumbo,* or homestead, centered on the *eumbo* owner with his wives, children, and other family members.[54] Physically the homestead was composed of three sections: a living compound, a corral, and fields. The heart of the homestead was the kitchen, where meals were made, and its head was the *ochoto,* or big room, where the entire homestead gathered for evening meals and ritual ceremonies.[55] The daily pattern in the homestead began with everyone taking a grain drink in their individual houses and milking cows for butter. Then the women left for the fields and the males took the cattle out to pasture, while small boys remained behind to watch the calves. The homestead came together again for the evening meal followed by various forms of relaxation, including martial arts.[56]

The apparent monotony of the daily subsistence pattern was broken up by the year's agropastoral cycle, which the Kunene calendar divided into thirteen months.[57] In the wet season the cattle were grazed in local pastures. For the rest of the dry season, however, they had to be driven to distant pastures called *etunda.* There the males, sometimes accompanied by their wives, lived in *hambos,* or temporary abodes. Unlike during the normal pastoral year when the homestead functioned as the basic unit of production, travel to the *etunda* required the uniting of various homesteads together as a ward group for the military defense of cattle from raids and thieves.

Wards and Rites of Passage

While the homestead was in many ways a self-sufficient unit, members of numerous homesteads were linked through their clans and wards, the latter enacting the rites-of-passage ceremonies that helped pass martial traditions from generation to generation. Clans (*eanda*) determined inheritance and provided connections over vast regions.[58] However, more important to daily activities and the ritual contexts for martial arts was the ward. The ward (*omikunda*) was composed of fifteen to twenty homesteads that coordinated their efforts without regard to clan membership. It was at least nominally led by a headman (*mukunda*) and united neighbors in collective work projects, wars, and trade.[59]

The ward also hosted many important communal rituals and performances marked by music and dance. These included dances accompanied by transverse drums. A few courtship dances took the form of opposing lines of boys and girls. However, in the most common form participants would form a circle and two dancers would enter the ring to dance, then touch or indicate other members of the circle to replace them. Couple dances might reflect courtship, while the movements of two dancers of the same sex could be complementary, competitive, or both. Particularly in dances between two men, brinkmanship was common, and martial arts skills were also exhibited in some dances. Beyond the *kandeka* and *engolo* that will be detailed shortly, various war dances with spears or whips and stick dances and games were practiced among different Kunene communities. For example, one dance used short sticks and the dancers hit each other's sticks in imitation combat, while another was a dynamic stick-fighting game. In the latter the two competed with sticks while the "talking" of the *ngoma* drum was used to "stimulate the performers and communicate instructions to them."[60]

These courting and competitive dances took place at a wide variety of gatherings, including celebrations of births, initiations into adulthood, deaths, and harvests. One particular context in which competitive dances were highlighted was during the seasons in which the cattle were best fed. These were times when cattle were compared socially as at a fair but also when men competed, trying to outdo others through orating and dancing out the superiority of their cattle over others. While these fairs were important for building community and exhibiting individual achievements, arguably the most socially meaningful of Kunene festivals were the male and female rites of passage.

The male rite of passage was known as an *ekwendje* ("important thing to a boy") or an *etanda* (big encampment).[61] The *ekwendje* took place only under the orders of the king, who first made sacrifices to bless the renewal of the community with the birth of new soldiers into the society. Then all the boys ready for the ceremony in the kingdom were taken by wards into encampments in the bush. The day after the boys entered the camps, each was circumcised by an experienced surgeon who carried the title "leopard." Thereafter they covered themselves in white ash and were called *ovingolongolo* (the striped ones). When the wounds were fresh, elders responsible for the education of the boys would instruct them in history, songs, and lore. Once the wounds healed sufficiently they began dance and military school. The boys learned various dances, particularly those to be performed on their return to society. These circumcision camps were also used for military preparation.[62] The boys were trained in the use of bows, throwing sticks, and other martial arts.[63] During this period a hierarchy would be established among them for leadership on the battlefield or in public works. After four to six months of relative isolation, the boys returned to the home of the headman or chief for the concluding rites, in which their mothers danced the *ondolo,* a reenactment of giving birth to these boys now being reborn as men in society.

The female rite of passage was called *efico* and included a much smaller group of initiates than the *ekwendje*. The exact phases of the *efico* varied substantially by region but usually began with a ritual in which the initiates entered a mock battle with the young boys, who would overcome them and carry them to the ceremonial place in the corral, where the rite took place.[64] On some level the rite linked the initiates to cattle. They danced in the corral, and at least one ox was killed for the initiates to eat. The girls then wore the kidney fat of the ox as collars for days. The festival concluded with a ritual washing of the girls' bodies and the braiding of their hair into a special form. As with the *ekwendje,* the mothers danced the *ondolo,* signifying the birth of the initiates as women. From the completion of the *efico* the women were now free to marry and bear children.

If one of the newly emerged women married immediately after the *efico,* a special nuptial ceremony, called the *omuhelo,* was held. The term *omuhelo* means "war dance" or "mock battle," possibly highlighting the importance of prowess in the marriage ceremony.[65] This was one important context in which *engolo* competitions took place among at least some Kunene groups. Among these groups the male *etanda* and the female *efico* were at times arranged so that the men and women emerged at the same time. Only when marriages followed directly after the *efico* did the full version of the *omuhelo* marriage ceremony take place. Martial arts were an important aspect of males demonstrating their valor and prowess in these ceremonies. In these cases the "essential condition for the parents to consent to the wedding" was that "the groom be wealthy and valorous (*valente*)."[66] In addition to other displays of martial virtuosity, including war dances and the exhibitions of *engolo* that could accompany any wedding festival, Albano Neves e Sousa suggests that in these cases special *engolo* tournaments were held; the young man who was declared the champion was not required to pay a dowry for his bride.[67]

While both the *efico* and the *ekwendje* were carried out at ward and district levels, they were also linked with the centralized political structure. Pregnancy before the completion of the *efico* was a grave crime punishable by death, as it was believed that such a birth was an omen of the death of the king (*ohamba*). The *ekwendje* could be commissioned only by the king and could take place when the king had a son or nephew ready to undergo the ceremony. One of the king's central duties was to ask the royal ancestors for the proper time and blessings to execute circumcisions in the kingdom. This began with the king consulting the house of the holy relics or emblems of power. Then the order was officially declared to the kingdom by a special minister, the *mwene mpembe,* whose messengers went from chiefdom to chiefdom informing the chiefs of the upcoming ceremony. In order to ensure the success and safety of the ceremony, all the chiefs then traveled to the ruler's palace (*ombala*). There the king conducted a ritual sacrifice to the ancestors and sparked a sacred fire, which was taken back to the various provincial areas by the chiefs. The belief was that a new era for the kingdom was initiated with a new generation of adults born into the kingdom.[68]

Ombala *and* Ohamba

The largest of the Kunene social systems was the *ombala,* or kingdom. This complex bureaucratic system impacted all levels of social life from local rites of passage to large-scale resistance of Portuguese military encroachment until the mid-nineteenth century. While the term *ombala* designated the central territory of a kingdom, in its narrowest meaning it referred most specifically to the capital palace of a kingdom.[69] The palace housed the royal family and numerous ministers and councilors[70] and from as early as the sixteenth century was protected by a stone-walled fortress.[71] These fortresses, called *kimpaka,* made the court a refuge during periods of war and slave raiding that swept over the area in the eighteenth century. The outer circumference of the fortress housed the king's wives and children, maternal relatives, the permanent council, guests, and young men who had been drawn into the king's service. Among these were the *ovikola,* the king's elite troops, who were handpicked by the king after he observed groups of aspirants giving demonstrations of their constitution, dodging ability, and martial competence.[72] The central palace housed the king and first wife along with the *kalunga* and *etoko* ritual areas, which linked the king to the royal ancestors associated with his power to make rain.

In addition to royal fields, the basis of the king's material welfare rested on raiding, tribute, and the control of trade.[73] The king claimed half of the cattle and captives taken in any cattle raids, which also ensured that his cattle numbered above the tens of thousands.[74] The vast majority of these were not kept in the royal corral but distributed to subordinates throughout the territory. The king also profited from a system of compulsory gifts, which funneled trade surplus into royal hands, and maintained tight control over long distance trade.[75]

This control became even more crucial once these regional trade routes were linked with the Atlantic trade. The Humbe region participated in the transmission of Atlantic goods as far back as the mid-sixteenth century, if not earlier. Trade goods passed through the Humbe to the Nama and other groups to the south.[76] Yet, the practice of royal trade control and the ability to use cattle rather than European goods for redistribution to subordinates allowed the lords of Mutano to retain significant control over the trade. Mutano kings sent out their own trading parties to the coast and Kakonda, funded their own operations, and had royal officials vigilantly oversee the trade. Such was their independent control over the trade that even as late as the mid-nineteenth century the *ohamba* could force visiting traders of European descent to wear skirts as a sign of his domination over trade relations.[77]

Martial Arts in Kunene Society

While long distance trade was a royal monopoly, it also provided socioeconomic advancement to a select number of the most talented fighters as royal caravan guards. While only the most select fighters of the kingdom would become royal caravan guards or join the king's elite *ovikola* military unit, the majority of younger skilled fighters still had the opportunity to work in the service of wealthy local figures, protecting their herds from attack and enriching both themselves and their patrons during cattle raids on others. Thus, there were ample opportunities for young Kunene men to advance themselves socially through martial prowess. These skills were honed through the practice of martial arts such as *kandeka,* which utilized short sticks, and *engolo,* which transformed the human body into a weapon. So great was their ability in these arts that Kunene peoples were widely renowned for their lethal potential. George Tams, a British observer at the coastal port of Benguela in the 1840s, noted that due to the dangerous nature of the trade, "trains of caravans, which have to pass through numerous districts, are often quite overburdened with weapons of every description." Yet, he marveled at one unusual group who "used no other weapon than the club though they carry on the most bloody wars with the Giagas, who are, at the same time, skilful in the use of the bow and arrow. I have often seen individuals among the caravans from the interior, who were merely furnished with war-clubs, which were suspended at the left side of their waist cloth, whereas, others are, as I said before, quite laden with diverse kinds of weapons."[78] Other visitors to the interior noted that it was above all Kunene men who were best known for their emphasis on stick fighting, which was elevated to an art form called *kandeka.*

Kandeka

Kandeka was a central concept in Kunene martial traditions and could refer to stick fighting, slap boxing, or a war dance. Primary among these was the art of stick fighting. Tams describes the deadly combat stick: "They never exceed two feet in length, and are seldom above an inch in diameter at the butt-end, while the thickest part is only double the circumference; but as they are made of heavy wood, generally *guajak,* this circumstance renders them doubly dangerous, by the facility with which they are handled, and apparently it does not require much strength to inflict a fatal blow."[79]

This weapon was also the basis for the hatchet, which was constructed by simply adding a blade perpendicularly through the thick end.[80] Even when their users did not resort to attaching the hatchet blades, these sticks were formidable weapons in the hands of skilled adepts. The Kunene men were renowned for their preference and expertise with this stick, which could be thrown or wielded in the hand with great efficiency. As a Portuguese observer noted in the 1840s, "They are the people most certainly known for the game of stick fighting, by this they are most respected. There are Negroes so experienced that [when throwing the stick] and wanting it to hit with the head of the stick or the butt end, can do so when hitting a little target at the distance of sixty to eighty feet!!"[81] Later observers such as Möller, writing in the 1890s, also noted their renown for the use of this weapon.[82]

Kunene stick fighting was quite versatile. It could employ one or two sticks held in the hands or thrown via different hand patterns to kill or take an opponent off his feet.[83] Kunene society placed great value on mastery of stick fighting, while fighters treasured their sticks. Great care went into choosing and preparing a stick. Tams notes that the "butt end is usually oblong, and is cut into sharp angles and edges, and the whole club is covered with carved figures."[84] The particular decoration of the stick may have acted as an ethnic marker as well.[85] It was a prominent symbol of masculinity, and a Kunene man never left his compound without at least one stick.[86] Sticks were indispensable for two important and overlapping pastimes of Kunene males: pursuing a pastoral subsistence and maintaining social respect in a society of honor. At the center of both were the Kunene cattle.[87]

Cattle had evolved over centuries into a centerpiece of subsistence, trade, and social mobility in the region. Close connection to cattle made bovine social systems very immediate to Kunene people. Cattle, like many other mammals, were organized into a hierarchy, with every herd member having a dominance relationship with every other member and the most dominant male leading the herd. Those higher up in the pecking order of a given herd had greater access to food and, among the bulls, dominated the sexual reproduction via access to receptive cows. However, these relationships were never static, and subordinated individuals regularly challenged those above them. Younger bulls sought to establish themselves by challenging the dominant bulls as they grew in strength. Thus, the alpha males maintained their status only by overcoming the constant challenges of subordinates and at times reinforced it through unprovoked attacks or threats in order to reinforce domination.[88]

Human control over such cattle required entry into their social world as a dominant individual. Domination over cattle began early in the lives of both herder and herded. Kunene children too young to lead the cattle to pasture remained at the homestead to look after the calves also left behind. To accomplish various tasks, these boys of four and five years old could find themselves pitted in vigorous struggles against calves at least equal to them in weight and strength. In these early contests of resolve boys were encouraged not to give in until they prevailed.[89] Through such struggles cattle would learn to recognize individual pastoralists as dominant; yet, the natural tendency of cattle to continuously test those above them as they grew stronger necessitated the maintenance of dominance through aggressive behaviors with sticks. Cattle often threatened other cattle or even herders through broadsiding or turning at right angles to their opponents.[90] Although describing the struggles of West African Fulani, the following words could also be describing a Kunene response to such challenges: "The Fulani recognized this threat and responded to it by threatening in turn with an upraised or flourished herding stick and a yell, often in combination with a brisk charge toward the bull. If the bull did not signal submission or retreat he was hit with the stick. While selection during domestication has undoubtedly reduced their wildness, Fulani cattle, especially the bulls, are far from timid and violence towards them carries the potential of reciprocal attack."[91] Such potentially dangerous displays of bravado with a stick were essential to remain dominant within the herd's hierarchy.

Male children and adolescents spent most of their time unsupervised with part of the herd. Despite often being as young as six, these youth were expected to exhibit the courage to dominate bulls many times their size. Once the cattle were settled into a grazing area, the boys used the long hours of idle time to establish their own hierarchy among themselves through matches with sticks. Skill in stick fighting allowed younger boys to rise in the pecking order of the group. These matches were part of a lifelong maintenance of mastery of stick fighting through both the throwing of sticks and dueling with them.

Stick throwing was developed from a young age through target practice. As soon as young boys were old enough to watch over cattle, around age six, they were expected to be able to defend the cattle from attack. Younger boys could test their throwing skills by hunting small game with their sticks as the cattle grazed. Older boys could lead the herd from a distance by throwing the sticks so that they would barely graze the head bull on one side and cause it to veer to the other direction.

Boys trained informally from a young age through games of mock battle. The process of formal training for individuals began with *ombundje,* a training game in which youth practiced their attacks and defenses while using switches covered in soft leaves. These allowed the novice fencer to spar with a partner without risking any serious pain or injury. As the leaves fell off, the blows came with greater speed, and when a child could effectively defend himself against the attacks of the switch, he could move on to training with real sticks in *kandeka.*[92]

Sparring with sticks was a Kunene youth's constant pastime. In many ways Kunene stick fighting resembled that of the pastoral societies of the Pondo and other Ngoni peoples, who trained from a similarly young age: "Fighting with sticks is as constant an occupation of the Pondo as is playing with a ball of the English. I have seen a mother playing with her son of 2 or 3, pretending to hit him so that he put up one arm for defence and tried to hit back; boys of 4 and 5 have their knobkerries and begin to scrap. When out herding the elder boys arrange contests, pairing off couples and forcing them to fight; the combats between individuals are constant."[93]

Among other Cimbebasian youth, and likely Kunene youth as well, *kandeka* skills played a role in courting behaviors. Loeb describes a partner *kandeka* game among the neighboring Ambo to impress young girls: "A favorite game, called *onhandeka,* consisted of fights between pairs of boys who wished to show off before the girls. Each pair fought another pair with knobkerrie sticks an even number of rounds, odd numbers being unlucky, until the vanquished pairs admitted defeat. Then each victor performed a jumping dance, called himself by the name of a favorite warrior, and challenged all other boys of his age group to fight him."[94]

Similar shows of bravado occurred when groups of boys would encounter each other in their fields. Various challenges would incite contests between individuals of a similar age or teams contests. Younger boys who refused challenges would often be beaten severely by older relatives for cowardice. Group training matches prepared the boys to act as a more coordinated fighting unit as adult soldiers.[95] When these encounters took place between boys of different wards and clans, the battles would take on a more competitive nature. As their ages increased, such battles would become more potentially dangerous and the spilling of blood became a more common occurrence. The cumulative effect of these various levels of training was that by the time they passed through *ekwendje,* Kunene youth were well-seasoned fighters. The most talented of these had the ability to rise socially through their own prestige and economically through service to wealthy men. It was this latter kind of relationship that provided poor males with the eventual possibility of building up their own large herds, perhaps enough to become patrons with clients and young fighters in their service.

The number of contexts for stick fighting was somewhat reduced among adult males. Men continued to exhibit their skills publicly in dances such as *okusela,* which could feature numerous variations, including one dancer throwing rocks at the other, who defended himself by blocking them with his stick. In *okutana,* another dance practiced by some Kunene peoples, two men with sticks faced each other in danced competitions that were imitations of real duels but circumscribed by ritual and aesthetics.[96] Beyond these danced modalities, however, adults had to give up random contests and unprovoked challenges for the reserve and self-control expected of a Kunene man.

Yet, *kandeka* would remain a central component of the adult honor system's *code duello.* For adults self-control and emotional restraint were the social standards. However, under certain contexts the use of aggressive violence was regarded as legitimate and necessary by Kunene society. These included performing in the service of their chief/patron's military exploits or in the settling of personal disputes between men. António Nogueira, who lived among the Humbe for a decade in the 1850s, describes these *kandeka* bouts: "The duel among them has an original form that is worthy of mention. When two men become infuriated to the point of seeking aggression, however rare, the relatives or friends of both give them a stick prepared in the moment from any tree, remove any [other] weapons that they may carry, and invite them to fight in order to remove the fury from their hearts. Then both champions cudgel each other until one of them or both feel satisfied, and usually end up the combat by mutual reconciliation."[97] This legitimized stick dueling acted as a form of conflict resolution, but it was also tied into a larger social system of a reflexive honor code that required Kunene men to be constantly ready to defend their linked honor and herds.

The Kunene attachment to *kandeka* was in part tied to a larger culture of honor linked to pastoral systems in which herds were subject to raiding. Because herders risked losing their bovine wealth in such raids, they had to be constantly prepared to defend their cattle, advertise this preparedness, and react to any insinuation that they were too weak to defend their property. Reflexive honor was a cultural code demanding that a man whose honor was impugned mount a counterattack in order not to lose his honorable reputation within his community.[98] Insults were considered a challenge to a herder's ability to defend his cattle and therefore required the abused to confront the insulter and fight bravely with a stick in order to defend his honor. As Brochado notes, "if there is any small dispute between two individuals, they resort immediately to [stick] dueling."[99] In this reflexive honor system, men were socially compelled to violently redress any insults through combat since a man's right to own cattle was intricately linked to his ability to defend his reputation and his cattle through the violent enforcement of honor.[100] Cattle actually embodied honor, so to lose one's cattle in a raid was to lose one's honor.[101] Thus, mastery of *kandeka* remained a lifelong necessity for Kunene males.

Kandeka was also a cultural constant that spread over a wide spectrum of social roles. The stick was a Kunene man's primary form of self-defense against surprise raids, wild animals, or their prized bulls. *Kandeka* could serve as a community performance, a solitary recreation, an innocuous sparring match, or a bloody conflict over cattle or honor. A mother might be her son's first trainer, and he would continue to carry his fighting sticks into his old age.

In addition to being a stick-fighting contest, *kandeka* also referred to a slap-boxing match practiced primarily by young males. The term *kandeka* is clearly related to *okukandeka,* meaning "to avoid or prevent," stressing the defensive nature of the art and reminiscent of the centrality of agility in defense.[102] Youths developed their defensive skills through slap boxing in different social situations. Informal matches took place in the household *ochoto* as a form of

Figure 1.1 (left): *Kandeka* slap boxing. Originally titled "Nyaneka boys wrestling." From Carlos Estermann, *Etnográfia do sudoeste de Angola* (Lisboa: Junta de Investigações do Ultramar, 1957); Figure 1.2 (right): Open-hand *kandeka.* Photograph by the author

entertainment. Edwin Loeb, in his sketch of an *ochoto* among the Kwanyama, depicts a pair of boys slap boxing, with the caption "African Boxing."[103] Often more intense slap-boxing matches took place among groups of boys who passed time as cattle grazed. Although not nearly as imbricated into the social fabric as stick fighting was, slap boxing may have had some reverberations on the informal hierarchy among the boys. Away from the purview of family elders, these matches certainly had the potential to be more highly charged.[104]

More public ritual displays took place in dance circles at various parties and festivals, often preceding the *engolo* proper.[105] In this more ritualized public display, slap-boxing *kandeka* matches among the Kunene took place in a large circle of boys and men who were both musicians and at the same time potential combatants, with an outer circle of community members who participated musically. The music consisted of a steady clapped rhythm while individual fighters took turns leading call-and-response songs in which all those present answered back with the chorus. These songs served to encourage the fighters. Once the music had taken hold of the crowd, a fighter would enter the circle and raise his open hands above his head as a challenge to all present.[106] Another fighter, usually one who felt he was close to or above the skill level of the challenger, would enter the circle with dancelike steps and raise his open hands, palms forward, demonstrating his guard.

Once partnered off, the two fighters attempted to slap each other in the face or body while dodging and parrying to keep the rival's blows from reaching their target. The encounter could turn into a hailstorm of attempted blows and ended when one person landed a blow clean enough to dissuade his rival from continuing. When there was a clear winner, he was allowed to stay in the center and might stay until he had defeated all potential rivals. When nobody else was willing or able to face him, he rejoined the circle and allowed lesser fighters to challenge each other. This slap fighting was an opportunity for younger boys to participate before the more serious *engolo* matches of older boys and men began.

Engolo

While *kandeka* trained young fighters in the art of combat using sticks or open-hand slaps, the *engolo* honed their whole bodies to be able to launch acrobatic kicks and sweeps with great dexterity. This training prepared soldiers for both armed and unarmed combat through the development of acrobatic evasiveness.

The *engolo* matches, like those of *kandeka,* could take place in a wide variety of social settings. It was practiced informally among older boys as a form of entertainment while at pasture. It was also performed in ritualized public displays that took place inside dance circles that accompanied all festivals, the most important of these possibly being the female (*efico*) and male (*ekwendje/etanda*) puberty rites. Yet, *engolo* contests could be used as athletic contests, as sacred healing ceremonies, or as a form of dueling between rival champions from distant wards. *Engolo* matches could be friendly amusements or deadly contests when personal or group rivalries were on the line. Thus, it is important to distinguish between the matches that formed part of the training ground for more serious encounters in the ritual circle and those in the open battlefield. For example, in ritual practice the art used kicks exclusively, while outside of ritual contexts, for example in general brawls, *engolo* experts could also call upon knee strikes or deadly head butts. Similarly the dance element of the art was key in ludic contests but relegated to peripheral importance during real combat.

In its ritual practice the *engolo,* like most African combat forms, was inseparable from music and dance. Language evidence indicates that the art's early history included inverted kicks, sweeps, and evasions. However, our description of how these techniques played out in ritual practice must rely on twentieth-century ethnographic evidence. Neves e Sousa documented the ritual practice of *engolo* as taking place in a circle of singers / potential combatants, which was at times controlled by a *kimbanda,* or ritual specialist.[107] The music began with clapping and the call-and-response songs that accompanied the practice circle.[108] In some songs a rhythmic humming could take the place of a response of a chorus. Soon after the mantra-like song was fully established, a practitioner would enter the circle dancing and often shouting to accentuate the techniques he would begin to demonstrate. When a contender joined the challenger in the circle, the two would continue to dance to the music as they squared off while sizing each other up until one adept launched a kick or sweep at the other. This attack was defended by dodging or "blending" in such a way that allowed the defender to launch a smooth counterattack. Ideally the two continued in a cycle of attacks, defenses, and counterattacks in a smooth, continuous flow. The interaction would end when one adept accepted defeat in the case of a disparity in ability, when one of them felt that the match had come to completion, or perhaps when a *kimbanda* who oversaw the match called for its end. The two then rejoined the circle and allowed other fighters to enter.

Origins and Techniques

The *engolo* was believed to be a sacred pastime handed down from the ancestors. The practice probably evolved from the cosmological understanding of *kalunga* as an inverted ancestor world. The only story of the *engolo*'s origin in the oral history of the Kunene is that it was passed down to each generation by the spirits of their deceased ancestors. Therefore, if Neves e Sousa is correct in suggesting that the art was linked to the fighting style of the zebra (*ongolo*), *engolo* would have been associated with zebras well after the art's inception. Zebras were noted for being especially abundant in Kunene lands by Brochado in the 1840s and by Möller, who hunted there in 1895.[109] The zebra may not seem a likely role model to emulate for combat, but they are quite adept at defending themselves:

> Zebra foals love to play. These activities are important since they help develop speed, strength, reflexes, and agility, which can mean the difference between life and death in an emergency. Adult zebras play-fight with their offspring to prepare them for possible confrontations with predators or other zebras. . . . Since zebras do not kill other animals for food and are sought by a variety of predators, they are classified as prey. Yet zebras are not an easy kill. . . . If a mare and her foal are attacked, a call for help brings five or six stallions racing to the rescue. . . . As noted, zebras do not always run at the sound of a lion's roar. Nevertheless, they are extremely wary of this enemy. . . . If more than one lion attacks a herd, zebras use a different defensive tactic. They huddle together, stallions protecting the sides and rear. Any lion that penetrates the stallions must contend with the mares, which defend their foals and themselves to the death. . . . Furthermore, a stallion is a deadly adversary when cornered. He can stomp a lion to death, or crush its vital organs with a well-placed kick.[110]

The zebra as a role model for combat also makes sense in the context of the all-important evasive ability of dexterous defenses in combat, since for the Kunene, the zebra was the symbol of nimbleness. In fact, some Kunene took on the name *ongolo* in hopes of having the gift of agility conferred on them through the ritual name change.[111]

The tournament-style *engolo* that Neves e Sousa suggests was a part of the *omuhelo* wedding also had fascinating social parallels in the ritual combat of zebras. A young bachelor zebra that wishes to take a stallion's young foal to start his own herd must first prove himself in ritual combat against the other young bachelors. This combat consists of a match with kicks and "neck wrestling" (head butting) that can last up to an hour. After winning, the elect bachelor is then tested by the father in battle. The stallion's intention is not to keep his daughter from mating but to test the bachelors to ensure that the strongest takes his daughter. The other bachelors watch and imitate in anticipation of the day they can become the elect and challenge a stallion for his daughter.[112] Thus, Neves e Sousa's *engolo* tournament to choose the most able bachelor among a Kunene ward group after an *efico* ceremony would have had clear similarities to the practice of zebras.

Even the techniques of the *engolo* closely resembled the fighting style of the zebra. The zebra's combined ability for lethal kicking and nimble defense relate it to the practice of *engolo*. Neves e Sousa argues that the *engolo* was named after the zebra and that the kicks executed with the hands on the ground were direct imitations of the kicking of the zebra.[113] These "zebra" or inverted kicks executed with the hands on the ground were the most distinctive and characteristic kicks of the *engolo*, as well as its American derivatives.

Despite these parallels between the *engolo* and the fighting style of the zebra, linguistic evidence suggests that the ultimate origins of the art lie in an ancient Bantu cosmological system. The martial art under the term *e/ngolo* can be dated to the close of the settlement of the Kunene floodplains sometime before the twelfth century.[114] This historical linguistic dating would link the art's origins to the time of the developing military culture in the region. While this militancy explains the emergence of martial arts as part of the culture, it does not explain the unique form the art took. While the zebra's fighting style may have come to be symbolically linked to the art, the term *engolo* does not appear to have evolved from the term *ongolo* for zebra. Tonality plays an important role in Bantu languages, and the term *ongolo* for zebra has a "high-low" tone (óngólò), while the term *engolo* for the martial art has a "low-high" tone (òngòló). Rather the term for the art and its related meanings may derive from **-gol,-* an ancestral Bantu root word meaning "to bend a joint, twist, or bend over."

While this term appears unrelated to combative activity, its meaning become clear when we consider the cosmological worldview of the Bantu culture of the floodplain area since late in the first millennium. African art historians such as Patrick McNaughton have put forward an understanding of African art as being about form managing power: "The aesthetic choices an artist makes are about creating the most efficient vehicles for containing and delivering that power to achieve a desired outcome."[115] Working from this understanding, the unique combat aesthetics of the *engolo*'s inverted kicks can be understood as a stylistic manipulation of ancestral power.

Like most savanna Bantu-speaking groups, the Kunene shared an inherited cosmological view of their spiritual and physical world ordered around the concept of *kalunga*. The widespread use of the term from Cameroon to South

Africa attests to its antiquity. Ultimately the term was derived from the ancestral proto-Bantu term **-lung-*, meaning "to put in order / to put straight."[116] Also derived from **-lung-* were words for the Creator God, appearing in Njila languages as *Kalunga*, which might roughly be glossed as "the one who put [the world] in order."[117] *Ka* is a prefix often used for people or offices, reflecting the fact that they conceived of *Kalunga* as a singular personalized God.[118] Beyond directly signifying "the Great Bringer of Order," *Kalunga* also referred to the cosmological order that God created. At the center of their understanding of the universe was the *kalunga* as the threshold between the lands of the living and the lands of the dead. Good ancestors were believed to live beyond, or more accurately below, the *kalunga* in an inverted underworld that could be accessed via bodies of water or even through sacred caves. The passage through the *kalunga* was a transformation linked with the color white, the color of the sea bottom or the dust rubbed onto a soul as it squeezed through the small portal in sacred caves. One then emerged into the world of spiritual power, where the ancestors walked inverted with their feet up and hands down.

The martial art may have first emerged among the ritual specialists since its constituent elements would remain linked to *kimbandas/ngangas* in the wider chain of Njilia, Bantu-speaking peoples. For example, among the Pende ritual specialists of the Kipoko masquerades, the most important physical movement was a semicircular kick identical to the *engolo*'s *okupayeka* kick (see appendix, image 5). The Kipoko masqueraders threw this kick over sacred medicines to activate them in the protection of the village. The sick of the village would crouch down to their knees so that the masked spirit could kick "each leg over them in the same semicircular kick to cover them with a shell of protection that will block the entry of the evil spirits or sorcerers who may be responsible for their afflictions."[119] Cavazzi, writing in the mid-seventeenth century, describes the equivalent of the *engolo*'s inversion movements among ritual specialists in northern Angola. In describing the behaviors of the *nganga ngombo* ritual specialist, he notes that "in order to augment the reputation of his excellency, he frequently walks turned upside down, with his hands on the ground and his feet in the air."[120] Thus, throughout the wider Njila language group to which the Kunene belong, these inversion techniques were linked to ritual specialists who clearly gained spiritual power through physical imitation of the ancestors. They may have been the first to turn flips to draw on spiritual power and use head butts to deliver medicinal payloads in their duels among themselves.[121] From these ancestral specialists the art may have spread to the general population, although in Kunene lands the inverted art remained overseen by ritual specialists in some situations.

Whether they were developed by the ritual specialists or by Kunene fighters, the techniques of the *engolo* appear to have evolved as a combative reflection of the *kalunga* paradigm with fighters predominantly using their feet to fight. Circular kicking may have been drawing on cognitive body mapping that linked the lower body with the use of ancestral power for defensive or protective objectives.[122] Most illustrative, however, was the use of inverted kicks, with fighters often supporting their weight on their hands and kicking while upside down (see appendix, images 2, 9, 11, 13–16). In this way they ritually mirrored the ancestors, as the world of spiritual power was believed to be an inverted one. These kicks from an inverted position were considered among the most powerful techniques in the *engolo* arsenal. From another perspective, the effectiveness of such attacks was at least partially compromised by the precarious nature of such an inverted position. However, the power referred to by *engolo* exponents was the more important spiritual power derived by harmonizing the body with those of the ancestors. The resulting aesthetic that valued such acrobatic inversions often dictated that the hands be used for supporting the body weight while kicking, evading, or lunging very low to duck under an attack. This constant bending over into these central positions explains how the term *engolo* could have come from an ancestral term meaning "to bend down or twist down." (See Figure 1.4 below.)

Not only did the *engolo* originate from a cosmological understanding of ancestors, but it also remained a practice strongly linked to belief in ancestral powers. The Kunene viewed the *engolo* circle as a sacred space. The *elola/ovahakelela,* or practice circle of the *engolo,* was a socially special place that evoked powerful images of the sacred status of strength. Understandings of the *engolo* stood in sharp contrast to the usual social customs of the Kunene of the eighteenth and nineteenth centuries. Among the Kunene, as with their Cimbebasian and many wider Njila-speaking neighbors, even unintentional homicide had to be rectified with a proper burial and a blood debt paid back to the clan or family of the victim, often in the form of cattle. Not giving a proper burial was believed to have spiritual ramifications, which is why the Imbangala of the *kilombos* "ate" their fallen comrades since they did not bury their dead. In the 1840s Brochado found that in order for a murderer not to be killed in retribution, the offender had to pay "six head of cattle for the body, a measure (*pedra*) of salt for the head, and eight yards of fabric for the intestines."[123]

In contrast to these practices of burial and retribution, the circle of *engolo* was seen as a liminal space where ideally more martial concepts prevailed. Vestiges of this ideal were enshrined in a line of a common *engolo* song:

> Wankya kengolo mutanbo kwapkwapo
> (who is killed / struck down in the *engolo* does not make a wake)
> Wankya kengolo kalilwa
> (who is killed / struck down in the *engolo* is not cried for)

Thus, those killed during ritual *engolo* matches were not, at least according to the lyrical ideal, allowed to have wakes, which were considered an essential part of proper burial rites. Furthermore, the *engolo* theoretically did not stop for the death of a fighter; nor was the killer required to pay the victim's family.[124] The *engolo* was also understood as a sacred space because it was watched over in a special way by ancestral masters of the art.

Full mastery of the *engolo* was limited to those who were initiated into the art as a sacred vocation. In this sense *engolo* masters were part of professional networks similar to those of *kimbandas,* sacred hunters, and blacksmiths.[125] Of such networks based on achieved status, the historian Jan Vansina notes, "All we know is that these professional statuses were highly rated, that they were acquired through individual initiation conducted by older members of the profession, that deceased members were buried with special ceremonial by their fellows, and that from time to time a group of fellows convened on other occasions."[126]

The masters of *engolo* became members of such networks and acquired full spiritual mastery through a special ritual process called *okukwatelela.* As with other sacred professionals, this calling could begin with the initiate falling sick. A diviner would then determine that the cause of the illness was an *okutumbwa* spirit, an ancestral master calling the initiate to carry on his legacy in the art. Only the ritual initiation would cure the illness and open the initiate to the direct inspiration of the ancestral master. This ritual ceremony began with the *kalunga* line being drawn across the initiate's face in white powder (*ompeyu*), symbolizing the portal to the inverted ancestral realm. The ceremony culminated in an *engolo* circle under the direction of a *kimbanda* in which the initiate became possessed by the ancestral *engolo* expert, who inspired the physical techniques and reactions of the living practitioner. From then on the initiated professional was understood to fight *engolo* with supernatural power from across the *kalunga.* This social practice also kept technical innovations developed by great masters circulating as part of the larger repertoire of the art.

Martial Techniques

While in the ritual circle, *engolo* experts relied primarily on the kicks of the art, just as supervised *kandeka* slap boxing relied primarily on slaps and hand trapping. These and other techniques might come together as a form of fighting skills when adepts skilled in multiple disciplines found themselves outside of ritual contexts in brawls or battlefield situations.[127] Of these auxiliary fighting techniques, the most socially grounded and important was the use of the head in butting contests, which constituted a separate ritual practice as well. Combatants would literally charge at each other headfirst and clash heads. These head butts took on special ritual and aesthetic significance in Kunene cattle culture. Kunene people saw cattle as representing the well-being of the nation.

Figure 1.3: Head-butting games. Photograph by the author

As individuals they valued their cattle above almost all else, named each one, and danced to mimic their bulls' movements, which symbolized masculine strength. Head-butting skills were first developed in childhood games and later applied to head-butting contests. One missionary described these as "games in which they imitated bulls butting each other."[128] This practice served as a distinct form of recreation and dueling, as stick fighting linked Kunene masculinity to the clashing of their powerful cattle.[129] The techniques of *engolo* were additionally linked to the inverted realm of ancestral power.

The *engolo* was also linked to pastoral social values. Some of the movements of the art were drawn on within the realm of pastoralist honor in dance. This was most evident when men competed in dances such as *kankula* and *omutjopa,* in which they entered the dance circle as individuals and in pairs, respectively. In both, men danced with their hands raised in "horn" positions and stomped to exhibit the characteristics and superiority of their own cattle. When they wanted to exhibit their personal flair and impress onlookers, they would punctuate these cattle movements with kicks, lunges, and jumps highly reminiscent of the attacks of the *engolo.* These movements were linked to ancestral power though ritual initiation and physical inversions.

The foot-fighting tradition of *engolo* had a distinct arsenal of inverted and circular kicks and evasive maneuvers. Unlike the kicks of many Asian martial arts, *engolo*'s kicks were not snapping, kicks and thus allowed the opponent to blend with the attack and counterattack in a smooth succession of exchanges. Most kicks were circular, and when straight kicks were utilized, they tended to be pushing kicks (see appendix, images 16, 17).[130] The most characteristic group of techniques in the *engolo* repertoire included the inverted kicks with the hands on the ground, particularly in the handstand position. There were numerous possible variations; these could be grouped into *okuminunina / okusanene komima* (spinning kicks with hands on ground [see appendix, image 15, and fig. 1.4]), *okusanena-may-ulu* (using handstand/cartwheel to kick [see appendix, images 9, 11, 13]), *okusana omaulo-ese* (using handstand/cartwheel to kick down [see appendix, image 13]), and *okuyepa* (using cartwheels to escape). These techniques were considered the best in their armory. Other important leg attacks included foot sweeps either from a standing position or from a low crouch (see appendix, images 18, 19). While individuals often created variations of the various acrobatic techniques, they all drew off the same basic vocabulary of movement and aesthetics of power.

While *engolo* fighters utilized kicks and sweeps for attacks, they relied on acrobatic evasion for defense. Unlike the slap-boxing *kandeka*, there were no blocking movements in *engolo*. Rather, the *engolo* adept had to be able to go over, under, or nimbly blend to escape any attack or situation. The beauty of the art was in the defensive agility. The all-important ability was to dodge oncoming blows and escape from attempted traps. This was highlighted by the *engolo* song "*Kauno tchivelo kwali tolondo,*" which could be glossed as "You don't have a door, maybe jump over" but spoke to finding an agile way out of any attack as well as to the wider trait of cunning in the sense of executing creative solutions to difficult situations. An *engolo* expert was expected to be able to gracefully dodge kicks and arrows aimed at him or evade the charge of a bull with flips. It was this ability to defend oneself with ducks, twists, leaps, and even flips when necessary that made the *engolo* a practical part not only of unarmed self-defense but also of battlefield combat.

Figure 1.4: Kicking from an inverted body position and crouching defense. Photograph by the author

Figures 1.5 and 1.6: Foot sweep as counter to a circular kick. Photographs by the author

Kunene fighters, like most soldiers of the Angolan savanna from the fifteenth to the nineteenth centuries, did not use shields as part of their military tactics. Shields would have made fighting in structured battle lines efficient, and their absence encouraged the use of fighting without formations, which maximized each individual fighter's combat skills. Battles were fought in a spread-out formation in two phases that tested each soldier's abilities of evasion and hand-to-hand combat, respectively.[131] The first phase involved a brief exchange of missile weapons, often only a single volley of arrows. In order to survive this exchange, soldiers relied on their ability to dodge projectile weapons.

This skill in dodging was recorded by missionaries in northern Angola as "sanguar," a European derivative of *nsanga*.[132] While "sanguar" was also exhibited in the individual or collective war dances (*sangamento*), its main purpose was self-defense on the battlefield. Pero Rodrigues, a missionary in Angola in the late sixteenth century, described this style of defense: "They do not have defensive arms, all their defense rests in *sanguar*, which is to jump from one place to another with a thousand twists and such agility that they can dodge arrows and arms (*pilouro*) aimed at them."[133] This missile phase quickly gave way to the hand-to-hand melee, as Father Rodrigues noted: "the most brave bring only one or two arrows, and take great pains not to loose the first shot, because if they loose it, the enemy is on top of them with such speed that it does not allow them to prepare (*embeber*) a second arrow before they are knocked down."[134] Thus, the most decisive phase was that of hand-to-hand combat, which occurred with open military formation. The *engolo* helped develop the seemingly fantastic ability to dodge, which was central to surviving the missile phase of combat, and would also be helpful in the hand-to-hand phase to avoid an enemy's weapon in the absence of a shield.

In Cimbebasia, dodging remained a key concept in cattle raiding even as late as the colonial period. Cattle raids were often seen as omens for the group, so chiefs and *ohambas* chose their raiders carefully through tests of agility. One such test among the Ambo was described by Loeb: "Imitation cattle raids formerly enabled the king to select the young men who might become good warriors. . . . Then the boys paired off and fought with knobkerrie sticks. Others formed rival groups armed with bows and unpointed arrows and practiced warfare by shooting at one another and dodging the arrows."[135] These tests represented the two attributes central to the style of warfare in Cimbebasia: the ability to dodge arrows and the ability to overcome in hand-to-hand combat, particularly by wielding a fighting stick.

Among Kunene peoples, military training encompassed five major pillars. As one missionary noted, "They practiced archery, rock throwing, fencing with sticks and knobkerries, hand-to-hand combat, and games in which they imitated bulls butting each other."[136] Each of these five arts had its place in combative situations. Archery was important for initial long-range attacks in open warfare, and lances could serve as an alternative. However, in the case of surprise raids, fighters might be called to fight from tending their herds and without their bows. In this case proficiency in rock throwing would be their backup as rocks could be collected on the way to the fight and serve as missile weapons to cover their entry into close-range combat. At these ranges fighters prided themselves on their mastery over their culturally valued sticks. In the late nineteenth century Peter Möller noted that the weapons of Kunene soldiers were the "dagger, kerries [fighting sticks], bow with arrows, and spear" but that they were "especially known for their skill in throwing the terrible throwing club, 'kerri' of which they often carry three or four in their girdles."[137] If they lost their preferred fighting sticks, they could adapt their stick techniques to the dagger.

Yet, even if completely disarmed, some Kunene fighters were still a force to contend with after years of honing their skills. Slap boxing and numerous other training games helped in this process, but the most prestigious ritual combat practices were head butting and foot fighting. Head-butting games taught each to transfer his entire body weight into formidable blows with the head. Beyond its dynamic inverted kicks, the *engolo,* along with other dodging practices, prepared soldiers for warfare by developing sharp reflexes and intuitive acrobatic defenses, both being constituent attributes necessary for dodging arrows, rocks, or throwing sticks. *Engolo* also helped develop the hand-eye coordination and improvisation necessary to triumph in hand-to-hand combat even when armed. Although Kunene soldiers would gradually adopt the use of firearms, these skills remained at the core of their martial system in the nineteenth century, when one observer noted their vast superiority over Europeans in close-quarters combat.[138] Kunene combat tactics reflected their gorilla-fighting approach to cattle raiding. In the late nineteenth century one missionary noted that their military "strategy consists in carrying out an ambush, hiding to get close, and suddenly jump out at a surprised enemy; if they are attacked in an open field, they disperse and regroup elsewhere."[139] These individual martial skills and collective tactics would prove a formidable challenge to Portuguese attempts at military domination of the region.

The Slave Trade and Portuguese Encroachment

The lords of Mutano were able to resist the waves of predation that marked full integration into the slaving system of the Atlantic commerce until the mid-nineteenth century.[140] However, the Portuguese economic and military penetration into the Kunene heartlands was a gradual process that began in the seventeenth century. It was nearly drawing to a close only toward the end of the slave trade in 1860. This conquest that took centuries was marked by endemic warfare that undoubtedly sent Kunene war captives into the Atlantic world after each battle along the way.[141]

Conflict between the Portuguese and Cimbebasians began from the very founding of the colony of Benguela in 1617. The Portuguese began sailing to the coast of southern Angola in the 1490s and intermittently traded alcohol and weapons with local Africans near the Loanga River for cattle, ivory, and copper jewelry. Gov. Manuel Cerveira Pereira, who likely bought into Portuguese fantasies of rich ore deposits inspired by this jewelry, established the town of Benguela in the Bahia das Vacas, or Cattle Bay. As the nascent colony grew roots and settlers ran out of any trade goods they may have brought with them, warfare quickly became the primary method of acquiring African goods.

The Portuguese attacked local lords such as Peringe, Kangombe, Mulondo, and others and enslaved their prisoners of war. They raided for cattle near the middle of the Koporolo River and at its mouth took by force the saltpans of the Ndombe people. The Portuguese used this salt to trade with the interior, and the vassaled Ndombe were forced to provide food and labor for the town. Portuguese then took by force the copper-producing area of Hebo from the lord Hebo, a Kalunda, who had grown powerful controlling the distribution of copper to the interior via Kilenges.[142] However, the control of these mineral resources did not satisfy the ambitions of the governors of Benguela, who began refocusing their attention on attaining more captives from above the escarpment.

From the founding of Benguela the Portuguese at the coast had heard stories of great kingdoms such as Mwila and Humbe Inene. In 1627 and 1628 Gov. Lopo Soares Lasso led two profound military operations into the interior. One went to the headwaters of the Kunene, and the other followed African trade routes to the heartlands of the Kunene people. These raids captured more than a thousand Africans and six thousand head of cattle, and they established indirect trade relations with the interior along the existing route from Benguela via Kilenges to Kipungo.[143]

Soon after these expeditions to the Kunene, the growing flow of Portuguese trade goods along these routes began to destabilize Humbe Inene. With its political center far to the south of the main route from Kipungu to Benguela, the Humbe Inene overlords in Mutano were ill-positioned to remain in control of this growing trade. As a result, the earlier political balance based on cattle redistribution was shaken as subordinate kings and provincial lords (*ovipundi*) moved to take advantage of this trade and acquire trade goods for their own redistribution to subordinates.[144] While the Portuguese at Benguela were providing the international goods flowing back through these routes in exchange for African resources, they did not initially control the interior trade.

Standing alone the Portuguese had limited military power beyond the coast. Although their armor made the Portuguese the only heavy infantry in the region, European firearms were loud and spectacular to Africans although too bulky and inaccurate to prove decisive in battles.[145] Maintaining a small cavalry was a military preoccupation for the governors of Benguela, but this force proved most important for chasing down would-be deserters or fleeing enemies.[146] Rather, the real heart of the Portuguese power was the mass armies of their African allies, called the *guerra preta*.[147] In southern Angola the Portuguese could exert military power only after the 1630s, when they gained the aid of an Imbangala ally, the lord Kakonda. Kakonda helped them to exercise lasting power between the Katumbela and Koporolo rivers, which led to the highlands. Governor Lasso envisioned extending his influence into the highlands toward Humbe Inene.

However, when they ascended the escarpment the Portuguese encountered formidable opponents in the Kunene peoples. Until the 1770s the Kunene rarely used firearms in their warfare; rather, they fought primarily with arrows and *l'arme blanche.*[148] Yet, backed by years of developing virtuoso levels of mastery over these weapons—and over themselves through *kandeka, engolo,* and a social system of reflexive honor—these Kunene soldiers proved to be formidable enemies. As one Portuguese official would report in the following century: "From the establishment of Benguela, they have tried to open Humbe Grande [Inene] and Pequeno, the entrance of which whites have not so far the power to achieve, and nor will they achieve without great power. So much so because these blacks are brave and in great number, and of much willingness. . . . Thus they let their valor be known, and their disattachment to life, such that far from fleeing in the wars that they lose, they stand firm waiting for death along with their leaders."[149] This was a lesson learned too late by Governor Lasso, whose dream of controlling the wealth of the Kunene heartland was cut short when he and all his men were killed by Kunene soldiers from Kilengues in 1639.

On December 21, 1641, the town of Benguela was taken by the Dutch, and the Portuguese were forced to withdraw inland to a fort at Massangano where they were cut off from the salt that had been a staple of their trade. As a result, they increasingly turned to slave raiding as their primary source of wealth. When Brazilian forces restored Benguela to the Portuguese in 1648, Benguela's settlers returned to the coast but remained focused on slave trading under Brazilian influence.[150] In 1650 they again attempted to ascend the plateau under the command of Duarte de Lemos, but they were defeated by the Kunene of Kilenges in the same place as Lopo Soares Lasso had been routed and killed two decades before.

Undaunted, in 1682 the Portuguese attracted new allies. These allies aided them in setting up a garrison in the interior, establishing the first *presídio* (Portuguese military administrative district), Kakonda, in the lands of the lord Bango. After years of warfare Kilenges fell under the influence of Kakonda, and by the end of the seventeenth century the Portuguese attempted to establish a parish called Santana in Kilengues.[151] However, the combined effects of drought and the Portuguese slave raiding would not allow for much tranquillity on the interior.

Conflicts in the central highlands had a profound effect on the way the Portuguese conducted their slave trade. In the period between the 1680s and the 1720s, as the Portuguese were just emerging above the escarpment, they found the polities of the central highland in the midst of a process of transition that had begun as early as 1600. Following the imposition of Imbangala leadership among the Ovimbundu, many of these lords abandoned the wandering life to dig themselves into the most defensive mountain redoubts available. These served as bases to expand their control over a series of Ovimbundu states on the plateau.[152] Although droughts induced military conflicts in Portuguese-controlled areas, Portuguese direct slave raiding began to be overshadowed by the number of captives that the expanding Ovimbundu states were trading to the Portuguese traders in Kakonda and Kilenges.[153]

These changes in the central highlands only heightened conflict and instability in the Kunene region. Recurrent warfare remained the norm and was characterized by the construction of numerous *kimpaka,* or stone-walled fortresses, throughout the highlands and the Kunene floodplain. Raids by the new Ovimbundu states on the Kunene cattle lords were met by defensive measures. Mwila cattle lords walled themselves up in the best defensible mountains of the Humpata plateau, and Humbe Inene lords retreated to the stone *kimpaka* of Mutano. They would disperse their normal cattle herds and sacred cattle to allies and clients for the duration of the raids.[154] Some Kunene lords of Mwila, who wanted to trade cattle and ivory rather than captive Africans prior to 1760, appear to have been forced to engage in heavy trading of captives from the 1760s in order to obtain firearms, which had already been utilized by Ovimbundu raiders for over a century. Most of the captives sold by Mwila lords originated in or passed through the Kunene and Kakulovar floodplains. This trade caused the Mwila lords to lose their overlordship of their empire as their subordinate lords in Njau took advantage of their control of trade down the Kubal River to declare their independence from Mwila in the 1770s. In this same period the Kilenges Humbe lost their vassals, the Kilenges Muso, who were in much closer contact with Portuguese traders.[155]

In this period Humbe Inene alone preserved its sovereignty by not allowing Portuguese or their traders to enter the lands south of Kipungu. Instead they sent their own traders up the established trade route to Benguela via Kipungu to trade their ivory, cattle, and captives. According to Portuguese reports in 1770, Humbe Inene still had a reputation as a wealthy and powerful kingdom: "These blacks are brave [to establish their own caravans of trade to come to the coast] as well as because it is against their laws to allow the entrance of whites into their territories or even blacks dressed [in European clothes] or with shoes. . . . from there comes yearly a great number of slaves and the largest part of ivory that your majesty has account of."[156]

In addition to trading along these northern routes with the Portuguese, the kings of Mutano financed their own trading diasporas radiating down the Kunene and Kubal rivers, where royal traders dealt directly with French and English ships calling at Cabo Negro and the mouths of the Kunene and Kubal rivers. Far from being sporadic smuggling ventures suggested by Portuguese sources, this far-southern trade constituted a fourth major commercial network after Luanda, Loango, and Benguela.[157] This southernmost system reached its height in the last quarter of the eighteenth century following the Seven Years'

War (1756–63), when the French made regular calls. Especially significant were French ships returning from the Indian Ocean with the most desired trade items sold for captives in Angola, Asian cotton textiles.[158] At its peak around 1780, the number of captives sold on this southern coast reached more than half of the number of captives sold out of the port of Benguela.[159] This efflorescence corresponded to a militaristic phase of expansion in Humbe Inene in which settlements and raiding parties were sent up the Kunene to get war captives from the populous highlands and trading parties were sent down to the mouth of the Kunene.[160]

The lords of Mutano were able to maintain their independence from the Portuguese throughout the highest points of the slave trade. As some Portuguese in Benguela lacked trade goods to compete with the Asian textiles of the French, British woolens, or Brazilian *aguardente,* they made their goods available on credit to traders and African customers.[161] This tactic helped flood the central highlands with traders and indebted chiefs. In contrast to the growing indebtedness of the Ovimbundu to Lusophone traders, the lords of Humbe Inene financed their own operations. By the 1780s Humbe Inene was supplying most of the ivory reaching Benguela. At the same time the Benguela trade was approaching its peak. Between 1770 and 1790 over half of the twenty-five thousand to thirty thousand captives shipped per year from Angola came from or passed through the Ovimbundu and Kunene routes.[162] The Benguela trade peaked in the 1790s, when it was forcibly emigrating over nine thousand captives per year. After this the southern trade to French and English ships allowed the lords of Mutano briefly to compensate for the declining exports at Benguela. Then their wealth in cattle allowed them to resist the opening of their borders to Portuguese traders until the mid-nineteenth century, after the Portuguese had abolished the slave trade.

Local Portuguese did not easily accept the metropolitan decision to stop the Atlantic slave trade. Despite earlier attempted reforms of a few individual governors, Angola had for centuries relied primarily on the slave trade and was in many regards more linked to Brazil than to the metropole. The Lusophone populations of Luanda and Benguela, which had a tradition of subverting metropolitan interests, continued the trade illegally. The Palmerston Act of 1839 posed a serious challenge for this illicit trade as it gave British cruisers the right to stop and seize all Portuguese vessels suspected of carrying enslaved Africans. This led to a temporary decline in the trade, but also to lower prices for captives in Angola at the same time that the prices Brazilian planters were willing to pay reached an all-time high due to a coffee boom.[163] The illicit traffic then took on a North American character to bypass British control and began to soar after 1842, reaching its height of sixty-seven thousand in 1847.[164] While the Mutano lords' southern trading network had fallen into sharp decline, with only a few French ships calling along the southern coast after the 1820s, these southern embarkation points revived somewhat during the illegal phase of the trade. Portuguese and British naval repression helped redirect traders from Benguela to the less patrolled sites of Lobito, Moçamedes, and the mouths of the Kubal and Kunene rivers. It was in large part due to widespread slaving near Little Fish Bay that the Portuguese founded Moçamedes there in 1840.[165] Only after the Brazilian government enforced the end of the traffic in 1850 did the illegal trade completely come to a close in the 1860s.[166]

We have seen how the origin of the *engolo* can be linked to the cosmological paradigm of *kalunga,* the inverted ancestral realm understood to be accessible through bodies of water. In Cimbebasia the *engolo* became linked to recreation, community rites of passage, and sacred networks of initiated masters. The disruptive effects of Portuguese military invasions and intensive trading in human captives reached the Kunene region in the second half of the seventeenth century. During the following century the penetration of the Portuguese above the escarpment caused major political and social disruptions among these populations. Many Kunene and other Cimbebasian soldiers, responsible for the defense of their communities, were enslaved and marched to Portuguese trading entrepôts or Humbe trading outposts on the coasts, where they were shipped against their will across the Atlantic. In 1770 one Portuguese officer reported from Benguela that enslaved Kunene peoples could become faithful servants but were "the ones that most resist embarkation to America."[167] We can only imagine that the various forms of such resistance by enslaved Kunene people at times drew on ingrained martial arts such as *kandeka* and *engolo.*[168] If so, this would not be the last time they would call upon this weapon to resist enslavement. Indeed, despite their resistance, many Cimbebasians were forcibly taken across the Atlantic *kalunga,* where they would continue to rely on their marital traditions to help them overcome the onslaught of racial slavery. They would ultimately pass significant elements of this tradition to their new communities, thus extending the technical tradition of the *engolo* into the Americas.

Two Bloodless Duels

Combative Custom in Biafra to 1860

Just as the *engolo* evolved within the historical context of the *kalunga* cosmology and cattle culture, so too Biafran martial arts developed within a particular cultural context. Biafran martial arts—and here we will focus mainly on Igbo traditions—were part of a much wider tradition of grappling arts spreading through much, if not all, of West Africa. Yet, the form that they took and their social meaning evolved from a cultural complex including yam-based agriculture, the recognition of a moral code of conduct sanctioned by the Earth Spirit, and the use of paramilitary societies. In contrast to the series of large, centralized states that marked the history of the Kunene region, Biafrans gave birth to an equally vibrant sociopolitical system but one marked by the political independence of each village or village group. Far from limiting sociopolitical development, this system was marked by democratic ideals, a complex trading system, and one of the highest population densities in Africa. In this village system of Biafra, and in particular that of the Igbo, the martial art of *mgba* was a nonviolent form of wrestling utilized within and between villages during times of peace. However, a separate martial tradition of "head hunting" dominated during times of sanctioned conflict, particularly on borderlands under the influence of non-Igbo neighbors, while a more "pacifist" Igbo social complex emanated out of its highland heartland of Nri.[1]

Out of Nri: Igbo Sociopolitical History

In order to understand the evolution of *mgba,* it is important to look at the Igbo cultural systems that united large areas of Igboland together through a shared cosmology linking them to the land and, in many areas, the ancestral highland society of Nri. The Igbo-speaking people stem from speakers of the wider Niger-Congo language family that took up yam-based planting agriculture and began spreading through the West African rain forest around 5000 B.C. The Igbo language groups are believed to have diverged from other related Niger-Congo languages such as Yoruba and Edo around four thousand years ago.[2] The Igbo appear to have separated from these other members of the Kwa-language branch in the region of the Niger-Benue confluence. From there the

Igbo or proto-Igbo gradually settled the highland plateau known as the Nsukka-Okigwe cuesta.[3] The population density grew as the Igbo developed their agricultural techniques based on yam cultivation.

This early cradle of Igbo settlement was gradually transformed from rainforest vegetation into a derived savanna, a process that would later spread with the Igbo as small groups spread to the east and west. The intensity of their agricultural production led to increased population pressures on the land. J. E. Flint remarks on the efficiency of early Igbo agriculture, to which he attributes the fact that the Igbo "developed a density per acre only matched in Africa by that of the Nile Valley."[4] As a result of this population pressure, small groups responded by traveling out from the areas of the Igbo heartland to form separate villages. During the development of their agricultural system the Igbo were simultaneously developing some archetypal social institutions and cosmological systems, the rudiments of which were already in place before the slow dispersion from the early cradle on the Nsukka-Okigwe highlands. This slow migration appears to have begun before the last centuries B.C.E.[5] From the highlands the Igbo gradually settled to the west as far as the emerging Bini Empire and east until peoples in the Cross River area hindered their advance.

Throughout Igboland the subsistence basis remained agriculture. Yet, the economic vitality of the region was reflected in its market system and currency. The market structure was based on the ancient four-day week (*izu*) that may have been part of the early core culture spread during the emigration from the highlands. This four-day week was later also fitted into an eight-day cycle known as *izu ukwu*, or "the big week."[6] Each market name combined its location and the day of the week on which it occurred. In this way Igboland was covered with a vast network of interlocking markets arranged physically and temporally to avoid overlap. Local markets were dominated by women trading surplus foodstuffs and local manufactures on *eke* day, a customary day of rest. Each village "owned" its own market, which fell under the jurisdiction of the village's patron deity. The "senior" markets and fairs (those based on the big week) were also dominated by general provisions but attracted longer-distance trade and a greater diversity of goods.

Regional trade linked various parts of Igboland, bringing fish from the Niger-Anambra valley, salt and fish from the Cross River areas, and iron and iron manufactures from the Igbo plateau. Trade within Igboland was marked by the use of important currencies.[7] The primary trade with external groups was formed along a north-south axis through which international trade goods coming from as far as India entered Igboland via the Sudan and the Igbo's northern neighbors the Igala and continued through Igboland to the Ijaw area to the south. These imports included horses, beads, and bronzes. A secondary east-west route consisted of trade in beads and cloth that went from the village of Aboh through Benin and Yorubaland as far as the areas of the Akan heartland. Aboh served as an important emporium visited by traders from outside Igboland; they traded foreign goods for Igbo salt coming from eastern Igboland and beads, horses, and iron wares from the Igbo plateau.[8] It is difficult to date precisely the development of such trade until further archaeological work is done. However, the work done by Thurstan Shaw at Igbo Ukwu confirms that these regional and international routes were already well established by the ninth century.[9]

Despite the economic vitality reflected in early Igbo market and currency systems and high population pressures, the village or village group remained the largest unit of Igbo political life. It is impossible to generalize in terms of Igbo political systems since there was a wide range of diversity over the societies, particularly in the borderland areas.[10] Yet, it is clear that the Igbo never developed large territorial states, which are often equated with political complexity. Rather, by the ninth century the Igbo had developed the basis of a democratic government based on individual freedom to achieve success and with social interactions regulated by a system of divinely enforced honor and respect for the ancestors. Elders, priests, war heroes and other individuals carried preeminence socially, but they could not rule politically. While Igbo speakers in different areas exercised distinct political systems, a common pattern particularly in the core regions was a system based on kinship models, with its largest unit being a group of villages claiming descent from a common ancestor. Villages were in turn made up of lineages claiming common descent, and these were divided into sublineages or wards based on extended families. This system may be best described as a gerontocratic democracy because elders were given respect and preeminence while each individual was allowed to maintain a political voice. Although each village group had its own intricacies, the general pattern was that each consisted of households tracing their descent to a common ancestor. In turn the village comprised ward sections or ward lineages that were descended from the sons of the original founder or cofounder of the village.[11]

The eldest man in each lineage or sublineage was considered a living link to the world of the ancestors and held the position of *okpara,* or lineage head, who had special duties involving the distribution of land. Therefore, the *okpara* of a ward's sublineage commanded a great amount of respect and could influence or arbitrate within the sublineage through moral pressure. However, all matters of political or legal weight went to the council of the sublineage, which was open to all the adult householders in the unit. This council was autonomous in matters with repercussions solely within the unit. Matters affecting other units went to the village assembly. The assembly was chaired by the *okpara* of the senior lineage and officiated by the sublineage heads, but any adult member of the village could take part in the decision-making process of this direct democracy. Similarly each village was autonomous in its own affairs, but matters that involved outside interests went to the village-group assembly, which was chaired by the *okpara* of the senior lineage head of the senior village. Even in this largest Igbo political unit, which often functioned as a representative democracy, attendance and participation were open to all who cared to attend.[12] Although both men and women could participate in these general assemblies, Nwando Achebe has shown that, at least in Aku, a complementary women's assembly, presided over by the eldest woman in the village, managed female concerns and could overturn the decisions of the general assembly.[13] Such political complementation reflected conceptions of gender balance at the core of Igbo religious beliefs.

Religious custom, or *omenani,* was at the heart of Igbo political and social interactions. While each individual would have given first loyalty to his or her family, local village, or village group, that person would have also undoubtedly felt a sense of shared cultural background with neighboring villagers. At least part of this affinity would have been based on the shared interlocking social and cosmological system that had been formulated during the early expansions from the plateau cradle. This cosmological system posited the existence of numerous spiritual forces that framed an Igbo's personal, social, political, and religious lives. Again, while unique combinations of practices could be found in various regions of Igboland, over all the spiritual forces of the religious system can be seen as forming a continuum from the most personal, an individual's own "personal god," to the most remote, Chineke, the abstract godhead that set all in motion.

The spiritual force that was believed to play the most central role in an Igbo's life was called *chi,* or destiny. Every person in the land of the living had his/her *chi* that was believed to have been chosen by that person before birth. Before a soul waiting to be born could enter the world as a child, it went before the Creator and had to choose a *chi.* While the Creator was conceived of as "the great *chi*" or the "ultimate self ordering the course and character of the universe," the personal *chi* was a spark from this great *chi.*[14] This *chi* acted in some ways as the Creator's agent (much like a guardian angel) and in others as a chosen destiny. One of the components of *chi* for males in many regions of Igboland was called *ikenga,* which represented the essence of a man's will to succeed and was symbolized by the machete. According to Victor Uchendu, this emphasis on the success of the individual fostered a "conciliar and democratic" sociopolitical system.[15] Together the *chi* and *ikenga* created a worldview that was oriented toward achievement. In a sense, the concept of *chi* obstructed the development of *okpara* lineage heads into autocratic rulers who could impose their will over the voices of individuals in the community or their ability to achieve success. As Uchendu explains, this success orientation extended even to the concept of leadership, which for the Igbo is achieved, not ascribed: "The Igbo leader 'emerges': he is not born or made. The Igbo saying that 'everyone is a chief in his hut' must be understood in the proper context. What is meant is that a dictatorial leader of the Igbo is inconceivable. A leader may be a dictator if he likes, but his leadership must be restricted to his household. A leader is supported by his followers as long as 'he does not govern too much.'"[16] Thus, an *okpara* did not "rule" per se, as that might interfere with others' drive to succeed. Rather, they acted as spokesmen for village councils while exerting influence from their association with the ancestors (*ndichie*) who lived in the world of the spirits.

The Igbo believed that when elders died and were buried close to the village, they would become *ndichie,* benevolent ancestral spirits that would observe and protect their living children. Even while in spirit form, ancestors were believed to uphold oaths and laws by punishing those who broke either. The *okpara,* usually the oldest living male of a lineage, was believed to be in communion with the ancestors and wielded the *ofo* staff of ancestral authority. While the ancestral spirits were usually protective and beneficent, they were also unmerciful in revenging wrongs when angered. The *ofo* staff was a common instrument of oath taking since swearing on the *ofo* called upon the vigilance of the ancestors to punish an oath breaker.

Ancestors were not the only spiritual forces to punish misconduct. Another class of spirits known as *alusi* were created by Chineke, the High God, to act as guardians of certain parts of the physical world. These *alusi* were the most feared spiritual forces in the Igbo worldview, and their jurisdiction transcended lineages and clan groups. These included Ifejioka, the yam spirit; Anyanwu, the sun spirit; and Igwe, the sky spirit. Of the numerous *alusi,* primacy was given to the pair Amadioha and Ana, said to have been the first *alusi* created. Amadioha, god of thunder, was conceived as a fair-skinned, titled gentleman of cool temper who was patron of "light skinned Igbos" and "men of exalted rank."[17] However, the most feared and respected was Amadioha's paired opposite (either as his wife or mother), Ana, the earth deity.[18] Ana was conceived as a dark-skinned female and the caring mother of all her Igbo people, but she could be a mother of a quick and terrible wrath when offended. Her central role in the Igbo worldview came from her association with agriculture and moral codes.

As the Earth Mother, Ana was a provider and protector ensuring fertility and agricultural productivity, the cornerstones of Igbo success. She also imposed proper actions between people by establishing *omenala,* conduct sanctioned by the land. Ana was "the most ubiquitous spiritual moral agent" because her sanction was inescapable.[19] All highly valued social norms were considered "things of the land." Among these, two separate violations were distinguished: *nso,* or forbidden acts; and *nso ani,* those that defiled the land. The Igbo believed that any *nso ani* abomination such as homicide, suicide, adultery, or kidnapping, for example, would incur Ana's wrath and bring the violent punishment, if not death, of the offender. Not only were such crimes against Ana immediately punished, but they also required special rites to cleanse the land.[20] Thus, Ana ensured that her Igbo children treated each other with proper behavior.

The most removed spiritual force was Chukwu (Chi-ukwu, "the great *chi*") or Chineke. The name Chineke implied a concept of God as the unity of the cosmic harmony of the male (*chi*) and female (*eke*) principles.[21] Chukwu was the ultimate creator and overseer of the universe. However, prior to the seventeenth century developments among the Aro, Chukwu may have been considered a removed observer of the world who entrusted humans to their individual *chi*, ancestors, and spirits such as the various *alusi*. In addition, Chukwu instituted human specialists who could balance these spiritual forces. Such specialists also played a central role in pan-Igbo relations. In this way the same religious system that mitigated against the creation of polities larger than village groups also allowed for interactions between distant and unrelated villages and village groups. The most widespread system of ritual specialists emanated from Nri, which had been linked in the early core cosmology with the Ana Earth Mother prior to the widespread emigration from the early Igbo heartland on the plateau.[22] As various Igbo groups spread out settling Igboland, they took with them this concept of Nri as a holy city linked to the earth forces. The Nri were considered the oldest ancestors or the elder brothers of all Igbo. Their sacred head, the *eze Nri,* wielded the original ancestral *ofo* staff of authority. As they were connected to the introduction of *ofoism,* yam cultivation, abominations, and Igbo titles, the Nri were considered the arbiters of custom (*omenani*).[23]

This special role of Nri in the Igbo cosmology acted as a pan-Igbo force in two ways. First, representatives of the *eze Nri* traveled from village to village performing rituals to ensure fertility of the soil and to restore harmony in local affairs. In particular, whenever abominations against the land were committed, only a Nri man could remove the ritual pollution of defiled land. Thus the Nri ritual specialists would be called in to perform the special rituals required to "cover" such an abomination and thereby ensure the future productivity of the land.

Second, local men could purchase the right to affiliate themselves with the *eze Nri* by taking a series of ranked *ozo* titles. The highest of these ranks was the *eze* title that allowed its holder to bear special *ichi* facial markings and other insignias of exalted rank. The *eze* titleholder thus attained access to supernatural forces and as a result would wield great influence in village affairs. Not only did such men gain respect in their own villages and village groups, but they would receive deferential treatment in unrelated villages as well. Thus, like the ritual specialists of Nri, local men could achieve the *eze* title and travel freely throughout Igboland despite the highly localized nature of the Igbo political system.

The Nri system was widespread but not the only crosscutting institution based on ritual specialists. *Dibia* associations and closed societies were two more religion-based organizations that helped maintain links between unrelated groups while enforcing custom in a society without rulers. *Dibia* (or *ndi obia*) were the specialists consulted in most cases of sickness or calamity. They were initiated people who could communicate directly with the spiritual realm. This ability was often combined with a practical pharmacological knowledge so that a *dibia* could divine what was ailing a person and determine how to rectify it via sacrifice to the offended spirit or medicines. There were various methods used by different *dibia*, but their common link was membership in the *mitiri dibia* association. This required a rite of ordination called *igwo aja*, which conferred on the *dibia* the power of vision into the spirit world. Their powers entitled them to widespread respect, and members of the *dibia* fraternity were able to travel outside their communities, thus linking unrelated areas of Igboland.[24]

Similarly, other closed societies linked various regions of Igboland. These groups consisted of masking societies in which the ancestors returned physically as *mmanwu*, or incarnate dead (masquerades), to inspect and judge the community. These societies often acted on behalf of the elders of the community and were used as an executive branch that might be asked to enforce the decisions of the village council.[25] The most common society was the *mmo* in central Igbo areas, the *odo* and *amabe* in the Nsukka area, and the *ekpe* or *okonko* leopard society from the Cross River area that spread throughout Igboland with Aro traders.[26] Members recognized each other through their ritual emblems such as their *ekpe* hats, and some developed mastery of a writing system called *nsibidi* and a corresponding gestural language called *egbe*, which allowed for ritual communication between members who spoke different languages.[27] In some regions of Igboland, particularly those closest to Ibibio and Efik influence, these closed societies also acted as a parallel form of leadership in the covert sphere, thus linking separate village groups over much wider areas and exercising great influence over trade.[28]

Custom and Conflict

These archetypal social and cosmological systems that spread out of the Nri heartland never remained static. Each Igbo community's experiences shaped these widespread prototypes into unique local variations. Ideally these local social practices continued to encourage the individual to strive for personal achievement but at the same time maintaining democracy and peace. In most local communities there were likely a few restless young men eager to gain a reputation as "head hunters" (a topic we will return to shortly).[29] Yet, on the whole, according to Afigpo, the Nri religious complex acted to limit violence. This was symbolized by the transformation of weapons, such as the club into the staff of ritual kinship authority (*ofo*) and the machete into a ritual emblem of the yam and *ikenga* cults.[30] The most common form of warfare between related groups, *ogu okpiri,* was extremely curtailed.[31] It was even an abomination for people to quarrel verbally or speak in loud voices during certain times in the growing season.[32] Even when conflict was allowed during certain days after harvest, it generally abided by a unique set of principles that guided most intervillage and intravillage warfare. In conflicts between groups with real or putative blood relations, the drawing of blood, let alone killing, was abhorred and avoided at all costs.[33] Therefore, most fighters used *nkpo* (fighting sticks) and *abariba* (wooden machetes).[34] Coupled with protective helmets, this type of warfare ideally led to few deaths or serious injuries. The use of *ogwu,* or medicines (such as poisons or offensive charms), was not allowed; nor was the attacking of any females who were not directly acting as warriors, which allowed some women to carry out spying and intelligence activities to ensure that none of the parties were able to carry out schemes that could lead to the death of people.[35] In all, these limited skirmishes were so regulated that they may have taken on a sportive quality. As M. D. W. Jeffreys opines, "war was a friendly but exciting display of human force employed to break up the monotony of the dry season."[36]

In the borderlands, however, where their non-Igbo neighbors' modes of conducting war could not be regulated by a shared cosmology, Igbo communities often developed fiercely martial cultures. This occurred most prominently in the northern, western, and southeastern frontiers of Igboland, where the desire for achievement focused on a second type of war called *agha* or *ogu egbu ebi isi,* "the war in which it is possible to kill and cut off the head."[37] In the Cross River region some martial societies, including the Ohafia, Adda, and Abam, produced large numbers of highly skilled warriors who specialized in head hunting with machetes.

These warriors were the products of a militarization of their society, reflected in their gendered social hierarchies.[38] For men in these societies, honor and class status were linked to martial valor, creating powerful social pressure on young men to develop into successful warriors. Male youths were not considered full men in the society until they had decapitated worthy opponents with deft strokes during "justified" wars.[39] These *ufiem,* or honorable warriors, were predominantly men who had taken heads, although the rank could also be given to a male who had similarly killed a leopard. *Ufiem* alone could carry their machetes in leopard-skin sheaths and wear *ufie,* the color red.[40] The rest of the males, who were branded *ujoo,* meaning "coward," were considered to have failed to establish their masculinity and were barred from active participation in many activities of adult men. While women more often chose honor through their achievements in agriculture, trade, and motherhood, some women chose the path of warriorhood.[41] Such women took on the ascriptive status of warriors.[42] These brave warriors (whether biologically male or female) were awarded great respect in their communites.[43] Among other honors, they alone could qualify for admission into the most prominent "secret" or closed societies in their communities.[44]

Among the most prestigious of the closed societies were the paramilitary leopard and war societies, which held mastery over lethal combat arts. Throughout Biafra such societies often guarded the village against thieves, collected fines, and punished transgressors of group norms.[45] The *ekpe* was a graded leopard association that originated among Cross River peoples including the Ejagham, Ibibio, and Efik, but eventually spread throughout Igboland with the Aro traders.[46] As the voices of ancestors, the *ekpe* masqueraders could execute convicted murderers without fear of the abomination of drawing blood.[47] Like leopard societies elsewhere, those of Biafra marked their victims in ritual forms of execution, but more common was use of decapitation or fatal mutilations, which were the marks of justified killings.[48]

This martial subculture was most pronounced in war societies such as the *ekpo, ite odo, ogbu isi, ebie-owo,* and *ekong* societies.[49] Like some leopard societies, war societies allowed full membership only to those who had killed men in justified battles.[50] At the same time, these war societies were effectively professional combat schools. Youths in the Cross River area began martial training as children early under the apprenticeship of their fathers, uncles, or age-grade leaders.[51] During initiation ceremonies of war societies the older members expanded on this training and "taught the novices various aspects of the martial arts."[52] Boniface Obichere notes that some groups taught an unarmed martial art known as *ntele ukwu. Ntele ukwu* was best known for its scissors kicks, in particular flying head scissors that could maim or kill an opponent.[53] Among other combat skills, initiates learned "hand-to-hand combat, techniques of ambush, methods of taking cover," coordination of movements without verbal speech, and the use of war medicines. These societies also instructed youths in the art of fighting with machetes, the primary weapons of combat for young soldiers. Part of the selection process into war societies involved dancing with a machete in order to display newly acquired skills: "Any candidate not sufficiently adept with his knife or that appeared to lack courage was rejected, causing life-long disgrace to himself and his extended family."[54] This reflected the stipulation among head-hunting groups that the head had to be taken in hand-to-hand combat and not after death by long-range weapons such as firearms.[55] These war societies were especially prominent in borderland areas, and some spread back into heartland areas during the slave trade.[56]

It is important to note, however, that the paramilitary violence carried out by these closed societies was limited to certain spheres. An act of violence by masquerades did not call down religious repercussions on humans, as the actor was believed to be an incarnate ancestor. Likewise, while hand-to-hand combat and the taking of heads were valorized in Igboland, these activities were limited to spiritually sanctioned, legitimate wars. Full-scale wars in which it was possible to collect heads were most common on the frontiers, but even then they were not frequent. It was this scarcity of such wars that sent restless youth from the Cross River area to travel far and wide in search of battles.[57] In the Igbo interior, such full-scale wars were especially discouraged. Related groups risked spiritual retribution if they drew each other's blood, let alone took lives.[58] Thus, neighboring villages or wards usually looked to other alternatives. One such alternative form of conflict resolution was *mgba*, or Igbo wrestling.

Mgba: Igbo Wrestling in Biafra

The origins of wrestling are difficult to trace. In his seminal work that made him the doyen of modern hoplology, Sir Richard Burton traces the spread of various arms and armaments of the world to ancient Egypt.[59] A similar reconstruction of the spread of wrestling, however, is almost impossible as wrestling in one sense seems to be one of the oldest sports in the world and is almost ubiquitous. The oldest record available on wrestling dates to 2800 B.C.E. and is found on the walls of the tomb of Governor Amenemhat in the Egyptian province of Mahez (now Beni Hasan). This tomb includes over five hundred illustrations of the complex system of Nuba/Egyptian wrestling.[60]

Scholars have attempted to explain the remarkable similarities between some Igbo cultural traits (use of mummification, sun worship, and dual organization) and those of the ancient Egyptians and Israelites by positing that the Igbo migrated from Egypt or Israel. Olaudah Equiano, G. T. Basden, M. D. W. Jeffreys, and numerous Igbo writers suggest that the Igbo are of Egyptian or Hebrew ancestry.[61] However, many of these notions among European scholars stemmed from racist and the now-debunked Hamitic myth that plagued early European and European American studies of African history in the twentieth century. Claims by Equiano and other insiders, however, are clearly important and meaningful.[62] However, relative to the historical study of martial arts, we will defer to linguistic evidence showing the Igbo language to be unrelated to Afrasian or Semitic languages. Glottochronology dates to five thousand to six thousand years ago the Igbo separation from the Kwa branch of the Niger-Congo language family to which it belongs. That information together with archaeological evidence that Igbo-speaking people were already occupying their highland plateau by the third millennium B.C.E. shows that Igbo wrestling is not likely traceable to the Egyptian system of Beni Hasan.[63]

Rather, given the widespread centrality of wrestling to almost all West African groups prior to the Islamization of West Africa, it is probable that wrestling was already a cultural trait of the Niger-Congo–speaking peoples prior to their separation into the various language families of West Africa. However, from this "protoculture" each differentiated group came to develop its own particular wrestling systems and traditions.

Etiological stories often allude to the fact that in earlier times wrestling was a potentially lethal activity. One example is "The Origins of Man's Furrow-behind":

> Once upon a time, human beings and spirits were neighbors and had many things in common. One of the bonds holding them together was the annual wrestling contest held in the land of the spirits. This particular annual event was much anticipated by all concerned because each community fielded its best wrestlers. The human society sent six stout men . . . with Akpi as their leader. The special feature of this contest was that any contestant whose back touched the ground died instantly.
>
> Akpi was the one to open the competition; his opponent was a three-headed but one-legged spirit. The wrestlers appeared to be evenly matched. . . . Akpi killed the leader of the spirits and defeated the rest of them, but all his companions were killed. Akpi stole a magic horn from the spirits, restored his men to life and they fled. Akpi was on the verge of crossing the boundary between the lands of the spirit and human beings when the spirit caught up with him and scratched his back with his claws. This accounts for the man's furrow-behind or the hollow at his back.[64]

The oral tradition of the Edo, a group just to the west of the Igbo, suggests that wrestling in antiquity was a lethal martial art used for the survival of the fittest but over time evolved into the more "sportive" art of African wrestling.[65] Although hand-held weapons made it virtually obsolete on the battlefield, wrestling was considered an important part of African military training for building strength and reflexes for hand-to-hand combat.[66]

Although this association between wrestling and combat preparation can be found in many areas of West Africa, in order to write a meaningful social history of Igbo wrestling, it is necessary to focus on its unique social functions in Igbo society. Wrestling was a shared cultural trait of almost all West African groups, but its forms and social roles varied greatly in different parts of West Africa. In Igboland wrestling, or *mgba,* had five major social functions: group identification, ritual fertility, intravillage seniority and intervillage relations, spiritual transcendence, and conflict resolution.[67]

Group Identification

Wrestling served as a means of group identification. Despite the ubiquitous nature of wrestling in West African societies, many variations and styles existed. An adept of wrestling can distinguish in the ethnographic accounts between "hooking" (brutal wrestling intended to maim the opponent) and the tamer "sportive" or ritual forms of wrestling. Even within the latter there were numerous styles of wrestling in Africa. Some allowed opponents to lock grips before the competition ensued; in others the two sides stayed outside and would dive for each other's legs; and in still others the two would fight sitting down.[68] In fact, Frank Salamone, researching on the plateau to the north of Igboland, found that the various wrestling styles served as means of group identification between various ethnic and smaller social groups.[69] The same holds true for the Igbo; even local village groups had distinguishing methods of wrestling. In my own village of Nnewi, for instance, there were two forms of grappling: the more general Igbo ethnic style of *mgba;* and *ebenebe,* which specialized in ankle picks.[70]

Establishing the particularities of Igbo ethnic styles is somewhat difficult to do from ethnographic sources, especially given that most writers knew too little about wrestling styles even in Europe to make such distinctions and parallels. G. T. Basden admits as much in his attempt to distinguish the Igbo wrestling style: "I am not sufficiently acquainted with the various schools of wrestling to be able to pronounce definitely what styles chiefly prevail amongst the Ibos, but should be inclined to class them generally as 'Catch-as-catch can.'"[71]

The "catch-as-catch can" style refers to the more properly defined Lancashire wrestling.[72] It is unlikely that Igbo grappling resembled Lancashire wrestling beyond a throw or two that Basden may have seen, since in Lancashire wrestling throws were followed up with ground wrestling, and this was rare in formal bouts among most Igbo groups. Similarly Talbot claims that the Igbo style was "Greco-Roman."[73] Yet, the modern style defined as "Greco-Roman" wrestling in Europe prohibited leg techniques, while Igbo wrestling was based principally on the use of the legs and wrapping or grabbing an opponent's legs to execute a throw.

Mgba took many local forms. Many were "out-play," or styles in which contestants started apart and then one struggled to seize the other's legs, arms, or head. A few were "in-play," or styles in which adepts grappled from preestablished grips. Here, focus will be on a stylistically particular subform of "in-play" that will be referred to as leg-wrapping *mgba.* This substyle, practiced at least among the western Igbo, was paralleled by some Edo regional styles that shared the ideal of leg wrapping.[74] Today this style remains popular among some older master wrestlers (*di mgba*) but has fallen out of use among the younger wrestlers, who have been influenced by European wrestling styles. The antiquity or centrality of this approach among the Igbo is supported by the fact that the only named technique in *mgba* that I encountered referred to leg wrapping.[75] While leg wrapping as a defensive technique was known in many

Figure 2.1: The leg-wrapping position of "in-play" wrestling. Photograph by the author

forms of West African wrestling, including other styles of *mgba,* among this substyle leg-wrapping techniques formed the central core of the arsenal. This style ideally involved the two wrestlers beginning in or working their way to a side-by-side position. The idea was to lock up side to side with the far arms holding each other extended while the near arms were around each other's arms, necks, or waists. Then one wrestler would wrap his near leg around his opponent's inside leg. The wrestler with this grip had an advantage because, barring certain countermoves, he would have been able to land on top if both should fall. The techniques of this specific leg-wrapping style may have varied among various Igbo groups, but in the regions where I conducted my research local styles were composed of variations of ten to twenty central techniques and countertechniques.[76]

Thus, the local and regional styles of *mgba* were unique and served to distinguish Igbo communities from each other and their non-Igbo neighbors. For example, in contrast to Igbo leg wrapping, the Hausa style to the north, *kokawa iri na maza,* dictated that a Hausa wrestler could "use his feet in order to help him stay erect, but can not use them to hook, sweep, or lift up an opponent."[77] Similarly, the Nupe to the northwest also had a very different wrestling style; like the Hausa *kokawa,* the Nupe style made use of deadly wrestling bracelets.[78] While contests between wrestlers with such unique backgrounds were not unheard of, the different approaches served to designate wrestlers from different areas and thus acted as social markers.

Ritual Fertility

Wrestling played an important ritual function among Biafrans. Sigrid Paul suggests that wrestling was used "to ritually revitalize the earth, especially if young, sexually potent (and perhaps celibate) people engaged in it."[79] This was the case in Igboland, where ritual wrestling was associated with the New Yam festival, one of the most widespread and solemn of Igbo festivals.[80] The event varied by region but always included numerous rites to ensure the future fertility of the soil (such as sacrifices to Ana) and was concluded by wrestling.[81] These matches were far from simply recreational; according to Talbot, they were an important part of fertility rituals: "The most important social events of the year are the wrestling matches, held with the idea of strengthening the crops by sympathetic magic. . . . This is continued on every big Eke day for about three months or more until the New Yam festival, during which the feast of the ancestral spirits is also celebrated. Later, wrestling matches are held in Omopo Quarter in honor of the new corn juju Mbara, after which all wrestling finishes for the year. A curious point about these matches is that the onlookers at once interfere and separate the players if either of them seems to be growing angry or tired. This is possibly done with the idea that such a result might, by sympathetic magic, have an ill effect upon the crops."[82] Thus, in such festivals the wrestling acted as part of the rituals that ensured the new vitality of the earth.

Wrestling matches varied by region but often included constituent elements. The formal activities began with a practice called *ichu ama mgba,* in which a crowd clearer would wave a palm frond to clear the crowd from the wrestling area.[83] In some areas virgin girls would follow this with dances, as it was believed that the virgins would spoil the power of any evil charms brought to the contest.[84] The community then formed a circle around the wrestlers, many of whom had their own drummers. These drums were played three at a time and could be accompanied by two rattles (*ahia/oyo*), a large wooden gong (*uhia/iroko*), and a small gong (*ekwe*).[85]

Drums sounding special wrestling rhythms and then songs, often provided by female vocalists, charged the area. Then the ritual taunts and challenges between the wrestlers began. Talbot noted that after a contender accepted a challenge the two would "bend down and touch the earth with their fingertips, apparently to beg for help from Mother Earth."[86] Then the two would square off dancing; each looking for the moment to engage in the actual grappling contest until one person was thrown. These ritual matches were community events in which all members of society participated. In many communities women participated as wrestlers in local bouts, and during the New Yam festival they issued challenges and wrestled women from rival villages as well.[87] Older males who had retired from wrestling acted as judges (*atamaja*), and even spectators participated by singing call-and-response songs to urge the wrestlers on. These events often began with lower ages wrestling and concluded with one or more matches between men in their late twenties, the premier wrestling grade.

Intravillage Seniority and Intervillage Relations

Wrestling also served to determine status and seniority in village affairs while training champions for intervillage contests. Most Igbo communities grouped youths into formal or informal age grades. As this cohort aged, they moved through age-grade levels until they became the elders of the community. In the early levels wrestling was a common pastime and helped to establish the leadership of the group.[88] Intravillage wrestling was not only recreative; as Paul notes, it was also "a means of establishing internal rank order, male leadership roles, and friendship bonds as well as promoting social solidarity within the village."[89] Before entering the organized village set of leadership service, each Afikpo man had to win a match in the highest wrestling grade known as *ikpo*.[90] Linked to the ancient practice of head-hunting as a prerequisite stage toward manhood, an inept wrestler who wanted entry into the formal age set had to pay a fee to arrange for someone to "take a fall" for him.[91] The matches between the ward's best wrestlers were also the training grounds of village champions and leaders. By rising to the status of champion of one's age grade, a wrestler could become the village representative, thus gaining increased wealth, status, and deferential treatment by defending the village honor in intervillage contests.[92] Successful wrestlers could also rise to social influence through their acquired respect.[93] In addition, while the victors of wrestling matches between rival villages were praised, intravillage matches involved a separate ideal of cooperative competition since the matches were intended for the good of the entire community. The winners of these communal wrestling matches were not publicly praised or glorified; nor were they socialized to boast of their valor publicly, as such behavior was thought to engender envy, resentment, and group conflict.[94]

While competitive, wrestling also fostered stronger intervillage relations among the Biafrans. Such matches usually occurred in the dry season after the harvest so that there was enough food to ensure proper hospitality. The village hosts were responsible for feeding and lodging visiting wrestlers and their supporters, thus assuring continued good relations between the two villages. In promoting intervillage contact, wrestling helped form alliances, fostered interaction among unrelated Igbo villages, and impressed on their constituents a sense of commonality. In addition to emphasizing mutual interdependence and potential solidarity on a wider level, wrestling was closely linked with courting. As a whole these matches could present the entire community as one worth being allied with in marriage. As Sigrid Paul explains: "During the match each party displayed its potential in strong young men, who, at least in former times, could have been viewed as an army of future warriors. But these wrestlers and their judges also had an opportunity to demonstrate fairness, expert command of rules, and readiness to compromise, thus exhibiting qualities sought after in potential marriage partners and allies in economic or martial enterprise."[95] Individual wrestlers could use such opportunities to demonstrate their skills in the presence of females from another village. Because wrestling was such a source of prestige and wealth, successful wrestlers were often among the most sought after in marriage.[96]

Spiritual Transcendence

For some wrestlers, grappling was a vehicle for potentially transcending mortal limitations. This form of personal elevation was reflected in the more immediate use of celibacy and medicines to overcome physical barriers to personal excellence. Most wrestlers did not engage in sexual relations for a week before a contest in an attempt to rise above their ordinary limitations. Some combatants further prepared themselves by consulting a ritual specialist for special medicines, which were worn in the *odogo* loincloth when wrestling. Others drank liquids believed to empower them or used external salves designed to harm an opponent who touched them.[97]

More important, however, wrestling offered a means to become a transcendent hero. Through the application of masterful wrestling in intervillage contests, a wrestler brought honor to his or her village and would be recognized as a *di-mgba* and a candidate for heroism. Retaining this recognition demanded that the *di-mgba* continue to exhibit a keen sense of justice and socially appropriate behavior both in competition and in daily life.[98] Those who maintained their heroic character without blemish throughout their lives could have their burial ceremonies marked by the presence of an *Agaba* masquerade symbolizing heroic strength and vigor, marking their candidacy to become an ancestral hero. In a process somewhat akin to canonization, these ancestral heroes became special ancestors who were invoked to continue their heroic activities among the living. They were unique among ancestors in that they alone could be reincarnated through masquerades and yet retain their position among dead ancestors.[99]

Conflict Resolution

Wrestling among Biafrans could be used as a form of conflict resolution. Such wrestling can be viewed in a continuum of combat forms among the Igbo. The most dangerous was *agha* or *ogu egbu ebi isi*, in which machete blades, firearms, and even spiritual weapons were used. Such weapons were prohibited in the more frequent *ogu okpiri* between groups thought to be related.[100] Wrestling could be seen as the safest form of conflict. The importance of the practice in this continuum was the fact that drawing the blood of a relative or clan member was an abomination against Ana, the Earth Mother. Although the ideal in *ogu okpiri* was to limit injury, occasionally bloodshed and death occurred.[101] Such uncleanliness would result in Ana's vengeance on all the members of the offending community, not simply the one who drew the blood. If such an abomination was not removed, the particular lineage, village, or village group, in addition to facing the wrath of Ana, would find themselves in a state of "ritual siege," and no one would trade with them until the situation was fixed. Such abominations could not be undone and could be "covered" only through a set of rituals conducted by a representative of Nri.[102]

For this reason the elders of a region at times sanctioned the settlement of disputes over land or personal offenses by a wrestling bout.[103] In this way they tried to avoid potential bloodshed. Such bouts were usually set in an open place, often a market that was both neutral ground and thought to be protected from bloodshed by spiritual forces that would severely punish such an offense. There the two representatives would meet with their numerous supporters. As they were fighting for the community rather than just for themselves, the community supported, fed, and in all ways encouraged their champions prior to the engagement. Unlike the intravillage contests, these matches were accentuated with taunts and boasting on the part of the wrestlers and their supporters. In these dispute matches, village champions often wore charms to ensure victory and to intimidate their opponents. The wrestlers would face each other and begin displaying their charms while reciting incantations in attempts to frighten the opponents into submission.[104] If this did not produce a victor, the two men fought until one was thrown onto his back. The thrower was declared the victor, and his community claimed the prize in question.

Thus, *mgba* was an integral part of Igbo society and culture. It served as a distinguishing marker of local groups as well as Igbo as a whole. *Mgba* played a ritual function that helped to insure the fertility of the land; established age-group seniority; linked villages through the hosting of contests; and served as a form of conflict resolution that helped to avoid the unnecessary shedding of blood that would be an abomination against Ana. Although the Igbo cultural system was designed to avoid bloody warfare, armed conflicts grew more common as the effects of the slave trade on Biafra intensified in the seventeenth century.

Biafra and the Atlantic Slave Trade

The area of the African coast and hinterland situated between the Niger delta and Cross River, now referred to as the Bight of Biafra, came to be known as "Calabar" by the European slave traders calling at its ports. Ethnically the people of the Calabar region could be divided into three major groupings: Ijaw, Ibibio, and Igbo, while other important groups included the Efik and the Ejagham.[105] The Ijaw lived in mangrove swamp areas along the western edge of the coast to the Opobo (now Imo) River. They had since around the ninth century been involved in long-distance trade with their northern Igbo neighbors, producing salt and dried fish in exchange for Igbo agricultural products and manufactures, as well as international trade items from across the Sahara, such as beads. The Ibibio were an agricultural people living on the coast between the Imo and Cross rivers. The Igbo living in the coastal hinterland constituted the largest and most populous group and acted as a conduit of trans-Saharan trade items to these coastal groups.

The arrival of the Portuguese on the coast in the 1470s radically altered the position of the coastal peoples in relation to long-distance trade. The Ijaw and Ibibio groups went from being on the extremities of the trade to a position on the forefront. Yet in the sixteenth and early seventeenth centuries, the trade remained sporadic, particularly in the Ijaw area, where newly formed trading towns raided villages in the delta region for captives. During the early to mid-seventeenth century this pattern of coastal traders raiding nearby villages was giving way to a more systematic slaving that drew enslaved Africans from the interior. This led to the rise of the primary trading sites of the coast, which the Europeans came to refer to as "Calabar." The Efik, related to the Ibibio, were particularly quick to reorganize and specialize in facilitating trade between the coast and the hinterland. As a result, some Efik trading towns on the Cross River developed into the area later known by slave traders as "Old Calabar." Following this pattern, the previous era of widespread raids and disruption in the Ijaw area began to settle with the consolidating expansion of "New Calabar" under King Amakiri I.[106] Then in the late seventeenth and early eighteenth centuries the trading town of Bonny rose to prominence by building trading connections with the Igbo on the headwaters of the Opobo River. Many of these towns turned from procuring captives by raids to acquiring them from the largely Aro-run Igbo markets of the interior.

By the late seventeenth century three overlapping trading systems linked the Biafran interior to the activities of European slave traders on the coast. The first, to the east of the Cross River, was a long overland route connecting Old Calabar through the town of Mamfe to the grasslands of present-day Cameroon. Despite the length of this route and its temporary rise in the 1820s and 1830s due to Fulani raiding in the grasslands, it remained a relatively marginal supplier to the trading town of Old Calabar.[107]

The second, and more significant, trading system was based in western Igboland among the riverain village-towns on the Niger River. These Igbo villages had been in trading contact with the Ijaw and Edo since at least the fifteenth century. They had developed a growing trade network that linked the Igala, Ijaw, Edo, and Igbo economies. With the expansion of trade stimulated by European trading activities on the coast, some of these Igbo villages turned increasingly to canoe trading along the Niger. Under the influence of the Edo kingdom of Benin, some adopted an Igboized version of Benin's king, the *oba*. This form of polity featured a figurehead (*oba* or *obi*) who, as with general Ibgo polities, sat more as chairman of the village council than an absolute ruler. While these specialized polities had more centralized authority figures than the village groups in most of Igboland, these mini-monarchies "were village communities and each was inhabited by even fewer people than was the case in an Igbo village-group."[108]

These village monarchies facilitated trade up and down the Niger, acting as middlemen connecting the delta states such as Warri and Brass with the interior kingdoms of the Nupe and Igala near the convergence of the Niger and the Benue.[109] The trading system was quite effective as it used canoes for transport and cowries as currency. Together the Igbo of these riverain trading towns became known as Anioma, and their towns of Aboh, Asaba, and Ossmari rose to prominence. However, the vast majority of enslaved Igbo reached European ships on the coast by the separate Aro trading system that tapped the majority of Igboland and came to dominate even the Bonny trade.

The trading system of the Aro, an Igbo group from the Cross River area, had been developed prior to the arrival of the Portuguese at the coast. The Aro, along with other Igbo groups on the heartland plateau, began to experience a relative overworking of the land due to the length of settlement and intensive agriculture relative to those of the more recently settled areas to the east and west. In response to these deteriorating environmental conditions, the Aro combined trade with their dispersion as traveling agents of the Ibini Ukpabi oracle.[110] The Aro trading system was poised to dominate the majority of the slave trade in Igboland once Europeans began trading on the coast. Their prominence can be attributed to three factors: the Ibini Ukpabi oracle; their trading linkages; and their use of military forces to overcome obstacles.

The most famous oracle in Igboland in the era of the slave trade was the Aro Ibini Ukpabi oracle at Arochukwu. This oracle was presented by the Aro in this era to be the voice of Chukwu, the Creator God. The Aro traders who were spread out throughout Igboland acted as the oracle's agents. When disputes arose in communities in which Aro traders were residing, they encouraged the contesting parties to consult the oracle. The trader would bring them to Arochukwu to receive a judgment from Chukwu. The impartiality of the oracle and its association with Chukwu made it quite popular.

This oracle system served the Aro in the slave trade in two ways. First it helped protect the Aro, who referred to themselves as the "children of God," by giving them the divine sanction of Chukwu in their travels. Second, when the Aro convinced Igbo from distant regions to travel to the oracle to settle a dispute, the Aro would pronounce judgments through the oracle and at times demand the guilty party provide human victims as a fine for the offense. These victims were supposedly sacrificed to appease Chukwu for the offense committed, but in reality they were enslaved and sold into the Atlantic trade by the Aro.

A second source of Aro trading dominance was their extensive trading network. Dealing in slaves was a dangerous occupation that required a large network of trading partners, suppliers, transporters, and escorts over long distances. Thus, the Aro's earlier patterns poised them for their dominance in the era of the slave trade. As the Aro spread out they established permanent settlements at strategic points in their diaspora.[111] These settlements then acted as collecting and distribution centers for their trade goods, as well as offering traveling Aro hospice on their journeys. From these settlements the Aro established relationships with the nearby communities, and through affiliation with the oracle, intermarriage, or via military might they gained political influence in these communities. At strategic points they established markets and large fairs such as Bende and Uzuakoli in the interior. This system not only spread to the interior but also deeply penetrated Ibibioland on the way to Old Calabar. Paralleling this physical dispersal was the spread of the leopard society *okonko,* which was derived from the *ekpe* of the Efik-Ibibio. This closed society spread deep into the interior, linking society members to both the Arochukwu oracle and the Aro commercial network. As part of a paramilitary organization, members maintained security on the roads and enforced credit contracts.[112] As the slave trade was often dangerous if conducted in the open, the meetings also allowed members to conduct the clandestine trade in kidnapped people.[113]

The Aro dominance over the slave trade was also based on their military dominance. Although they had direct access to firearms, with which they always traveled, their military dominance rested in their employment of martial specialists from the Cross River area. Any groups who rejected the oracle's decisions or interfered with Aro trading ventures might find themselves at the mercy of the Aro allies—the Abam, Ohafia, Arriba, and Ada. These warriors rejected the use of firearms for their young fighters as such use went against the spirit of battle.[114] Herman Kölar, a German doctor who visited Biafra in 1840, noted that by that time the flintlock had "become so common that even the inhabitants of Iboland are beginning to lose respect for it."[115] Yet, firearms did not create the fear in opponents that these Cross River soldiers did. Father Lutz was in Aguleri at the end of the century when the inhabitants fled their town in fear of an attack of the young men of Adda. He recalled that "in the past [the Adda] traveled across the land killing all in their path. Small in stature and armed only with small cutlass, they swoop down on their enemies with the fury of a tiger. They cut off their heads which they put in a sack hung around their necks. When the sacks are full, they return in triumph to their own people."[116]

Thus, despite the widespread use of firearms, these Cross River warriors remained the most feared opponents in Biafra well into the nineteenth century. The Aro, who existed in a symbiotic relationship with these men, tapped their desire to become full citizens through combat. The Aro acted as their guides through Igboland, allowing their fighters to prove themselves against worthy opponents, while the Aro benefited by being able to direct these armies to anyone who crossed them or failed to pay their debts. In this way Aro traders were able to expand their way militarily through most of Igboland.[117]

The Aro system then spread throughout Igboland. There were few areas that did not feel the effect of Aro trading ventures directly or indirectly. With their involvement in the slave trade, larger and larger numbers of Igbo were drawn into the transatlantic trade. Kidnapping and warfare were the primary sources of enslavement in Igboland.[118] As a result, instability became widespread and men never went out unarmed. According to Equiano, the situation was so grave that even the women of his community were called upon to defend it.[119]

As the Aro system extended into the Biafran heartland, Igboland became the primary origin of enslaved Africans leaving the ports of Biafra. By the mid-seventeenth century, as the regularity and volume of the trade increased, the majority of the enslaved were drawn from Igboland. This trend only intensified during the height of the trade. In the 1670s a European named James Barbot noted that the New Calabar traders acquired most of their captives from the "people of their inland neighbors," and in the 1690s he attributed the source of New Calabar's enslaved to "Hackbous" (Igbos) in particular. He noted, "In their territories there are two-market days every week, for slaves and provisions, which the Calabar Blacks keep very regularly, to supply themselves with both provisions and slaves."[120] Bonny eclipsed New Calabar at the end of the seventeenth century and remained the chief exporter of enslaved Biafran people through the nineteenth century. Eighteenth-century accounts remark on the reliance of Bonny and New Calabar traders on Igbo markets in the interior. John Adams estimated in 1790 that the sixteen thousand Igbo of the twenty thousand enslaved sold annually from Bonny were brought to the coast in great canoe caravans from Igbo markets in the interior: "Fairs are held every five or six weeks at several villages in the interior, to which the traders of Bonny resort to purchase them. Large canoes capable of carrying 120 persons are launched and stored for the voyage. At the expiration of the sixth day they generally return bringing with them 1500 or 2000 slaves."[121]

Although the exact numbers are debated, most scholars agree that Igbo comprised the majority of the enslaved sold to Europeans in Biafra.[122] In addition, some non-Biafrans from the far north were shipped out of these ports, particularly Fulani and Hausa. The latter carried with them a distinctively different form of grappling and a form of boxing called *dambe*. More numerous would have been the coastal peoples such as the Ibibio, many of whom had wrestling practices similar to those of the Igbo. However, the majority of enslaved people leaving these ports would have come from areas where leg wrapping or other styles of wrestling were a prominent social practice.

These Biafrans made up a large percentage of the enslaved population transported across the Atlantic to certain colonies. While the Portuguese and the French were also active in the Calabar trade, the British rose to be the dominant European trading partner well before the eighteenth century. Given the fact that most Biafrans were loaded onto British ships, on the whole Biafrans constituted a large constituent group of the enslaved population in the British Caribbean and North America.[123] This concentration was perhaps most pronounced in the area of Virginia, where Biafrans comprised over 44 percent of enslaved Africans brought into the region. Yet, Biafrans were visible and influential even in areas such as the Carolinas and Rio de Janeiro, where less than 10 percent and 1 percent, respectively, of Africans whose origins are known came from Biafra.[124]

Within the Bight of Biafra, then, two regional traditions of combat overlapped. When group bloodshed was unavoidable and ritually sanctioned, real conflicts were spearheaded by the closed societies found throughout Biafra but most characteristically represented in the Cross River and delta areas. In these regions closed societies were essential not only to trade and politics but also to combat. Such closed societies trained paramilitary tactics, above all the mastery of the machete to decapitate a foe in hand-to-hand combat. This feat would allow a soldier full entry into war and paramilitary societies.

Apart from these ritually sanctioned exceptions, however, a more "pacifist" approach to conflict dominated. In some ways distinct from elsewhere in West Africa, in the Bight of Biafra a refined approach to combat—spreading from the inland Nri heartland—was utilized to assure that bloodshed was avoided as much as possible. In fact, the art of *mgba* can be seen as a bloodless form of conflict resolution in situations that might otherwise escalate into the abhorred violence that could bring heavy religious and socioeconomic sanctions against the entire community.

In contrast at least to the "pacifistic" unarmed martial art tradition of Biafra, the martial arts of Cimbebasia were based on potentially bloody forms of pugilism. Mastery of the fighting stick was necessary for males not only to dominate their cattle but also to retain respect among their peers. Foot fighting, however, looked to the ancestral realm for inspiration. Thus, in these two regions, unique historical contexts gave birth to quite distinct approaches to combat.

As radically different as they were technically, when practiced as martial ways both *mgba* and *engolo* served similar social functions. When mastery of *mgba* was combined with adherence to a larger code of conduct, the great wrestler could attain the highest of all honors by becoming a transcendent hero. Deceased *engolo* experts could inspire living adepts' initiation into an association of masters for whom the *engolo* became a sacred tradition. As such, both martial art traditions were spiritual disciplines linking the living to the spiritual world. They could therefore be understood as social "medicines" designed to bring harmony to the living community through added connections to the spiritual community. Angolans in particular conceived of slavery as witchcraft, an unnatural transplanting of souls across the Atlantic *kalunga* to the Americas.[125] Understood this way, martial arts may have been appreciated for their ability to bring ancestral power to bear in countering this perceived evil, as well as for their utilitarian application (along with *kimpaka, kilombos,* and other martial tactics) to strengthen their communities against slave raids. Thus, the wave of turbulent chaos that swept over the Bight of Biafra and Angola with the arrival of the Atlantic slave trade likely brought these arts to a premium.[126]

Two

Across the *Kalunga*

Three Enslaved Honor

The Utility of Martial Art in North America

The Middle Passage did not strip Angolans, Biafrans, or other Africans of their combat traditions. Rather, they carried this valuable legacy with them in their minds and bodies. Not only did they keep hope of a return journey alive in their souls; they also remembered the martial traditions that could be called upon in times of need. In places where the trade tended to settle large numbers of Biafrans together in a region, Biafran-derived war dances and closed societies continued to act as vehicles for paramilitary actions in the Americas. These traditions can be seen in the Abakuá societies of Cuba and the "Igbo" war dance, which was taken as a call for rebellion, performed in early nineteenth-century Trinidad.[1] Similarly, as John Thornton has shown, elements of the Angolans' military heritage appear to have reverberated throughout the Americas, including war dances and military patterns that were evidenced in numerous rebellions from the Stono Rebellion to the Haitian Revolution.[2]

Certainly such collective military traditions may have been perpetuated in areas that concentrated Africans from certain regions together. Recent scholarship has shown that far from scattering Africans randomly, as is popularly believed to have been the case, the combination of trading patterns and preferences of European planters in the Americas for laborers of specific African ethnicities tended to lump together large numbers of captive Africans from certain areas into particular colonies in the Americas.[3] For example, Holloway and Wood have argued that Angolans constituted the dominant plurality of the enslaved population of South Carolina. Chambers and Gomez have argued that the dominant plurality of bondsmen arriving in Virginia during the eighteenth century was taken via the Bight of Biafra, while Gwendolyn Hall has similarly centered Senegambians as being the numerically and culturally dominant African ethnic group in Louisiana. Other works have shown the concentration of certain African groups in areas such as Rio de Janeiro, Cuba, Saint Domingue, and Jamaica, among others.[4] Such demographic trends were constantly shifting both in areas of enslavement and in the Americas. In times and places where Africans from certain areas constituted a significant percentage of the enslaved community in a given region of the Americas, these populations could at times call upon elements of their collective military traditions.

However, the fact remains that even Africans entering a given region in small numbers could leave their cultural mark on the future generations of the general bonded population. A clear icon of such minority influence can be seen in the legacy of Igbo Landing in the South Carolina and Georgia low-country. Despite the seemingly insignificant representation of Biafrans in this region, the widespread renown of Igbo Landing, its continued place in the folklore, and its popular acknowledgment to this day as a monument of African culture and resistance clearly show the potential of a tiny minority to impact the traditions of the entire bonded community.

Similarly, the unarmed martial arts were living traditions that could spread in the Americas even when only a few practitioners were introduced to a region. As these arts had served as a base of support in difficult times in Africa, under the exceedingly horrific experience of racial slavery in the Americas even lone martial arts masters may have been called upon to serve their new communities as sources of defensive leadership. These arts did not die with such masters but were effectively passed on horizontally (to peers rather than exclusively to progeny) even to those whose patrimony came from areas of Africa other than Biafra and southern Angola.

Combat as Ethnic Marker

Around the year 1745 young Olaudah Equiano was kidnapped from his parents' compound in the interior of Biafra. His narrative recounts his gradual movement to the coast, passing through the hands of many traders and potential patrons whose languages and cultures were distinct from his own but comprehensible to him. When he arrived on the coast some seven months later, Equiano met coastal Biafrans whose culture and language were completely unfamiliar to him. In expressing this difference Equiano noted the foreignness of their fighting style along with other traits: "All the nations and people I had hitherto passed through, resembled our own in their manners, customs, and language; but I came at length to a country, the inhabitants of which differed from us in all those particulars. I was very much struck with this difference, especially when I came among a people who did not circumcise . . . and fought with their fists among themselves."[5]

Equiano was not alone in using fighting style as a marker of cultural difference. As Frank Salamone has detailed in his study on the Gungawa, many Africans used combat forms as an ethnic marker.[6] Even in North America fighting styles would serve as means of setting various classes and communities apart. Through the group performances that established bondsmen as a new community, the martial arts of leg wrapping, foot fighting, and head butting were adopted as the black community's representative fighting styles, which proudly distinguished them from the various classes of whites, with their markedly different fighting styles.[7]

The distinctive fighting style called "gouging" was the most widespread fighting form of European Americans during the colonial and antebellum periods. While descriptions of enslaved blacks kicking and head butting each other may have appeared to the sensibilities of some European American contemporaries as bloody and "barbaric," these black fighting styles were no more brutal than white combat forms of the day. The term "boxing" was frequently used to describe the combat form employed by whites in Virginia and the Carolinas in the colonial period. Yet, this term did not refer to British bare-knuckled pugilism by Broughton's rules but, as a North Carolina governor described it in 1746, a "barbarous and inhuman manner of boxing."[8] By the early antebellum period this unique combat form had taken on the more fitting name of "rough-and-tumble" or "gouging."

While participants in rough-and-tumble rejected the use of weapons as reflecting unmanly fear, they specialized in maiming an opponent. Matches usually began with some perceived slight and ended when one of the combatants submitted or was unable to continue. The style was thus quite unique in

Figure 3.1: A street fight. From the *Crockett Almanac,* 1841. Courtesy of Lilly Library, Indiana University, Bloomington

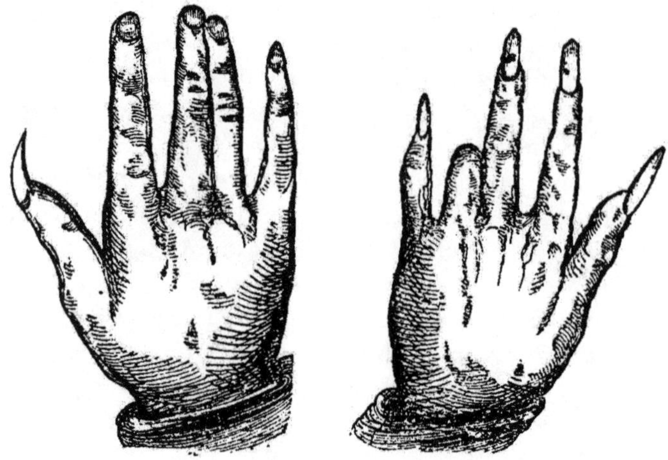

Figure 3.2: Hands of celebrated gougers. From Richard M. Dorson, *Davy Crockett: American Comic Legend* (New York: Spiral Press, 1939), 42

its emphasis on physical disfigurement by biting off appendages and eye gouging, which "became the *sine qua non* of rough-and-tumble fighting, much like the knockout punch in modern boxing . . . a fighter's surest route to victory and his most prestigious accomplishment."[9] To gain advantage, some fighters filed their teeth to bite off a nose, ear, or lip more easily, while others filed their fingernails into points and "hardened them every evening in a candle."[10] As a result, "saving face" in terms of reflexive honor often literally cost individuals their facial figures.

Linked with ideals of honor, the combat style was patronized and performed by southern gentry in the colonial period, although they gradually abandoned it in the antebellum era.[11] Many of America's founding fathers were accomplished brawlers, and even in the antebellum period elite men backslid into rough-and-tumble. While intending to settle their dispute in a "proper" duel, Savannah politician Robert Watkins and United States senator James Jackson reverted to gouging, and Jackson had to bite Watkins's finger to save his eye from being gouged out.[12] On the whole, however, during the antebellum period gentlemen slowly turned from gouging to the fencing of European aristocracy.[13] Rough-and-tumble, however, remained entrenched among the lower- and middle-class whites and spread with them geographically to Kentucky, Tennessee, Mississippi, Alabama, and Georgia. Separated socially and financially from the prestige of southern gentry, lower-class whites developed their own unique codes of honor to give them standing among their peers and to separate them from the servitude of black bondsmen: "As their own unique rites of honor, rough-and-tumble matches allowed backcountry men to shout their equality at each other. And eye-gouging fights also dispelled any stigma of servility. Ritual boasts, soaring oaths, outrageous ferocity, and unflinching bloodiness—all proved a man's freedom . . . where blacks could not jeopardize their value as property, poor whites proved their autonomy by risking bodily parts."[14] Gougers such as Davy Crockett spread this combat style of mutilation across the frontier south of the Ohio River, and rough-and-tumble boxing became an intricate part of the southern culture of poor and middle-class whites.

Meanwhile, southern upper-class whites moved toward the more "genteel" combat forms of the English aristocracy and when possible hired visiting British masters for fencing instruction. Sword duels slowly replaced gouging as the gentleman's redress of insult. The unarmed combat of the English aristocracy —British boxing by Broughton's rules—was highly esteemed but almost nonexistent in America before the Civil War.[15] The unarmed combat form of wrestling that filled this void among upper-class Americans had actually been a lower-class pastime in parts of the Europe.

David Fischer erroneously traces the origin of European American wrestling styles exclusively to the "back hold" combat traditions of the English northern border areas.[16] The fact is, however, that there were various styles both within that region and throughout the British Isles. In the British Isles wrestling was originally the esteemed form of unarmed combat and enjoyed royal participation and patronage. In the 1700s, however, wrestling began being incorporated into and replaced by boxing in the British heartland and urban centers. Thereafter, wrestling's popularity remained rooted only in the remotest areas of the kingdom: Cumberland and Westmoreland in the North, Cornwall and Devon in the West, and Lancashire south of Westmoreland.[17] Each of these areas boasted its own unique wrestling style. The Cumberland and Westmoreland style consisted of standing wrestling, in which the first to be off-balanced or thrown was declared the loser regardless of how he fell. These northern styles were marked by a distinctive wrestling position, resting one's chin on the opponent's shoulder and locking hands behind his back. In the south Cornish wrestling tended toward the use of bear hugs, while the Devon style stressed the use of trips; however, both shared the rule that an opponent must land flat on his back for the throw to count. The Lancashire, or "catch-as-catch can," style was a mixture of both standing wrestling and ground wrestling for a two-shoulder pin. Lancashire wrestling's use of torture holds, locks, and strangling made it appeal to the rough-and-tumble sort, and it took hold in many parts of the United States late in the antebellum period. After the Civil War, the Lancashire style would eventually be fused with the most widespread wrestling form in the late antebellum period, collar-and-elbow style.

The distinctive version of wrestling known as collar-and-elbow was developed in Ireland and northern England in the fifteenth and sixteenth centuries.[18] During the seventeenth century Irish wrestling was a common form of public entertainment, and successful wrestlers made their living off this trade.[19] The style worked from an opening stance in which "each contestant placed one hand on his opponent's shoulder at or near the collar line, and with the other he clutched his opponent's arm directly above the elbow."[20] This style also included groundwork and became popular in America because it gave the advantage to skill rather than size and allowed for contests between individuals of different sizes.

Although collar-and-elbow wrestling was seen as a common man's sport in Ireland, in several areas of the colonies it was considered a gentleman's pastime by the 1730s. Southern planters sent their boys to local wrestling schools.[21] Wrestling was even part of the curricula in finishing schools such as Rev. James Maury's academy in Fredericksburg, Virginia, which turned wealthy youths into polished young gentry and, as in the case of George Washington, into polished collar-and-elbow wrestlers as well.[22] Outside the walls of pristine finishing schools, this gentleman's art had a brutal side in the colonial and most of the antebellum periods. Collar-and-elbow matches in Ireland could be dangerous, and in America this style was often incorporated into rough-and-tumble sorts of matches that stressed arm breaks, chokes, and other torture techniques. The tamer version that eliminated the use of the more brutal techniques was introduced in Vermont, where the Catholic clergy adopted it in the 1700s after large-scale Irish immigration. In Vermont the clergy helped transform collar-and-elbow into a more docile form that spread with the Union army during the Civil War.[23]

In light of this discussion of European and European American combat styles in America, it is clear that the leg-wrapping wrestling style of African and African Americans derived from very different origins. The wrestling of Africans and their progeny was no mere imitation of the enslavers' style of grappling, as some may have assumed in the past. In the colonial era numerous African wrestling styles must have existed side by side in North America when Africans numerically dominated the bonded community. Some sources suggest that during festivities wrestling was often performed with music, as in Africa and in contrast to European norms. In such cases the African participants would have continued to perceive their wrestling as Wolof *laamb*, Igbo *mgba*, or Yoruba *gidigbo*, each with distinctive techniques and formats. However, a single style of African wrestling eventually took hold in the African American communities of the lowcountry, possibly by the 1830s, when the Africans and their immediate descendants were being outnumbered by those of the third generation.[24] Why this form of grappling came to dominate is not entirely clear; however, it may have been linked to the fact that side-hold wrestling like that of the Bight of Biafra region may have been familiar to other West and Central Africans as a widespread defensive technique, even if they did not have wrestling systems entirely devoted to it. Even after the percussive

Figure 3.3: Kicking a wrap, demonstrated by Deacon Robinson. Beaufort, South Carolina, 1990. Photograph by the author

music that accompanied it in Africa and in colonial America fell out of use, its African origins were evident in the techniques of this leg-wrapping style.

Details of the techniques of this style were never recorded in writing, but the geography of its twentieth-century practice suggests that it dates back to at least the previous century. Many older black men in regions of the Chesapeake and lowcountry remember engaging in or watching this type of wrestling as young men. In areas where boxing gyms did not appear until after the late 1970s, the cultural pattern of black wrestling continued into this decade. This style, referred to as "kicking a wrap" or just "wrasslin,'" was markedly different from the European wrestling styles in North America in terms of style, gender dynamics, and social usage. Like the leg-wrapping *mgba* and its cognates, kicking a wrap was quite distinct from either Lancashire catch-as-catch-can or Irish collar-and-elbow. This leg-wrapping system was a form of in-play (begun from certain starting positions) that did not include groundwork in formal contests. Unlike the styles of the northern British Isles, kicking a wrap used the identical techniques of the leg-wrapping *mgba* and its cognates. Wrap wrestling was executed from a side position with the far arms held out and locked at the hand. The techniques mirrored the *mgba* ideal to control an opponent by using a leg to wrap around the opponent's. From this position side-hold wrestlers used the same leg-wrapping attacks and countermoves described by older *di mgba* wrestling experts. Even the rules were similar to those of *mgba* in terms of what constituted a fall and how many falls constituted a win. Thus, technical elements of the leg-wrapping style of *mgba* and its various cognates were perpetuated in kicking a wrap.[25]

Beyond the combat techniques, the gendering of African American wrestling also paralleled practices in Biafra and possibly other areas of Africa.[26] In the European American tradition of gouging some female participation in wrestling may have occurred but was neither commonplace nor socially acceptable. Yet, in the bonded communities of North America, women played an active role in wrestling against each other and against men. In many Biafran communities women not only supported their wrestling sons but also wrestled themselves and trained young wrestlers. Some Biafran women often took part in wrestling matches against women from other villages during the ritual matches surrounding festivals.[27] Some societies encouraged the formal training of women in wrestling because they valued women as soldiers in times of warfare.[28] A parallel pattern took place, particularly in the lowcountry, where women were frequently wrestlers.[29] Even today in the lowcountry area there are women known as feared wrestlers in the community who are said to have humbled many men in their careers.[30] Together with the fact that Biafran women outnumbered Biafran men in the lowcountry, this gendering of wrestling raises the likely possibility that African women may have played a role in the perpetuation of leg-wrapping techniques in the bonded communities of the region.[31] In contrast, knocking and kicking was a male-dominated art in North America.

Knocking and kicking was a composite art that carried on the legacy of foot-fighting and head-butting practices of Cimbebasian and other Angolan peoples. A compartmentalized but important component of this art's arsenal, the use of head butting was likely drawn primarily from the experience of Angolan fighters. As in Angola, head butting in North America (and much of the Americas) was a much more widespread social practice than the kicking component. The establishment of this wider use of head fighting in North America may have been supported by the fact that head butting was also practiced among some northern Angolans from the overlapping regions of Kongo and the Greater Loango Coast.[32] Despite the possible ultimate Bantu providence of the practice, by the time detailed accounts of the tradition became known in the eighteenth century, it was already widely accepted into the cultural practice of bondsmen regardless of specific African ethnic origins.[33]

Although the term "knocking" could be applied in general parlance more broadly to any percussive blow, particularly a punch, in its more strict usage by practitioners the term also designated a specific type of head butting: a charging head butt from a more horizontal upper body position. Echoing the Kunene men's imitation of their prized cattle, black North Americans rushed at each other with bowed heads, and the impact of their clashing skulls produced

Knocking

Butting

Figure 3.4 (top): "The Sabbath among Slaves." From Henry Bibb, *The Life and Adventures of Henry Bibb: An American Slave,* ed. Charles Helgar (Madison: University of Wisconsin Press, 2001); Figure 3.5: Adaptation from "The Sabbath among Slaves" highlighting knocking and butting

the loud "knock" after which the technique was named. (See Figures 3.4 and 3.5.) One visitor to North America noted the skill of the black steward on the ship, *Ruthy,* who was "known as a champion of champions, having conquered a hero of his own colour by butting on all fours, like two rams, a mode of fighting common amongst blacks."[34] A second modality of head butting was called "buttin" and involved close-range head-butts from a more vertical position. (See combatants at the right side of Figure 3.4.) These could be freely applied in combat but were also practiced in games in which two competitors grabbed each other by the body or ears and butted each other until one party admitted defeat.

Numerous twentieth-century informants attest to the effectiveness of these head blows. Emory Cambell, director of the historic Penn Center on St. Helena Island, recalls being told by his father not to fight one of the Cohens, a local family, or they "will knock you down with their heads."[35] Mike Cohen remembers seeing his grandfather James Cohen butt many people and knock them out with one blow, and Perry White claims that Mike's grandfather could knock out a cow with his head.[36] Sam Toomer, an expert butter, stated that good butters know exactly where to hit a person to knock them out in playful competitions and where to hit to cause serious harm or death in a real conflict.[37]

A separate and more exclusive component of the art was kicking. Numerous informants attest to the destructiveness of these foot attacks. The son of a late knocking-and-kicking master remembers his father often kicking a doorpost with great precision and power developed by years of training. Sam Toomer explained that certain families of his generation knew this art and could "kick over your head like those karate guys."[38] The lowcountry historian Herman Carter explained further: "I used to know some men who are dead now who used to do it. Instead of using knives and guns and things they just get out and do it with each other's heads, or take the feet . . . now some of them were more talented than the karate [fighters] in Asia. I saw grown men have bouts. It was similar to karate kicks, but they were aware of where to kick you to put you out. . . . They would have certain places where they would hit you. If he was going to hit you in the chest with his foot, in the stomach, or under the chin he'd hit you places where it would really be a detrimental blow if he hit you right."[39]

The leg techniques of this art also included numerous *engolo*-style sweeps. Although knocking and kicking may not have been adapted to compete with British pugilism until the last decades of enslavement, twentieth-century practice suggests that its foot sweeps may have been effective against British-style boxing. John Anerum of Charleston demonstrated for me the "crosss-step," a versatile technique identical to an *okukondjola* (similar to image 19 in the appendix) in *engolo,* which cuts an opponent off his feet. Although usually used as a counter to a kick, the crosstep was used when confronting a boxer in order to "kick his feet out from under him," according to John Anerum.[40] Another such sweep was the "catman," akin to *engolo*'s *okukondjola olumbimbi* (similar to image 18 in the appendix).[41] Al Alston, Zora Dance, and numerous other lowcountry blacks remember learning these techniques by watching the trained, older fighters.[42]

In ritual use these skills of head butting and foot fighting were practiced separately. While kicking masters relied primarily on their dynamic kicks and defensive movements, like most men in their communities they were also trained in the art of head butting. Thus, while martial skills were compartmentalized in ritual practice, in real melees kicking masters could use all the offensive skills in their arsenal. They may have found head butts particularly effective in combat with people who fought with grappling. Thus, the presence of strong grapplers in the bonded community may also have encouraged the widespread use of head butts. Certainly their utility for kickers is highlighted in the stories of such mixed matches. For example, numerous elders on Lady's Island, South Carolina, recounted the memorable fight of "Heavy Dick" Miller, who was a feared kicker. He was known for his high and inverted kicks and usually won all his fights by kicking. Some elders have recalled the day when a strong wrestler had managed to elude his kicks, throw him down, and pin him on the ground. A woman named Nelly asked, "What's wrong with your head, Dick?" At that, Dick butted the wrestler and knocked him out with one shot.[43]

In summary, in North America fighting styles continued to demarcate different social groups. During the colonial period, elite European Americans distinguished themselves from the English elite by employing the violent fighting style of gouging. In the late antebellum period, they gradually moved to adopting European combat forms such as fencing, Lancashire catch as catch can, and Irish collar-and-elbow. Lower-class European Americans held on to gouging and used it as a statement of their honor and difference from the enslaved Africans. The bonded community must have originally housed as many different combat forms as there were African ethnicities represented in a given area. Thus, while enslaved Senegambians, for example, may have continued to distinguish themselves in the bonded community through their particular techniques, they also would have been keenly aware of their grappling styles' overarching similarities to other black styles in the bonded community, particularly in contrast to the radically divergent European American gouging, which was used while wrestling on the ground and looking to maim an opponent. Over time, at least three African American styles became widespread: the leg wrapping style of kicking a wrap, head butting, and kicking. As Fredrick Douglass noted in his 1855 work, *My Bondage and My Freedom,* fist fighting was being practiced, but the nature of this boxing remains to be explored. These African combative technologies were continued not only because they served as identity markers but also because they served practical uses in the lives of North American bondsmen.

The Utility of Martial Arts

Captive Africans who were brought to different parts of North America would have experienced related but distinct regional and subregional systems of bondage. In Florida a colony of strategic more than economic value for the Spanish, in addition to their use in agriculture and pastoralism bondsmen were often employed in militias for the colony's defense.[44] In the northern colonies many labored, for example, on cereal or provision farms or in ironworks, tanneries, or saltworks. A significant percentage of bondsmen in the northern colonies labored in cities, while forced labor in the lower Mississippi Valley became typified by urban bondage. A common feature of urban bondage was hiring out the labor of bondsmen.[45] In contrast, plantation economies dominated the Chesapeake and lowcountry regions.[46] Some bondsmen in both regions worked in semiskilled and skilled trades as, for example, domestics, craftsmen, artisans, and boatmen. Yet, the economy of the Chesapeake region was primarily dependent on tobacco (and to a lesser extent cereal) production. While bondsmen were dispersed across work units of different sizes, many worked in gangs to grow and process tobacco. The economy of the lowcountry was focused primarily on rice production, although indigo and cotton were important secondary crops. African traditions of rice cultivation and processing were crucial to the introduction and success of the crop in the region. Most bondsmen lived on relatively large plantations and worked under a task system of labor, which limited their forced labor to the completion of a certain daily objective or quota.[47] In the nineteenth century many of the descendants of enslaved Africans were drawn into the rapidly expanding cotton plantation system that swept across the lower South.

Although most of the examples in this chapter are drawn from the lowcountry and Chesapeake regions, it is important to note that blacks drew on martial art traditions in all regions of North America. These included forms of stick fighting.[48] However, the two longest lasting and most widespread martial arts were the "wrasslin'" art of kicking a wrap and knocking and kicking, also known as *yuna onse*.[49] Why these martial art traditions, of the many others that would also have been brought by African adepts, became prominent in North America is not entirely clear.[50] That African martial arts became entrenched in the Americas, however, should not be surprising since these technologies could potentially aid enslaved Africans and their descendants in a wide variety of contexts. Michael Gomez has pointed out that there were two major contexts of cultural interaction. The first was the "culture of volition," away from the presence of whites, "in which intra-African and African-African American cultural factors were at play." The second was the "culture of coercion," in which there was an unequal exchange between people of African descent and those of European descent in the realm of forced interaction.[51] Although Gomez suggests that in the presence of whites, "reinterpretation [of European forms] was the lone option available," on the level of combative culture this was not the case.[52] As we shall see, without any need to "reinterpret" European American gouging, the mastery of African martial art traditions had potential utility in multiple realms. In addition to their application in closed societies and in defense of honor (topics that will be discussed later), there were three overarching social spheres in which African martial traditions could prove beneficial in North America: on the outskirts of the slave system among maroons; within the bonded community's performance rituals; and in the service of European owners.[53]

Maroonage

The state of maroonage could be a permanent condition of individuals who liberated themselves from bondage or a temporary state in which an enslaved person left his or her plantation with the intention of returning after a brief respite. Those of the former often formed maroon communities of self-liberated people who fled bondage to live in inaccessible areas, particularly swamps and forests.[54] While some groups settled in distant areas, many maroon groups situated themselves just beyond the periphery of the plantations or towns. The latter remained a constant thorn in the side of the planter class since they often raided European American settlements and encouraged enslaved blacks to run away with them.[55]

As in other areas of the Americas, maroon settlements in North America often drew on African military traditions in developing the defense of their communities.[56] Although written documentation about the inner workings is scarce, sources clearly indicate that fighting was crucial to maroon survival and that African legacies undoubtedly informed maroon combat practice. An escaped bondsman named Jacob was presumably drawing on an African combat legacy when he defended himself with "sharp pointed darts of a sufficient length and size to kill a man at great distance" in order to escape capture by six whites.[57] An expedition against one maroon group in a swamp on the Savannah River in 1765 encountered a lookout post set up on a scaffold, on which one black was "hoisting Colours" and another was "Beating a Drum" to warn the members of the community—who escaped before the expedition could reach them.[58] John Thornton found that during the 1739 Stono Rebellion in South Carolina, rebels danced the Angolan *nsanga* war dance before battle.[59] Maroons may have also practiced the related unarmed arts that were considered essential to war preparation, a theory that is supported by examples of martial arts use by maroons throughout the Americas. For example, the Colombian maroon groups called *palenques* all had their own martial art styles; and in Brazil, if martial arts styles were not always present in maroon groups, *capoeiras* at times helped defend captured maroons.[60] In North America oral histories note the use of knocking and kicking being used by maroons for self-defense. This account is not surprising since knocking and kicking was practiced by the Gullahs, who formed the numerous maroon groups that fought in the series of Gullah wars up to 1858.[61] Similarly, knocking and kicking was deeply rooted in the black communities in Surry County, Virginia, particularly the area once known as the "Great Dismal Swamp," which housed many maroon groups.[62]

Although such maroon settlements could be found in many regions of colonial North America, the most common form of maroonage was temporary visits off the plantations to see loved ones or attend gatherings. Sometimes planters would grant passes to some slaves to leave the plantations. For those who left without a pass, encountering a patrol or an overseer on another plantation was a recurring threat. While resisting white overseers and patrols could lead to severe punishments, including death, some bondsmen chose to fight them and return to their own plantations, where they might escape punishment.

Drawing on martial art skills for self-defense could be especially effective if the bondsman's enslaver chose to protect what he saw as his personal investment. Benjamin Johnson was visiting a lady friend on the Brady plantation when Brady tried to give him a whipping. Johnson defended himself and immediately darted "home," where he eluded future retribution for his act: "'Bout dat time, ole man Brady had done got dere, an' he tole de marster dat I wus on his place de night befo', an' de marster say to 'im, 'Dat wus his game. if you had im, you shoulda whupped 'im. Dat's de law. If you had whupped 'im, dat woulda been yo' game. But you let 'im git away, an' so dat wus his game.' Ole man Brady's face turned so red dat it looked like he wus gonna bus'."[63]

Austin Steward recounts how another bondsmen named Williams not only escaped a beating but also gave one to the overseer of another plantation, where he was spending time as a temporary maroon:

> The overseer called at the cabin of one of the slaves, and was not a little surprised to find there the refractory slave, Williams, in company with three other men. He immediately walked up to him and asked him some questions to which Williams made no reply. Attended, as he always was, by his ferocious bulldog, he flourished his cowhide in great wrath and demanded an instant reply, but he received none, whereupon he struck the slave a blow with the cowhide. Instantly Williams sprang and caught him by the throat and held him writhing in his vise-like grasp, until he succeeded in getting possession of the cowhide, with which he gave the overseer such a flogging as slaves seldom get. Williams was seized at once by the dog who endeavored to defend his brutal master, but the other slaves came to the rescue, and threw the dog in to a huge fire which was nearby, from which, after a singing, he ran off, howling worse than his master when in the hands of Williams. He foamed and swore and still the blows descended; then he commanded the slaves to assist him, but as none obeyed, he commenced begging in the most humble manner,

> and at last entreated them as "gentlemen" to spare him; but all to no purpose. When Williams thought he had thrashed him sufficiently, he let him go and hurried to his boat and rowed down the bay instead of crossing it. The overseer no sooner found himself at liberty than he ran out, calling to a servant girl to bring his rifle, which was loaded. The rifle was brought, but before he could get to the bay, Williams had gone beyond his reach.[64]

Such bested overseers were often hesitant to seek legal retribution, for reasons that will be discussed below.

More feared than the overseers of other plantations were the patrollers, groups of white men, often armed, who policed the plantation countryside capturing and punishing temporary maroons, usually individuals who had left their plantations without passes to visit loved ones or attend social events. These patrollers were despised by bondsmen in the Chesapeake region, who called them "pattyrollers" and in their secret codes described them as insects.[65] Like overseers, these patrols had an ambiguous relationship with the planters. Clearly they were necessary to maintain order, but they were lower- or middle-class whites and thus at times were in discord with the landed elite. While the elite supported them in theoretical terms, planters would often react negatively toward patrollers whom they perceived as overstepping their bounds by damaging the planters' personal investments in captives.[66] While skilled fighters could turn the tables on a single overseer, one fighter's odds of overcoming a group of armed patrolmen were slim. Frederick Douglass remembered offering no resistance but watching in awe the untamable spirit of his companion Henry, who attempted to fight five armed patrollers. While he managed to knock their guns from their hands, Henry was overpowered in the subsequent struggle.[67] When bondsmen worked together, however, they could offer serious resistance to such patrols. According to the former bondsman Jeff Davis, "Lots of times when de patterollers would get after the slaves dey would have de worse [of the] fight an' sometimes de patterollers would git killed."[68] One relevant account relates how a group of Colonel Alexander's bondsmen threw a large social event. A huge crowd of bondsmen from all the nearby plantations attended, only some of whom had come with permission. They were well into their night's activities of dancing and eating when discovered by a patrol. Many bondsmen fled, but the core group, led by a native African, resisted the patrol with hand-to-hand combat, killing three or four of the patrollers. Colonel Alexander defended his bondsmen and refused to allow them to be put on trial.[69]

The lives of settled maroons near white settlements were filled with the frequent likelihood of violent encounters with whites who crossed their paths. Some traveled with firearms, but most, if armed at all, utilized *l'arme blanche*, such as the razor wielded by a maroon named George to cut out a would-be slave catcher's eye.[70] Temporary maroons rarely carried weapons and could rely only on their own fighting ability to defend themselves in a crisis. In many cases bondsmen acquiesced to their punishments; however, it is clear that on numerous other occasions they felt compelled to fight what they may have perceived as injustice or dishonor. In such cases martial arts could provide the fighting skills necessary to overcome these foes when bondsmen were willing to risk future legal ramifications. Given the serious dangers posed by patrols, the fact that large numbers of bondsmen without passes still chose to attend nocturnal community gatherings, such as the one thrown by Colonel Alexander's bondsmen, shows that they must have been important events.

Performance Rituals

Performance rituals of the bonded community were a second social sphere in which martial arts thrived. These performances were central to bonded life, although scholars have largely overlooked their importance by approaching them from the European American perspective. Therefore, the commonly used term "slave leisure activities" will be replaced in this discussion by the term "community performance rituals," or "plays," as bondsmen often referred to them.[71] There was nothing leisurely about it; the enslaved engaged in these activities with much more vigor and perceived importance than they did their work in the fields. These were not the equivalent of the white enslavers' pastimes. The enslaved intentionally chose not to simply "pass the time" in resting or in less strenuous activities; rather they valued their rituals so much that they often pushed themselves to exhaustion by performing all through the night: "Instead of retiring to rest [at night, the Virginia bondsman] generally sets out from home, and walks six or seven miles in the night, be the weather ever so sulky, to a negro dance, in which he performs with astonishing agility, and the most vigorous exertions, keeping time and cadence, most exactly, with the music of the banjor (a large hollow instrument with three strings), and a quaqua (somewhat resembling a drum), until he exhausts himself, and scarcely has time, or strength, to return home before the hour he is called forth to toil next morning."[72]

Bondsmen took advantage of their evenings to attend plays, hunt opossum, or visit relatives. Some observers referred to evening as bondsmen's "daytime," and in some respects this was when they came alive as individuals.[73] Through these rituals, the enslaved defined themselves as individuals and united themselves as a cultural community. While whites proved their public worth and distinguished themselves as individuals through their work (success of a plantation or a private practice), for most blacks their labor took place in the "culture of coercion," the sphere of guarded and forced behaviors.[74] Thus, public performance became *the* activity through which they asserted and maintained their individuality and self-worth.[75] As in Biafra *mgba* matches and dances highlighted individual competence but also united the village/ward as the unit of cultural production while linking it to related groups through shared performative style and hospitality, in a similar way enslaved Africans and their descendants in North America united and defined themselves as a new community via performance rituals. Thus, far from being mere "leisure," bonded performance activities were nothing short of African-based community-forming and individual-empowering rituals.

Such performances usually took place during weekends and holidays. In the eighteenth century some planters gave their bondsmen Saturdays to themselves and others made them work throughout Saturday, but by the nineteenth century bondsmen typically worked a half-day each Saturday.[76] Sundays and major holidays also provided respites from forced labor. Withholding such days could be seriously counterproductive as it would bring about indignation, disobedience, and insubordination.[77] Frederick Douglass saw these holidays as a type of opiate: "I believe these holidays to be among the most effective means in the hands of the slaveholders of keeping down the spirit of insurrection among the slaves. . . . But for these, the rigors of bondage would have become too severe for endurance, and the slave would have been forced up to dangerous desperation."[78] During these weekend breaks and holidays, planters usually left the enslaved to their own activities unless these interfered with regular work or the safety of the plantation.[79]

Music, dancing, and competitive games were important elements of these plays. A wide variety of musical instruments was featured at these gatherings. Contrary to popular opinion, drumming was widespread in North America, particularly during the colonial period. Allen Kulikof points out that Virginia bondsmen used drums to communicate over long distances and to call bondsmen together for celebration.[80] Similarly, we have evidence for a vibrant drumming tradition in Georgia, and there are numerous accounts of African-style drumming in New Orleans's Congo Square.[81] Musical poles or slapping one's own body often took on the various uses of the drum, allowing the continuation of African polyrhythms without drums.[82] In the eighteenth century scattered references indicate the presence of balaphones (keyed percussion instruments widespread in Africa), while more common instruments were the banjo and reed pipes.[83] In the nineteenth century the fiddle became a popular addition to the music at plays.

The bonded community exhibited many types of dance forms. Some reflected African traditions; some were innovations, such as the cakewalk, that were particular to North America; and some appear to have been variants on Atlantic-wide black dance forms. Many dances were employed for their religious importance, such as the ring shout of the lowcountry or the Vodun dances of Texas.[84] During the colonial period, when enough individuals from certain regions of Africa were present, they danced in styles that reflected aesthetics from specific regions of Africa and the historical processes by which more localized ethnic groups came together into larger collectives in the Americas called nations. These new African nations evolved in the Americas and were often not equivalent to an individuals' birth nation or ethnic group.[85] Urban settings often pulled together enough African-born bondsmen for such "nation" dancing. "At the time of fairs and other great holydays" bondsmen congregated in Philadelphia's Washington Square "to the number of one thousand of both sexes, and hold their dances, dancing after the manner of their several nations in Africa, and speaking and singing in their native dialects."[86] Yet, bondsmen also participated in new styles shared by the entire bonded community.

Competitive games were also an important element of plays. In addition to frequent competitions between musical composers or dancers, plays featured one-upmanship via storytelling, ritual insults, oratory skills, and athletic competitions.[87] African pugilistic and wrestling traditions formed part of this larger genre of competition. In the performance circles of closed societies, knocking and kicking was performed by two competitors exhibiting their kicking prowess in ritual contests before a closed community. In these cases the art was performed to the rhythms of drums or clapping or was accompanied by reed pipes called "quills." Movements such as the cross step, cartwheels, and the dynamic inverted kicks of the art done to music made knocking and kicking inseparable from dance.[88] In these society gatherings, the art's combative potential was openly displayed among trusted members of a closed community. In other contexts, the art's martial side could be disguised within dance and thus safely demonstrated in the open. For example the kicks were openly shown in a covert form in a lowcountry dance that to the uninitiated supposedly represented "a fisherman dramatically kicking mud off his shoes after fishing."[89]

Wrestling also played a part in community performances. John Pierpont, a tutor employed on a plantation in Georgetown, South Carolina, described a community festival in 1804. He noted that while the American-born bondsmen danced to the fiddle and drum, "Some of them who were native Africans did not join in the dance with the others, but, by themselves gave us a specimen of the sports and amusements."[90] Wrestling may have been among these sports practiced by Africans, given the fact that it was arguably the most prominent sport in most of Western Africa. A vivid account from the 1650s describes African bondsmen wrestling in Barbados, a region from which bondsmen would later be taken to form the founding black generation of South Carolina.[91] According to the account,

> On Sundays in the afternoon, their music plays, and to dancing they go, the men by themselves, and the women by themselves, no mixed dancing.

> When they have danced an hour or two, the men fall to wrestle, (the music playing all the while) and their manner of wrestling is, to stand like two cocks, with heads as low as their hips; and thrusting their heads one against another, hoping to catch one another by the leg, which sometimes they do: But if both parties be weary, and that they cannot get that advantage, then they raise their heads, by pressing hard one against another, and so having nothing to take hold of but their bare flesh, they close, and grasp one another about the middle, and have one another in the hug, and then a fair fall is given on the back. And thus two or three couples of them are engaged at once, for an hour together, the women looking on: for when the men begin to wrestle, the women leave their dancing, and come to be spectators of the sport.[92]

Two hundred years later in North America, Frederick Douglass wrote of his fellow enslaved that "the majority spent the holidays in sports, ball playing, *wrestling, boxing,* running foot races, dancing and drinking whisky"(emphasis added). He goes on to explain that not only were such "wild" pastimes allowed; they were condoned: "It is plain, that everything like rational enjoyment among the slaves, is frowned upon; and only those wild and low sports, peculiar to semi-civilized people, are encouraged."[93]

Despite the frequent references to wrestling and fighting in the narratives of the enslaved, one historian argues that the bonded children "spent very little of their leisure time in combative activities." This contradiction stems from his inability to reconcile his idea of combative activities with the "slave code." This code dictated that "[p]hysical abuse of one child by another was considered unjustifiable and a veritable threat to the general well-being of the group" and that adults "ran the risk of being banished by their peer group if they unfairly abused other slaves."[94] However, from the African perspective, the use of combat forms was not necessarily in contradiction to the honor code. Biafrans held clear distinctions between ritual/recreative wrestling and serious conflict wrestling. This distinction was even clearer among other African groups for whom combat wrestling employed a fuller range of destructive techniques.[95] In the bonded contests of North America, sanctioned wrestling during plays was of the ritual and community-affirming type. These public displays gave young wrestlers the ability to gain notoriety not only for their strength and skill but also for their style. From the enslaved's perspective, combat display was important not only in establishing group status through personal display and mastery of form but also for distinguishing oneself for potential leadership or courting.

Displays of physical prowess could help bondsmen attain leadership positions in the community. Despite the limitations of bondage, Africans and their descendants in the Americas often honored their own freely chosen leaders.

Throughout the Western Hemisphere in colonies such as Argentina, Brazil, Cuba, Venezuela, Mexico, Barbados, Saint Domingue, and New Orleans the enslaved held annual festivals to induct and honor black kings and queens. William Piersen has shown that even in New England, where blacks represented less than 5 percent of the population, on blacks' election day bondsmen chose their own leaders known as governors or kings. More than just ceremonial, many of these New England kings headed informal black governments to which even whites appealed for justice to be served.[96] Pierson has shown that along with selecting Africans born of royal lineage, bondsmen looked to men of great physical prowess, which often placed powerful fighters in positions of leadership.[97] For example, black sailors imprisoned in Dartmoor prison during the War of 1812 inducted to leadership the fighter Richard "King Dick" Crafus, who made the black barracks the most organized in the prison. This was due not only to his impressive physique but also to his mastery of combat, as he was a prize-fighting champion and even ran a prize-fighting school in the prison. Potential rivals to his leadership tried to establish themselves in combat with him but were always defeated. After the war King Dick returned to Boston and remained the "master of ceremonies" during blacks' election day until around 1830.[98]

Even more common than attempts to gain leadership status were aspirations of men to win the admiration of single females. As in Africa where the martial arts were used in courtship, the arts continued to be a way that male fighters could attract females in the Americas. The public displays of martial arts strongly reinforced the threatened concept of manhood by providing status and respect for males in a bonded society linked by honor. Although women also wrestled, wrestling and knocking and kicking likely played a more accentuated role in male courting of females given that men greatly outnumbered women in most bonded communities.[99] Expert fighters could gain a wide reputation that may have helped win favor with single women. As Douglass notes, "the great wrestler can win laurels."[100]

In this sense, combat arts were among many other forms of performative dueling reinforced throughout the African diaspora. However, unlike musical dueling, competitive oration, or "playing the dozens," martial arts had the potential to move out of the performative sphere and into the combative sphere. Suitors competing for the hand of a woman at times may have turned to wrestling as a form of resolution, echoing practices in Biafra and likely other areas of Africa.[101] For example, two romantic rivals of a bondswoman called Elle settled their differences in a decisive wrestling bout.[102] If such courting competitions occurred in the Chesapeake region with one of the most balanced sex ratios in the Americas, then the importance of male displays becomes apparent when one reflects on the social ramifications of gender ratios across the diaspora. In many areas high male to female sex ratios were the norm. Marriage partners were scarce, and competition could be significant.[103] In such contexts, performative displays to enhance chances in courting were reinforced demographically.

Thus, in holiday and nocturnal plays, men and women united themselves as a community through performance rituals. Like dancing and music, combative displays allowed individuals to display their own style and grace through mastery of aesthetic forms. The prestige that enslaved males could attain through martial displays of their prowess could also help them attain leadership positions in the bonded community or aid them in courting. While the martial arts were put to use within the bonded community for community enjoyment and prestige, these potentially counterhegemonic arts were also put to use at the orders of the plantation owners.

Service to Europeans

A third social sphere in which martial arts found utility was in the service of planters, who exploited the combat skill of bondsmen as soldiers, gladiators, and strongmen. African fighting traditions were at times put to use in wars on behalf of European American interests. Many Africans and their descendants served in colonial militias, often fighting against Indigenous American groups.[104] Two illustrative examples may also be found from accounts of the American Revolution, an era of dramatic opportunities from the perspective of the enslaved black population. When the British offered freedom to black Americans who fled their enslavers for the British lines, many flocked to promised freedom, some took advantage of the general disorder to escape and form maroon communities, and others remained to seek manumission on the American side. Among the latter were skilled fighters who put their talents to use for the Continental army. One of these was Zachary Molineaux, father of the famous pugilist Tom Molineaux, who came from a family of fighting bondsmen. In 1788 Zachary Molineaux was hauled before a Philadelphia court for assaulting Silas Freeman. Although the details of his service are sketchy, apparently he put his fighting skills to good use in the Revolutionary War; newspaper articles described him as a "warlike hero who was the conquering pugilist of America" and who "fought for the Colonists in their recent strife with England." In the end, his record of loyalty and reputation as a fighter won out, and he was dismissed after an apology.[105]

Another enslaved black who used his combat skills in the service of North America was Jack Sisson. Sisson was described as remarkably small, and yet he was an expert head butter. He was an enslaved man of Lieutenant Colonel Barton, who led the daring capture of British major general Richard Prescott at his headquarters in Newport, Rhode Island, in July 1777. Barton led a group of volunteers on a secret expedition in a few boats (one being steered by Sisson) that slipped past the British forts and warships to reach Prescott's headquarters.

An account in Sidney Kaplan's book reads, "The col. went foremost, with a stout active Negro, close behind him, and another at a small distance." Barton and Sisson took out the single sentinel at the door, and with "the rest of the men surrounding the house, the Negro, with his head, at the second stroke, forced a passage into it and the generals chamber." Thus, with the help of Sisson's head-butting skills (an act subsequently immortalized in ballad), Prescott was taken captive and later traded in an exchange for American general Charles Lee.[106]

In addition to using blacks as colonial soldiers, whites exploited blacks' fighting ability by using bondsmen as gladiators or bodyguards. White-sponsored contests between champions of different plantations are noted in the narratives of the enslaved and circulated in both black and white folklore traditions. Such contests, like the intervillage competitions of Igboland, tended to be seasonal. They usually coincided with corn shuckings and log rollings, when large numbers of enslaved were gathered together on one plantation, providing both a pool of fighters and a large audience. In *Singing the Master,* Roger Abrahams notes, "Indeed, at the center of the pastoral drama of the plantation were combat displays, with the workers used as contestants."[107] While acknowledging such gladiatorial events, some scholars have downplayed them due to their misunderstanding that it was in conflict with the honor code of bondsmen.[108]

Eliot Gorn, in his pioneering studies of combat sports in North America, also doubts that such matches occurred frequently, for two reasons. First, and understandably given the dearth of scholarship on African-derived martial arts, he assumes that such contests would have been based on western boxing and that, except for rough-and-tumble fighting, boxing was not popular in the pre–Civil War South. Second, he argues that masters would have shied away from risking their investments in bondsmen under damaging circumstances: "Even brutal masters recognized the need to protect the investments, and in the name of productivity slave owners generally discouraged violence among their bondsmen."[109] However, both of these widely held but erroneous assumptions are easily corrected by the testimony of former bondsmen. According to Henry Bibb, such planter-inspired bouts often took place on Sundays, when bondsmen would drink, gamble, and fight each other. Note that there is no mention of British-style boxing or gouging: "This is often encouraged by slaveholders. When they wish to have a little sport of that kind, they go among the slaves and give them whiskey, to see them dance, 'pat juber,' sing and play on the banjo. Then get them to wrestling, fighting . . . and butting each other like sheep. This is urged on by giving them whiskey; making bets on them; laying chips on one slave's head and daring another to tip it off."[110] Frederick Douglass confirms that plantation owners encouraged wrestling and pugilistic matches along with other merriments as "among the most effective means in the hands of the slaveholder in keeping down the spirit of insurrection."[111]

It is important to distinguish between two types of planter-inspired contests: matches between bondsmen on the same plantation for amusement and prizefights between two fighters with different owners as a form of gambling. In the case of the former, matches were not necessarily damaging to the contestants or in conflict with the bondsmen's honor code. The fullest written description of such a match (from the narrative of Henry Bibb) reveals that blacks did not fight with imitations of British boxing but with knocking and kicking. Furthermore, it shows that the matches—while serious—were not necessarily life-threatening events: "Before fighting, the parties choose their seconds to stand by them while fighting; a ring or circle is formed to fight in, and no one is allowed to enter the ring while they are fighting, but their seconds, and the white gentlemen. They are not allowed to fight a duel, nor use weapons of any kind. The blows are made by kicking, knocking, and butting their heads; they grab each other by the ears and jam their heads together like sheep. If they are likely to hurt each other very bad, their masters would rap them with their walking canes, and make them stop. After fighting, they make friends, shake hands, and take a dram together, and there is no more of it."[112] Thus, like intravillage wrestling in Biafra, these competitions did not necessarily jeopardize group solidarity and utilized African-derived combat traditions.

Prizefights between representative fighters of different plantations, however, could certainly be violent. Such contests probably came closest to the ugly fictional picture of enslaved prizefighting painted by Faulkner in *Absalom, Absalom!*: "in the center two of his wild negroes fighting, naked, fighting not like white men fight, with rules or weapons, but like negroes fight to hurt one another quick and bad."[113]

Yet, even under these conditions the potential injury to their fighters was a relatively minor risk compared to the extremely high-stakes betting that took place over horse racing. As Timothy Breen has shown, by the early eighteenth century southern gentlemen, forced to work together to preserve their domination over local affairs, turned to rampant gambling as a safe outlet for expressing their extreme competitiveness without threatening social tranquillity. The exceedingly high wagers were designed in part to exclude common planters from openly participating in this elite betting culture. Thus, rather than being a deterrent to pugilistic matches, as Gorn suggests, the risk to the health of their enslaved made such gladiatorial matches attractive by virtue of making such contests a display of their status above common planters, who could not contemplate such risks.[114]

Given the potential danger, fighters who impressed their enslavers in recreational plantation matches may have been more reluctant to enter violent prizefighting matches than competitive planters with an eye on gambling profits. Yet, there could also be great rewards for blacks who fought well in such white-sponsored contests. First, such black gladiators would have been fed much better than the mass of malnourished bondsmen and released from hard labor during the training periods prior to the bouts. Second, such fighting would give the individual a certain reputation that may have entitled him to special recognition from the black community and the plantation owner. Some evidence suggests that respected fighters were at times promoted to positions of authority because they had the respect of the bonded community and could physically enforce order if necessary. According to Charles Brown, "they always have one strong colored guy on all the plantations. He's given a lot of consideration by the boss—usually he be foreman. Can put two or three of the others in his back pocket."[115] Nancy Williams recalls that after her father fought the overseer, the plantation owner let him then run the plantation.[116] Jeptha Choice links drivers and fighting ability: "In the field was always a big strong nigger to keep peace among the hands. . . . He had to be good with his fists to make the boys who got bad in the field walk in line."[117]

A third potential benefit for such gladiators was that in rare instances a black fighter might be released from bondage. The world-famous black boxer Tom Molineaux was popularly believed to have won his freedom in such a match:

> At a party given by one of the neighbors, Randolph Peyton, young Molineaux heard a boast made that not a slave in any of the Virginia families could take the measure of a Peyton slave, Abe, by name. Tom's master, Squire Molineaux . . . asked for volunteers from among his chattels and Tom immediately responded. The Master promised freedom for Tom if he won the battle and with that as an inducement, a merry contest was assured. A considerable sum was wagered on the outcome. Squire Molineaux, one of the wealthiest Virginians, bet a huge sum on young Tom. . . . To further interest Tom in the fight, Squire Molineaux made an added inducement—he promised him besides his freedom, the sum of $100. That seemed to make a complete change in the Negro. He went about his task with agility and his training was conscientious. On the day of the fight, Molineaux was in fine trim. He entered the ring strong as a bull and full of vim and he was master of the situation at all times. He handed Abe a frightful beating. He pounded Abe into submission in a few bloody rounds.[118]

While such potential for manumission was rare at best, these images clearly captured the popular imagination of blacks.[119]

Fighting experts might also be put to use as coercive toughs, bodyguards, or hit men.[120] Peter Wood found that tough blacks were used to dragoon and regulate seamen in the early eighteenth century: "others exploited Negro strength in more dubious ways. When sailors were being pressed into service against pirates in 1718, it was four slaves who executed the pressmaster's orders for a month. In later years Negroes were encouraged to take part in the apprehension of white sailors who deserted their ships, and owners were promised compensation from the Public Treasury 'if any Slave shall be killed or maimed in apprehending such fugitive Seamen.' Slaves themselves were often put to work on local privateers, and occasionally while at sea, captains allowed or even forced slaves to beat European crewmen."[121]

Black toughs were also used at times to control other blacks. Jeff Stanfield recalled one bondsman who beat up his master and then fought off town officers; he was held down for a beating only after the services of a tough bondsman named Jim were employed.[122] Blacks acted as hit men to settle personal scores among whites, such as the planter who used his bondsman to punish his wife's lover in 1736.[123] An overseer sent a bondsman to physically reprimand a white man who had beaten the overseer's pig.[124] Also common was the use of bondsmen to resist governmental seizure of goods for outstanding debts. Thomas Lowndes, ex–provost marshal in South Carolina, complained that when attempting to make seizures outside of Charleston, frequently "the Negroes are let loose upon him," and he is left without legal recourse since it cannot be proven "that was by their Master order tho' every one knows it could not be done without it."[125] A year later an equally frustrated provost marshal chose to fight fire with fire and employed his own group of black strongmen.[126]

Not unique to the Carolinas, the practice of having bonded bodyguards was also common in the Chesapeake region. Josiah Henson developed widespread notoriety as a wrestler and a dancer. Due to this reputation, together with his diligence in exposing the corruption of the former overseer, Henson became the "superintendent" of his Maryland plantation. The one part of his job for which he felt no reluctance was his position as bodyguard of the plantation owner. His fighting skills were often called upon, particularly during assemblies of neighborhood planters on the weekends to drink, debate politics, and gamble over horse races and cockfights. Henson wrote: "Of course, quarrels and brawls of the most violent description were frequent consequences of these meetings; and whenever they became especially dangerous, and glasses were thrown, dirks drawn, and pistols fired, it was the duty of the slaves to rush in, and each one drag his master from the fight, and carry him home. . . . It was a rough business, and I went in roughly, shoving, tripping, and doing my best for the rescue." His proven skill as a wrestling champion served him well in such frays, earning him the respect of the other bonded bodyguards as well.[127]

Martial arts, then, served multiple functions in the lives of bondsmen. They were important tools for self-defense among both temporary and permanent maroons. They were one of many performative displays that allowed bondsmen to display their grace as individuals and define themselves collectively as a community.

Blacks used fighting skills at the request of plantation owners as soldiers, gladiators, drivers, and bodyguards. Martial arts also played important roles in two other contexts: in closed societies and in reflexive honor communities.

Knocking and Kicking and Closed Societies

In North America knocking and kicking was also perpetuated by closed societies.[128] While not linked to any particular African institution, these did echo some of the characteristics of numerous African prototypes. As shown earlier, in Biafra the use of hand-to-hand combat was glorified and played a central role in many closed societies, a pattern widespread in Western Africa.[129] Even in southern Angola, entry into full mastery of the *engolo* required initiation into an association of professionals who pursued the art as a sacred practice.

While Betty Kuyk clearly points to a Biafran legacy in the black fraternal organizations in Virginia, I am not suggesting that Biafran practices necessarily influenced the closed societies linked to knocking and kicking.[130] However, in interviews with informants in the lowcountry, other than the term "Gullah" (which at one point referred specifically to Angolans), the only African group mentioned by name was the Igbo, the name with which most Biafrans would have been associated despite their actual specific Biafran ethnicity.[131] While this likely may not reflect any historical connection between the Biafrans and North American closed societies, the numerous references to Igbo among members of these societies at least raise the possibility that Biafrans may have influenced cultural life in the lowcountry.

In light of the current historiographical trend to understand African-derived culture in the Americas as being determined by demographic concentrations of certain African ethnicities in certain colonies, one might not expect that Biafrans would have had much cultural impact in the lowcountry, given that they were represented in the region in low gross figures. The fact that a group was not present in large numbers, nor clustered at the beginning or end of the slave trade to a given area, does not necessarily mean that they would not influence the culture of the region. William Pierson has shown that even though Africans as a whole constituted less than 3 percent of the population in New England, they maintained an impressive cultural presence.[132] The same may be true of specific African ethnic groups in the Americas.[133] The question of how the Biafrans may have made a cultural impact despite their small numbers may not be resolved here, but an initial approach might consider three factors.

First is the time of arrival. When slavery spread to Georgia in the 1750s Biafrans represented over 18 percent of the founder generation.[134] Gerhard Kubik's work shows that despite their tiny proportion among captive immigrants to Brazil, Mozambicans left a strong cultural mark on Brazilian culture due to their late arrival.[135] Biafrans may have similarly grown in representation during the illegal trade in enslaved Africans to the lowcountry. The trade in captives from the Bight of Biafra fell markedly between 1811 and 1815, but the illegal trade revived there between 1816 and 1835. In this period the Bight of Biafra was exporting more captives than anywhere else on the Atlantic apart from the Angolan region, which continued to dominate even the illegal phase of the trade.[136] The fact that the exact spot of Igbo Landing on St. Simon's Island is so well known throughout the lowcountry suggests that the landing of that group may have taken place in the illegal phase of the trade. If so, it could explain a pronounced Biafran legacy since latest arrivals sometimes left a strong cultural mark.[137] However, even during the middle phase of the trade, the arrival of the largest wave of Biafrans came at a time ripe with potential for cultural impact. Prior to the Stono Rebellion, Angolans were numerically the largest among captive immigrant groups in South Carolina. Yet, in the 1740s Biafrans represented almost a third of all Africans brought into the colony.[138] Biafrans arrived in large numbers with their legacy of closed societies just after the uprising, when the freedoms that had earlier been exercised openly had to be done "secretly, and since informants were well rewarded, it was necessary to be as covert among other blacks as among whites."[139]

A second factor may have been a higher percentage of Biafrans in local areas and in motherhood roles. Even if their percentage was low overall, the Biafrans may have been highly concentrated in local areas. Wadmalaw and Edisto islands in South Carolina appear to have had high concentrations of Biafrans, as did the nearby Savannah communities of Canebreak and Burris.[140] This would have made it possible for Biafrans in these microcommunities to influence the later lowcountry culture that grew out of these microcultures.[141] On any given tidewater plantation Biafrans and Angolans may have been concentrated in the field due to planters' beliefs that those groups were best suited for such work.[142] Biafrans likely also had a significant impact on the American-born generation since many of the women in the lowcountry were Biafran. Littlefield suggests that Biafran women may have acted as a cultural bridge between other groups as men of many other ethnic groups married and had children with Biafran women.[143]

A third factor to consider involves both the nature of specific Biafran practices and the means by which they were introduced to the lowcountry. Not all cultural forms have equivalents in other cultures, and a particular practice brought by a minority group may have been seen as valuable or useful and thus was adopted by other bondsmen. In addition, African factors involved in the transmission of cultural practices may have affected their influence in the Americas. The linguist Victor Manfredi has argued that Igbo speakers may have been responsible for introducing the ritual language of the Abakuá societies into Cuba, which explains both the impetus behind the spread of *ekpe* to Cuba and the simultaneous lack of a separate Igbo language there.[144] Whatever the ultimate reasons are, it is clear that despite their small numbers, Biafrans were quite visible and certainly left a legacy in the lowcountry.

This Biafran impact is especially clear in counterhegemonic activities such as revolts and maroonage.[145] A clear example is the case of Igbo Landing, from which Biafrans arriving by ship were believed to have walked back across the Atlantic to Igboland. Whether read as a testament to their spiritual power to walk back across the *kalunga* or as a form of collective suicide, this act of defiance continues to reverberate in lowcountry culture.[146] Despite their small demographic numbers, Biafrans appear prominently in the documentation of the 1822 Denmark Vesey conspiracy, which was organized along ethnic lines. Although Senegambians certainly participated, it is significant that apart from the dominant Angolan unit led by Gullah (Angola) Jack, the second most clearly identified ethnic contingent was the "Igbo" society led by Monday Gell.[147] Even more telling of their role in resistance was their representation among maroons. While other groups were represented in proportion to their numbers as runaways, Wood found that "the only marked exception was among the Ibo tribesmen from the Bight of Biafra, who represented only several per cent of the incoming slaves but who constituted more than one tenth of the colonial runaways whose African origins are known."[148] This disproportionate representation becomes even more marked when viewed by gender. Littlefield calculated that in general American-born bondsmen ran away more often than African-born; however, Biafran women completely defied this categorization: "There were a number of ethnic and regional compilations that approached and exceeded this norm—Congo-Angola (9 percent), Guinea (12 percent), Windward Coast (14 percent), and Kisi (15 percent)—but none to measure the Ibos, who surpassed the norm by 142 percent. So in their identity as Ibos and as women, Ibos stood out among runaways."[149] Thus, there were clearly factors that made the Biafrans influential in levels far beyond their gross demographic numbers.

Again, this is not to suggest any necessary connection between Biafran and North American closed societies but to point out that overall numbers do not dictate cultural impact. By the same logic, it is possible that individuals of other African ethnic groups influenced the development of early closed societies in the lowcountry. Indeed, Margaret Washington Creel has described the legacy of closed societies in lowcountry Christianity in terms relating to the Poro and Sande societies.[150] Ras Michael Brown has recently pointed out that these same traits also parallel West Central African initiation societies.[151] Bondsmen may have drawn on any or none of these prototypes in forming their closed societies, which were in many ways unique to North America. However, given the overlooked importance of closed societies in the African diaspora, future research should try to illuminate the haze that currently surrounds the history and function of these societies.

Historians intending to write about such closed societies in North America face a serious challenge, but the topic should be pursued. Carter Woodson was the first to write of the enduring legacy of African closed societies among African Americans, but he viewed these as mutual aid organizations meeting predominantly economic needs, such as burial: "The orders in Africa conformed to the requirements of meeting a social need felt in Africa; and so have they developed in America. . . . Drawing upon the African Negro's penchant for burial pomp, many Negro secret societies have been developed mainly around the idea of taking care of the sick and burying the dead."[152] Clearly, African American societies did perform practical functions such as collective economics. Yet, taken together with Thompson's emphatic suggestion that "nowhere is Kongo-Angolan influence on the New World more pronounced, more profound, than in black traditional cemeteries throughout the South of the United States," perhaps the cultural and spiritual aspects of the societies responsible for such cemeteries also deserve further investigation.[153]

Finding sources to trace the historical development and functions of closed societies among bondsmen is a formidable task. Secrecy was a common defense of the enslaved to protect them from their oppressors. When outside the gaze of whites, blacks lived out a parallel society in which they expressed themselves more freely. This "polycultural rather than syncretic" culture of bondsmen was reflected in numerous examples, such as their having one set of lyrics for a particular tune when among themselves but another, "safe" set of lyrics for the same tune while in the presence of whites.[154] Robert Smalls, who had escaped bondage in 1862, was asked by an agent of the Freedman's Inquiry Commission whether "masters knew anything about the secret life of the colored people." Smalls responded, "No sir; one life they show their masters and another life they don't show."[155]

While bondsmen usually exhibited a high level of reserve when around whites, an even deeper level of secrecy covered closed societies. Smalls also revealed to the agent of the Freedman's Inquiry Commission that he had belonged to clandestine societies. Scipio, a bondsman in All Saints Parish, South Carolina, was hired out to a northern visitor named James Gilmore just prior to the Civil War. After overhearing a conversation Gilmore had about the impending secession of South Carolina, Scipio confided in him that this had been the topic of a nocturnal meeting with other bondsmen the previous night. When Gilmore expressed concern about Scipio's safety because other bondsmen might report him, Scipio responded, "Tell! Lord bless you, massa, de bracks am all free-masons; dat are old men and women who would die 'fore dey's tell."[156]

In rare cases whites did encounter clandestine meetings, such as in 1770 when an anonymous visitor to the lowcountry witnessed a group of bondsmen engaged "in a secret council [that] had much the appearance of Doctors, in deep and solemn consultation upon life and *death*."[157] White fears of insurrection often led them to view such societies as expressly designed toward revolt. Given the role that closed societies played in the Denmark Vesey conspiracy, these fears were not completely unfounded.[158] Yet, beyond such potential counterhegemonic objectives, closed societies also served the internal needs of the bonded community. Many such groups were ethnic based and may have provided a place for bondsmen from certain regions of Africa to make sense of their experiences as a collective. In addition, the African American societies growing out of these ethnic sodalities could have provided spiritual counseling, forums to discuss relevant issues, and community leadership.

Some North American closed societies may have continued masking traditions, a prominent part of many African closed societies. Chambers suggests that the Jonkonnu masking dance in North Carolina and Virginia may have been the public face of closed societies: "In effect, moreover, the *jonkonu* troupe may have served as a slave 'secret society' much like a masking version of *okonko*. . . . The *jonkonu* performance at Christmas was a buffoonery; the rest of the year it may have served as a secret and Americanized re-creation of the title societies of historical Nri-Akwa and Isuama (the most populous areas of Igboland)."[159]

Although this dance was not necessarily of Biafran derivation, Chambers's suggestion that there was more to the society is well founded. Ken Bilby's Atlantic-wide research on Jonkonnu suggests that it was tied to Myal in Jamaica, from whence it seems to have spread to the Bahamas, Belize, Honduras, and North America along with burial societies and ancestral veneration.[160] John Mathews, a former bondsman, may have been referring to similar masking societies when he said, "I believe in spirits. I is seed many one, but it is against my religion to tell bout dem; dat is a sacred thing. In fact I have acted de part of de spirit, but dat was a long time ago. I don't belong to dat sect any more an' cant tell deir secrets."[161] Given that Mathews experienced the oppression of enslavement at the end of the Antebellum period, his apparent reference to participating in masking ceremonies suggests that such traditions retained their salience among North American bondsmen well into the middle of the nineteenth century.[162]

Until further research is conducted, it will not be possible to tell to what extent the practices still carried on by such societies in the twentieth century date back to earlier practices. The roles of elders and the *dala* staff (a sacred cane or staff) likely relate back to African traditions. Although they are not necessarily of Biafran provenance, these practices show some similarity to the Igbo practice of "ofoism." The African American closed societies I encountered share the Biafran social pattern of a gerontocracy. As respect for elders was common to all West and Central African societies, it is not surprising that Blassingame found that Africans and elders played special roles in the bonded community: "The social structure of the [slave] quarters also reflected African influences: the most revered slaves were native Africans and aged blacks. Joseph Cobb acknowledged this when he reported that the Africans on one Georgia plantation 'were treated with marked respect by all the other negroes for miles around.' Often the oldest blacks constituted a council who were called upon to settle disputes in the quarters."[163]

This practice of a gerontocracy appears to have continued after abolition in the context of closed societies. These African American closed societies were groups of extended families sworn to the obedience of their elders. Another parallel with the Igbo social system was the *ofo* staff of authority.[164] Its use among these closed associations was linked to the concepts of the left and the right hands, echoing the Igbo *ikenga,* "the cult of the right hand."[165] In Igboland the *ofo* staff was *the* symbol of ancestral authority, and the elder who wielded it spoke for the ancestors. African American elders in authority also wielded *dala,* which signified their authority.[166] Depending on the hand in which the elder, or his staff-bearer, held the *dala* while openly giving orders or verbally complying with a white person's wishes, the members of the group knew if the order was to be followed or should be feigned but not actually carried out.[167] Beyond these structural practices, at the heart of these closed societies was the perpetuation of a system of physical and spiritual empowerment that gave bondsmen a sense of control over their lives.

Tricknology

These African American closed societies perpetuated what they termed the "Old Time Religion,"[168] and they utilized an arsenal that included both knocking and kicking and root doctoring.[169] This association linked the martial art and medical knowledge together as parallel means of attaining power. It was not uncommon for bonded fighters to rely on sacred medicines provided by elders of the Old Time Religion or root doctors in general.[170] Conversely, elders of the Old Time Religion societies, who served roles akin to those of root doctors, also relied on knocking and kicking for their physical protection.[171] According to Gwaltney, "the original use of knocking and kicking was holy. It was to defend the elders [of the Old Time Religion]."[172] The closed societies of families following the Old Time Religion would continue to perpetuate the martial art in the twentieth century, explaining the closed nature of the art. While certain aspects of the art, particularly head butting, were practiced widely in the bonded community, after emancipation the complete art was often hidden from other blacks as well as whites. Willie Nelson explained that "not everyone used to do it, just certain circles of blacks," and as a boy he was afraid to cross those who knew it.[173] Practitioners at the end of the last decade still used separate terms to distinguish between blacks in general and blacks tied to the remnants of these closed societies. As the historian Herman Carter explained: "The world didn't know about it, but they brought [knocking and kicking] from Africa and disguised it in the context of religion to cover it up . . . to keep the white man from getting at it. And that was their weapon to fight with. They couldn't have any guns or weapons to fight with and to defend themselves they had to use something, so they used [knocking and kicking]. . . . It was mostly a secret undercover thing for the slave because that was his way of defense. But see, if he could have carried it out in the open like karate and the martial arts from Asia it would have been a momentous thing. But this was undercover and most of it you didn't hear about . . . over here [America] they didn't pass it around, only in the secret ranks that they were training under them."[174]

Gwaltney defines knocking and kicking as "the ancient martial art practiced by slave clergy and their followers."[175] This "clergy" of elders encouraged the open practice of the art only in their clandestine gatherings. As Johnathan David describes them, these societies "consisted of cults organized around local extended families that met also in larger, public festivals."[176] These larger, yet still clandestine festivals were often referred to as "drum meetings." The fact that in these ritual contexts kicking contests included physical inversions, together with the continued association of inversion with the "crossing of the water," suggests the possibility that knocking and kicking may at one time have continued to serve a ritual function in the Old Time Religion by accessing spiritual power from across the *kalunga*.

Through these Old Time Religion societies, knocking and kicking was linked to a larger arsenal of psychological and spiritual weaponry. Old Time Religion societies promoted many spiritual traditions, such as wood carving, drumming, and herbal healing.[177] Yet, given the harshness of bondage, at the forefront of these societies was a set of tools that allowed bondsmen to exercise some semblance of power in relation to white society. According to Gwaltney, these societies were "the social cult which black people created to free themselves from the wickedry [of whites]."[178] Whites were understood to have employed powerful witchcraft, evil, and deception in the enactment of the transatlantic slave trade. This was often coded into stories passed down in North America about the experience of individuals having been tricked into boats by white sailors or their African agents using red cloths. Not meant to be understood literally, these accounts document the collective moral judgment of the essential wickedness enacted by Europeans in the slave trade.[179] As a result of this evil committed by whites that was akin to "witchcraft," Africans found themselves cast into the horrors of racial slavery, where they were systematically disempowered in perpetual bondage.[180]

In order to counter this wickedness, members of Old Time Religion societies often turned to an arsenal of redemptive violence that included knocking and kicking, poisoning, and root doctoring.[181] From the African and African

American perspective, the latter two were inseparable, and all three worked in conjunction with the bonded philosophy of defense through the art of trickery, which here will be referred to "tricknology."[182] Trickery provided a theory of resistance through the continuation and elaboration of African tricksterism as portrayed in the model of the African and African American trickster hero.[183] As one bondsman recalled, "The only weapon of self defense I could use successfully, was that of deception."[184] So resonant was this concept of tricknology that a Central African proverb relating to it was passed on in the black communities of North America. Lowcountry bondsmen repeated the proverb in its entirety or just the essential phrase "kum yali, kum buba tambe," meaning "he is tricky, so I will win by being tricky too!"[185] In the nineteenth century, when numbers of African-born were dropping significantly in relation to those of American-born blacks, Africans were closely associated with root doctoring and African languages were believed to have spiritual power. This proverb was utilized ritually as an incantation in a process that was believed to allow certain Africans to literally fly back across the *kalunga* to Africa. While many Africans were believed to have this power, the gift could also be passed on to American-born blacks through incantations such as this.[186] However, for the majority of the bonded community, who would have to wait until their funerals to pass back across the *kalunga,* the assertion and philosophy behind the proverb provided a blueprint for overcoming the obstacles of life in bondage.

In knocking and kicking, the importance of trickery was most evident in the use of head butting to overcome attackers in self-defense conditions. Knocking duels between members of a black community often began with an acknowledgment of the imminent conflict by a mutual charge from a distance. However, when fighting from some physical disadvantage or when defending oneself from a white oppressor, the ideal was to strike a butting-style head blow and finish the fight before it even developed.[187] As such butts had to be delivered at close range to be effective, a fighter had to use trickery to close the distance under some innocuous guise. Once at a close range, the head butt's effect could be extremely traumatic. Jack White related how, with this skill, small-statured practitioners of knocking and kicking could defeat opponents twice their size and drop a man unconscious before he could reach for his weapon.[188] Just as Brer Rabbit feigned fear of being thrown into the briar patch, so might a smaller-statured underdog feign fear of being grabbed by an overseer with a whip held overhead, only to turn the tables by not resisting the attack. Rather, the adept would allow himself to be pulled into an overseer's grasp and then deliver a knockout blow, to which the aggressor would have no defense as his arms were already engaged.

While knocking and kicking employed trickery, root doctoring stood at the spiritual heart of the tricknology complex—so much so that "tricking" was a vernacular term for "root doctoring."[189] Not surprisingly, tricking or root doctoring drew on African precedents and was also known from Virginia to Georgia by Biafran terms such as *mojo* and *ober* and Bantu terms such as *hand, wanga,* and *gopher.*[190] According to W. E. B. Du Bois, the first African American institution was an association that was linked to African traditions related to root doctoring and was "not at first by any means Christian."[191] Although the Old Time Religion societies that were formed around African spiritual traditions gradually adopted more Christian elements, likely in the nineteenth century, conjuring traditions remained central to these societies because they provided empowerment over the practical circumstances of their bondage.[192]

Like other forms of tricknology, root doctoring had multiple uses, but most salient among these was "arbitrating the day-to-day conflicts in which slaves were confronted with white slaveholder domination, which was often directed and enforced through violent means."[193] The circumstances of the oppression that bondsmen endured included sickness, destitution, forced labor, random acts of violence, separation from loved ones, and general dishonor and disempowerment. W. E. B. Du Bois describes the root doctor as "the healer of the sick, the interpreter of the Unknown, the comforter of the sorrowing, the supernatural avenger of wrong, and the one who rudely but picturesquely expressed the longing, disappointment, and resentment of a stolen and oppressed people."[194] Thus, trick doctors sought to "cure" the symptoms of bondage through using medicinal knowledge to cure disease, using their knowledge to earn a sizable income, using special plants that would cause feigned sickness so that a person could avoid work, or controlling the excesses of white oppression through the threat of spiritual vengeance or poisoning.[195]

Just as mastery of knocking and kicking could allow a bondsman to advance in the culture of coercion to a position as driver or bodyguard, root doctors could find themselves with much greater respect and freedom of movement than was afforded the average field hand. Although skeptical of such trick doctors, one South Carolina plantation owner acknowledged that on every plantation there was at least one root doctor, who was among "the most powerful and significant individuals on the plantation."[196] The Reconstruction legislator William Councill experienced the fact that elder root doctors, male and female, often looked after white children as well as black children, instilling a fear in both.[197] While some root doctors were at times targeted by the agents of white domination, at other times they were allowed to travel freely as doctors as long as they paid a portion of their earnings to their plantation owners. This was the case for Jack, who was allowed by a Tennessee landowner to travel through the region practicing medicine, as well as for Jeff, who was hired by a South Carolina planter to "doctor some of his Negroes."[198] William Wells Brown recalled a root doctor named Dinkie who was "his own master." Dinkie did not work, did not get whipped, and did not get stopped by patrollers. Indeed, even some of the most upper-class white women visited him for consultations, and white men tipped their hats at him.[199] Skillful trick doctors stood as potent symbols of the power of tricknology as they lived in effect as their own masters in a society in which bondsmen were mere tools for labor. Not only were bondsmen such as Dinkie free of demands for their physical labor, but they also often held as much sway over other bondsmen as did their enslavers.[200]

Thus, root doctoring and knocking and kicking acted as related sources of empowerment. Root doctoring was a much more powerful weapon in the Old Time Religion Society's arsenal in that it could provide a buffer from a much wider array of dangers than knocking and kicking could. Yet, both provided for defenses against the physical brutality of bondage. Knocking and kicking could provide some control over the random beatings that were the central symbol of white domination. Similarly, among the most popular of sacred medicines in North America were those used to keep from being whipped.[201] These two legs of tricknology often worked in tandem, as in the case of Frederick Douglass. Douglass was armed with a charm provided by the trick doctor Sandy when he entered into a bold physical confrontation with his overseer.[202] Yet, Douglass also chose to resist his oppressors physically. In doing so, he was able to prevent further beatings. Thus, he attained a status similar to that of the root doctor Dinkie but by physically demanding respect from his overseer, which simultaneously rekindled his own sense of honor.

Field of Honor

Enslaved Africans carried strong concepts of honor to North America. As we have seen, the pastoral Angolans held a tradition of reflexive honor in which affronts to honor were settled in stick fights. The agricultural Biafrans organized their entire society through honor of communal rules rather than laws imposed by a political leader, as did numerous other African groups. This legacy was continued by Africans and their descendants, who fought for a sense of honor despite slavery's threat of social death. Although blacks were systematically treated with dishonor in the culture of coercion, in their own voluntary culture the core of the community founded its own honor community. The bonded communities' dominant honor system, like that of Kunene herdsmen, was a reflexive honor code in which insults and infractions among peers had to be responded to, often with violence, in order for honor to be retained.[203]

Europeans and their descendants in North America did not always recognize this bonded honor code, but southern elites lived by their own reflexive honor system that led to violent gouging matches and later duels.[204] This elite form of honor likely influenced that of bondsmen in some ways, and yet they were distinct in other ways. Like the white code, the honor system of Africans and their descendants in North America was most clearly exhibited through loyalty to peers, personal displays, vengeance, and resistance to dishonor. The most fundamental element of the enslaved code of honor was loyalty to fellow bondsmen. John Willis, whose work has best explored the history of honor among bondsmen, describes the foundation of the honor code as being a "steadfastness" manifested by bondsmen "in the many ways they aided fellow bondsmen, punished traitors, and cooperated to frustrate the intentions of whites—often at great personal risk."[205] The enslaved showed this respect to one another by hiding and feeding runaways and refusing to betray other bondsmen. Steadfastness was also exhibited in the ways bondsmen kept their plans for secret meetings closed through a covert means of communication and elaborate steps to keep from being discovered.[206] John Brown experienced the weight of loyalty while enslaved: "I am sure that, as a rule, any one of us who would have thought nothing of stealing a hog, or a sack of corn, from our master, would have allowed himself to be cut to pieces rather than betray the confidence of his fellow-slave."[207] Even status in the master's culture was not always enough to override steadfastness; Wyatt-Brown highlights examples of black drivers who felt compelled by the honor code not to carry out ordered whipping if the plantation owner was not immediately present.[208]

The most overt element of the honor of the enslaved was personal display, expressed through individual appearance and performance abilities. Such display was ubiquitous for those with eyes to appreciate the gait of their walk or the ways they transformed their simple clothes into fashion statements. These styles were particularly on display during plays, which began with the preparation of wardrobes for the event. Shane and Graham White have explored how the enslaved expressed themselves through clothing, and Willis has shown how this vital concern for appearance was a reflection of their honor.[209] Once at the play, an enslaved woman could gain honor in the eyes of the community for her ability to sing, hypnotize the community with engaging stories, or dance with grace. Some bondsmen gained communal recognition for their demonstrated intellectual abilities during verbal contests involving riddles, orations, or humorous insults ("playing the dozens").[210] Others commanded respect for their demonstrated skill in physical contests such as climbing poles, wrestling, or knocking and kicking. Through these various forms of display, enslaved Africans and their descendants exclaimed their individual worth and honor. The desire to seek such communal honor was clearly strong.

Bondsmen valued plays to such an extent that they would walk miles, risk severe beatings, and sacrifice sleep despite an abusive work routine because their participation was a badge of honor. Collectively these community rituals, with their inheritance of African traditions and aesthetics, can be understood as countervailing forces against European Americans' views of enslaved Africans as deracinated with no culture of their own and no cultural pride. These plays provided the enslaved with a context in which to overtly display their honor and participate in group membership. Skin color alone was not enough for full inclusion. Black individuals who stayed clear of these community-forming rituals would not necessarily be completely trusted as clear members of the honor group. While not always the case, at times even those bondsmen who held some status in the coercive culture, such as drivers, domestics, or artisans, were hesitant to break peer loyalty since doing so brought them the risk of vengeance.

In Africa fighters often exhibited their power on behalf of the enslaved community in the enforcement of honor. Although elements of reflexive honor/vengeance could be found throughout West Africa, this principle was especially apparent among Biafrans and numerous other societies without centralized states, in which closed societies rather than rulers controlled behavior through vengeance, the enforcement of honor through violence. Samuel Crowther and John Taylor note that in comparison to the Yoruba and Hausa, "the law of life for life among the Igbos is very strong, and is more to be dreaded than any other."[211] Dishonorable behavior was punished through individual combat or the fierce masquerades of the closed societies. C. K. Meek describes an example of a Biafran man who failed to show proper respect to an elder. In order to fix this breach of honor a *di-mgba* (master wrestler) was sent to enact physical vengeance on the violator.[212]

In North America breaches of honor among bondsmen often led to violence and retribution. Bondsmen were sensitive to the *point d'honneur,* and many responded by physically confronting their insulters.[213] "Them as wont fight," Lewis Clarke recalled, "is called Poke-easy."[214] While defense of personal honor could lead to physical conflict, often more serious forms of retribution fell on those who betrayed the steadfastness of the larger community. According to Charles C. Jones, the code of honor among bondsmen assumed a "sacredness," and transgressors would, among other retributions, have "their names cast out as evil from among their brethren, and being subjected to scorn, and perhaps personal violence."[215] North American bondsmen could face lethal vengeance in the form of root doctoring or poisoning. Daniel Hundley was confounded by what he perceived as the "trivial" causes that lead the enslaved to kill their fellow bondsmen.[216] Peter Kalm, a Swedish visitor to North America in 1748, could more clearly see that tricking, particularly the use of poison, was used by the enslaved "on such of their brethren as behave well [to whites], are beloved by their masters, and separate, as it were, from their countrymen."[217]

Even more disconcerting to European Americans was the use of reflexive honor against whites. In taking an overtly physical stance against whites, bondsmen risked heavy retribution. Many excellent studies, including Hartman's *Scenes of Subjection,* highlight how the various levels of domination of the black body physically, legally, and socially circumscribed people of African descent under slavery.[218] Focus here is on the atypical situations in which the black body was turned into a weapon used to fight for honor. This focus in no way minimizes the harshness of slavery or legal repercussions. Bondsmen who resorted to physical means were often met with inordinate if not lethal levels of legal and physical repression. Capital punishment was a common sentence for bondsmen who injured whites in former British colonies. In the French Caribbean and Brazil expulsion from the territory was at times a more common sentence than capital punishment. Yet interestingly, as Diana Paton points out, in the case of Jamaica, where the frequency of the death sentence was much closer to that in North America, many whites still found the legal system out of their control.[219] Other whites, whose sense of honor made them avoid seeking aid from the state, turned to administering extreme physical punishments.[220] This range of repression, which I am assuming most readers will already be familiar with, makes the effective struggles of some exceptional individuals all the more illuminating.

Because redress against whites drew disproportionate opposition, some bondsmen chose to mask their impugned honor and retaliate clandestinely. In general, insults by whites did not require redress under reflexive honor since whites were not part of the same honor group. Yet, when an enslaved person who did take offense chose to respond, he or she often waited until interference by uninvolved whites was less likely. This remained a part of the philosophy of knocking and kicking into the twentieth century. According to some, Old Time Religion and knocking and kicking shared a concept similar to *taqiya* in Islam, which allows Muslims to conceal and deny their faith when it would bring repression to themselves or coreligionists.[221] Similarly, knocking and kicking practitioners among the Old Time Religion could conceal their fighting ability and sense of honor to postpone direct response until an opportunity of relative strength presented itself.[222] A bondsman who felt his honor impugned by a white could swallow the insult and retain honor among his peers, or he might get his revenge by means other than a direct challenge to the insulter in a public setting. This revenge might take the form of sabotage at a later date. The plantation owner Edward Ruffin was confused for years about how some of his buildings had burned, but he later came to realize that he had been the target of vengeance by bondsmen against the actions of a cruel overseer.[223]

Understood in this light, many cases of "passive resistance," such as the murder of prized animals, might be alternatively read as acts of personal vengeance. Similarly the numerous assassinations of white plantation owners by bondsmen in Virginia, as noted by Phillip Schwartz, could have been acts of delayed vengeance, as evidenced by the statements of justification and lack of remorse by many blacks who took justice into their own hands.[224] More often, however, the prime targets of vengeance were not plantation owners but patrollers and overseers. Their horses and dogs were often killed clandestinely, while patrollers and overseers were often tripped by vines, pushed into rivers, showered with hot coals, pushed into fires, or beaten.[225]

Most bondsmen would have to mask their honor when confronted with affronts and wait until a potential window of opportunity to seek redress; others displayed their honor at times by resisting dishonor. Bondsmen might respond with immediate violence at insults, especially when dealing with overseers. Nancy Williams recalled that when an overseer verbally dishonored her father, "[he] got mad an' cuss my pappy, den is de time dat ole po' white trash got jumped."[226] Given the oppressive nature of racial slavery, few could respond this way to every insult, and no bondsmen could resist every dishonor. However, many of the enslaved could draw a line at physical violence.

Many bondsmen resisted the dishonor of whippings, which was one of the most widespread and degrading features of slavery.[227] These individuals turned to counterviolence to prevent the beating or raping of themselves or members of their families. Reverend Jacobs recalled that when an overseer was beating his Uncle Charlie excessively hard, "Uncle Charlie made up his mind he wouldn't stand it any longer, so he jumped the nigger-driver. They fought and Uncle Charlie won."[228]

The use of fighting skills was not limited to men. African bondswomen carried a legacy that linked womanhood to assertive action in the fields of agriculture, trade, and even combat when necessary.[229] As mentioned earlier, black women engaged in wrestling against men as well as other women. Over the course of the late nineteenth century, prevailing gender conventions among whites that linked womanhood with passivity and domesticity appear to have been adopted or imposed as black masculinity began to be defined in oppositional terms to black womanhood. Until the end of the Civil War, however, the combative prowess of women was recognized and admired by the black community.[230] In his fateful combat with his overseer, Frederick Douglass was successful in part because a bondswoman named Caroline disobeyed orders to help subdue him. Douglass openly acknowledges that "she was a powerful woman and could have mastered me easily."[231] Lucy Galloway fondly recalled with admiration the fighting ability of an African woman named Luce: "We wuz all crazy about 'Little Luce.' Dat wuz what we called her, cause she wuz little, but my! she wuz strong and could whup anybody that fooled wid her."[232]

Bondswomen could turn their fighting ability against their oppressors, as when Silvia Dubois exacted revenge for years of her mistress's brutality by beating the mistress severely, which intimidated white spectators and allowed Silvia to fly to freedom.[233] Many bondswomen may not have had the ability to defend themselves effectively. Yet, some successfully resisted the dishonor of rape. Mrs. Fannie Berry remembered the example of Sukie:

> She used to cook for Miss Sarah Ann, but old Marsa was always trying to make Sukie his gal. One day Sukie was in the kitchen making soup. When ole Marsa come in . . . he tell Sukie to take off her dress. She tole him no. Den he grabbed her and pull it off 'n her shoulders. When he done that he grab hold of her and try to pull her down on the flo'. Den dat black gal got mad. She took an' punch ole Marsa an' make him break loose an' den she gave him a shove an' push his hindparts down in the hot pot o' soup. Soup was near to boilin' an' it burnt him near to death. He got up holding his hindparts an' ran from de kitchen, not darin' to yell, 'cause he didn't want Miss Sarah Ann to know 'bout it. Well, few days later he took Sukie off an' sol' her to de nigger trader. Marsa never did bother slave gals no mo.[234]

Other enslaved women, such as Lizzie and Fannie, also were able to protect themselves from rape at the hands of their enslavers.[235]

Enslaved men often felt compelled, despite the legal fiction of natal alienation, to protect their female family members. Allen Wilson, as a child seeing his mother being beaten, prayed he would grow powerful enough to kill their overseer and "prayed Gawd dat someday he'd open a way for me to protect mother"—fighting ability was one way that this prayer was answered for some; Francis Henderson's intimidating abilities kept his enslaver from beating his child.[236] J. D. Green recounts how a bondsman named Dan killed his master for trying to rape his love, Mary.[237] Robert Elliott from Virginia remembered how his father's combat skills were used to protect his family: "In those days if you was a slave and had a good looking daughter, she was taken from you. They would put her in the big house where the young masters could have the run of her. . . . Paw was very mean and always said just what he wanted. He met you half way and expected you to meet him the same. One day a strange white man came down around our cabin and tried to get my sister out. Father jumped him and grabbed him in the chest. He pointed at the big house and said, 'If you don't git in that house right now, I'll kill you with my bare hands.' The white man flew."[238] Despite his direct confrontations with whites, Elliott's father was never beaten: "My master was a Garret and an old devil. He was the meanest man out, but my father wouldn't let him beat him. I've seen him try time and again to beat my father an' I always heard my father say, 'I'll die before I'll let you beat me!'"[239] Elliott's father was one of numerous enslaved people who refused to be beaten.

While many such bondsmen risked being sold or killed, others were begrudgingly awarded the concession of being exempted from physical punishments. Eugene Genovese estimates that one or two bondsmen on every plantation would not submit to whipping; some even made known their refusal to be beaten before there was any danger of being whipped.[240] William Davis was one who refused a beating. When the overseer realized he could not force Davis into complying, he ordered three others to assist him, but Davis dissuaded them with a stern warning, "if either of you touch me, I'll kill one of you."[241] If not exempted from a beating or successful in his physical defense, a bondsman could be punished even more severely for resisting. While artisans, foremen, and other "special" bondsmen could effectively get away with not being beaten due to their valued position, others were exempted by their fighting ability. Laura Smalley remembered her uncle being a fighter who would not be taken by force even in the face of multiple assailants; in the end his enslaver could punish him only by reducing his rations.[242] Similarly, Frank Bell remembered the power of his Uncle Moses: "Everybody skeered of him, even ole Marser. Never whip him, don't believe he ever had a whippin' in his life." Even after running away nine times, Bell's Uncle Moses was never beaten: "If it had been any other slave he give him a good whipping, but not Uncle Moses. Just want going to whip him. don't know why, ah guess he was little bit skeered."[243] Such resistance earned these men hesitant respect by whites and honor in their own communities.

It is often popularly believed that physical resistance against an owner would not occur since it would be punished by death, but a death sentence was possibly no more effective at stopping capital crimes in the nineteenth century than it is in our own society. A planter also had the legal right to kill a bondsman who struck him, but the economic loss the owner could incur by such a policy mitigated against its universal use. J. W. Loguen recalled such an incident when a bondsman named Jarm resisted a beating and decisively threw down his plantation's owner, Manasseth:

> this transaction greatly disappointed and embarrassed both parties. Jarm [who had been severely beaten days before] was in no condition to attempt an escape, and Manasseth in no condition to dispense with his abilities and labors. This extrodinary and daring onset on him, opened his eyes to the positive, manly, and promising character of his slave and awakened his respect. To pursue and punish him, he saw would be to drive his chafed spirit to a desperate extremity, and that he should therefore lose him. He concluded therefore, not to pursue him. Left alone, he believed Jarm would wander in the fields until his passion cooled, and then return to his labors, where he was greatly needed. Thus was Manasseth disciplined to submission by the decision and bravery of his slave.[244]

Such physical resistance, when the planter did not want to seek legal action, could lead to better conditions for a resister. Planters could punish powerful fighters only if they had assistance or could maneuver the bondsman into a weakened position. Blassingame suggests that otherwise, "the only way he could be punished was to shoot him. Realizing this, many slaves parlayed it into better treatment."[245] If they were valuable workers, like Jarm, however, planters often avoided future attempts at beatings. Bondsmen who fought back found that they came to an understanding with their masters and were thereafter given a certain amount of distance and respect. Elijah Marrs, after fighting his master rather than receiving a flogging, found that from then on, "I do not remember that he ever gave me an unpleasant word or look."[246] Other bondsmen who fought back evoked the same reaction.[247]

Blacks were successful at resisting the dishonor of whippings by overseers with even greater frequency. An overseer was often hired, and the ambiguous relationship between an overseer and a planter could be exploited by bondsmen. On the one hand, if the overseer beat a bondsman so badly that he could not work, the overseer might have to answer to the planter, who was losing labor. The overseer did not have options available to planters such as selling the bondsmen, and an overseer who shot a bondsman might lose his salary for the entire year.[248] Legal records, travelers' accounts, narratives, and journals reveal that blacks often turned on their overseers. Physical self-defense could be especially effective as protection against an overseer from another plantation, who had limited recourse to retribution. As Benjamin Johnson explained from his experience as a bondsman, "If you git home, den dey couldn't do nothin' to you."[249] Ironically, some bondsmen who used force against overseers and escaped punishment may have been protected by the strength of the overseers' sense of honor. It was certainly possible for an overseer to seek legal or other punitive measures for such an assault. However, this may have cost the overseer even more dearly than the original beating, since to admit to the white establishment that he had been bested by an "inferior" bondsman would have cost him respect by his white peers and those of the planter class.[250] Thus, when they thought they could effectively use master-overseer divide to protect themselves or were angry enough to risk the consequences, bonded fighters might react to overseers' insults with violence and suffer only those consequences their antagonists could inflict.

Such resistance not only liberated the bondsman from physical dishonor of whippings but could also liberate him from mental bondage. While focus here has been on outer or objectified honor as judged by an honor community, such resistance could also affect a bondsman's honor in the basic, inner sense of self-worth. Thus, an important result of resisting the dishonor of whippings was the psychological freedom and feeling of self-empowerment it could give to those in bondage. While the system of enslavement sought to disempower and psychologically subdue the descendants of Africans into believing they were inferior, striking back bodily could reaffirm their independence and self-dignity. Frederick Douglass had been abused by his overseer Covey for some time and had submitted to many whippings. Yet, on one fateful day he snapped and fought Covey off, trying not to hurt Covey but only to defend himself from being beaten until Covey relented. Later Douglass eloquently reflected on the profound liberation he found in his combat:

> This battle with Covey . . . was the turning point of my "life as a slave." It rekindled in my breast the smoldering embers of liberty . . . and revived a sense of my own manhood. I was a changed being after that fight. I was *nothing* before: I WAS A MAN NOW. It recalled to life my crushed self-respect and my self-confidence, and inspired me with a renewed determination to be A FREEMAN. . . . It was a resurrection from the dark and pestiferous tomb of slavery, to the heaven of comparative freedom. I was no longer a servile coward, trembling under the frown of a brother worm of the dust, but, my long-cowed spirit was roused to an attitude of manly independence. I had reached the point, at which I was not afraid to die. This spirit made me a freeman in *fact*, while I remained a slave in *form*. When a slave cannot be flogged he is more than half free. He has a domain as big as his own manly heart to defend, and he is really "a power on earth."[251]

Given that physical self-protection had such a powerful potential for liberation of the spirit as well as the body, it is not surprising that martial arts remained among the African traditions that African Americans continued with such determination.

Although any bondsman might find the determination within himself to resist beatings, specific martial art skills did often play a role in such forms of resisting dishonor. Wrestling skills could be turned against a master or overseer. William Lee remembered how, when his mistress tried to beat him, he "carried old missus out and thro' her on the ground jus' as hard as I could."[252] Similarly, when a bondsman named Johnson was visiting the plantation of a Mr. Brady, Brady tried to whip him and Johnson employed tricknology. Johnson stooped over pretending to take off his coat to receive the whipping and then suddenly used a wrestling move to throw Brady into a puddle.[253] Kicking was also associated with resisting the dishonor of whippings. In his battle with Covey, Douglass was not trying to hurt Covey and did not employ any offensive skills. However, when Covey's cousin Hughes tried to intervene and Douglass decided to attack him, it is telling that Douglass neutralized him with one powerful kick.[254] Even more common in such skirmishes was the more openly exhibited art of head butting. Reverend W. P. Jacobs recounted how head butting was practiced by bondsmen and used by them to prevent abuse by overseers: "One way slaves had of fighting was by butting. Some of the slaves had very hard heads. Albert Soods was a great butter. Niggers fought by butting all the time. They would grab each other by the ears and shoulders and just butt. Colin Hodgeins, a slave, was a great butter also. He had scars on his arms, back, and the other sides of his head from the lash. Just wouldn't be whipped after he was seventeen years old."[255]

William Grimes similarly recalled how his head-butting skills saved him from a beating and gained him the respect of the other blacks on a new plantation:

> [The driver] came to me, and asked why I did not rake up my oats, or those I had cut. I replied that I had a large boil under each arm and was unable to do it. He swore that I should do it, and went for a stick to beat me, in order to compel me to do it. I heard him coming back, and when he burst open the door, I let him have it old Virginia style. I drove my head against him, (hardly knowing what I was about, being so much terrified) until he could scarcely stand or go. I then compelled him to give up the stick to me, which I kept in my hand, walking to and fro, while as soon as he recovered from the bruising I had given him, called aloud to the other slaves to come to his assistance. They immediately gathered together, to the number of about twenty. He ordered them to seize me, and was in hopes they would; but one of the stoutest of them, on whom he placed the greatest reliance, came up to me to inquire what was the matter, and why I treated the driver so. I asked him how I had treated him. He replied, how you did. I then seized him by the shoulders, and said to him, I will show you. So I served him in the same way I had the driver, and almost as severe. The other negroes seeing me use this stout fellow so harshly, were afraid to touch me. . . . They did not attempt after that to touch me.

Grimes eventually gained the respect not only of the other bondsmen and the overseer but of the master as well.[256]

Even as free people, blacks continued to rely on their fighting skills to resist dishonor. For example, William Smith, a free African American in Canada, wished to return to the United States, where he had previously been in bondage and worked as a sailor. However, he was constantly denied the money for his Canadian land by a fraudulent land agent. After much mistreatment, Smith vowed to settle matters his own way and head butted the agent. The agent, Longworth, an extremely large man, recovered his composure after the blow. Undaunted, Smith "administered two or three more effectual butts with his hard head into the lordly agent, when the subdued and now silent English gentleman, drew from his pocket book, and carefully counted out, every dollar Smith had at first demanded."[257]

All of the seemingly disparate uses of African martial arts in North America can be brought together in the concept of honor among the enslaved. Martial arts helped bondsmen mark their honor and declare their humanity in numerous ways. In their plays, martial arts allowed adepts to gain honor through their mastery of the art in performance contexts. Such honor could serve them well in courting or in attaining leadership positions in the community. Even in the white culture of coercion, some bondsmen could gain some level of respect from whites when they turned their African fighting skills against the foes of the colonies in the American Revolution. The recognition of Zachary Molineaux's fighting ability and showing in the war released him from a possible lawsuit, while Jack Sisson's use of head butting in the capture of General Prescott led whites to immortalize him in praise songs. A more common nod of acknowledgment took place when black fighters were promoted to positions of distinction such as drivers, overseers, prizefighters, or bodyguards. Even legally free black people would continue to use their fighting arts to insist on their right to respect, as in the case of William Smith in Canada. Maroons also would have called upon available combat traditions to resist capture. Yet, the potential use of martial arts in exhibiting honor was most potent within the context of bondage.

Orlando Patterson defines slavery as the "permanent, violent domination of natally alienated and dishonored persons."[258] In this sense, martial arts were potentially powerful tools in resisting the core principles of the slave system. Martial arts could help bonded people psychologically and physically prepare themselves for the unforeseeable risks of escape and the defense of maroon communities. Within bondage they could be used to confront the violent domination of whippings, protect family members with blows against natal alienation, and claim honor through personal display. Of these, resisting the dishonor of whippings was a particularly powerful statement of honor by the enslaved as it denied their oppressors the central means of physical discipline. As Douglass experienced, resisting one's oppressor physically was linked to a profound sense of honor and a feeling of self-worth. In this sense the martial arts could help some bondsmen mark their honor and thus declare their humanity. Bondsmen who refused to be beaten asserted their will above that of their "owners"; they denied that they were mere chattel. Thus, African martial arts were potent weapons against the physical and symbolic violence of plantation slavery in North America, just as they would be in the Francophone Caribbean.

Four Return Passages

Ritual and Revolutionary Liberation from Bondage in the Francophone Caribbean

Many Africans arriving in the Caribbean Islands were forced to work in one of the most life-consuming labor systems of the Americas: sugar plantations. Yet, even on these islands the experiences of bondsmen were quite varied, as were their ethnic backgrounds.[1] Unlike in Rio de Janeiro, where the vast majority of Africans hailed from Central Africa, bonded populations of the Francophone Caribbean were often much more diverse. In a sense this made those populations not entirely unlike the frontier communities of Africa. African societies were constantly in a flux that produced a continual shift of populations to borderlands, where small groups, often from different language and culture communities, joined together to create new societies.[2] As in these African frontier societies, the African communities in the Francophone Caribbean incorporated people of many different backgrounds. Unlike African frontier societies, however, bonded communities of the Caribbean suffered social pressure on an unprecedented scale. Most lived under one of the most extremely coercive labor systems of the Americas.

Yet, their island plantations were surrounded by the sea, a constant reminder of the possibility of the freedom they had known across the *kalunga*. Martial arts served as another reminder of this past embodied in postures and movements. Black communities of the Francophone Caribbean, particularly Guadeloupe, Martinique, and Saint Domingue, performed combat styles that helped them cope with these historical realities of bondage.[3] Martial arts were commonly used for performances in drum circles that helped bondsmen create a sense of individual honor and collective solidarity. For many bondsmen, death was the only lasting respite from oppression, and martial arts played a role in wake rituals that aided the deceased spiritually to make the return passage across the *kalunga*. For others the social tension inherent in their position as an enslaved labor force resulted in the wielding of African combat traditions against the slave system in revolts such as the Haitian Revolution.

Sugarcane and the French Antilles

Although the French Antilles were originally used as bases for privateering, the spread of sugar production transformed the islands from coastal outposts surrounding Native Amerindian communities into plantation economies dependent on the influx of large numbers of captive Africans. Each island changed at a different rate and by a different historical process. Martinique, for example, began this alteration in the mid-seventeenth century. Although Martinique remained a French colony, it was the Dutch who initiated the island's sugar plantation economy. In the 1640s Dutch settlers from New Holland (now Pernambuco, Brazil) began introducing modern milling and production techniques and providing credit for local planters to acquire enslaved Africans. Dutch vessels later hauled the finished sugar to refineries in Amsterdam. Following the return of New Holland to Portuguese sovereignty in 1654, many Dutch refugees resettled in Martinique, firmly establishing a plantation system on the island.[4] Although Dutch settlers also settled in Guadeloupe, physically the largest of the French Lesser Antilles, the island remained legally subordinated to Martinique through most of the following century.[5] While sugar production increased on the island, this growth did not match that of Martinique, which became France's wealthiest Caribbean holding in the later seventeenth century. In the following century a diverse group of less wealthy investors, including recent immigrants, poor whites, and free people of African descent, who could not compete with the wealthy sugar planters for the expensive flatlands near the coasts, turned to growing cocoa or coffee in the highlands with varying levels of success.[6] Other alternate crops included indigo and rocou.[7] Yet, sugarcane plantations dominated both the island's economy and the lives of most Africans and their descendants on the island. As a result, plantation owners of Martinique and Guadeloupe began to forcibly immigrate large numbers of enslaved Africans to meet the high labor demands of their various cash crops. By the 1670s these islands, populated primarily by native Caribs just fifty years earlier, were now demographically dominated by enslaved Africans.[8]

French planters of the Caribbean held strong stereotypes about different African nations, which affected their purchasing patterns; yet, no single group appears to have demographically dominated across the French Lesser Antilles.[9] In Guadeloupe the largest number of Africans arrived from Central Africa, and yet these comprised only roughly 22 percent of the bonded population. Those taken from Biafra were the next most numerous group on the island, representing about 20 percent. The next largest group, from the Bight of Benin, had a significantly smaller representation at 10 percent.[10] Guadeloupe had a reputation as a market for captives unwanted elsewhere, and this may partly explain the high numbers of West Central Africans and Biafrans, as these two groups along with Africans from Sierra Leone and the Windward Coast were stereotyped by French planters as not well suited for sugar production.[11] The absolute numbers of Africans brought to Guadeloupe were relatively small compared to those in Martinique. It is difficult to directly extrapolate the ethnic makeup of Martinique's bonded community from slave trade data because Martinique, as the easternmost French island and administrative center, was also a major center of reexportation to other islands.[12] Ship records suggest that no region of Africa supplied much more than 35 percent of the Africans sent to Martinique, but a detailed analysis of documents on the island would be necessary to confirm these indications.[13] It is clear, however, that Africans from certain areas of Africa were not as heavily clustered in the French Lesser Antilles as they were in Virginia, South Carolina, Rio de Janeiro, or even Saint Domingue.

The colony of Saint Domingue made the most dramatic transition into a thriving plantation economy. In 1697 the colony, situated on the western half of the island of Hispaniola, was still an outpost for privateering. Yet, during the first quarter of the eighteenth century sugar plantations spread rapidly on Saint Domingue. By the 1740s it replaced Martinique as France's wealthiest Caribbean colony, producing more sugar by itself than all the British islands combined.[14] A decade later average plantation sizes in the colony surpassed 200 acres and the population of enslaved Africans exceeded 117,000.[15] The North Province had the largest bonded populations and sugar output, followed by the West Province, while the South Province lagged somewhat behind. In the second half of the century, sugar plantation sizes were quite large, particularly in the North Province. As a whole, a majority of bondsmen on sugar plantations found themselves living with at least 200–300 others.[16] After the 1730s, when restrictions against exporting Caribbean coffee to Europe were lifted, coffee production increased across the colonies, reaching its height from 1763 to 1791. Coffee became the most important secondary crop in Martinique and Guadeloupe but remained far behind sugar in scale and value there.[17] In Saint Domingue, however, coffee production grew dramatically in the mountainous regions of the island and came close to rivaling sugar production right before the revolution. By this time Saint Domingue had become the world's largest producer of sugar and coffee, a feat that required a constant influx of enslaved Africans to provide labor.

While Africans who embarked from the Bight of Benin and Biafra were brought to Saint Domingue in significant numbers, Angolans had the strongest demographic presence there. Individuals taken from the Bight of Benin were brought to the island in a steady stream and carried with them many elements of what would later become the most widely visible religious tradition on the island, *vodun*.[18] Yet, West Central Africans alone represented around 50 percent of forced immigrants in the eighteenth century.[19] The use of the blanket terms "Angole" in the slave-trade data and "Congo" on the island masks the more specific ethnic identities of these West Central Africans. The majority were from the coast north of the Kongo River, but certainly captives taken from Cimbebasia at the mouth of the Kunene River were among them.[20] By the second half of the eighteenth century Angolans constituted the largest minority of Africans on sugar plantations and a majority of adult Africans on coffee plantations.[21] These West Central Africans had a reputation for being better suited to the less strenuous coffee plantations, which engaged almost as many bondsmen as sugar plantations by the eve of the revolution.[22] At this time, despite a large population of young, locally born bondsmen in some regions, over two- thirds of the enslaved population was African-born.[23]

Regardless of their specific origins, the vast majority of Africans who were brought to these French islands suffered from the harsh demands of plantation slavery. Gabriel Debien calculated that only around 10 percent of immigrant Africans would end up in urban-type slave systems in the towns and cities of the French Antilles;[24] the rest were destined for the plantations.[25] In many ways sugar plantations were ideally established to be separate social systems. Set up like little villages, each included a sugar mill, a boiling house, a curing house, a distillery, a planter's house, an infirmary, bondsmen's quarters, cane fields, areas for livestock, and provision gardens. Additionally cassava fields were needed to meet the requirement of the Code Noir (the code outlining treatment of bondsmen for all French colonies), which stipulated that each bondsmen be given two and a half pots of cassava per week for food.[26] Father Jean-Baptiste Labat, a Dominican missionary in Martinique from 1693 to 1705, ran a plantation on the north side of the island for many years. Labat left in his memoirs a detailed description of his plantation, which he intended as a model for others to follow. He held 120 captive Africans on his plantation, and as many of these were Aradas, he learned their language to communicate with them.[27] Labat calculated that about a third of newly arrived Africans died within the first year due to the new climate, the disease environment, and the harshness of the workload. Labat allowed them to acclimate for a week before being gradually introduced to the labor regime, and he was critical of the typical practice of most planters, who sent newcomers straight to work.[28]

The types of labor done on sugar plantations were quite varied. The plantation utilized bondsmen as domestics, nurses, cooks, and midwives.[29] Bonded tradesmen included blacksmiths, coopers, wheelwrights, carpenters, masons, and others who were essential for keeping the buildings, machinery, and equipment in good order. Canoemen and fishermen aided in transport and provided protein toward the Code Noir's stipulation that each bondsmen receive three pounds of fish or two pounds of salted beef, the latter of which would otherwise have to be imported.[30] Labat, like many other owners, chose Africans from pastoral backgrounds to serve as herdsmen over the horses and oxen, which among other tasks powered most mills in the first half of the century.[31]

Working in the mill, boilers, and distillery was prestigious but undoubtedly uncomfortable due to sweltering heat around the boilers and the risk of industrial accidents.[32] Labat may have been atypical in selecting bonded women to work in the mill extracting juice from the cane and in the distillery.[33] Certainly, he reflected a common practice in selecting a bondsmen to act as a driver overseeing the field gangs.[34]

Throughout the French Antilles these field gangs, or *ateliers*, employed the largest group of bondsmen and did the most backbreaking labor of the sugar plantations. The *grand atelier* was the center of the production process. It was composed of the strongest men and women among the enslaved group.[35] The second, or *petit atelier*, was composed of bondsmen who lacked the capability to work in the *grand atelier*.[36] In the growing season these gangs worked in the field clearing land, planting cane, or tending the fields from early morning until sundown, when they returned to their houses to work a few more hours on other tasks such as preparing manioc flour.[37] Different fields were planted to mature in rotation, typically producing a harvest period of over five months. Work in the harvest season was extremely oppressive, and work hours were extended. Because the cane had to be processed immediately after being cut, the mill and boilers worked twenty-four hours a day for the season. This hard labor took a toll on bondsmen. An official in Martinique investigated the extremely high mortality rates in 1725. He concluded, "This slave mortality appears to be caused by the heavy labor that the planters make them perform without adequate nourishment. Some planters give them nothing except to let them work for themselves on Saturdays to earn their sustenance for the week; others give them only half the rations that are required by the ordinances of the king; and others give them even less. Still others give them neither the half rations nor the free Saturday. To be fair, there are some planters who give their slaves everything that is required by the Code Noir, but such planters are rare. The others, in contrast, are very numerous."[38] The disease environment and work-related injuries also took a toll on plantation laborers.[39] Even those on smaller coffee plantations, where physical labor was less strenuous, had their share of hardships and comparable mortality rates.[40]

Many bondsmen who were manumitted found themselves drawn into another sector of the system: military service. Militias were absolutely essential to the survival of plantation-based economies, in which enslaved Africans were the staggering majority. A 1790 census in Guadeloupe reported some 3,125 free people of color; 13,969 whites; and 90,134 bondsmen. Around the same time Martinique had 5,000 free people of color; 10,600 of European descent; and 83,000 bondsmen. Although Saint Domingue hosted much larger numbers of free people—30,000 whites and 28,000 free people of color—these were demographically overwhelmed by the 465,000 bondsmen.[41] The task of policing this overwhelming population fell to the local militias and *maréchaussée*, or colonial police force. In addition to poorer whites, many such units were composed of the *gens de couleur libres,* or free people of color. This group was composed of free people of African descent born in Africa and the Caribbean, the latter of whom often also had some European ancestry.[42] Although these individuals had been granted liberty from bondage, their lives and opportunities were still severely circumscribed by other legal restrictions. As a result, many of these free people of color entered the local militias and police forces, where they could access some institutional protections and possibly rise to officer status.[43] In the second half of the eighteenth century new taxes were introduced; these charged heavy fees on owners who freed their bondsmen directly but were waived if the bondsmen first served out an eight-year term of military service.[44] As a result of these social pressures, the ranks of militias and the police forces were swollen with bondsmen and free people of African descent.[45] These forces, along with militias during the Haitian Revolution, provided a potential context in which some bondsmen's previous martial experience may have been put to use in service of the colony.[46] The primary task of these troops was the internal policing of order breakers and especially bondsmen.[47]

Even under the rigors of this extreme plantation labor and policing by patrols, Africans and their descendants under bondage created some space for economic and social autonomy. Despite the legal fiction of the enslaved not being able to own property, in social practice bondsmen gained control over their provision grounds, often even passing them on to their descendants.[48] Bondsmen worked on their provision gardens to balance out their diet and traded their surplus in an underground economy.[49] This black market network of bondsmen connected with those of smugglers and people from other islands.[50] Many Africans and their descendants chose to face the dangers of escape to pursue a life of rural maroonage, which appears to have expanded dramatically along with the plantation system.[51] Although free of plantation labor, these maroons remained in contact with the bonded community for supplies and information. Others sought anonymity on neighboring plantations or in large port cities, which also offered the possibility of maritime maroonage.[52] Perhaps the most common form of respite from the plantation was *petite maroonage,* the short-term leaving of the plantation confines to engage in independent economic activities or attend social gatherings such as *bamboulas.*

Bamboulas in the Lesser Antilles

Although early descriptions of unarmed martial arts in the French colonies are sparse, it is clear that in the French Lesser Antilles separate combat techniques, both open-handed and armed, coexisted. The most visible context for the practice of these combat styles was community performance rituals akin to the plays of North America. These were generally called *kalendas,* or for the purposes of the current discussion, *bamboulas.*[53] *Bamboula* referred specifically to the small drum of these dance circles. Father Labat describes (likely from his plantation on the north side of Martinique) a dance circle accompanied by two drums: "the big one beats calmly, whereas the one who touches the baboula [*bamboula*] beats as fast as he can."[54] This essential action of the *bamboula* to improvise and respond to the dancers'/fighters' movements was likely the reason that the term *bamboula* was often extended to describe the entire performance-ritual event.[55]

Some of these *bamboulas* were semiprivate rituals conducted by associations called *sociétés* in Guadeloupe and *convois* in Martinique. These closed societies combined ethnic, religious, and economic functions.[56] In their role as mutual aid cooperatives, they generated common funds for funerals, purchasing freedom of members, or for sponsoring community performance rituals (such as processions and dances on festival days). These organizations appear to have grown out of groups of African nations in the Lesser Antilles. In Martinique closed societies had a hierarchical organization led by a queen or king and court.[57] In 1829 there were some seventeen such societies in Saint Pierre alone.[58] While there is little written documentation to illuminate the participants' understanding of the *bamboulas* of closed societies, it is likely that many of the dances had specific religious implications, particularly when connected to particular nations.[59] In Martinique the covert rituals of some closed societies may have been the context most associated with the pugilistic arts, which, according to Jacqueline Rosemain, was "the most secret dance"; only those initiated into the closed societies knew the martial art form, and noninitiates knew it only by its distinctive rhythms.[60] Similarly, in Guadeloupe some of the martial drum dances were believed to emanate from closed societies, possibly "Kongo" societies.[61] Thus, some African martial traditions of the French Caribbean may have been at one point linked to closed societies. Some of these societies, like the Old Time Religion societies of North America, provided resources for counterhegemonic activity, such as the society that a bondswoman led in Guadeloupe in 1845 and that was dedicated to helping bondsmen escape slavery.[62] While closed societies sponsored *bamboulas,* possibly requiring oaths to attend, others were events by and for the entire bonded community.

The largest *bamboulas* usually took place on weekends and holidays. Almost all bondsmen were relieved of forced labor to attend to their provision gardens and so were free on Sundays as well as holidays including Christmas, Lent, New Year's Day, and All Saints' Day.[63] The livestock and produce of these provision grounds (in some instances stolen from the plantation) were often served to *bamboula* participants. Despite successive prohibitions against such gatherings, bondsmen in Martinique would travel great distances to participate in nocturnal assembles. Labat notes that these assemblies often took place late at night in remote locations: "When the masters do not permit them to dance on the plantation, after they finish their work in the sugarcane fields they will walk 3 or 4 miles (*lieux*) on Saturday night at midnight to meet in a place they knew they could have a dance." According to Labat, the most widely popular dance of bondsmen was centered around a belly-bounce between dancers of the opposite sex:

> What pleases them most and is their most common dance is the *calenda*. The dancers are arranged in two lines, the one before the other, the men to one side, the women to the other. Those are the ones who dance, and the spectators make a circle around the dancers and drums. The most skilled sings a song that he composes on the spot, on such a subject as he judges appropriate, and the refrain, which is sung by all the spectators, is accompanied by a great beating of hands. As regards the dancers, they hold up their arms a little like those who dance while playing castanets. They jump, they spin, they approach to within three feet of each other, they leap back on the beat, until the sound of the drum tells them to join and they strike their thighs, [the midsections of] some beating against the others, that is, the mens' against the womens'. To see this, it seems that they beat their bellies together, while it is however only their thighs that support the blows. They back away immediately, pirouetting, to recommence the same movement with completely lascivious gestures, as often as the drum gives them the signal, which it does several times in succession.[64]

The structural features of this dance all appear to have Angolan provenance, particularly the opposing lines of men and women, pelvic isolation, and courtship gestures leading to a leg/belly bounce, called *semba* in Angola.[65] It was the courtship gestures and *semba* that both fascinated and revolted European observers of the dance.[66] Planters were also concerned that clandestine *bamboulas* could lead to open revolt and that some bondsmen would dance until daybreak. As a result, some planters sponsored local dances that would take place in a controlled location after Sunday Mass until midnight.

Whether covert or overt, these events united the bonded community while also allowing for the expression of ethnic diversity. Labat notes that while all bondsmen came together in their appreciation of the *semba*-style belly-bouncing dance, each nation also danced according to its own tastes in separate circles at the common *bamboula*. The Congo nation had a ring dance structurally similar to the North American ring shout, the Mina dancers turned dynamic pirouettes, while the Gambie (Senegambians) and other nations had quite distinct dances of their own.[67] Half a century later the practice of separate dance circles continued but with the integration of locally born bondsmen, who numerically rivaled African-born in the second half of the century.[68] A report from 1793 reveals that Martinican dance rituals were divided into nations that were distinguished by their dances, dress, and musical instruments: "The Negroes gathered by nation to dance during the public feasts. Their flag revealed that such and such group was composed of Caplaus or of Igbos; who, besides, could be recognized by their costumes and their musical instruments. Finally, this custom was adopted by the creole Negroes."[69] The saliency of these separate "nation" dance traditions continued into the nineteenth century.[70] An 1838 description of a *bamboula* in the capital city of Fort Royal showed that the participants divided themselves into many separate circles.[71]

Similar patterns were present in the *bamboulas* of Guadeloupe. William Butterworth, an English sailor who passed through Guadeloupe in 1787, described one such *bamboula* in some detail.[72] Having noted from his experiences in Grenada that "Sunday was the negroes' holiday, which they devoted to festivity and manly exercises," Butterworth "took every opportunity" to witness them in Guadeloupe. "The ground appropriated to festive scenes was well chosen, being pleasantly situated on the summit of a hill, a little out of the town [Basse-Terre]." As noted above, the community united, but "the greatest order prevailed in forming the respective circles, each knowing to which he belonged." Different nations were represented and marked by flags "of different colours," and people of mixed African and European descent, whom Butterworth called "mustees," also had their own circle. These events were open to the entire community, and children sitting on the ground formed the innermost ring of every circle, implying a potential for generational continuities.[73]

In addition to nations and colors, these dance circles also reflected gender distinctions. Butterworth noted groups composed of women "particular in keeping themselves select, not a male of any description being allowed to interfere with them." Yet he was certainly not the only male who enjoyed watching them from beyond the circle. Most of these women worked as domestics, but as the *bamboula* witnessed by Butterworth took place just outside the urban center of Basse-Terre, this may not have reflected status divisions as sharply as it may have in rural contexts.[74] According to Butterworth, in these circles women claimed honor through personal display of dancing "executed with taste and judgment" and style of dress: "They added gracefulness to personal flexibility, and pliancy of limbs, which appeared to the greatest advantage, when performing the evolutions of the mazy dance, which, together with singing, constituted the whole of their amusements."

An orchestra of drums, rattles, and "an instrument somewhat like a guitar" provided music. This same music was the backdrop for the male combat games that took place in other circles. Although the combatants were predominantly male, women likely played an important role in these circles as well. Bernard Moitt notes that women played a dominant role in many of the *sociétés* that sponsored such *bamboulas,* and since some were known to be exclusively female, women may have often provided leadership for the overall events.

Figure 4.1: "A Negro fight in South America." *Harper's Weekly,* August 15, 1874, 673

Women also sang for these dance circles and "competed with one another over the merits of the compositions."[75] Thus, while Butterworth is silent on the subject, it is possible that women were competing vocally in the same circles while men were competing physically.[76] These physical contests were also public displays of masculinity. The competitions began with the winner of the previous week's competition "strutting about" with a "dignified appearance" before initiating the actual competitions, according to Butterworth.[77] The intended audience of such bravado certainly included women, many of whom may have also played an active role in egging men on in their performance.

Butterworth notes distinct "manly exercises" in the *bamboulas* of Guadeloupe. One of these combat sports was a form of grappling set to music. It began with an opening ritual of posturing and challenge that led to a physical contest in which "the man who brings his adversary fairly to the ground claims the victory." Although Butterworth does not give us the local term, what he glosses as "wrestling" may have been a precursor to the art later called *sové vayan* or *lévé-fessé*.[78] If this early form was similar to these twentieth century forms, then the stylistically open nature of this art would have allowed Biafran wrestlers to continue their *mgba* techniques, at the same time allowing Senegambians or other African groups to continue their grappling techniques as well. Thus, these contests would have been an outlet for all the various African ethnic groups that came to the Caribbean with their own unique forms of wrestling.

If the formal wrestling competitions of the *bamboulas* had been foreign to Kunene men from Angola, Butterworth also describes contests that would not have been. Among these were stick-fighting competitions akin to the ones in which Kunene men grew up participating. Butterworth also mentions head-butting duels he calls "tupping." The head-butting games described here were reminiscent of the Kunene dueling with head butts in imitation of their prized cattle:

> Another favorite amusement is tupping, generally practiced by Negroes. . . . The ring being formed as before, the music again strikes up, and the victorious tupper of the last Sunday's encounter enters the ring, endeavoring to surpass in dignified appearance the champion of single sticks. Anyone wishing to try the hardness of his head enters the circle, marches up to, and shakes hands with the fortunate tupper: after which the music changes to a common jig tune, to which the opposing combatants dance with careless gaiety, frequently exchanging smiles, and significantly nodding their heads at each other. They then separate, withdrawing a few yards from each other, still dancing, jumping, and nodding the head: now stooping forward, with hands clasped upon their backs, they advance towards each other, with the spirit and caution of game cocks, that have been pitted before, each panting for victory. When within a yard and a half of each other, the music ceases; the tuppers pause for a moment, and eye each other with the steadfast gaze of scientific pugilists; when, as if by mutual impulse, both dart forward, head against head, like two rams![79]

Butterworth also mentions circles dedicated to boxing contests, but it is impossible to tell what type of pugilism he witnessed since he did not leave a detailed description.

Pugilism in the Lesser Antilles

Even more so than in North America or Brazil, references to unarmed combat in the French Antilles are extremely rare, particularly for the nineteenth century.[80] In Martinique pugilism was being practiced, as were head-butting contests. Dr. Etienne Rufz de Lavision notes that "in their brawls, the negroes seldom use offensive weapons although they constantly have their cutlasses. They resort to their fists or hurl themselves at one another head first just like rams."[81] While it is clear that head butting was a constant, the lack of details concerning other nineteenth-century unarmed pugilistic systems makes it difficult to connect the pugilism witnessed by Butterworth directly to the martial art styles of the early twentieth century.[82] With this caveat, it may still be worthwhile to examine what can be tentatively gleaned about the forms of pugilism as they existed in the early twentieth century.

Beyond head butting, there were at least three types of pugilism practiced throughout the French Lesser Antilles: *kokoyé, bèrnaden,* and *danmyé/ladja*. The first, *kokoyé,* was a unique form of pugilism based on the round, haymaker-style swinging punch. This contest took the form of a war of attrition in which both combatants met with their front feet touching each other. Without moving their feet, they then threw powerful swinging punches at each other until one was knocked down or forced to step back.[83] The term *kokoyé* also appears in Cuba, where bondsmen also practiced boxing combat styles such as *maní.*[84] A possibly related term, *kokovale,* was used in Puerto Rico to describe combat art.[85] The unique punches of this style might have been developed locally, perhaps influenced by other Atlantic World forms of pugilism such as English boxing or a pugilistic art called *biboto* with very similar strikes.[86]

A second form of pugilism was *bèrnaden,* a practice that would have been familiar to Kunene people arriving at these islands. This was a slap-boxing contest much like that of open-handed *kandeka.* As with the Kunene slap boxing, the beauty of the art was in the defense.[87] These blows of *bèrnaden* were different from those of *kokoyé,* with the latter's strikes demarked as *wonpwen,* or "swinging fist" (*rond de poing*).[88] In contrast, the *kandeka*-like slaps of *bèrnaden,* with their straight-line trajectories, were referred to as *filé dwa* in Martinique.[89] As with *kandeka,* the usual objective was to exhibit defensive skills as the two participants tried to slap each other in the face or body, with the lips being the primary target.[90]

The third pugilistic style was the kickboxing art in Martinique that will be referred to here as *danmyé.*[91] According to Julian Gerstin, these were "noncombat duels, in which the contestants attempted to demonstrate mastery without injury."[92] Although some punches were used later in the twentieth century as the lines between *danmyé* and the composite art became blurry, previously at least one strain of this tradition was predominantly foot fights involving an exchange of acrobatic defenses, sweeps, and kicks, the latter often thrown from an inverted position.

The inverted kicks of the art, called *wolo* among other names, were linked to the *kalunga* through their use in an aquatic game of the same name. The term *wolo/woulo* designated both inverted kicks "delivered from a crouched position with the hands on the ground" in ritual combat on land and an aquatic game involving a contest between two players in the ocean or river. According to Ed Powe, in Martinique players at times attached weapons to their feet in these contests. The two combatants would flip themselves over to try to kick the opponent in the head or upper body with one or both feet (aquatic variations of images 9, 11, 13, and 14 in the appendix). As on land, the defense was to dodge or turn with the strike. This game was practiced on many other islands of the Lesser Antilles, where it was also known as *libo.*[93]

A related composite art called *ladja* was formed in Martinique, purportedly as a human variant on cock fighting.[94] According to popular stories, Africans were used as gladiators for entertainment and gambling akin to fighting cocks.[95] This practice may have been an important factor in the development of *ladja.* In Martinique, particularly, the more destructive side of the martial arts may have been common in planter-organized fights. This practice was referred to as the *lan mò* or *ladja de la mort* (*ladja* of death) because participants were often reportedly forced to fight to the death, the enslaver hoping to overcome in winnings the financial damage he had incurred with the injury of his enslaved.[96] As with the black strongmen in North America and the Brazilian *capangas,* bonded fighters were at times used as overseers in Martinique. According to Gerstin, "owners frequently paid certain slaves to act as overseers and to police the other slaves. These overseers, called *majò* (majors) used *ladja* in their work."[97] Even after abolition, masters of *ladja* continued to be referred to as *majò*.[98]

Although written evidence is lacking to corroborate their existence, it is possible to hypothesize that if forced death matches between bondsmen did exist under slavery, then the serious nature of the *ladja de la mort* may have acted as a catalyst in the breaking down of barriers between the previously segmented combat components.[99] In the Kunene region, slap-boxing *kandeka, engolo,* and head-butting contests were practiced separately just as such combat rituals continued to be in the "manly exercises" described by Butterworth. Yet, such skills were often all contained in the corporal vocabulary of an individual fighter, who could obviously combine such skills when efficacious. Perhaps the danger of death or serious injury to the losing party during *ladja de la mort* fostered the integration of these separate combat forms into an all-inclusive style; that is, fighters had to draw on anything and everything in their arsenal in order to ensure their victory and survival. Thus, the hand-fighting arts of *kokoyé* and *bèrnaden* were merged with the kicking art of *danmyé,* the throws of *sové vayan,* and the head butts of *tupping*. In addition, in some death matches it was purportedly not unknown for the *majò* in these fights to hold razor blades with their feet, making their kicks even more deadly.[100] The result was a composite form that used any means available to overcome an opponent in combat.

While forced death matches would have ended after emancipation, nonlethal prizefights of a similar nature continued in Martinique. The fighters, who like most blacks were forced to work in cane fields for meager wages, were drawn into these fights as means of added income. For the higher classes, this served as a form of entertainment akin to the highly popular cock fighting. These matches went on as late as the mid-twentieth century when Vidiadhar Naipaul visited Martinique. He was taken to a pit surrounded by two tiers of seating where gambling and cock-fighting matches went on all afternoon. In the evening the cocks were taken out and *ladja* fighters brought in to take their place.[101]

This style was practiced in ritual matches as well in the twentieth century.[102] The style of *ladja* came to be used in ritual sites that may previously have been marked by *danmyé*. *Ladja* took place at dance performances, on the docks, and at festivals. In northern Martinique thatched pavilions were built for *bèlè* and *ladja* performances, and the latter was also practiced on the docks of Fort-de-France.[103] *Ladja* was performed spontaneously at communal festivals but was most associated with Carnival and Samedi Gloria (the day before Easter Sunday). The latter usually hosted the largest *ladja* matches. During Lent all *ladja* stopped, and the fighters went into a period of physical and ritual preparation in anticipation of Samedi Gloria, which represented the annual regeneration of the art form.[104] During Samedi Gloria the *ladja* matches recommenced with a night-long competition that took place on riverbanks or the seashore, a continued link to the crossing of the *kalunga*.

In these contexts, as with the other combat arts, the *ladja* took place in a circle of singers/fighters known as the *won*. The main musical elements were the percussion provided by a drum called *tanbou alendjé*, musical sticks (*tibwa*) that played on the backs of the drums, and soloists who led the chorus in call-and-response songs. The ritual began with the *kouri lawon*, in which the drums called a fighter to enter the circle in a stylized counterclockwise run.[105] The combatant began the *monté tanbou*, in which he danced to the drummer, saluted the instruments, drew energy from them, and tried to intimidate his adversary with the agility of his dance. After appraising the challenger's skill level, another adept would emerge from the circle to perform his own *kouri won* and *monté tanbou*. The two then faced each other and engaged in ritual combat in which they danced to the music while attacking and countering with a series of kicks, evasions, sweeps, swinging hand blows, head butts, throws, and cartwheels. In this controlled ritual environment, the fight continued until the musicians called for the two to break and then called for another pair to begin their *kouri rond*. Less experienced adepts usually fought first, with fighters gradually working in skill levels to the *majò*.

A few scholars have suggested that *ladja* is a continuation of West African wrestling traditions, particularly Igbo *mgba* or the wrestling of ethnic groups in the Bight of Benin.[106] However, while West African wrestling certainly influenced the combat form, *ladja* was much more accurately described in terms of the Central African pugilistic tradition. This is suggested by the art's musical and religious elements and confirmed by a technical analysis.

If *ladja* was originally a gladiatorial system, it eventually came to be practiced in the drum circles formerly utilized for the practice of *danmyé*. Musically the ritual practice of *ladja/danmyé* seems to fit the pattern of the Central African pugilistic arts in the diaspora. The *ladja* drum is long and cylindrical and is played on its side, with a drummer playing the skin-covered end and another musician striking the cylinder with two sticks called *tibwa*. By sitting or standing astride the drum the drummer can employ the feet to intensify the sound, thus heating up the fighter for whom he is playing, a technique also called *danmyé*.[107] The drum and style of play are strikingly similar to those used by the Kunene at times to accompany *kandeka* and *engolo*. Although not exclusive to the Kunene, this transverse drum style (played horizontally on the ground) has been noted by ethnomusicologists as being of Central African origin, as was the playing of musical sticks on the back of the drum.[108] In Brazil, the visiting Austrian artist Rugendas in the 1820s depicted a similar style of transverse drum being used in the *jogo de capoeira.*[109] A similar drumming style with accompanying sticks playing on the back of the drum for the martial art of *maní* was practiced in Cuban *yuka* drumming, which also came out of Cuba's Central African tradition.[110] The transverse drum and *tibwa*-like sticks of another Central African–derived martial art in Brazil called *punga* were also strikingly similar to those of the *danmyé*. Thus, the *danmyé* drum and its style of play are clearly part of a wider Central African diaspora of a linked martial and musical tradition.

Central African–derived religious ideas continued to play a role in an understanding of the *ladja*. For example, an opening pose called the *parada* (standing with the left arm akimbo and the right hand upward) was believed to throw the spiritual power of the fighter against his opponent, as in the Central African religious gesture *telama Iwimbanganga.*[111] Robert F. Thompson also notes a strong sense of the Central African cosmogram in the *kouri rond* of *danmyé:* "The first thing players of *ladja* do is to run in a mystic circle to 'close' their bodies off from emanations of jealousy and envy, according to Eugene Mona, himself a deeply versed player with a Kongo tree-shrine to his ancestors in his yard."[112]

Writing about the United States, Sterling Stuckey examines this Angolan circle in the religious lives of slaves and concludes that the counterclockwise circle is foremost a Central African– derived ritual danced to invoke the ancestors.[113] As in the *engolo,* ancestral *ladja* fighters are believed to watch over *ladja* fighters and offer them power, which could be tapped into by *ladja* fighters. In addition, as in the *engolo,* it was the inheritance of this ancestral power, referred to as *ladja* secrets, that separated true masters from casual practitioners. Raoul Grivalliers thoroughly believed in the power of his *ladja* secrets imparted by his ancestors: "With prayers and *ladja* secrets I could lift my house. It has happened that people have had such strength despite small size."[114]

The Central African pugilistic essence of the combat form is confirmed by an analysis of the style. The various defensive dropping positions, cartwheels and spin kicks, and danced ready position all mark the *ladja* as derived primarily from a pugilistic base. Dunham's descriptions of one of the central kicks of the *ladja* show that it is clearly derived from the tradition of inverted kicking, being thrown with the hands touching the ground. It was accompanied by a song:

> Gade' Mile' a
> (Look at that mule)
> Kon I ka vréye' pyé
> (How he Kicks his feet).[115]

Dunham's analysis points out that at the heart of the *ladja*'s aesthetic were the interactive blows and defenses characteristic of the Central African pugilistic styles: "The fascination of the real [*ladja*] lies not in the lust of the combat, but in the finesse of approach and retreat; the tension which becomes almost a hypnosis, then the flash of the two bodies as they leap in to the air, fall in a crouch, and whirl at each other in simulated attacks, only to walk nonchalantly away, backs to each other, showing utter indifference before falling again into the rocking motion which rests them physically but excites them emotionally."[116]

This insightful passage from Dunham also highlights another aspect of the Central African aesthetic, the theatrical breaks and feigning of disinterest in order to fool one's opponent and gain the element of surprise. This practice fostered trickiness and delighted the audience by highlighting the exchange of attacks and counters.[117] While some grappling was incorporated into *ladja*, it played only a minimal role in the matches filmed by Dunham in the 1930s.[118]

Although our understanding of the historical evolution of these pugilistic practices is for the moment hindered by a lack of documentation, there are two important comparative points to be gleaned from the martial arts of the French Antilles. First, although the dating and causes for ladja's formation remain unclear, it unquestionably stands as an example showing that hybrid art forms could be developed in the Americas. Unlike North American kicking or the *jogo de capoeira*, which can be discussed as direct continuities of the *engolo* tradition, the *ladja* clearly represents a merger of previously separate forms. This was not, however, the result of acculturation in which African arts adopted or creatively reconfigured aspects of the French martial arts of *savate* or *la boxe française*, which were popular in the nineteenth and twentieth centuries.[119] Rather, it reflects primarily a historical blending of the pugilistic styles of bondsmen with some influence from West African wrestling.

Second, in both the eighteenth-century practices observed by Butterworth and in early twentieth-century practice, multiple combat arts coexisted side by side without any need for hybridization. Most of these certainly drew inspiration from African combat traditions, but further research would be needed to determine the possible influence of specific African styles. The *wolo* inverted and circular kicks of *danmyé* most likely derived from the *engolo*. *Bèrnaden* may have been inspired by the slap boxing of southern Angola. While pugilistic arts of northern Angola seem to have provided some strikes to *kokoyé*, other Atlantic World combat arts may have influenced its development as well.[120] It is clear that these various combat arts continued to be practiced long after the development of *ladja*, in part due to their important ritual functions in wake ceremonies.

Return Passage across the *Kalunga*

The combat arts of the bonded community played a critical role in rituals helping bondsmen's souls make return journeys across the *kalunga*. Many Africans and their descendants in the Francophone Caribbean died as a result of the work conditions on plantations. Disease, overwork, accidents, harsh punishments, dietary change, and malnutrition took huge tolls on the African populations of the French Antilles. In an average group of Africans brought to these islands in the eighteenth century, as many as half would be dead within eight years.[121] For them, this death was not the end but rather a return passage to their natal communities across the *kalunga*. Enslaved Africans did not forget their homelands and kept alive the dream of returning there. For many this preoccupation manifested itself in the avoidance of excess salt, an element that Central Africans believed would prevent them from returning home. The salt was associated with acculturation, which might jeopardize their connection to ancestral power that provided the ability to physically "fly back" to their natal communities.[122]

The belief in the ability of Africans to fly back out of slavery was clearly widespread across the Americas. In Cuba this ability may have been most associated with Central Africans, the Musundi in particular, who were also associated with stick fighting in Saint Domingue. According to Esteban Montejo, "they went flying, flying in the sky, and headed off for their homeland. The Musundi Congo were the ones who flew the most." In North America, "flying" was perhaps most associated with the Igbo, who were believed to have flown back after arriving at Igbo Landing. However, any African was believed to have the potential for flight. For some it required special rituals such as the North American ring shout, in which bondsmen danced in a counterclockwise circle to re-create the crossing of the *kalunga*.[123] While for many, the ring shout allowed the living to traverse the *kalunga* spiritually to access ancestral power, it was believed that others were able to use it to fly back to Africa: "Duh slabes wuz out in duh fiel wukin. All ub a sudden dey git tuh-gedduh an staht tuh moob round in a ring. Rond dey go fasternfastuh. Den one by one dey riz up an take wing an fly lak a bud. Duh obuseeuh heah duh noise an he come out an he see duh slabes riz up in duh eah an fly back tuh Africa. He run an he ketch duh las one by duh foot jis as he was bout to fly off. I dohn know ef he wuz neeah nuff tuh pull um back down an keep um from goin off."[124] Rosa Grant from Georgia remembered the story of her grandmother, who took flight back to Africa. Her mother "wuz standing right deah wen it happen. She alluz wish dat uh mothuh had teach uh how to fly. She try an try doin duh same way but she ain nebuh fly."[125]

If flying back in the flesh was a power retained and shared only by some Africans with strong spirits, return to ancestral homelands was a reward to be shared by all Africans after their physical deaths. For Africans death could signify their escape from the brutality of racial slavery and their return to Africa. Proper burial was essential for an African to return to his/her homeland safely. For this reason, burial services and burial markers were of central concern to enslaved Africans and their descendants. Grave sites throughout the Americas reveal a long tradition of burial marking based on the cosmology of crossing the *kalunga*. In Guadeloupe graves were painted white and marked with seashells, symbols of the crossing of the waters.[126] Similarly in North America, bondsmen's graves were often marked with iconographic representations of the *kalunga* with items placed upside down, in continued appreciation of the fact that the world of the dead was an inverted one.[127] This tradition was maintained and passed down through generations. Charles Ball recalled the burial of an American-born child, whose African father buried him with "A small bow and several arrows; a little bag of parched meal; a miniature canoe and a little paddle, (with which he would cross the ocean to his own country), small stick and a piece of white muslin by which his relations and countrymen would know the infant to be his son, and would receive it accordingly, on its arrival amongst them."[128] Thus, at least in parts of the Americas, even American-born would recross the *kalunga* to ancestral families if the proper connections were ritually maintained. Belief in this return passage made burials happy occasions. As one planter reported, "great rejoicings [were] made by African Negroes at the funerals of each other, from a belief that the deceased are going to their own country again."[129]

Similarly in the Francophone Caribbean, rather than being viewed as sorrowful occasions, burials were seen by enslaved Africans and their progeny as moments for celebration. Slave communities took heart in believing that their loved ones were not leaving them but going to join the ancestors, where they could become a guiding force in their lives from across the *kalunga*. Some Africans, particularly Biafrans, were seen as believing this so strongly that they had a reputation for committing suicide to speed their return passage rather than remain in an oppressive state. Michel-René Hilliard d'Auberteuil, who lived in Saint Domingue in the 1760s, opined that death did not frighten bondsmen, and Moreau de Saint-Méry noted of the Igbos in particular that death, "far from terrifying them, seems rather to offer something alluring because they believe in the transmigration of souls."[130] To counter this, French plantation owners from Martinique to Saint Domingue mutilated the bodies of African bondsmen who committed suicide and tried to frighten the rest from following this course by claiming that their mutilated bodies would not be able to complete the return journey.[131] This spiritual terror waged by the planter class highlights the belief that death was not enough to ensure a safe passage back. The spirit, in order to make this joyful journey home, first had to travel through stages and be appeased by a proper send-off. An unappeased spirit that did not return to join the ancestors was believed to linger around the living causing illness and harm.

In the Francophone Antilles martial arts were, alongside various forms of storytelling, hymns, games, and dance, an important part of the wake ceremony that sent the soul on its way contented.[132] *Sové vayan, bèrnadin,* and *danmyé/ladja* played unique roles in the wake ceremonies of Guadeloupe and Martinique. These ceremonies were known in Guadeloupe as *véyé boukousou* (*veillée mortuaire* in French) and were elaborate ceremonies divided into inner and outer circles of participants. Burial rituals could be ethnic- or trade-specific, such as the Igbo wake described by Félix Longin in 1848 or that of an African fisherman described by Abbé Dugoujon in 1845.[133] By the early twentieth century, the more general form, however, began with an announcement via the trumpeting of conch shells.[134] The wake proper began in the evening and lasted through the night, with the entire community coming together with refreshments to help send the departed into the next world. The corpse was laid in a house, where those present chanted for the soul of the deceased.[135] The door of the house was left open so that the deceased could observe the displays of oral and physical prowess that took place directly outside. In some circles, men of words (*met frazè*) exhibited their talents at storytelling, riddles, word games, and jokes.[136] In other circles, men of action displayed their physical prowess in dances, rhythm games, and combat games such as *bèrnadin* and *sové vayan.* The latter two were performed to the rhythm of hand clapping or transverse drumming. In *bèrnadin* the fighters in the center of the circle tried to hit their opponent's mouth, which was defended with arm parries and dodging movements. *Bèrnadin* was accompanied by songs, such as "Zombi-la," which spoke of a *zombi* who tries to block someone's passage, perhaps paralleling the spiritual challenges that the departed soul would meet on its journey home.[137] This song also was telling, as the term *zonbi* or *zombi* signified a person who for various reasons, including an unsatisfactory burial, did not make the journey back to the ancestral community but remained in the area causing possible harm.[138]

Sové vayan was another combative contest in the *véyé boukousou.* In these funeral grappling matches, as in the intervillage wrestling of Biafra, the winners were not overly praised. More important than who won was the fact that both fighters showed strength and courage. These attributes linked *sové vayan* to fertility. Just as the Igbo wrestled *mgba* as a symbol of fertility and an offering to the Earth Mother during the New Yam festival of renewal, so too *sové vayan* matches could be seen as essential offerings of fertility and strength to the deceased. Enslaved Africans attached great importance to such ceremonies, believing that "a dead man's send off will affect his status on the other side."[139] Just as the American-born child described by Ball was sent on his journey with a miniature bow and arrow to provide protection and courage for the long journey back, so too the offering of *sové vayan* was intended to strengthen and fortify the deceased while at the same time also possibly symbolizing fertility and renewal of life for those who remained behind.

Danmyé/ladja was also at times a component of wake practices in Martinique.[140] Like the other "manly exercises" of *sové vayan* and *bèrnadin,* the kicking arts of Martinique may have symbolically offered strength for the return journey. In *bèrnadin* the matches between contestants trying to slap each other's lips ended with ritual torches being inverted at the end of the competition. The inverted kicks of *danmyé/ladja* may have served as a similar symbol of return passage. In Françoise Montreuil's study on Martinican funeral practices, she suggests that in this context fighters were not allowed "to hit with the fist, but only with the foot and heel" and tried to kick as high as possible.[141] When inverting themselves to kick in this context, *danmyé/ladja* fighters may have represented the continual cycle of life and death, and also the ability for the living to draw on ancestors as sources of power for the living. Thus, these unarmed martial arts aided in the smooth passage of the deceased to the inverted world, as did contests using sticks.

The stick-fighting art of *kalenda* was highly associated with these funeral ceremonies throughout the Francophone Antilles. In Trinidad, "French Creole"–speaking stick fighters ritually adorned themselves in outfits made from funeral shrouds.[142] *Kalenda* was also done at wake ceremonies in Trinidad, while in Martinique danced stick clashes were an important part of wakes.[143] Similarly on the island of Grenada, among "French Creole"– speaking bondsmen and their descendants the *kalenda* was "danced at 'wake houses' to ensure the passage of the dead person through purgatory."[144]

The role of the *kalenda* in these ceremonies may have also been tied to the art's role as a fertility dance and link to the passage across the *kalunga.* In addition to the obvious phallic symbolism of the sticks, songs sung during its performance equated the blows to sexual penetration. For example, the sung passage "you cannot enter my bedroom" was a statement that "you cannot penetrate my guard."[145] The marriage of symbols of fertility and funerals was natural in Central African cosmology, which married death and birth through the counterclockwise movement of souls across the *kalunga* in a harmonious pairing of opposites.[146] The implication was that just as the person was passing through the *kalunga* line into death, so other ancestors, and possibly even the deceased, would return through the *kalunga* into the land of the living through birth. Furthermore, the sticks, which functioned both as walking sticks and weapons, were also symbolically linked to courage in the minds of some Central Africans. "It allowed an elder to walk upright, so it functioned metaphorically as a bridge across the water between the worlds of the living and the dead. With it, the elder could cross into the realm of the dead without fear."[147] In the context of the French Antilles, bondsmen were strengthened by the thought that the deceased might now become a source of power for the living community, and they were reminded that they too would one day make the journey home across the *kalunga* to be free from the toils of bondage.

Kalenda and Revolutions in the Greater Francophone Caribbean

If stick fighting helped the smooth transition into the ancestral realm, it also remained a tool of honor for those who sought liberation in their lifetimes from the oppressive system of racial slavery that bound them.[148] Under this system, they would use stick fighting as a vehicle to fight for individual honor through dueling, and, under the right circumstances, to fight for their collective honor in revolts that sought to topple the oppressive system outright.

Stick fighting was a widespread social practice by Africans and their descendants throughout the Americas. In Rio de Janeiro, the stick was a widespread weapon used both within *capoeiragem* and in separate stick-fighting dances, as described by Rugendas.[149] In Venezuela a stick-fighting art called *garrote* was simultaneously a religious dance in the Tamanangue festival and a form of self-defense used by people of color.[150] Stick fighting was known in South Carolina, where one lowcountry-born man was described as sporting scars on his face and chest from "fighting sticks" and "single combat."[151] Even in New England the festivals surrounding the election of new leaders among blacks were marked by combat games including stick fighting.[152]

Yet, stick fighting was perhaps most prevalent in the Francophone Caribbean, where it was present from the mid-seventeenth century and was tied to bondsmen's sense of honor. Labat was quite aware of the reflexive honor of bondsmen, whom he describes as "strongly proud" and "extremely vindictive." This honor was often defended in stick dueling, but in some cases its defense led to large-scale feuds, such as the one Labat describes between the bondsmen of his and two adjoining plantations. As the situation escalated, meetings between these groups of bondsmen resulted "in their coming to blows." At the insistence of Labat, the battles gradually died down, but an accusation of witchcraft insulted the reputations of the Africans of Labat's plantation. They satisfied their honor by giving the other group "a sound beating" with sticks. The following week the other plantation's owner and overseer drew their swords and led their bondsmen into a return attack. Forbidden by Labat from carrying weapons, his bondsmen "were defending themselves with sticks that they had taken from their aggressors and by throwing stones. . . . The master of the attackers and his white driver both had their heads broken, the former with a stone, the latter with a stick, and they were obliged to run away."[153] Thus, as among the Kunene peoples, this is an example of bondsmen in the Francophone Caribbean utilizing the stick as their primary weapon of self-defense and honor.[154]

Labat's bondsmen would have been almost exclusively African-born, and many of them likely grew up in cultures where stick fighting was elevated to an art form. The art of fighting with sticks and rocks was well ingrained in Cimbebasians and other Central Africans. Beyond Angolans, the Fulani of West Africa were well versed in a stick dueling that grew from their pastoral lifestyle.[155] Likewise, the fighting stick was also the primary weapon in the "bloodless wars" of Biafra. They also played some role in the combative arsenal of other regions of West and Central Africa, including the states of Dahomey, Oyo, and the Sokoto Caliphate.[156] This technical familiarity and the stick's ready availability made it the common arm of bondsmen in the Francophone Caribbean. In the seventeenth century enslaved individuals likely utilized fighting sticks in different styles according to their ethnic background and training.

However, one particular style of employing the stick became widespread by the second half of the eighteenth century. This style was often referred to as *kalenda*, although other names were utilized as well.[157] The term was likely derived from the name of a wider musical form or ritual and was thus often applied to other dances and rhythms as well.[158] While all Africans with stick-fighting legacies would have found ways to segue into *kalenda*, the art was ritually tied to the Angolan peoples, who were usually joined under the ethnonym "Congo."[159] Many sticks were "mounted" with Central African ancestral powers and then had to be "fed" in order to keep the spirits pleased. In Martinique the wood for fighting sticks was named after the Central African nation of Mongongue, and some sticks were ritually prepared from the late seventeenth century to cause chronic pain from the slightest touch.[160] Similarly, in Saint Domingue they were often made of a special wood called *koko makak* and associated with *zam kongo* (Central African spiritual weapons).[161] Even the Kromanti combat unit of the Surinamese maroons, widely purported to be predominantly of Gold Coast derivation, referred to their fighting sticks as "Congo sticks."[162] In the 1780s a bondsman in Saint Domingue named Jérôme (nicknamed "Pôteau") was arrested for selling Central African–derived religious paraphernalia "but above all [fighting] sticks called *mayombo*, in which were placed powdered *maman-bila* ['Congo' medicines] by means of a drill. This gave the ability to fight, without danger to oneself, another slave whose stick had no *mayombo*."[163]

The techniques of employing these sticks may have also been influenced by Central African ritual body postures. These postures were utilized while holding the stick at both ends as a means to guard the body physically and spiritually simultaneously.[164] This distinctive defensive method was at the core of the *kalenda* style and was evident from the second half of the eighteenth century. However, if the particular style of using sticks was acknowledged as being related to Central African traditions, it was adopted by black communities

Figure 4.2: A cudgeling match between English and French blacks on the Island of Dominica, by Agostino Brunias. Courtesy of the John Carter Brown Library at Brown University, Providence, Rhode Island

throughout the Americas regardless of African ethnic origins. Thus, *kalenda*-style stick fighting was one of the performance arts shared by all males in *bamboulas,* reflecting its role in community building. The distinctive *kalenda* style was clearly captured by Agostino Brunias, an artist from Rome, who painted a stick-fighting match during his stay on the island of Dominica from 1765 to 1775. The print depicts a match between English- and French-speaking bondsmen, showing that the style spread to Anglophone bondsmen as well.[165] Although their techniques were quite distinct, bondsmen's employment of these sticks paralleled the honor-driven use of bladed weapons among the Europeans on the islands.

The courts of Renaissance "Italy" outlined a code of behavior regulating the competition for honor via the duel, which spread in modified forms throughout Europe.[166] Elements of this tradition were carried to the Antilles, where among Frenchmen fighting duels was a way of life. In Martinique's urban center of Saint Pierre the public garden was the favored location, but duels were fought all over the island. Frenchmen of all classes were involved with formally dueling their peers—officers, doctors, police, shopkeepers, and even fishermen. According to Geneviève Leti's study of violence in Martinique, the locally born whites were equally "sensitive to provocations" but did "not always have the patience to wait to settle their difference by fighting a duel." Bypassing the elaborate ritual procedures established in France, they "walked around with small canes fit with daggers, swordsticks or even pistols" to settle their disagreements on the spot.[167] While the legal codes of the islands theoretically stripped Africans of their honor, they displayed a similar sense of honor when wielding their fighting sticks.

Bondsmen displayed their honor through the bold carrying of sticks, employing them in performative displays, and brandishing them in duels. When not in use as weapons the sticks were utilized in personal display as elegant canes, particularly those called *bangalas*. "The bangala is a short metal-headed baton with which the Negro is accustomed to fight."[168] The use of nails to garnish the head of the fighting stick was likely tied to the activation of "Congo" medicines in the most highly valued sacred sticks in eighteenth-century Saint Domingue.[169] These combat sticks showed a high level of artistry in their composition "of extremely hard wood which have many knots on them, and whose upper end is well ornamented and then set with little gilded nails. Over this is a covering and binding made of a bit of leather, of a third of its length, i.e. for about ten inches, and with another piece of leather for a cord."[170]

Despite the craftsmanship of these sticks, colonial officials viewed them as constant threats from the seventeenth century. In Martinique the law established on October 4, 1677, forbade any bondsman to "carry a baton or *bangala* under pain of the whip for the first offense."[171] In 1685 article 15 of the Code Noir forbade bondsmen in all French territories to be found in the possession of firearms and "big sticks."[172] Such prohibitions were perpetual throughout the eighteenth century in all the French islands. In Saint Domingue, for example, the carrying of fighting sticks was continuously prohibited by various ordinances of the colony, including those of 1717, 1758, and the 1780s.[173] The numerous complaints and repeated issuing of prohibitions only highlight the inability of such ordinances to eliminate the widespread use of these sticks. Indeed, bondsmen blatantly disregarded these ordinances and, at the risk of punishment, publicly displayed their *bangalas*. Bondsmen cited their need to defend themselves from snakes as their excuse for possessing these *bangalas*.[174] Yet, beyond such utilitarian functions, bondsmen carried these weapons also as badges of honor.[175] Despite a century of repeated prohibitions in Martinique, in the second half of the eighteenth century Pierre-François Dessalles could still note that bondsmen "rarely leave on Sundays without being armed with a *bangala;* it is their primary offensive and defensive weapon."[176]

Bondsmen also utilized these sticks to display their honor through participation in closed societies and community performances. In Saint Domingue *mayombo* fighting sticks acted as badges of membership in rural closed societies, which appear to have drawn on "Congo" precedents.[177] Certainly, Jérôme and his assistants insisted that participants hold secret the activities of their nocturnal assemblies, called *mayombe* or *bila,* in the northern parish of Marmelade in the 1780s.[178] As in the Kongolese tradition, the term *bila* here appears to have referred to divination rituals that took place in these closed associations to discover the causes of misfortunes.[179] Participants received general protection against plantation owners through participation and *mayombo* fighting sticks that made them invulnerable in hand-to-hand combat against those without spiritual armament, and when the latter were gilded with nails making them *bangalas,* they were sold at high prices.[180]

Yet, even outside their links to such closed associations, *bangalas* and other fighting sticks were common at community *bamboulas,* where they were used in performative displays. The prevalence of these sticks among bondsmen attending *bamboulas* and other gatherings continued to worry white colonists throughout the eighteenth century, as in the 1715 report of groups of two hundred or more bondsmen meeting in Martinique on weekends and holidays "all armed with large truncheons."[181] Agonistic displays were a common element at drum circles in Saint Dominque in the second half of the century.[182] These displays echoed the structure of the Kunene stick-fighting dances accompanied by drums that urged the fighters on. Although he did not describe the interactive role of musicians and fighters, Butterworth noted in detail the honor-laden elements of these matches in the weekly *bamboulas* of Guadeloupe:

> the person who proved victorious the preceding Sunday enters the circle, assuming as much consequence as an Eastern nabob; strutting about in fancied greatness, and surveying the sticks, which are placed on the ground, without baskets or anything else to guard the hand. Seldom has he long to pace the "circle's bound," before he meets with an opponent, who also enters the circle; two tellers are then appointed, who act as umpires. The combatants, after taking up the sticks, approach each very gracefully, shake hands cordially, separate, take their ground, and commence the contest, to the sound of "sweet minstrelsy," if such it may be called: the music playing all the time, and keeping the whole in good humor, Men of equal science often contend a considerable time; without either obtaining any advantage over the other.[183]

Formalities such as the use of umpires and handshakes may reflect the influence of French duelists, highlighting the fact that such combatants were competing for respect by their honor community.[184]

Stick fighters displayed their craft in other modalities, such as training exercises and actual duels. Medéric Moreau de Saint-Méry, a member of the Superior Council of Saint Domingue in the 1780s, described the use of the *koko makak* fighting sticks in Martinique and Saint Domingue in some detail. In one training practice under the term *Jan-coulibé* in Martinique, a fighter would practice mastering his defense. The ideal was for a fighter to withstand attacks from a training partner continuously for up to fifteen minutes without being touched.[185] This training would be called upon when a bondsman felt compelled by the *point d'honneur* to defend his honor through stick dueling that often went to first blood. Moreau de Saint-Méry notes that such a duel was often preceded by a ritual challenge and oath. Interestingly, while men in the Lesser Antilles were noted for fighting with unarmed pugilism and head butts, Saint-Méry suggests that these modes of fighting were gendered female in Saint Domingue.[186] In contrast, he describes male bondsmen as typically avenging impugned honor with the stick: "It is by blows of the fist or the head that these differences are settled, at least among the women. . . . But [among men] it is a fight with sticks. The blacks handle this club with great skill and since they always aim for the head, the blows which they receive are always serious. And so, the combatants are soon all blood."[187] Although these duels could be sanguine, stick-fighting techniques became even more lethal when combatants utilized machetes.

The tradition of stick fighting could be modified for use with the machete, a tool that, like its African prototypes, could serve various ends. Given the role of the machete in the forced production of sugar, the status of this instrument may have become ambiguous even for some bondsmen. Yet, at the same time separate African traditions elevated this instrument to a powerful religious symbol. To the numerous followers of the Yoruba/Fon/Ewe/Aja religious traditions, the machete was revered as the icon of Ogun, the *orisha* of iron and warfare known as Ogun Féray in Saint Domingue.[188] For many Catholic Kongolese and Mbundu, it was the symbol of Saint James the conqueror, whose cult was established in the kingdom of Kongo before 1506 and whose feast day was celebrated every year with a large collective *nsanga*.[189] For Biafrans, the machete was the symbol of *ikenga,* success in both agriculture and the "head-hunting" arts institutionalized by paramilitary closed societies throughout Biafra.[190] In the *mayombe* ceremonies of Jérôme, an altar was set with two candles and crossed machetes. Participants drank a ritual medicine that caused them to fall unconscious, symbolizing death. Blows with the flat of the machete to revive them symbolically rebirthed initiates. Such ritual practices ensured the continued association of the machete with the supernatural in Saint Dominque.

This potentially sacred instrument could also be turned into a lethal weapon in the hands of Africans versed in bladed combat techniques or bondsmen who developed stick-fighting skills in the Francophone Caribbean.[191] In Martinique there were numerous cases of assaults with machetes. At times these were directed against each other, as when two bondswomen, Céleste and Marthe, had a battle with machetes that ended in the death of Céleste. In July 1839 a bondsman named Joseph killed the owner of his plantation, and in 1840 in less than one month three bondsmen turned their machetes against plantation managers. In August 1838 the governor proposed a ban on the carrying of machetes outside of work hours for free people of color as well as bondsmen. However, the council rejected the proposal in light of the difficulty in stopping such an entrenched and widespread practice.[192] As a result, stick-fighting skills could be applied to machetes in real fights. In the late eighteenth century Lafcadio Hearn noted that ritual combat could give way to lethal conflicts: "The caleinda [*kalenda*] is danced by men only, all stripped to the waist, and twirling heavy sticks in a mock fight. Sometimes, however—especially at the great village gatherings, when the blood becomes overheated by tafia—the mock fight may become a real one; and then even cutlasses [machetes] are brought into play."[193] Such serious fights were not uncommon and were termed *goumages* in the Lesser Antilles.[194]

The use of the stick in collective skirmishes, such as the one described by Father Labat, and the ability to transfer that use to the machete suggest that the widespread mastery of the stick and the machete as weapons played a role in large-scale slave revolts, such as the Haitian Revolution. The role of disease and the genius of individual leaders such as François-Dominique Toussaint-Louverture in the revolution have rightfully been highlighted in previous studies;[195] however, the mastery of stick fighting and other African fighting traditions must also be recognized as success-aiding factors. In addition to any previous military experience they may have had in Africa, many bondsmen who rose up in 1791 were well trained in hand-to-hand combat from their years in the colony.

Despite legal prohibitions against the carrying of sticks, it is clear that stick fighting was thriving among people of African descent in Saint Domingue in the years before the revolution. Distraught over the potential of such fighting sticks, Saint-Méry lamented that the "police have indeed forbidden these clubs and keep confiscating them, but they are so easily replaced that it does no good."[196] Clearly, he would have been even more worried had he realized how easily these techniques could be applied to the machete.[197] However, while he was worried by the implications of this practice, Moreau de Saint-Méry was begrudgingly impressed by the high level of skill attained by bondsmen: "This fatal club serves also to make the negro's skill dazzling in one sort of combat. One cannot help admiring with what speed the blows are launched—and avoided—by two practiced men. They maneuver around each other to gain the advantage, while holding the club and swinging it with both hands. Then, suddenly, a blow is directed, the other parries, and attack and riposte alternate, until one of the fighters is hit by the other. This normally ends the fight. The sport has its own rules, just as fencing does. A new athlete takes the place of the beaten one and the palm goes to the most adroit."[198] Such a high level of virtuosity made enslaved Africans and their descendants masters of *l'arme blanche*.

From this perspective, it should be acknowledged that the legacy of African martial traditions in a wide sense contributed to the success of the Haitian Revolution. These legacies included African-derived war medicine, African guerrilla warfare tactics, and this mastery of *l'arme blanche*. Although this study is not the place for a full-scale exegesis on the role of African religious traditions, these traditions did play numerous important roles in the Haitian Revolution.[199] In that revolution Angolan-style battle tactics also prevailed, predominantly in the early years of the war. Many bondsmen not drawn into the large armies such as those of Toussaint-Louverture or Jorge Biassou split up into ethnic bands under their own leaders. A good example would be the Biafran band led by a Moko captain, Cherit, or the numerous armies and bands described as "Congo" that played important roles in the revolution.[200] Many groups spread across the plantations on the plains like *kilombos*, aiming to recruit and initiate new members of any ethnicity into the band by persuasion or force. As one writer noted, those who resisted this levy were "cut to pieces."[201] Reminiscent of the Imbangala as well as maroon tactics, these groups then often retreated, in the words of one white planter, "into the inaccessible mountains, where it would be imprudent to search for them."[202] This strategy made it almost impossible for the colonists or European armies to secure a solid victory, "for when strategically encircled or militarily overpowered, the slaves would disband and retreat into the mountains, only to attack again at different points with replenished and reorganized troops."[203]

Even on the level of troop formations, as John Thornton has shown, the revolutionaries fought in ways remarkably similar to those in Angola, and which supported their use of *l'arme blanche*.[204] Paralleling the Kunene and Imbangala *kilombo* pattern of dividing the army into smaller tactical squadrons or platoons, the revolutionary armies were usually split into small bands, which harassed European armies with short but constant skirmishes. Felix Carteau, who experienced these tactics, noted that they harassed French forces "day and night."[205] Like Central Africans, they fired from a prone position or from behind trees and other natural obstacles. As one soldier experienced, these small bands "took to their heels after saluting us with a volley of bullets."[206] They avoided heavy losses by firing from dispersed positions and would soon return to continue their constant harassment. The revolutionaries often advanced in small units to African-inspired martial music, and if they did not see an opportunity to dominate in close quarters, they would quickly disperse.[207] However, like Angolan armies, they would amass when they felt they could enter into a decisive hand-to-hand engagement. When they did so, like the Imbangala, they usually attacked in three columns, as in the three-pronged attacks that hit the Breda plantation, Port Marigot, and Petite Anse in the second month of the war.[208]

In contrast European soldiers fought in closed formations that made rapid maneuver and retreat extremely difficult. To make up for the inadequacy of their individual muskets, which were "barely accurate at 100 yards," European troops packed together in tight ranks and fired together in volleys. These massed volleys and artilleries between ranks standing directly in front of each other at relatively close ranges led to concentrated carnage.[209] Revolutionaries, however, rarely provided such a static mass target. In the Angolan and early Haitian Revolutionary models, the real carnage was the result of *l'arme blanche*. There are countless examples of the use of *l'arme blanche* in the early years of the revolution. Bryan Edwards details the opening night of the rebellion on August 22, when the vast majority of whites in the parish of Acul, particularly the plantations of Noe, Clement, Flaville, and Gallifet, were hewed "into pieces by their [revolutionaries'] cutlasses."[210] Even with the capture of an arms supply originally intended for Vincent Ogé, the leader of the free coloreds, two-thirds of the revolutionaries were armed exclusively with *l'arme blanche*, particularly machetes.[211] Some were able to advance safely close enough to enter close-quarters combat through stealth and wile. According to one European soldier, "under cover of the brush, they come as near as a pistol's range without even being seen."[212] One ingenious group advanced on Le Cap covered in light, cotton-filled mattresses, which bullets could not penetrate. European forces "fired three times, but without the least effect."[213] A white soldier described in detail how Jean François's Congo band took Le Cap, armed "with torches and knives [machetes]."[214] One of these Congo knocked him out with his fighting stick in the battle, but he was left for dead and managed to crawl into hiding. There he witnessed many people falling to the fighting stick and machete and even overheard the boasting between two of Jean François's men over how many they had killed and how they had taken down their foes with these weapons.[215] Thus, the same weapons of honor that bondsmen had mastered under slavery were turned against their former oppressors at the outset of the revolution. As in the ancient rebellion of Spartacus, a Roman gladiator, the years of training in stick fighting aided former bondsmen during the Haitian Revolution, particularly in the crucial early years, when access to firearms was relatively limited.[216]

In the Francophone Caribbean, then, martial art traditions served members of the bonded community on various levels. These combat styles played a prominent role in the *bamboulas* through which peoples of various origins celebrated their diversity and came together as a unified community. Activities related to these traditions were understood as crucial in aiding the souls of departed community members to cross the *kalunga* back to ancestral communities. While combat arts' connection to these wake services was arguably of primary importance, such spiritual roles did not preclude their use in social resistance against slavery. Whereas the enduring fighting styles used in wake ceremonies allowed bondsmen to envision flight from the oppressions of bondage by spiritually or physically journeying back across the *kalunga*, other martial traditions, particularly stick fighting, provided means for transforming the world in which they had been forced to settle. Keeping martial traditions alive helped bondsmen imagine a world in the Americas beyond slavery and then aided them ultimately to rise up and create that world for themselves through revolution.

Five Urban Inversions

Combat Societies in Rio de Janeiro

Southern Angolans and Biafrans who were brought as captives across the Atlantic *kalunga* to Rio de Janeiro found themselves in a thriving urban environment. While the economy of seventeenth-century Brazil was largely focused on sugar production in the regions of Bahia and Pernambuco, a gold rush in Minas Gerais in the 1690s sparked a diversification of the economy and the rapid growth of its main port city, Rio de Janeiro. Rio took the place of São Salvador (hereafter Salvador), Bahia, as the capital of Brazil in 1763 and then became the capital of the entire Portuguese Empire in 1808 when Dom João VI relocated his court from Lisbon to Rio to escape a potential French invasion. The city became the second-largest in the Americas after Mexico City, in part due to the fact that over a million enslaved Africans were taken to or through the region's ports.[1]

This metropolis was driven by African labor. Bondsmen constructed buildings, cleaned houses, unloaded ships, delivered merchandise, traded food, produced crafts, and worked in factories. Each household required the services of African bondsmen, who balanced barrels on their heads to bring water for daily needs and to carry away human excrement for disposal into the sea. Most Africans were introduced to the brutalities of racial slavery in Rio through their sale at Valongo, the largest market of enslaved Africans in Brazil. From this first sale, some were transported further into the interior to work on rural sugar and coffee plantations, significantly lowering their life expectancy, while many others would live out their lives struggling under bondage in the sprawling city. Urban slavery, however, was by no means benign. Squalor and poor sanitary conditions marked the urban experience of many bondsmen, leaving them vulnerable to infectious diseases and recurring epidemics that resulted in high mortality rates among them as well.[2]

Despite the brutality of bondage, these Africans and their progeny established new communities that significantly outnumbered those of the European settlers they served. In the early nineteenth century about two-thirds of the city's population was of African descent.[3] Many Africans arrived without extended families but created new bonds with their shipmates, referring to each other as *malungu*, a Bantu term meaning "brother" or "shipmate." However, the widespread practice of calling each other *malungu* may have signified much more than this. The fact that they intentionally chose not to use more literal terms for "brother" reveals a quite different conception of their identities. Among the Mbundu of Angola, *malungu* was the name of an ancestral symbol believed to have come from the *kalunga* and that had the power to establish new lineage relations in an area. This word choice may have reflected their awareness of their own ability to found new lineages in the area to which they had been brought across the Atlantic *kalunga*.[4]

Various Njila-speaking peoples from southern Angola formed the majority of Africans brought to Rio in the second half of the seventeenth century.[5] Various waves of different groups of Africans followed, reflecting wars and surges in enslavement in West and Central Africa, but the vast majority hailed from the region of Angola.[6] Captives taken via Benguela were again the most numerous in the nineteenth century.[7] Angolans from the interiors of Luanda or the Greater Loango Coast were also present in large numbers. Of the West Africans in Rio, the most widely visible nations were the Biafran Calabars and Minas, the latter term most closely tied to the region of the Gold Coast, but in Rio often used as a catch term for all other West Africans who were not Calabars. However, even all together these West Africans were in the numerical minority as nearly 80 percent of the African population originated from Angola.[8] Together, the Angolan Kongo and Njila speakers carried with them cultural traditions that would take root in the streets of the city.

Thus, despite the culture shock of racial slavery that would have struck recent arrivals in Rio, Africans and especially Angolans would have encountered at least some familiar African traditions. In addition to hearing the Bantu languages spoken and sung throughout the city by Angolan porters, Central Africans could go to *zungu* houses to buy Angolan-style food, particularly *angú*.[9] More than just restaurants, *zungu* houses were also cultural centers, places where Africans could come together to speak in African languages, sing, dance, rent rooms, or hide from authorities. Many would have frequented communal dances called *batuques*, in which people organized themselves into nations to perform according to aesthetics norms that were at least somewhat familiar. Perhaps most important, Africans arriving in the eighteenth century would have encountered the Central African religious institution of *kalundus*. James Sweet has shown that these religious institutions, based on Angolan divination ceremonies, were widespread in Rio.[10] The Central African ritual specialists who directed the *kalundus* also continued to invert themselves ritually in order to gain more direct access to power from across the *kalunga*.[11] Along with this cosmological system that linked physical inversions to spiritual power came the Angolan martial art that arose from it. By the second half of the eighteenth century the Kunene unarmed combat tradition of *engolo* was firmly entrenched in Rio as the basis of the *jogo de capoeira,* or game of *capoeira.*[12]

The term *jogo de capoeira* was used to describe the art as performative ritual. As with the *engolo,* these matches could be playful and dancelike in their grace or quite agonistic. In either case, the *jogo de capoeira* remained primarily rooted in the use of the circular and push kicks (often from an inverted position), sweeps, and acrobatic evasions of the *engolo* and its cognates.[13] Eighteenth- and nineteenth-century sources, particularly by those outside or in confrontation with the tradition, are not always consistent in their use of the other terms relating to the art. However, in order not to confuse the reader, I will attempt wherever possible to be consistent in my use of the terms. The term *capoeira* will mean a person who is an adept of the *jogo de capoeira,* most specifically one fully initiated in the societies that dominated the art. The term *capoeiragem* will indicate most specifically the fighting skills used by members of *capoeira* societies in street fights. Yet, a wider use of the term referred to the entire cultural complex of these societies; thus, the police documents at times equate *capoeiragem* with any activity related to these societies, including dressing like their members.

The *jogo de capoeira,* like its North American counterpart, was practiced in various social contexts, possibly including maroon communities. Maroon groups were widespread in Brazil, both in remote regions and just on the outskirts of cities such as Rio. These communities were called *kilombos* (spelled *quilombos* in Portuguese), after the Imbangala *kilombos* that appear to have provided some of the institutional frameworks for the most famous of these communities, Palmares.[14] Limited anecdotal evidence suggests that Angolan pugilistic traditions were utilized in at least some of these communities.[15] While a lack of written documentation by members of maroon communities compromises our understanding of the extent to which *capoeiragem* was practiced in specific *quilombos,* police records reveal that the martial art was used on the outskirts of the city to rescue captured *quilombolas* (*quilombo* members) being brought back to Rio from the surrounding areas.[16]

The *jogo de capoeira* was a documented part of the artistic tradition at dances that took place both in the *senzalas,* or slave quarters, on rural plantations and among urban black communities in Rio. Like the *bamboulas* of the French Antilles, these performance circles were common in the evenings on Sundays and holidays, when bondsmen came out in large numbers. In Brazil these dances were often called *batuques,* although the term was at times applied to specific dances and martial arts as well. Local planters often allowed these *batuques* to occur even though official policy swung between repression and support of such gatherings, the motivation behind support being to promote the continued division of African nations in Brazil in hopes of keeping the enslaved from uniting as a single force.[17]

Figure 5.1: *Jogar Capoëra* (or *Danse de la guerre*), by Johann Moritz Rugendas. Courtesy of Photographs and Prints Division, Schomburg Center for Research in Black Culture, The New York Public Library, Astor, Lenox and Tilden Foundations

As with *bamboulas,* repression could not stop these dance circles. In the suburbs of Rio these dances could attract as many as two thousand bondsmen dancing in separate circles by nations.[18] These nations danced according to distinct aesthetic tastes in their separate circles but also came together for dances that seem to have been adopted by all bondsmen, including variants called *batuque* and *lundu.* As in the Francophone Caribbean, these common dances often utilized the Central African dance elements of undulating hips and the bumping of midsections.[19] The *jogo de capoeira* was among these dances adopted by all bondsmen, regardless of nation.[20] A French journalist located the *jogo de capoeira* in the performative context of the *batuque* circles on a rural plantation: "On Saturday, at night, after finishing the last task of the week, and on festival days, that bring rest and repose, the slaves are granted one or two hours for dance. They meet at the yard, they call themselves together exciting themselves and the party begins. Here is the *capoeira,* a species of combat dance, of daring and combative spins to the sound of the Congolese drum. There is the *batuque* with its cold and lewd attitudes, which the *urucungo* accelerates or slows. Beyond it is a crazy dance, with the provocation of the eyes, of breasts and hips; a species of intoxicating convulsion that is called *lundu.*"[21] In these dance circles the martial art's performative aspects were highlighted as adepts exhibited thrilling demonstrations of inverted kicks, sweeps, and acrobatic defenses set to percussion.

The *jogo de capoeira* was also performed in urban contexts, such as entertainment for sailors and other tavern patrons or for large crowds during public festivals and religious processions.[22] The martial art was likely practiced in much more informal settings as well: as recreation by enslaved Africans, as a temporary break from their labor demands at factories, as a way for day laborers to pass time while waiting for work, or as a form of violent combat in street fights. However, the primary context of the art that will be explored here was its use by closed societies formed by enslaved Africans trained in this martial art. While the art's use among maroons and *batuques* may have taken place on the outskirts of Rio or deep in the interior, these closed societies appear to have been exclusively urban phenomena. The colony's authorities were highly preoccupied with trying to exterminate these groups that stood in defiance of the slave system from at least the second half of the eighteenth century, when existent documents first allowed a view of the art.

Adão: A First Glimpse of *Capoeiras*

An early substantial reference providing insight into the world of *capoeiras* is a judicial record from 1789. According to the document, Manoel Cardoso Fontes purchased an enslaved *pardo* youth named Adão,[23]

> who grew into a robust type, a hard worker who was obedient to his master, serving him in the household chores. Manoel resolved to take advantage of him by renting him out to third parties as a laborer for public works, as a porter, or for any other physical labor. In this way Adão became a good source of income for his master. With the passage of time, the timid slave, who before had always lived humbly, became more self-confident and independent and began to arrive home much later than the end of his day's work. After Manoel questioned Adão about his change in conduct, the *senhor* found his excuses to be most inconsistent. Eventually what Manoel had long feared happened: Adão did not return home. Manoel thought that certainly he had escaped to some *quilombo* in the suburbs of the city.
>
> To his surprise, he was to encounter Adão behind the bars of the district prison. He had been arrested along with other disorderly people who had practiced [the *jogo de*] *capoeira*. On the day of Adão's arrest a fight had occurred between *capoeiras*, and one of them had been murdered. According to the law of the kingdom, the gravest of crimes was the practice of *capoeiragem*, and even more so when it resulted in death. In the course of the proceedings it was established that Adão was innocent regarding the murder charge, but his status as a *capoeira* was confirmed. As punishment he was to receive five hundred "lashes" and "two years in public works." His *senhor*, after Adão had served some months of service and had

received his punishment on the whipping post, petitioned the king, in the name of Christ's mercy, to wave the rest of the penalty, arguing that he was a poor man and dependent on the income that his slave brought him. He promised to take care that Adão would no longer return to fraternize with *capoeiras* or become one of them. Manoel's request was granted by the tribunal.[24]

This, the fullest known eighteenth-century document specifically referring to *capoeiragem,* is quite revealing about its social position in Rio de Janeiro during the second half of the eighteenth century. First, it is clear from this document that *capoeiragem* was completely criminalized by the second half of the eighteenth century. Despite the numerous forms of violent crime, crime against property, and crimes against public order, *capoeiragem* was singled out as the gravest of crimes in the document. This may not have been a mere emphatic statement; in the nineteenth century *capoeiragem* and escaping to *quilombos* were the two crimes that were met with the most repression.[25]

The case of Adão also highlights the ability of *capoeiras* to take advantage of their position as the breadwinners of their *senhores*' households. Harsher punishment of *capoeiras* in the form of imprisonment or forced labor for the state hurt *senhores* by depriving them of their income. Thus, *senhores* such as Manoel would often take the side of their bondsmen in legal proceedings, pressuring the authorities for a lighter sentence. This was an annoyance to the policing agents of the society, who were fixated on eliminating *capoeiragem.*[26] While forced labor and prison sentences would later be extended to three months, no *capoeiras* in the nineteenth century seem to have received the number of whippings that Adão was forced to withstand. This can be attributed to humanitarian reforms and the influence of *senhores,* who feared a dramatic loss of wages when beatings led to incapacitation or death.[27]

This document also illuminates the relationship between *capoeiragem* and the profile of enslaved Africans who worked *de ganho,* or "for hire." Unlike extremely wealthy rural plantation owners, each of whom made a profit off the agricultural labor of more than a hundred enslaved laborers, urban lower- and middle-class Brazilians tended to profit from the toil of only a handful of bondsmen.[28] Those with small shops or trades might capitalize on the labor of these bondsmen directly in their businesses, but for most, profiting from these enslaved Africans meant sending them out during the day into the city to work for wages.

These *ganhadores* competed with each other, and later other immigrants, for the most menial of tasks available in the city. They were expected to pay their *senhores* a large proportion of their earnings on a daily or weekly basis and use the rest to feed and clothe themselves. *Ganhadores* labored under a system critical to the economy of large cities such as Rio and Salvador since they unloaded ships and transported almost all the goods that moved through the city.[29] Whites delivered mail through them, avoided the heat of the sun and strain of walking by being carried in sedan chairs, and were able to supply their houses with water only because members of this urban enslaved labor force could be called upon to carry the numerous and heavy water jars on their heads. Despite the physical demands and the psychological stress of constantly having to make their quota or face beatings, the work of *ganhadores* allowed for some physical and social mobility relative to rural gang labor on sugar estates.[30] They moved about the city during the day, and it was not unknown for *senhores* to allow them to live outside the homes in rooms rented by free blacks.[31] Although they had to pay for much of their own maintenance, they were often able to save any income they made above their *diaria,* or daily quota. Working away from the watchful eyes of their *senhores, ganhadores* often found time to socialize and engage in activities such as *capoeiragem.* While many *capoeiras* followed other forms of employment, the negative image of *capoeiras* was popularly associated with *ganhadores* like Adão. As will become clear shortly, the *capoeiras* took advantage of the realities of urban bondage.

The case of Adão also highlights the fact that the world of *capoeiras* was attractive to a large segment of the enslaved population: young enslaved males. This demographic group would dominate the practice of *capoeiragem* for at least the next six decades. These youths may have been drawn to the art in part by the extreme physical abilities of the *capoeiras,* perhaps not unlike the way modern athletes draw legions of imitating fans. However, more than their physical abilities, *capoeiras* offered to any enslaved male youth trying to find his way and identity in a difficult world an alternative lifestyle that provided a sense of belonging and honor. The transformation in Adão's character from timidity to self-confidence highlights the role of *capoeiras* in providing youths with rites of passage into a proud manhood.

Figure 5.2: *Ganhadores* (coffee carriers). *Harper's New Monthly Magazine* 7 (1853): 729

In addition, the document implies that the dominant class was aware that *capoeiragem*, more than just an art form of individual expression, was also a collective activity into which individuals were initiated over time. The apparent contradiction of Adão's being confirmed as a practitioner of *capoeira* and Manoel's later promise not to let him *become* a *capoeira* suggests that whites were quite aware that youths served out an elaborate training and initiation process before becoming full members of these *capoeira* societies. These groups of *capoeiras* were organized into societies that the authorities referred to as *maltas, confraria, badernas, ranchos,* or simply *groupos de capoeira*.[32]

Capoeira Societies

Maltas *as Closed Societies*

There are some indications that the early *capoeira maltas* may have grown out of ethnic-based associations in the city. Hahner suggests that early clashes between *capoeira* groups were based on "tribal divisions," and perhaps Walsh is referring to *capoeiragem* battles when he notes the different ethnic groups of Rio engaging "in feuds and combats, where one, or even two hundred of a nation on each side are engaged."[33] From the early nineteenth century it seems that each nation used unique symbols to represent their *capoeira* societies.[34] In this way *capoeira* societies were like many other associations formed along ethnic lines by Africans in Brazil's large cities in the eighteenth and nineteenth centuries. For example, Catholic brotherhoods of the enslaved were lay sodalities, often ethnically based, dedicated to a particular Catholic saint, with an elected king and queen who sponsored dances and played central roles in African burials.[35] Even *ganhadores* organized themselves by "nations" into territorial work associations called *cantos,* each of which functioned as an early labor union.[36]

While the early *capoeira* societies may have initially formed along ethnic lines, the structure taken by the societies was not one of an ethnic mutual aid society but rather one of a closed society.[37] The closed nature of their practices makes detailed evidence of their clandestine activities scarce, and with no surviving legacy we are also deprived of a contemporary insider's perspective to provide details into the inner workings of these societies. However, the shards of evidence that are available suggest that *capoeira maltas* were similar in structure to closed societies.

Capoeira societies shared many of the outward functions of brotherhoods and *cantos*. Many scholars have chosen simply to gloss these *maltas* as "gangs," and in fact they were similar to some gangs.[38] However, the imprecision and cultural baggage of the term invites misunderstanding and obscures the meaning and form of these sodalities. Therefore, these *capoeira* societies can be more fruitfully compared to "secret" societies in the broad sense that their members claimed mastery of a special knowledge, in this case of martial arts.

As such, *capoeira* societies displayed the diacritical characteristics of closed societies in general and paramilitary societies in particular.[39] I am not suggesting that *maltas* were in any way continuations of any particular African closed society. Indeed, comparisons with Chinese paramilitary societies would prove fruitful for highlighting the fact that to equate *maltas* with street gangs is to miss out on a nuanced understanding of their inner workings. Thus, it is only because *ekpe* is one of the best documented of African closed societies that it will be used as a point of comparison, but with the awareness that these characteristics would have been shared by any of the hundreds of paramilitary societies in Western and Central Africa. This comparison will prove useful for unpacking some facets of *capoeira maltas*.

As previously noted, in Biafra, among the most prestigious closed societies were the paramilitary leopard societies such as *ekpe,* which was in many communities open only to those individuals who had proved themselves in battle.[40] *Ekpe* was a graded society with levels of initiation that played various roles in Biafra, including facilitating trade, artistic development, and law enforcement. The *ekpe* had a segmented organization, with each community having its own "lodge" and each lodge existing as part of a far-reaching network that allowed for coordinated efforts and safe travel of initiates to other areas of Biafra. This format allowed the *ekpe* to maintain order between independent areas and therefore exercise great authority over trade, especially in the interior of Calabar.[41] Thus, beyond the paramilitary roles being emphasized here, it is important to note that at times *ekpe* played economic, judicial, and political roles as well. However, at the ritual heart of *ekpe* was the tapping of the leopard's lethal grace for authority through both artistic and paramilitary power.[42] Artistic power was developed through ritual emblems such as special hats, knowledge of dance, combat, and literacy.[43] Although society meetings were closed, occasional public dances used to entertain the general community and display grace in dancing masquerades were important to the ritual functioning of *ekpe*.

The awe inspired by the use of leopard hats and dancing only enhanced the threat of very real juridical sanction as the *ekpe* was "devoted to the making and keeping of law." These societies often enforced legal codes in their communities through the enactment of secret vengeance. The leopard society was "the traditional executioner society—men who killed convicted murderers or launched peremptory strikes against outside enemies."[44] Like other leopard societies throughout West and Central Africa, those of Biafra often used special knives to kill their victims in ways that appeared to be leopard attacks.[45] The *ekpe* also collected fines from transgressors of societal norms and violently punished both internal offenders and external enemies.[46]

Rio's Biafrans were not unique in their previous experience with potential institutional prototypes for closed societies. Many of the "Bengulas" in Rio carried with them an experience with initiation schools from east of the Kunene that could have provided relevant blueprints, as was the case with many of the Congos, Cabindas, Minas, and individuals of other new nations in Rio.[47] Because many of these institutions were similar in structure and function and available data on the early development of *maltas* are lacking, it would be impossible to trace any direct influences from particular regions of Africa. What is clear, however, is that African *capoeiras* built their associations along a similar organizational model as *ekpe* and these other West and Central African closed societies. Rio's *maltas* shared common elements with such paramilitary closed societies, particularly graded initiations, esoteric knowledge, segmented organization, ritual emblems, periodic recreation, and the enforcement of communal justice.

Structure, Organization, and Knowledge

Rio's *capoeira* organizations were graded societies with at least five stages of initiation. The first level was that of *moleques,* who were usually youths attached to *capoeira* societies. The term itself (*muleke*) was widespread in northern Angola, where it signified a youth who had not yet been initiated into adulthood. The term was adopted by Portuguese and Brazilian slave traders and used to describe any child of a certain value in the trade.[48] However, it was likely used by *capoeiras* in the African sense of an uninitiated youth, often children who looked up to *capoeiras* and hoped to emulate them through initiation into *capoeira* societies. These youths served as auxiliaries, helping out with tasks such as carrying weapons for *capoeiras.*[49]

The second stage of participation in *capoeira* societies was to become a *caxinguele.* This Bantu term was used in Rio to designate an apprentice in the martial techniques of the art.[50] As one journalist noted, this training took place in public squares under the tutelage of experienced masters: "It appears that the roundabout of Sé is the chosen ground for the exercises of the recruits of the art. Yesterday at 2:30 in the afternoon, José Leandro Franklin, experienced veteran, and the novice Albano, the former teaching and the latter learning the arts and agility of *capoeiragem* were surprised in their studies by the municipal guard that sent their studies to the jail."[51]

Training of *caxingueles* involved a series of instructional stages. Developing leg attacks and acrobatic defense in the *jogo de capoeira* was undoubtedly fundamental as it was understood by authorities to be inseparable from *capoeiragem.*[52] In the second half of the century at least, *l'arme blanche* formed part of their training. Like the training of Kunene stick fighters who progressed from soft to real weapons, *caxingueles* graduated from wooden practice weapons to real blades: "The practices were regularly done on Sunday mornings and they consisted of exercises of the head and foot and blows with the razor and knife. The most famous *capoeiras* served as instructors to those that were beginning. At first the blows were rehearsed with wooden weapons and finally they were supplied with the real iron; often the training area was stained with blood."[53] In addition to attending their lessons, during their forays *caxingueles* went "ahead of *maltas* to provoke rival neighborhoods" or chosen victims.[54]

After attaining an acceptable proficiency in their training, the *caxinguele* could move into the next grade of the society. Aspirants who reached this next level of membership were described by some sources as *amadores* or *capoeira jubilados*. These were adepts at the martial art but not yet full members of the society. These *amadores* could later become initiated as professional *capoeiras* by passing through an oath ceremony.[55] These initiations took place in church towers, away from the view of the uninitiated; this secrecy made them quite distinct from the pubic ceremonies of the Catholic brotherhoods or the inauguration of the chiefs of the *cantos*.[56] After this closed initiation the individual became a full *capoeira* and could don the ritual emblems of the society publicly. This was the highest grade most society members attained.

Progressing to the level of leadership was in a sense the most selective process as each group had only one publicly acknowledged chief, a respected member who had to be a true master of the martial art. "The status of leader was only achieved," according to Filho, "by that one whose bravery could not be overcome."[57] Rev. James Fletcher, who visited Rio in the 1850s, described *capoeira* chiefs as those with the most kills.[58] Advancement to this stage also may have required some level of cultural mastery. This was indicated by the central role of Africans in the societies during the second half of the nineteenth century, even after the close of the international trade in captive Africans. Carlos Eugênio Líbano Soares, in his study on *capoeiras* in the second half of the nineteenth century, suggests that even after the reduction of African-born populations, it was standard for each *capoeira* society to contain at least one African, who normally held the office of society chief, "or at least the most experienced *malta* member, the carrier of cultural memory, and that had an important role in the symbolic reproduction of the group."[59] In addition to this possible cultural consideration, complete mastery of the martial art system was also essential for the office of chief because in certain situations conflicts between societies were ritually resolved through single combat of their chiefs.[60] Above them, at least in the second half of the century, were the overlords or chiefs of chiefs, positions attained only by "the boldest among these [the chiefs], the most considerate and wise."[61]

"Secret" societies are defined by esoteric knowledge, and in the case of *maltas*, the knowledge of the *jogo de capoeira* and *capoeiragem* was guarded and perpetuated. Additionally, at least some society chiefs appear to have controlled related forms of spiritual knowledge, particularly rituals of protection.[62] Such was the case for Aniceto Borges, a well-known *capoeira* who was found in possession of magic paraphernalia upon his arrest.[63] Soares notes that the special hats with pins stuck through them worn by some *capoeiras* were strongly reminiscent of Kongolese sacred medicines called *minkisi*.[64] Maya Chvaicer argues that *capoeiras* "used amulets that protected their bodies from injury and practiced special rituals and ceremonies that assured their safety outdoors."[65] It can also be argued that the inverted kicking of the art may have been strongly linked to esoteric knowledge in the eighteenth century.

As noted among the Kunene, only those initiated into the *engolo* as a sacred profession could claim true mastery of the art. Even in Brazil the *jogo de capoeira*'s inverted kicks—despite their application in seemingly profane street fights—may still have been associated with special access to ancestral power. Just a few years before Adão's arrest, a free black in Rio was denounced to the Inquisition for "witchcraft." One of the telling signs of his profession as a ritual specialist was his practice of walking "with his head toward the ground and his feet in the air."[66] Witnesses from an earlier Inquisition case from Bahia described another free black named João, who could become "possessed" and speak for those on the other side of the *kalunga*. However, in order to do so, he first had to "walk on one foot, throwing the other one violently over his shoulder."[67] Thus, in eighteenth-century Brazil these inverted and dynamic kicks continued to be linked to the crossing of the *kalunga*. Even though this explicit understanding of the spiritual nature of inverted kicks would be forgotten by later generations, the kicks remained at the ritual core of *capoeira* societies. Thus, in terms of both form and content, these *capoeira* societies corresponded in many ways to paramilitary closed societies.

Space, Aesthetics, and Spheres of Belonging

Like closed societies, *maltas* were segmented in that they operated in terms of both local "houses" and larger networks or "provinces."[68] The police were aware of this, describing the network of *capoeira* societies as "a regularly organized association, subdivided into groups with their own special signs and slang terms."[69] The local organizations were all linked to certain spaces within the city. Although some of their insignia and rituals may have been linked to African cosmological systems, their geographical boundaries appear to have been tied to Catholic parishes, with their churches and adjacent plazas.[70] Local societies situated their ritual headquarters in the bell towers of the parish church, made accessible by *capoeiras* who were also bellmen.[71] It was remarked that "not few of them became respected church servers (sacristães) and excellent bell ringers," and as such, they could and did use the bell towers as performance spaces and watchtowers.[72] Although *capoeira* societies performed secret meetings and rituals such as the oath ceremony in these towers that conveniently served as lookouts, their presence there was no secret to the authorities who raided churches looking for "*capoeiras* and ruffians."[73] *Capoeiras* had to be even more watchful of police while they made use of the open plazas for the training of their young aspirants and meeting places for their forays.

In addition to their occasional displays during public festivals, *capoeira* societies, like African leopard societies, usually extended their claim over an area during the evenings and nights while other residents were indoors. While their nocturnal skirmishes with police, soldiers, and rival *capoeira* societies often took place in open squares, the territory each claimed domination over reflected parish divisions in the second half of the nineteenth century. By this time the names of many of these groups were tied to their representative parishes. These names included "Cadeira da Senhora (the Lady's Chair) in Santa Ana, as Saint Anne is usually depicted seated; Três Cachos (Three Bunches) and Flôr da Uva (Flower of the Grape) in Santa Rita, referring to the grapes associated with that saint; Franciscanos in São Francisco de Paula; Flôr da Gente (Flower of the People) in Glória; Espada (sword) in Lapa; Lança (Lance) in São Jeorge, referring to the weapon used to slay the dragon; Luzianos in Santa Luzia; Ossos (Bones) in Bom Jesus do Calvário; Santo Inácio in the Castelo, where the Jesuit church was located; and Guaiamu in the Cidade Nova district."[74] Thus, it seems that each *capoeira* society acted as a fraternal paramilitary society "representing" the bonded community of an area somewhat akin to parish boundaries. These boundaries would temporarily disappear, however, when the need arose to fight together in the presence of a common enemy. For example, if two rival groups were interrupted by police patrols, "the two rival forces united in order to elude the public force."[75] At times these local societies also came together in larger formal meetings with the representative leaders of multiple local societies. Therefore, the relations between these spatially marked houses and provinces oscillated between rivalry and unity, depending on the circumstances. *Capoeira* societies had their own special emblems and ritual communication, making use of dress, colors, and whistles to announce their identity and belonging. *Capoeiras* were marked by characteristic clothing, particularly broad-rimmed felt hats such as *barretes* or *bonés*. The preferred colors were white or red, and to wear such a hat put a bondsman or free black at risk of arrest as the police recognized these hats as symbols of high-ranking *capoeira* society members.[76] For example, when two *capoeiras* were arrested on May 17, 1815, the report stated that this occurred at a "gathering of *capoeiras*, and a red hat was found, symbol of *capoeira*."[77] Joaquim Congo was arrested for "being encountered with a razor and a *barrette* of *capoeira*"; and presumably Joaquim Cabinda and Joaquim Nunez were similarly dressed when they were arrested for "walking as *capoeiras*."[78]

These hats were often adorned with colored ribbons that marked their owners as initiated *capoeiras* of specific local societies.[79] José Rebolo was arrested "for *capoeira* and having a white straw hat with a large yellow ribbon."[80] Even without the hats, colored ribbons were ritual markers of *capoeiras*. For example, José Cabinda and Antônio Pardo were arrested in 1814 for "playing *capoeira* with different colored ribbons," and Antônio Cassange was arrested for confronting Antônio Monteiro with head butts while "holding a colored ribbon in his hand."[81] These ribbons were also used to mark territory of respective societies, as when "Bernardo Moçambique tied a red ribbon to the pole in front of the church of Santa Rita in the parish of the same name."[82] These ribbons also marked communal action, as when various local groups came together for collective exercises while at the same time demonstrating their individual groups' colors.[83]

Another form of symbolic communication used within and between local groups was whistling. Whistling was identified by the police as a phenomenon exclusive to *capoeiras*. João Angola was jailed for "whistling like *capoeira*."[84] At times this was done with the aid of a physical whistle. Jose Benguela was arrested for "walking with a whistle and whistling *capoeira*."[85] This form of ritual communication may have been used to alert society members of the presence of danger in the form of rival groups or the agents of repression. It may also have acted as a form of communication between society members. During their night marches the leopard societies used various forms of ritual communication to coordinate their movements without speech and alert noninitiates of their nocturnal forays; one such communication was "a strange flute-like whistling" that warned people to go inside.[86]

While common people avoided *capoeira* societies during their nocturnal marches, they were drawn to the entertaining daytime activities of *capoeiras*. Like many African closed societies, an important aspect of *maltas* was to provide entertainment for the community at large during festive occasions and funerals. A French observer noted that *capoeiras* frequented all large gatherings, and in popular festivals they often preceded processions "executing a gymnastics or special dance also called *capoeira*."[87] A young bondsman named Antonio enjoyed such a diversion while at a public square, where he "was entertained . . . with acrobatic and agile exercises that the mob call *capoeiragem*."[88] In addition to the *jogo de capoeira* proper, individual *capoeiras* may have exhibited their skills in church towers by using their dynamic kicks to strike the church bells.[89] *Capoeira* societies made special appearances from these bell towers at funerals: "During the times when burials took place in churches and when religious festivals were frequent, the [church] towers were filled with *capoeiras*, famous bell ringers that, sitting on top of the bells, swung with the momentum of the strikes, blessing from the heights the masses that admired them, crowded in the plazas or streets."[90] Such periodic surfacing of closed society members publicly demonstrating their mastery helped establish their authority by flaunting their independence and power in the public sphere.

Capoeira societies served leadership and paramilitary roles among the larger bonded communities of Rio and thus, though they were closed, were important actors in the social and political landscape of the population. While no direct connection between these societies and uprisings has been documented,

Jules Itier suggests that part of the elite's preoccupation with Rio's societies was their potential to organize open revolts.[91] It appears that these societies played a judicial role in the inner workings of the bonded community and punished infractions of their code. *Capoeira* societies enforced a code of conduct, and like other paramilitary societies, these *maltas* enacted violence through ritually proscribed methods.[92] While Biafran societies utilized the dreaded four-bladed leopard knives, *capoeiras* punished malefactors with deft actions of their kicks, head butts, and blades.[93] Organized groups of armed men loyal to a code and a community that were unrelated and, at their core, ideologically opposed to European domination and the system of chattel slavery could only be viewed as a threat to the existing social order.

It should not be surprising that some closed societies, including the *maltas* of Brazil and the *Abakuá* of Cuba, were founded in the Americas. While the activities of these two groups were also more specifically linked to the nature of urban bondage, from a wider perspective their institutional formats (like those of their rural counterparts such as the Old Time Religion societies of North America and the *mayombe* societies of Saint Domingue) were quite appropriate to the context of American slavery. In Africa as elsewhere, closed societies often rose to prominence among communities experiencing forces of domination that were too strong to be openly opposed.[94] As George Simmel proposes in his seminal essay on closed societies, "As a general proposition the secret societies emerge everywhere as a correlate of despotism and of political control. It acts as a protection, alike of defense and offense against the violent pressure of central powers."[95] If this was truly a common cause for the formation of closed societies, the extreme domination of bondsmen by the arbitrary whims of *senhores,* lawmakers, and police provided a fertile ground for the flowering for such societies in Brazil.[96] This dialectical relationship was highlighted by the ongoing conflict between *capoeiras* and urban police and military forces.

State Repression: Controlling and Accommodating *Capoeira*s

Capoeiragem was one of the most persecuted African cultural practices in the nineteenth century. Ample documents from the police forces and related bureaucracies provide a detailed picture of the waves of repression that struck *capoeiras.* At the same time, *capoeiras* were also integrated to varying degrees into the structures of the dominant society, revealing a certain level of begrudging accommodation on the part of Rio's political institutions.

In 1808, fearing an impending French invasion, Portuguese emperor Dom João VI relocated his court from Lisbon to Rio. After his arrival, many African cultural practices, such as *kalundus* and *batuques,* came under systematic repression by a newly founded police force that had as its primary concern the supervision of bondsmen.[97] Under the monarch's auspices, the previously ad hoc use of military or private units to maintain civil order was replaced with a general intendant of police or the Royal Guard Police. In the absence of a clearly defined legal code, the police were preoccupied with the maintenance of public order, particularly the conduct of bondsmen, and were given authority to punish what they deemed as "unacceptable behavior." Especially when dealing with bondsmen, their responses were generally summary and violent. Police often beat bondsmen on their way to *pelourinhos* (pillories) in public squares. Once there, they were stripped down and whipped with a four- or five-tailed whip and then marched back to the Calabouço, the prison for bondsmen, where their wounds would be painfully washed down with vinegar and pepper.[98]

With the arrival of the royal court, many previously tolerated African cultural traits became viewed as a potential threat and "an offense of such . . . Africanisms to eyes . . . of 'perfectly civilized' Europeans."[99] The police authority to punish any "unacceptable" behavior was exercised on the large *batuques*. Despite this repression, these *batuques* continued in a clandestine form on the outskirts of town or on the beach. As the French wife of a Brazilian planter noted, "In spite of all this, however, they [*batuques*] take place. At the risk of being cruelly beaten, the Negroes go on at night, when the whites are asleep, to dance on the beach in the moonlight. They assemble in groups of the same nationality, either Congo or Mozambique, or Minas; then, in dancing they forget their ills and servitude, and only remember their native country and the time that they were free."[100] Rio's bondsmen developed strategies to protect the *batuques*. One of these was that participants would run when the police arrived and regroup elsewhere to continue until discovered by another patrol.[101] On other occasions some chose to meet police action with violence of their own.[102]

Police repression was particularly severe under Maj. Miguel Nunes Vidigal, the first commander of the Royal Guard Police. Although Vidigal personally spearheaded a war against *capoeiras*, it is interesting to note that he too was reputed to be "a competent *capoeira* . . . absolutely unbeatable with the blows of the head and feet."[103] This *capoeiragem* practitioner waged a war against *capoeiras*, *quilombolas* (members of maroon communities called *quilombos* on the outskirts of the city), and *batuque* enthusiasts. He instituted a special torturous kind of beating that would become a nightmare of violence for Rio's African population.

In this same period *capoeiras* may have increasingly turned to augmenting their unarmed skill with sticks, knives, razors, and rocks. The use of weapons by *capoeiras* led to greater resentment by the Brazilian authorities. In 1822 Emperor Dom Pedro I wrote a letter to the police reprimanding them for not controlling the *capoeiras*. In order to encourage the police in their battle against these rebellious bondsmen, Dom Pedro I promised four days leave to any soldier who caught a *capoeira*.[104] Even though there was no formal law against its practice, *capoeira* was punished with the severest measures legally available to police. Those caught would receive up to three hundred lashes of the whip and be sentenced to hard labor on Tijuca Street or in the navy yards on Ilha das Cobras (Cobra Island) for as long as three months.

Despite the animosity that *capoeira* societies engendered among the elite and police, in 1828 an event occurred that may have endeared the *capoeira* societies to some of the black and working-class people of Rio. Don Pedro I had contracted a large number of German and Irish mercenaries for his campaign to regain Cislatine Province for Brazil. While in Rio the idle troops offended locals with their arrogance and drunkenness. When on June 9 their officers attempted to impose more stringent discipline, many of the two thousand mercenaries broke out in revolt. During the five days it took to stop the uprising, *capoeiras* struck the mercenaries in heated battles, during which the latter suffered. Travelers noted that Rio's bondsmen were given virtual permission to kill the foreign troops with impunity.[105] Although the folk tradition holds that Major Vidigal summoned the *capoeiras* to fight side by side with police against the mercenaries, the *capoeiras* may have just taken advantage of the chaos to exact their own vengeance on the foreign whites. In any case the *capoeiras* were popularly remembered as indispensable in containing the revolt. In personally avenging the racist and obnoxious behavior of the European soldiers, bondsmen must have felt an emotional liberation not unlike that described by Frederick Douglass when he struck out physically against his owner. A German witness to these battles claims that bondsmen gained fifty years worth of confidence in three days because they could feel their power as men.[106] Collectively their actions established the *capoeira* societies as a force with which to be reckoned. Of course, many elites may also have feared that this force could easily be turned toward organizing rebellions against them.[107]

Despite *capoeiras*' popular acclaim for helping to quell the riots, the police began a new wave of repression against them in 1829. Beginning this year individuals were not allowed by law to administer more than fifty lashes on a bondsman per day.[108] Anything in excess of this was to be administered by the police at the Calabouço. It is significant in this context that the only exceptions were the two biggest perceived threats to the system: *quilombolas* and *capoeiras*, who continued to be whipped at pillars in the squares of Campo de Santana to set a public example.[109]

Yet, *maltas* continued, in part due to the system of urban slavery that in some ways encouraged illicit activity. Because they feared a loss of income caused by jail sentences or excessive whipping, *senhores* often defended their bonded *capoeiras*. Following the imposition of a criminal code that prohibited police from administering punishment without judicial review, Eusébio de Queiroz, police chief from 1833 to 1844, petitioned for the authority to punish *capoeiras* "even against the will of the masters, for experience has shown that often they are the first to try to excuse the bad behavior of their slaves."[110] Not only did some masters protect their bondsmen from punishment, but others were accused of indirectly encouraging the use of their fighting skills in illegal activities. As one critic of slavery in 1823 stated, "[w]e are not the least inventive because whoever possesses a slave sends him out to earn money; it does not matter if he robs, assaults, or kills, as long as he brings the stipulated daily amount."[111]

Violent crime was certainly a constant reality in a large city such as Rio de Janeiro. *Ganhadores*, in particular, depended on their own efforts to feed and clothe themselves, in addition to paying their *diária*, or wages due their *senhores*. Competition could be fierce, and wages were low.[112] James Henderson, who visited Rio early in the nineteenth century, noted that if bondsmen "do not bring a certain sum of money to their owners at night, the penalty is generally a severe castigation."[113] Some *capoeiras* who were *ganhadores* may have made money through their street performances of the *jogo de capoeira*.[114] Others turned at times to robbery or providing services as hired muscle and as assassins.[115] One *capoeira* chief was arrested for manipulating a bondsman into stealing the greater part of his *senhor*'s silver.[116] Assassins "were recruited, in general, among *capoeiras*," who for the right price would kill or simply beat a wealthy person's rivals in love, politics, or family feuds.[117] In turn, other elites felt the need to recruit similar individuals to serve as *capangas*, continuously employed strongmen and bodyguards.[118]

The middle of the century was a period of transition in the state repression of *capoeiras*. In 1849 police chief Antônio Simões da Silva instituted new tactics designed to get *capoeiras* off the streets, the most important being conscription into military service. This new tactic coincided with an important demographic watershed with implications for *capoeira* societies. The early 1850s saw the effective end of the Atlantic slave trade, which had been formally abolished in 1830 but renewed clandestinely since 1832. The ending of the Atlantic trade paralleled the growth of interregional domestic trade. Rising prices paid for bondsmen in the interior coffee plantations convinced many of Rio's *senhores* to sell their bondsmen to the traders, who then resold them to plantations in the Paraíba Valley. The joint effect of these changes would slowly begin to alter the demographic composition of *capoeira* societies, which in the first half of the nineteenth century were overwhelmingly composed of African bondsmen. During the second half of the century, Brazilian-born bondsmen, *pardos*, and free blacks would eventually grow to outnumber enslaved Africans in the *capoeira* societies.[119]

These changes had ramifications for police control of *capoeira*. Growing numbers of free *capoeiras* joined or were conscripted into the national guard, the fire brigade, and other bodies. While these new offices imposed limitations on their time and movements, they also offered *capoeiras* in these state institutions some form of protection from police repression. The political importance of the national guard made the treatment of free people of color in the guard a much more delicate issue than the punishment of bondsmen, whom the police could subject to immediate whippings as they saw fit. Furthermore, a national guardsman was immune to arrest by a policeman who did not outrank him.[120] Thus, in 1859 the chief of police could only appeal to the national guard to dismiss Felisberto do Amaral and allow him to be conscripted into the army because "he is very dangerous, and known to be the head of the *capoeiras* who gather in Santa Rita parish. He is the one who, during the pursuit of a *capoeira* gang there, threw a brick at patrolman Lúcio Feliciano da Costa, wounding him on the head."[121] *Capoeiras* conscripted into the army but not posted far from Rio continued to be active members of their *capoeira* societies and, like national guardsmen, enjoyed the protection of their new office. In 1859 the same chief of police, in anticipation of the feast of the city's patron, Saint Sebastian, petitioned the military to restrict off-duty soldiers to their barracks, suggesting that "the *capoeiras* are accustomed to taking advantage of the celebration to engage in their forays, committing crimes and alarming peaceful citizens, and it is undeniable that among them are a large number of soldiers in civilian dress."[122] Thus, the practice of conscripting *capoeiras* initially led to ambiguous results.

In the mid-1860s the authorities found conscription temporarily a more effective means of ridding the city of *capoeiras,* as they could be sent to battle far from Rio. The outbreak in 1865 of the War of the Triple Alliance, which pitted Uruguay, Argentina, and Brazil against Paraguay, came at a time when Brazil was severely shorthanded militarily. As Uruguay and Argentina were not prepared for an external conflict with Paraguay, most of the weight of the conflict fell on Brazil and lasted much longer than anticipated. The government was so in need of recruits that it eventually turned to coercive recruitment of guardsmen, civilians, and even enlisted bondsmen and convicts.[123] In Salvador and Rio the police took the opportunity to rid their cities of many *capoeiras.*

Capoeira societies were extremely hard-hit by this conscription, though they survived in a diminished form. During this anomalous period, foreign immigrants made forays into the world of the *maltas.* North American blacks, who had been present in *capoeira* societies as early at 1812, continued to be present in police sweeps of the 1860s.[124] More significant was the arrest in 1860 of seventeen-year-old Gregório da Rocha Moreira from Porto, who was the first white *capoeira* on record in the nineteenth century.[125] Other foreigners, including French and Italians, joined *capoeira* societies on occasion. Unlike the usual *capoeiras* of color, who were punished without the benefit of legal formalities, foreign nationals had to be charged with specific violations and treated with more delicacy.[126] In contrast to these other foreign groups, Portuguese entered the *capoeira* societies in uncharacteristically high numbers in the 1860s. This anomaly resulted from a huge influx of Portuguese in this decade at the same time that the *capoeira* societies were effectively drained of manpower by the war in Paraguay. The Portuguese who became *capoeiras* usually hailed from the lowest segments of white society. Many came as indentured servants to fill positions left vacant by bondsmen who had been sold to coffee plantations in the provinces. Some of these Portuguese indentured servants, particularly the youths, turned to the *capoeira* societies as a way of finding a place for themselves in the big city.

The defeat of Paraguay by the combined forces of Brazil, Uruguay, and Argentina in 1870 brought the return of many African and African Brazilian *capoeiras*. While some elites may have hoped that the *capoeiras* were sent to the front lines to be killed, they were instead, at least according to popular remembrances of the war, acknowledged for their military contributions: "During the Paraguay War, on the occasion of the final assault and the taking of the Itororó bridge, the Rio constituents of the legendary 31st Corps of Volunteers that proceeded in the vanguard . . . realizing they were out of ammunition in the middle of close quarter combat while overtaking the ominous bridge, they removed their sabre-bayonets and they threw the useless rifles away, rushing with unstoppable momentum against the enemy trenches, and attacking their defenders with *arme blanche* and *capoeira* blows."[127] In part as a result of their participation in this war, the relationships of *capoeiras* with each other and with the state took on new dimensions that shaped the history of *capoeira* in the 1870s and 1880s.

The return of these soldiers marked the end of the anomalously high representation of Portuguese in the *capoeira* societies. Soares suggests that the deaths of many interim *capoeira* chiefs marked the return of these blacks to their former positions of authority immediately following the war. With the decreasing number of bondsmen in Rio, the composition of *capoeira* societies became predominantly comprised of free people of color. Yet, bondsmen continued to comprise around 40 percent of *capoeiras* at a time when they represented only about 17 percent of people of color in the wider society.[128]

While each *capoeira* society continued to be affiliated with a certain parish of Rio, the umbrella organizations that linked various local societies into larger networks became more visible at this time. They emerged in the records after the war as two "families," known as Nagoas and Guaiamos. The Nagoas occupied the newest areas of the city, while Guaiamos defended the old city.[129] These two networks were similar to earlier cooperative structures linking various *capoeira* societies in the preceding decades. Yet, the emergence, or perhaps just the new visibility, of Nagoas and Guaiamos appears linked to the political role of *capoeiras* in the postwar era.

Figure 5.3: Types and uniforms of the old Nagoas and Guaiamos, by Calixto Cordeiro. *Revista Kosmos* 3 (March 1906)

The war in some ways seems to have politicized soldiers, whose participation in defending the country must have widened their vision of themselves as active participants in the country's affairs.[130] The ex-soldiers also returned to a politically divided city and few opportunities. In the tradition of earlier mercenary toughs, black fighters hired out their skills to politicians. *Capoeiras* protected polling places, intimidated voters, and attacked the rallies of the opposition. One of their specialties was a technique called "impregnating the polls," which involved creating a disturbance at the polling places and in the melee stuffing bunches of votes into the ballot boxes.[131] They quickly became a ubiquitous part of the political landscape with an alliance between the Nagoas and the conservative party and the Guaiamos with the liberal party. As an observer of life in the 1880s noted, "many of those in government rose by the flash of the razor, and the Senate and the Chamber supported themselves on the swarthy shoulder of the *capoeira*."[132]

These political connections frustrated the police as the ruling party commonly extended legal protection to their *capoeira* allies. The result was that a well-known *capoeira* leader such as Manduca da Praia, a smartly dressed *pardo* who owned a fish market as well as being the head of the *capoeira* society of Santa Luzia, could walk openly without fear of the police. He was arrested on numerous occasions but was always acquitted due to the political influence of his clients in the São José elections. In addition to political protection, *capoeira* chiefs may have received public funds for acting as "political shock troops" and bodyguards.[133] This reflected both a practice that frustrated police efforts to control *capoeiras* and a co-optation that may have limited the revolutionary potential of *capoeiras maltas* as a threat to the established order.[134]

However, the Nagoas and Guaiamos were no mere pawns of the conservative and liberal parties. These alliances were fruitful for the purpose of protection, and their collective strength was used for political leverage, particularly around the issue of abolition. Indeed, the two *capoeira* families united against the republicans, who were viewed as antiabolitionist.[135] Conflict between *maltas* and republicans dated from 1873, when a republican meeting in Brazil, inspired by the declaration of a republic in Spain, was broken up by *capoeiras*. In 1888 Brazil finally bent under the combined force of revolts by bondsmen, international pressure, abolitionist campaigning, and a large-scale flight of bondsmen from plantations. On May 13 Princess Regent Isabel signed the "Golden Law" ending legal slavery in Brazil. Abolition did not end the repression of *capoeiragem*, which would continue into the 1940s. Despite this repression that eventually broke down formal *capoeira* societies, the *jogo de capoeira* continued to thrive in Brazil.

Martial Traditions and Tactical Transformations

Kicking, Head Butting, and the Jogo de Capoeira

Though the details of the *jogo de capoeira* in the nineteenth century are limited, it is possible to compile a basic sketch of the practice during this time period. It is clear that, as in the ritual circle of *engolo*, the *jogo de capoeira* involved an interaction between a pair of practitioners, at times accompanied by a circle of spectators and percussion. This interaction in the *jogo de capoeira* emphasized kicks, sweeps, and acrobatic evasions. James Wetherell, who visited Brazil in 1856, describes what was clearly the *jogo de capoeira* as a dynamic foot fight: "A kick on the shins is about the most painful knock they give each other. They are full of action, capering and throwing their arms and legs about like monkeys during their quarrels."[136] It is possible to distinguish circular kicks, pushing kicks, sweeps, and inverted kicks from the latter half of the century. In particular the *jogo de capoeira*'s kicking arsenal was most associated with inverted kicks such as the *rabo d'arraia* and the *pentana*. As Filho notes, the *rabo d'arraia* was "one of the most rudimentary foundational movements" of the *jogo de capoeira*.[137] The *rabo d'arraia* was a kick launched by "turning over the body, rotating one of the legs to kick the enemy," while the *pentana* involved "turning over the body applying both feet against the chest of the adversary" (variations of images 15 and 9 in the appendix).[138] Such inverted kicks would have been central to potential spiritual symbolism of the art in the eighteenth century. Even though the following century may have witnessed the passing of any conscious connections between inverted kicks and drawing on spiritual power, they remained at the aesthetic core of the art's performative side in the *jogo de capoeira*. These dynamic kicks and their equally acrobatic defenses were likely the most captivating aspects of the spectacle that drew crowds of observers.

Figure 5.4: Blacks fighting. Nineteenth-century engraving

Also central to the *jogo de capoeira* was the use of acrobatic agility in order to defend against these kicks. As with the *engolo,* this began with keeping the body in constant motion with dancelike steps. By the late nineteenth century this motion was called *ginga* in Brazil, a Bantu term found in the Kongo and many Njila languages of Angola and meaning "to dance, sway, or play."[139] From this deceptive swaying dance, all attacks would be avoided through various dodging techniques. These often included ducking low under an attack. Such movements could simultaneously be defensive and counterattacks, such as with the *caçador,* in which the *capoeira* would drop low on his hands to avoid a blow and extend one leg to sweep out the opponent's support leg, sending him to the ground (see appendix, image 19).

Head butts too may have played a role within the *jogo de capoeira.* While Wetherell's description centers around kicking, Johann Moritz Rugendas, who traveled in Brazil in the early 1820s, highlights the role of head butts in his description of the *jogo.* Note the similarity to North American "knocking" in his description: "The Negros have another, much fiercer, war game, the *Jogar Capoeira:* two champions rush at each other, trying to strike with his head the chest of the opponent he is aiming to knock down. The attack is thwarted by leaping sideways or by equally skillfully parrying; but in springing at each other, pretty much like goats, they now and again butt each other's heads very roughly; so one often sees jesting give place to anger, with the result that the sport is made bloody with blows and even with knives."[140]

While kicks and head butts were associated skills, and certainly were integrated in the bloody street battles that could follow the *jogo,* it is difficult to establish any such integration within the *jogo de capoeira* in the early nineteenth century. Had the ritual that Rugendas observed contained the distinctive kicks of the art, it is not likely that his detailed description would have omitted them. Rather, Rugendas describes head butts being practiced in their own ritual context, as was also the case among the Kunene and in North America and the French Antilles. The possibility exists that Rugendas conflated ritualized head dueling, mentioned in the police records around the time of his visit as the *jogo de cabeçadas,* with the *jogo de capoeira.*[141] Another alternative explanation is that the term *jogo de capoeira* was used as a catchall term applied to two separate modalities, one specifically using head butts and another using kicks.[142]

While the techniques of the *jogo de capoeira* served as a foundational exercise for self-defense, during real conflicts *capoeiras* called on *capoeiragem,* a set of fighting skills that was quite distinct from the *jogo* in its wider arsenal, which relied on head butts, weapons, and other injury-inflicting maneuvers. Although *capoeiras* frequently used kicks in real combat, head butts were the most widely mentioned technique associated with the *capoeiras* who graced the pages of police registries. In fact, head butts were noted in one police document as the "principal weapon of *capoeira.*"[143] Representative of these *capoeiras* was Antonio Cassange, arrested for holding his society's colored ribbon while defying his victim with head butts.[144] As an English visitor to Rio early in the century noted, these head butts could have a lethal effect: "For the office of assassin, the very lowest order of Negroes are hired. . . . Their manner of setting to work is worthy of remark. They need no stiletto, bird cage awl (*ferro de gaiola*), or any other weapon. In lieu of all these, they use only the head; and with it they butt like bulls at the chest of their victim. I saw a field officer who had been murdered in this manner, and thrown over the wall into his garden, where his family found him in the morning: the upper part of the body had been flattened as if the implement of death had been a mallet."[145]

It is also important to note that the use of head butting was not limited to *capoeiras.* As in Cimbebasia and North America, kicking in Rio seems to have been the domain of trained specialists (initiated *capoeiras*) while head butting existed as a more widespread agonistic form among the general black population. This makes it difficult to determine if the *capoeiras*' use of head butts was distinct or a reflection of this wider bonded practice of head butting. The importance of the head butt as a characteristic weapon of bondsmen was apparent in the various names for that art (*cocada, chifrada, caveira no espelho, topete a cheirar*) depending on the blow's angle of approach and target.[146] For example, the *caveira no espelho* ("skull in a mirror") was a standing head strike to the face, while the *cocada* was an upward strike under the chin.

Nineteenth-century *capoeiragem* also included a much wider arsenal than did the *jogo de capoeir.a* The latter clearly consisted of a ritual space in which aesthetic and technical considerations dominated. While style may have been consciously demonstrated in the heated battles of *capoeiragem,* combat efficiency clearly took priority in more dangerous combat. The street fights that *capoeiras* engaged in could be lethal affairs. In these battles *capoeiras* with knowledge of combative styles from other areas of Africa or the Atlantic world, including punching and wrestling, likely would have called upon them when effective in melee. This may have been the origin of the few hand strikes noted in descriptions of late nineteenth-century street fights.[147] Of course, these may also have emerged spontaneously out of experience in such skirmishes. This could also be true for the antiblade techniques of *espada,* which used a circular kick to knock a knife from an opponent's hand, or *suicidio,* which ideally kicked an opponent's legs out, causing him to cut himself with his own blade.[148]

Weapons in Capoeiragem

Rugendas's description highlights the use of knives as a distinguishing marker between ritual practice and street fights. Although the unarmed martial art would remain at the core of the *jogo de capoeira,* the use of weapons became an auxiliary skill in the wake of escalating violence that erupted after the creation of the Royal Guard Police. The second decade of the nineteenth century appears to have been a turning point marking the *capoeiras'* more widespread adoption of weapons, including sticks, knives, razors, and even rocks. In 1809 Major Vidigal, in his quest to stamp out aberrant practices of enslaved Africans, handpicked his men for their large size and strength. He also armed each of his men with a special weapon: a heavy club with rawhide strips at one end, which was employed as both a club and a whip.[149] "Shrimp dinners"—the slang term referring to the severe cudgeling of unarmed individuals, which was seen as similar to tearing down the shells to access the pink flesh of crustaceans—were served in large portions to the "idlers" rounded up at *batuques, quilombos,* or *jogos de capoeira.*[150] Around this time there may have been an increase in weapons use among *capoeiras.* Although the cause may be overstated, Gilberto Freyre suggests that "the systematic persecution of the police turned these champions of kicking and butting into even more annoying dancers: dancers armed with razors and daggers."[151] Police records indicate that 1814 marked a watershed in the use of weapons by *capoeiras.*[152] Elysio Araujo's study of Rio's police points out that beginning in 1814, in a countermeasure by the police, the actions taken against anyone found in possession of a bladed weapon became more and more severe.[153]

Of the weapons that became common among *capoeiras,* the two that were the easiest to obtain were also those that were prominent in the Kunene arsenal: sticks and rocks.[154] Stick fighting was a natural auxiliary skill, particularly for the numerous West and West Central Africans with a rich tradition of stick fighting. Stick work in Rio was trained both through ludic stick-fighting dances such as one described by Rugendas in 1823: "It is important to also mention a type of military dance: two groups armed with sticks line up in front of each other and the talent consist in avoiding the powerful blows of the adversary." Stick also played a role in actual battles among *capoeiras*.[155] *Capoeiras* were frequently encountered with this weapon, as was the case with Elias Pereira, who was arrested "for having a stick on Pecho street, playing *capoeira* with others who escaped."[156]

Rocks were similarly dangerous, particularly in the hands of Kunene youth and others who were trained in their use as arms. Expert rock throwers could also substitute a brick or even a bottle as alternative missile weapons. Easy to leave around the city and pick up when necessary, these rocks could be quite effective weapons, and *capoeiras* used them to great effect. The sentinel at the fountain of Largo da Carioca was unaware that Manuel Congo had hidden two rocks in his barrel on his way to the encounter, much to the suffering of the sentinel.[157] Rocks were even used to attack targets in a crowd, as in the case of Manoel Quissama and Domingos Rebelo, who "were arrested for throwing rocks at the people in Largo de Sé as they were leaving the procession of the Rosary."[158]

The other main weapons were straight knives and *navalhas* (folding knives and razors). The early technical use of these weapons may have come from any number of sources, including Iberian blade work, Cimbebasian knife work, or even the tradition of knife fighting from the far northern region of Angola.[159] Certainly bondsmen would have noticed the knife-fighting skills of Portuguese and European Brazilians who fought in the cloak-and-dagger style of Europe. Henderson notes a thriving trade of special knives imported from England for this purpose.[160] However, the most common bladed weapon among African *capoeiras* in the first half of the nineteenth century was a simple awl-shaped knife called a *sovelão*.[161] Visitors to Rio noted the proficiency of bondsmen in wielding these weapons. As Walsh describes, "Their faka, or long knife, they use with tremendous effect. They sometimes hurl it, as an Indian does a tomahawk, with irresistible force, and drive the blade, at a considerable distance, through a thick deal board."[162]

Given the consequences of possessing bladed weapons if arrested, *capoeiras* had to be creative in not getting caught with these arms. In 1832 the minister of justice wrote a letter to the police recommending greater vigilance in searching for offensive arms: "Commander of Police in charge of the General Police Operations was informed of the recent possession by black capoeiras and other similar individuals, of *sovelões* and other instruments of that sort, hidden in marimbas [African musical instruments] and inside pieces of sugar cane and the butt of black whips made in the country. Therefore this information shall

Figure 5.5: Female *capoeira* with razor imagery. *Revista Illustrada* 289 (1882)

be communicated to all the Commanders of the National Guard so that they will be aware and shall warn the respective patrols to be most vigilant over these objects and to thoroughly examine such individuals, arresting them if found with such instruments and to be punished according to the prescribed law." When caught with weapons, some bondsmen tried to explain that they needed blades for their trades, perhaps to cut food if they were vendors, trim shrubs if gardeners, trim hair if barbers, etc.: "Make it known to whom read this editorial or hear about it, experience has shown that all the measures taken to avoid the abuse of pocket knives and knives, that in this city is principally committed by slaves under the pretext of being necessary tools that they use in their respective work."[163] Others tried to toss away their weapons while they ran from police, knowing that possession of such weapons would increase their punishments.[164]

The *navalha* was also widely used by *capoeiras* in the early nineteenth century, being the documented weapon in over 38 percent of arrest records.[165] Its clean cut and foldable blade likely made the *navalha* the preferred weapon. However, the *sovelões* were probably more common because *navalhas* were relatively expensive and thus out of reach for many bondsmen. In the second half of the century *capoeiras* would become most associated with the *navalha* in the eyes of the general public.[166] Yet, it is doubtful that the technical use of the *navalha* was introduced by Portuguese immigration in the second half of the century.[167] Rather, it probably reflects the increased number of free and other *capoeiras* with the economic means to purchase this weapon of choice. If assassinations were characteristically perpetrated with head butts in the early nineteenth century, they would be carried out with razors in the latter half of the century. An example of this was the 1872 case of the *capoeira* hired by Luís Teixeira da Cunha's group to cut a Portuguese barber with a razor.[168] One fascinating detail about the use of the razor, which first appeared in early twentieth-century documentation but may have been a much older practice, was its special use in the *jogo de capoeira.* While razors were often held in the hand during street fights, in the more ritually dominated context of the *jogo de capoeira* the razor was integrated as an extension of the foot-fighting tradition by being held in the toes.[169]

Even after the proliferation of *l'arme blanche* as auxiliary techniques of *capoeiras,* unarmed skill remained central not only to ritual practice in the *jogo de capoeira* but also to street skirmishes. At times *capoeiras* had to rely on their unarmed skills in combat situations against armed opponents. Against bladed weapons, *capoeiras* used the Angolan-style defensive agility. An unarmed master of the craft might even face armed opponents with confidence. This was the case in the fictional account by Plácido de Abreu in *Os Capoeira,s* in which the unarmed *capoeira* Fazenda defeats three armed rivals, providing a vivid example of how these various armed and unarmed techniques might have been combined in a real conflict.[170] However, the razor loomed large as a symbol of *capoeiragem* in discourse of the upper classes and was clearly used as such in political cartoons of the day. Yet, fewer than 30 percent of the *capoeiras* arrested in the nineteenth century possessed any weapons, suggesting that weapons use, let alone razor use, was not as central to the practice as it was a symbol of the potential of the art in the minds of elites.[171]

The *jogo de capoeira* was not the only martial art that proliferated in Brazil. *Capoeiras* also encountered serious rivals in the masters of a Portuguese stick-fighting art, who pushed *capoeiras* to develop new tactics in these clashes. Early waves of conflicts between *capoeiras* and Portuguese erupted in the turbulent years of Brazil's independence. Luiz José was arrested in 1833 along with a group of *capoeiras* attempting to kill Portuguese in the city.[172] Violence between these groups reached new heights in the 1860s, when despite the unusually high representation of Portuguese in the *capoeira* societies in this decade, tensions increased in general as the new waves of immigrants competed with urban blacks for the city's jobs. While Soares suggests that the similar conditions endured by immigrant Portuguese and bondsmen in Rio were a source of unity leading Portuguese youths into the *capoeira* societies, this shared oppression may more often have led to competition and rivalry.[173] As Thomas Holloway points out, the Portuguese "were more often the target of *capoeira* attacks than participants."[174] These tensions were reflected in the slang of the day. The widespread Portuguese antipathy for the blacks and *pardos* was reflected in references to them as "goat feet." People of color in turn referred to the Portuguese as "lead feet" or "ox feet."[175] Part of this animosity was the result of competition over resources such as jobs, living quarters, and women. While most Portuguese immigrants were by no means wealthy, their racial status allowed them to see themselves as superior in relation to people of color, especially the destitute bondsmen. This rivalry was purportedly heightened when the Portuguese used their status to attract women of color. According to Oliveira, this "offense" was avenged by the *capoeiras*.[176]

In their battles against some Portuguese, the *capoeiras* had to alter their tactics. The reason for this is that many Portuguese, especially sailors and those from northern Portugal and the Portuguese Atlantic islands, brought with them a fighting tradition called *jogo do pau*. The staff of the art was tapered and ideally long enough to reach the user's mouth when rested on the ground vertically.[177] Practitioners employed this weapon by grasping the narrow end and using the thick end for striking and parrying. The heavy staff could deliver lethal blows, and the methods of delivering them were honed in Portugal during the reign of King Dom Miguel (1828–34). Due to a conflict between the nobles and the liberals, the latter were prohibited from using or even wearing swords. In response the liberals turned to the staff art, which spread throughout Portugal and to both the lower and noble classes.[178] Numerous Portuguese immigrants who were versed in its methods brought this art to Brazil.

In order to meet this challenge, *capoeiras* adopted two tactics, one for less serious confrontations and the other for deadly encounters. When unarmed, the *capoeiras* relied on their defensive agility to wear out the staff-swinging Portuguese and goad them into leaving an opening so that the *capoeira* could close the distance: "To face the strong punch and the violent blows of the Portuguese staves, the tactics consisted of feinting before the opponent, looking to tire him and to distract him, until he offered the opportunity to be knocked down by an unexpected movement; sweep or head butt. Among the most skillful, there were some who took pride in fighting with their hands in their pockets, jumping from here to there, always making 'letters' (defensive footwork), and waiting until the opponent could be reached with a sweep, or floored with a good head butt to the pit of the stomach."[179]

Such matches did not always lead to serious injury and on occasion could lead to mutual respect. For example, when the famous Portuguese staff expert Santana came to Rio, he sought out the most famous of the *capoeiras*, Manduca da Praia. The two fought, and Manduca sent Santana flying with a well-placed kick. Afterward the two drank together and remained close friends.[180] However, in more serious, life-threatening battles, presumably in questions of vengeance, the *capoeiras* used pointed canes to inflict lethal wounds: "I heard many times, almost as a tale of a thousand and one nights, from the mouth of the older people, the stories of *galegos* [Portuguese] hurt by the hooligans [*capoeiras*], when not killed. The favorite weapons of these hooligans were canes of less than half inch of thickness, with a sharpened end that pierced, almost without pain in the first instant, the prominent stomach of the Portuguese. This cane was recovered from the main shaft of parasols as they were made in that era."[181]

Thus, *capoeiras* developed new tactics and adopted new combat strategies in the nineteenth century.

Post-Emancipation: Ongoing Repression and New Adaptations

A brief overview of the three decades after abolition in 1888, although beyond the range of this study, will help orient readers familiar with the modern *jogo de capoeira* and illuminate important phases of adaptation in the art, thus providing a fuller perspective on the process of continuity and change within the tradition. The social context of the *jogo de capoeira* practice was significantly altered after abolition. The continued repression all but eliminated the earlier practices of *maltas* in Rio and Recife. However, out of Bahia a variant branch of the *jogo de capoeira* would emerge due to the art's co-optation and relocation into regulated academy buildings in the middle of the twentieth century. This Bahian *jogo de capoeira* would later spread across Brazil, replacing the remnants of the older variations in the public eye.[182]

White planters were embittered since they perceived the monarchy's support of abolition in 1888 as a betrayal of their interests. Fearing further liberal reforms, they chose to back the republican movement growing out of the liberal party. With republicans threatening to remove the monarchy altogether, blacks became ever more allied to the monarchist conservative party as they feared that the republicans wanted to remove the princess in order to reinstate slavery. Becoming a core of the movement called the "Black Guard," the *capoeiras* continued their politics of violent opposition by attacking republican rallies and meetings.[183]

The fall of the monarchy in November 1889 signified the beginning of the most complete repression of *capoeiragem*, one that nearly eliminated the *maltas*. The new police chief of Rio, João Batista Sampaio Ferraz, was referred to by the *capoeiras* as "the steel goatee" (*o cavanhaque de aço*) because of his single-handed, ruthless campaign against *capoeiras*. Ironically some of those who persecuted the art, in this case republicans, had themselves been practitioners, as was the case in the preemancipation period of repression. This included the future provisional president Floriano Peixoto, and even Sampaio Ferraz was a *capoeira amadore*, although far from the most talented. Exemplary of this ultimate of ironies, in a discussion at Café Inglês between Ferraz and Luís Murat, general secretary of the governor of the state of Rio de Janeiro, Murat disagreed with Ferraz's campaign, and the two decided to settle the matter by the "sweep and head butt." Murat dominated Ferraz and sent him flying into a marble table.[184]

Although Ferraz's campaign also sought to clean the city of other "unsightly" phenomena such as African-based religious practices, his main target was the *capoeira* societies. Provisional president Deodoro da Fonseca gave Ferraz carte blanche to deal with the *capoeiras* as he saw fit. He began by compiling his "Turma da Lima," a list of names and addresses of the most fearsome and powerful *capoeiras,* including those who would have been responsible for passing the art down to *caxingueles.* This list included even the *capoeiras* in other areas of the country. Instead of trying to catch them in their *capoeira* society activities, which would have been difficult, Ferraz's plan was to approach them stealthily as they stood on their doorsteps talking or were engaged in other innocuous activities of daily life. The *capoeiras* were thus apprehended one by one, detained, provided no judicial recourse, and without a trial, deported to the distant island of Fernando de Noronha. Under slavery the *senhores* of incarcerated *capoeiras* would have pushed for their return, but under the republic most *capoeiras* never returned from the island. However, because *capoeiragem* had spread to some members of the elite in the last decades of slavery, Ferraz was criticized for being too heavy handed, especially in his arrest of Juca Reis, son of the Count of Matosinhos.

As a result of pressure from certain circles, Sampaio Ferraz was relieved of his office as police chief in late November 1890. By that year in office, however, Ferraz had managed to eliminate *maltas* as a political force by breaking the tradition of the societies. Even the many *capoeiras* who fled the capital to avoid Ferraz's campaign could not escape the arm of the new penal code of October 11, 1890. In article 402 the new code prohibited "practicing, in the streets and public squares, the exercise of agility and corporal dexterity known by the term *capoeiragem.*" This law acted not only against *capoeira* society members but also against the *jogo de capoeira* as part of a wider repression of all African customs.[185] This new expanded repression forced the adoption of new forms of the art in the early twentieth century.

The repression of *capoeiragem* in Rio did not end with the removal of Ferraz from office. The deportation of *capoeiras* continued under successive police chiefs, who were aided by the new penal code in preventing a resurgence of the open resistance presented by *capoeira* societies. With the removal of *maltas* from the political scene in the early twentieth century, the journal *Kosmos,* the voice of Rio's intellectuals, advocated that the *jogo de capoeira* should be accepted as a national art form on the level of British boxing or French *savate.*[186] Public support was rallied by the famous battle in 1909 between the Japanese jujitsu champion Sado "Koda" Miako and the *capoeira* "Macaco" Ciríaco Francisco da Silva. Macaco's agility kept Koda from grabbing him (jujitsu is a grappling art that seeks to seize and throw an opponent to the ground for a submission), and one swift *rabo d'arraia* won the fight for Macaco, who was carried out of the stadium on the shoulders of Rio's medical school students.[187] Although Macaco was hailed as a national hero in *Kosmos* and in the streets of Rio the following day, his victory did not win over the chief of police. In the years that followed, the once-thriving *maltas* would revive somewhat but without their former political influence.

In Recife *capoeiragem* had also been closely tied to the political system, and *capoeiras* were used as bodyguards and political shock troops. Following the war in Paraguay in the 1870s the societies of Recife were linked to military marching bands. Each marching band paraded with its *capoeiras* out in front demonstrating their physical prowess and gracefully daring any opponents to test them. Rivalry between marching bands, such as the Fourth Artillery Battalion band and the national guard band, often degenerated into bloody *capoeiragem* battles.[188] These battles continued until around 1910, when police chief Santos Moreira followed the example of Sampaio Ferraz. He deported the more experienced *capoeiras* to Fernando de Noronha Island, while many of the less experienced were held in prison or killed while resisting arrest.[189] While this repression rooted out most of the *capoeiras* in Recife, the *jogo de capoeira*'s legacy continued in the dance form called *passo*. *Passo*, born of the *ginga* dance of the *capoeiras* as they performed in front of the marching bands, also inherited the names of some techniques of the *jogo de capoeira*. While strictly a dance without self-defense techniques, *passo* grew out of and maintained much of the self-assured grace and combative feints of the *jogo*'s *ginga*.[190]

While *capoeiragem* was giving birth to *passo* in Recife, the *jogo de capoeira* was also undergoing contextual and musical transformations in Bahia. In Bahia the *capoeira* societies had been largely destroyed in forced conscription during the war in Paraguay. Many soldiers returned to Bahia, and yet the *capoeira* societies never regained their prewar momentum as societies had in the capital. However, *capoeiragem* was continued by individuals called *valentões* (also called *bambas*, or experts), who fought both in ritual games of the *jogo de capoeira* and in skirmishes on the street with each other and the police.[191] They continued their expertise of incorporating the use of sticks, knives, and razors in their street battles. These *bambas* also displayed their craft at popular festivals and *batuques*. A cycle of festivals leading up to Carnival, and particularly the Festas do Largo, were important contexts for the *jogo de capoeira*, but matches also took place spontaneously whenever players came together and had time on their hands, often in front of bars to accumulate drinking money for the fighters.[192]

Musical Transformations

During this time the musical accompaniment of the art was also undergoing change in Bahia. Around the turn of the century the main musical transformation was the switch from the drum to the musical bow as the art's primary instrument. The oral traditions collected by the musicologist Gerard Kubik reveal that prior to the twentieth century the *jogo de capoeira* in Bahia was accompanied exclusively by a drum to communicate to the trainees.[193] The drum would encourage one or more of the trainees through patterns and could warn all participants of the approach of whites. This oral tradition is affirmed by traveler accounts and police documents linking *capoeira* to the transverse drum. Rugendas's portrait of *capoeira* (fig. 5.1) shows a *jogo de capoeira* being accompanied by hand clapping and a transverse drum, while Ribeyrolles describes the *jogo de capoeira* being performed to a "Congo" drum.[194]

This drum was at some point in the late nineteenth or early twentieth century replaced in its central position in Bahia by a gourd-resonated musical bow. Prior to its incorporation into the *jogo de capoeira,* the musical bow was used in other contexts—at times by peddlers, who would play the instrument to attract customers to the wares they were selling. The instrument was a derivation of Angolan bows, particularly the *hungu* of northern Angola and the *mbulumbumba* of Cimbebasia. According to Kubik, the Brazilian *berimbau* and the "southwest Angolan variety called *mbulumbumba* are identical in the construction and the playing technique, as well as in the tuning and in a number of basic patterns played." Furthermore, the finger set used to play the bow in Brazil can be found only in southern Angola.[195] A seemingly related term, *bacumbumba,* continued to be applied to the instrument in Brazil along with other Bantu terms for musical bows, such as *urucungo, hungu,* and *madimba lungungu.*[196] By the twentieth century, when it became affiliated with the *jogo de capoeira,* the bow came to be called by the Portuguese misnomer *berimbau.* The Portuguese applied this term to their musical instrument the *guimbarde,* a "Jew's harp." Noticing some similarity between the *guimbarde* and the African musical bow when the latter was held in the mouth, the Portuguese referred to the musical bow as *berimbau* in the same way that the English called the African lemellophone a "hand piano" or a "thumb piano." The smaller African bow played while held in the mouth was termed *berimbau de boca* (mouth *guimbarde*), while the gourd-resonated bow was termed *berimbau de barriga* (belly *guimbarde*), a term eventually adopted even by many African Brazilians in the twentieth century.[197]

The question remains, why did this musical bow come to replace the Central African–derived drum as the central instrument in *capoeiras* around the turn of the century? Some *jogos de capoeira* began to incorporate other musical instruments, including the *bodge* (tambourine) early on and later in the century the *ganza* (scraper), the Yoruba *agôgo* (double cowbell), the *atabaque* (standing drum), and the *caxixi* (plaited rattle).[198] Kubik suggests that the adoption of the bow was in response to these additions in musical accompaniment:

> Projected on *capoeira,* the Yoruba concept would have stimulated the use of more and other instruments besides the traditional drum. At the same time the Angolan carriers of the *capoeira* tradition would have resisted too many compromising changes which would have led to the disappearance of the Angolan identity of this tradition. The compromise solution resulting from cultural pressure of the African group and intracultural resistance of the Angolans would have been that the carriers of

> *capoeira* were willing to include more instruments, but preferred to adopt an instrument *which was also Angolan:* the gourd-resonated musical bow. This might be the story of how the gourd bow, in Angola and Brazil of past centuries a solo instrument, became a group instrument in Brazilian *capoeira.*[199]

This ethnic rivalry resonates with other examples, such as the Angolans trying to maintain leadership in the brotherhood Our Lady of the Rosary in the face of a massive entrance of West Africans in the nineteenth century.[200] Yet, beyond the *bodge,* which may have been associated with the art much earlier, these other instruments were only systematically introduced in the 1930s–50s. Furthermore, the transverse drum was already affiliated with West Central Africans, if not exclusive to the particular southern Angolans who brought the *engolo* to Brazil. Therefore, the change may have had as much to do with resistance to police repression and the bow's use as a weapon.

The police repression ushered in by the republic brought unwanted attention not only to *capoeiragem* but also to other aspects of African culture in Brazil. The drum, which had for centuries struck fear of black rebellion in the hearts of many whites, may have been consciously or unconsciously targeted by police repression. The apparently innocuous musical bow did not have this legacy; nor was it affiliated with the equally repressed African-derived religious practices such as Candomblé. Therefore, a *berimbau* player may have been able to pass a policeman without evoking the same oppressive response caused by a musician carrying a large Bantu drum. Furthermore, when police broke up a gathering of *capoeiras,* the *berimbau* would have been much lighter to carry and aided the musician's chance of escape. In addition, unlike the drum, the *berimbau* served the dual utility of providing music as well as a potential armament. The *bambas* from the early twentieth century were unanimous in singing the praises of the *berimbau* as a weapon.

The late master Noronha (Daniel Coutinho [1909–77]) noted that the *berimbau* was a weapon of great utility to the *capoeiras,* a legacy of the masters of the 1920s who resisted police repression.[201] The *berimbau* was used as a weapon by itself with one end sharpened to a point or with a blade added to one end. The result was the longest-range weapon of the *capoeira* arsenal. If these factors help explain *why* the *berimbau* was adopted, the question of *how* may be answered by understanding the relationship between *capoeira bambas* and *batuque* circles.

The term *batuque* often connoted a suite of music and dance forms enjoyed by bondsmen. Among the various dance circles at these events were those dedicated to a combat game called *pernada* in Rio and *batuque* or more specifically *batuque-boi* in Salvador and the Recôncavo region surrounding it.[202] Although not enough is known about the history of this genre, these games may have evolved as a competitive variation of the *umbigada/semba* "belly-bounce" that was so popular in bonded dances throughout Brazil and indeed the Atlantic world.[203] The game involved one attacker and one defender. The defender stood with legs rotated inward to protect his genitals and root himself for the upcoming attack. The attacker then, after some possible feints, entered with one decisive attempt to knock down the defender with his hips, upper legs, or feet. If the defender fell, a new player replaced him, but if he stayed on his feet, he took the place of the attacker and the game continued. Edison Carneiro, who wrote in some detail on the topic of *pernada/batuque-boi,* notes that it was dominated by people of the "Angolan nation" and was practiced to the musical bow, tambourine, scraper, and songs. Carneiro also points out that many *capoeiras* also practiced *pernada/batuque-boi.*[204] Given this shared cultural space, the *jogo de capoeira* may have incorporated or co-opted the musical instrumentation of *batuque-boi* in Bahia. Furthermore, this game likely developed the use of new variations of sweeps that may then have been integrated into the *jogo de capoeira.*[205]

These contextual, technical, and musical adaptations in the Bahian *jogo de capoeira* did little to endear it to state authorities. *Capoeira bambas* encountered periods of repression, particularly in the 1920s under police chief Pedro Azevedo Gordilho.[206] Despite such postemancipation police repression, *capoeiragem* was clearly at its counterhegemonic height when used by bondsmen in the first half of the nineteenth century to declare their honor.

Capoeiras and Honor

Much of the violence surrounding *capoeiras* in the nineteenth century was the result of their sense of honor.[207] Yet, as Holloway notes, journalists and police officials were often mystified by the causes of seemingly random brutality, such as the assault on Mauricio, who "was attacked by a band of *capoeiras,* who fell upon him with clubs, striking him in the forehead, and gashing his thigh."[208] One police chief likened them to "the bloody sect of those who worship Siva, or the homicidal Druses," referring to the Indian Thuggee sect.[209] Another police report suggested that *capoeiras* attacked people for pure pleasure: "One of the crimes most common in this city, at least during the first three months of my administration, is murder and wounding that are more or less grave. It is singular that neither vengeance nor the desire to rob gives them cause. It is the joy of seeing blood run, or to use the term employed by this type of criminal, the desire to 'test their steel,' which raises them to the perpetration of such grave attempts, . . . the authors of these are known by the vulgar term of *capoeiras.* In only one afternoon of the month of February they committed seven murders in the parish . . . of Santa Anna."[210]

Capoeiras seem to have most often directed their attacks at each other in their battles to control certain areas of the city. However, according to police sources, their violence was also directed toward the general populace, particularly when they decided to shut down popular processions through terror tactics: "one could hear, along with screams of ladies fleeing in terror, of black women carrying the young master in their arms, of fathers seeking refuge for their wife and children, the horrendous 'shut down, shut down!' The *caxingueles* flew at the front, *capoeiragem* exploded without restraint, and the mayhem resulted in broken heads, shattered light posts, stabbings and deaths."[211] Because the victims of these *capoeiras* were often other blacks, these attacks cannot be conceived of as simple resistance directed at their oppressors.[212]

While *capoeiras* certainly engaged in some random violence, it is doubtful that most of their attacks are best understood as simple violence for the love of bloodletting. If this were the case, then the masses of Rio's bonded community would have lived in fear of them since they were as often as not their targets.[213] *Capoeiras* were well known in the city. For example, José Maria de Conceição placed an ad in the *Diario do Rio de Janeiro* calling for the return of his bondsman, Felippe, whom he described as "very well known by pedestrians" for "being a *capoeira*."[214] The worldview of police chiefs probably blinded them to the possibility that instead of being simply feared, *capoeiras* may also have been seen as men of distinction and possibly defenders of the community. While police and some elites wanted to eliminate demonstrations of *jogos de capoeira* as a public menace, to their amazement these *jogos* "attracted the attention of the transients to the curiosities of the diorama, also called a competition of *capoeiras*, just as a moth is attracted to light."[215] Thus, the common people of the city did not run in fear of *capoeiras* during daylight performances but rather flocked to their exhibitions, suggesting that the *capoeiras* garnered some level of respect or admiration from the larger community regardless of the violence of which they were capable.

The best way to conceptualize the ritual violence of *capoeira* societies, then, is through the lens of reflexive honor.[216] *Capoeira* societies, while not overtly aimed at overthrowing the slave system (at least not in the first half of the nineteenth century), should be understood as an equally powerful and probably more viable form of social resistance in claiming reflexive honor and enacting constant defiance of white control.[217] *Capoeiras* were able to claim honor through their membership in and propriety over a collective, in their performative display, in their vengeance of impugned honor, and in their refusal to acknowledge white claims of superiority.

Belonging and Honorific Displays

Capoeiras were able to claim a certain degree of honor by their very membership in societies that provided them protection. Beyond the utility of such protection, this membership may have carried meanings associated with a free identity, at least to some of the Africans who demographically dominated the city in the 1800s. These Africans may have continued to valorize such bonds as they spoke to both conceptions and realities of liberty enjoyed in their natal societies. Suzanne Miers and Igor Kopytoff suggest that African notions of "freedom" were strongly related to belonging to larger social networks.[218] These were often lineages but other times initiation-based networks such as the Imbangala *kilombo*. For example, through kinship and initiation into adulthood in their respective communities, Kunene males could claim full membership in this body that was the fundamental provider of legal, social, political, and ritual protection. While notions of "property" were central to some Western conceptions of slavery, they were also central to African understandings of kinship functions. In addition to "belonging in" kin groups, African members "belonged to" these bodies and were counted as part of its wealth. As such, an African lineage group could transfer its rights in a given person to another lineage in times of need or to pay compensation for a homicide, while transfers of marriage partners between lineages were conducted in terms somewhat akin to sales. According to Miers and Kopytoff: "neither the criterion of property nor that of salability can be useful then, in separating 'slavery' from simple 'kinship' in African societies, in which rights in wives, children, and kin-groups members are usually acquired through transactions involving material transfers and in which kin groups 'own' and may dispose of their blood members in ways that Westerners consider appropriate to 'property.'"[219] Thus, if Miers and Kopytoff are correct, a "sale"-like transaction (for a nonslave), while undoubtedly difficult, did not by itself necessarily induce the same moral trauma as losing one's "freedom"; nor did imposed labor since the lineage could make constant labor demands on an individual. Rather, the loss of "freedom" for Africans was most associated with a loss of belonging in a collective.

In what Orlando Patterson terms "Western culture," freedom—as the autonomy of an individual from constraint by another—was elevated as a cultural value.[220] In African societies, however, "freedom" was found not in individual autonomy but in attachment to a kin group, to a patron, or to another medium of collective power: "Among the Suku of Zaire, a man who had quarreled with his lineage and set up his own compound with his wife and children in isolation in the countryside was compared to a *muhika,* the term for outsiders acquired by a lineage [roughly an African equivalent of a slave]. His condition, which to a Westerner represents the height of freedom and autonomy, was considered to be analogous to that of a *muhika* because he had ceased to belong in, and to, a group, and thus lacked the protection of those who really 'belonged.'"[221]

This cultural understanding of the concept of freedom should not be overstated since on the level of actual human experience Africans likely found the entire experience of enslavement horrific. Yet, among other fundamental traumas would have been their loss of power to protect themselves through membership in collectives. While it is unclear if any elements of this understanding of freedom were passed on to American-born bondsmen in Brazil, this legacy nonetheless may have influenced the coping strategies of many Africans who sought to establish self-protection via new social relations.[222]

From this perspective, *maltas* would have been attractive to young aspirants not only because of the dynamic movements of the *jogo de capoeira* and the perceived status of *capoeira* chiefs as potential role models, but also because of the protective membership offered by *capoeira* societies. Initiation into such societies mirrored some aspects of initiation rituals for boys throughout many parts of Africa, such as the *ekwendje,* which was central to Kunene identity and sense of belonging. Through their initiation in the corporate body of Rio's *maltas* some Africans might have felt a sense of regaining one element that was traumatically lost in their initial enslavement. Yet, for all *capoeiras,* the practical protection and sense of solidarity provided by the *maltas* undoubtedly reinforced their sense of honor.

The physical appearance of *capoeiras* in Rio was also an important aspect of their sense of honor. *Capoeiras* were recognizable by their muscular bodies, developed through years of training, and their fashionable wardrobes. Manuel Antônio de Almeida's *Memórias de um sargento de milícias* is a fictional account set in the late eighteenth century but may capture the style of contemporary *capoeiras* in the character of Chico-Juca: "Chico-Juca was a tall brown man, corpulent, with reddened eyes, long beard, cropped hair, he always dressed in a white jacket, pants very wide in the legs, black sandals, and a small white hat leaned far to the side."[223] In the nineteenth century the style continued in the same spirit but grew to include pointed boots, neck scarves, and broad-rimmed felt hats.[224] The shoes were especially important because they were considered markers of freedom.[225] Dressed in their distinctive style, *capoeiras* were known to parade down the streets with a distinctive rocking, dancelike strut.[226]

Also important to their personal display were demonstrations of their physical dexterity in the *jogo de capoeira.* These exhibitions occurred in the cities' plazas throughout the year but especially on Sundays and during public festivals. Émile Allain, a French visitor to Rio, noted of the *capoeiras* that "they are present at all popular festivities, engaged in a gymnastic performance or special dance, also called *capoeira.*"[217] These *jogos* were played to the sound of Angolan-derived drums, which *capoeiras* carried with them for these occasions. This put the drummers at risk since to be caught by the police with these drums was cause for imprisonment. This was the fate of João Angola, who was arrested at a "gathering of *capoeiras* holding a small drum."[228] Even more dynamic were the demonstrations of dexterity that *capoeiras* performed on church towers. Soares suggests that *capoeiras* rang the bells with their bodies, perhaps their acrobatic kicks.[229] Mello Moraes Filho notes that these "most excellent of gymnasts . . . left the passers-by and faith-full stupefied in the face of the acrobatics that they performed precariously on the bells."[230] Although such bravery could lead to tragic results, *capoeiras* performing their games of aerial dexterity for crowds below greatly enhanced their social prestige.[231]

Even in the streets, the *jogos de capoeira* became powerful political statements when made by *capoeiras* in front of Catholic processions or state-sponsored marching bands. Chvaicer has shown that these "were a means to glorify and exalt the authorities through the demonstration of power, force, beauty, and order."[232] By disrupting this order, *capoeiras* provided their own alternative claim to honor and authority. When they shut down processions violently rather than simply disrupting them, *capoeira* groups were making powerful statements about their control over the streets, thus denying that control to the dominant power structure.

The same skills of corporal dexterity used to entertain crowds also served to protect *capoeiras* from random acts of violence or kidnapping. James Henderson, who visited Brazil in the early nineteenth century, noted the potential for such abuse faced by *ganhadores:* "There are men who profess to be catchers of runaway Negroes, and frequently detain and ill use them when they are proceeding upon their employment, keep them confined during the night, conduct them home tied in ropes, and pretend to have detected them running away, for which they demand certain charges and a recompense. . . . It is painful to observe, that if a Negro is stopped, or forced away, or in any manner ill-treated, nobody takes his part or believes his story."[233]

In cases of kidnapping, illegal conscription, or numerous other situations of abuse, a bondsman would be left to defend himself.[234] An anonymous Englishman visiting Brazil in 1819 gives an eyewitness account of a case of *capoeiragem* being used to resist another random violent attack:

> A carriage was drawn up at the door of the house, and the coachman and lacquey were lounging against the stone posts on either side of the door. A Negro slave going along the street passed betwixt the house and the carriage. So good an opportunity of mortifying a poor half naked Negro was too good to let slip, and the coachman gave him a very severe cut with his whip over the bare shoulders, which raised a welt as thick as my finger. The poor creature writhed in pain, upon which the blow was repeated; and the footman then seized the whip, and amused himself in a similar manner.
>
> I could not help expressing my astonishment at the Negro's remaining there under such evident suffering, instead of attempting to escape . . . Blacky had however his reasons for thus appearing passive; he was watching his moment, and having found it, a flash of lightning was not more prompt than were his movements. With his head crouched low, he butted at the coachman's stomach, who having the wall immediately behind him

> was settled in the twinkling of an eye; then turning suddenly at the lacquey the Negro gave him with the sole of his feet a kick in the stomach with such force and dexterity that he stretched him lifeless. Leaving both his victims, he then took to his heels with the swiftness of a deer, to our no small satisfaction at seeing such gratuitous and unprovoked brutality receive its due reward.[235]

Thus, *capoeiras*' refusal to be subjected to such abuse and action of turning the dishonor of physical abuse back on white oppressors was a powerful declaration of honor.

Some *capoeiras* put such skills to use not only in defending themselves but also in defending wealthy patrons, and in this way they also contributed to their own honor. Other bondsmen associated with powerful individuals at times thought of themselves as sharing the prestige of their patrons. For example, in 1821, when a patrolman ordered a bondsman named José Congo to keep quiet on the street, José boldly responded that his *senhor* was an important businessman and so he could make whatever noise he wanted.[236] Hired *capoeiras* claimed even more honor from their connection to their patrons. Adolfo Morales Filho describes *capoeiras* as men who gained wages as hired muscle: "Crusaders that are tavern going, in charge of crimes and beatings, politicians' helpers, body-guards of high society gentlemen and guardians of the women who were very solicited by the 'Don Juans' of Rio."[237] These positions provided *capoeiras* with a form of income that at the same time increased their prestige. Such ties were highlighted by *capoeiras* such as the *pardo* Joaquim Inácio da Cunha, better known as "Corta-Orelha" (ear cutter), who became widely famous as the bodyguard of José Bonifácio.[238] From the African's perspective, entering into such patron-client relationships was another avenue of attachment to corporate power. *Capoeiras* employed as bodyguards and assassins were often protected from full legal recourse by the political influence of their patrons. While this latter task added to the infamy of *capoeira* among the elites, from the perspective of an enslaved *capoeira* this was an opportunity to gain the protection of an influential patron, to make money, and at times to vent their frustration by beating and even killing white people with some impunity, thus promoting their reputation as men of honor among the enslaved.

Gender Relations and Black Masculinity

Black *capoeiras*, like their North American counterparts, lived by a strict code of reflexive honor that was bolstered by prevalent conceptions of masculinity. All bonded males would have encountered obstacles in trying to establish themselves as men under the social conditions of bondage in Rio, and African-born bondsmen may have experienced crises in their sense of masculinity in unique ways. On the one hand, whites tried to impose a patriarchal system that socially imprisoned bondsmen in a perpetual state of childhood. This presented a fundamental social crisis for African men such as the Kunene, for whom initiation into manhood was the central foundation of their sense of identity and belonging to a society.[239] Another threat, particularly to Africans' sense of masculinity, was the disruption of African gender balances. In Africa it was quite common for some men to have multiple wives, and this was a testament to their manhood and material accomplishment. However, the gender demographics in Brazil were skewed such that males greatly outnumbered females, thus often reversing African gender practices. Women, if they did not have multiple husbands, certainly had multiple suitors in Brazil's bonded community.[240] This may have caused a crisis of enslaved men's sense of manhood, leading them to embrace honor systems to the point of displaying hypermasculinity.[241] Such reflexive honor systems likely helped to fuel bondsmen's engagement in various violent contests, including the *jogo de capoeira,* stick-fighting games, and the *jogo de cabeçadas,* for which José Benguela and Crispim Quissamã were arrested.[242] *Capoeiras,* in particular, were sensitive to the *point d'honneur,* and any looks, words, or actions that impugned their honor were settled with violent contests, which acted as equivalents to dueling among elite Europeans in the eighteenth and nineteenth centuries.[243]

From this perspective, even the brandishing of weapons by African *capoeiras* in some assaults and fights may reflect a perceived connection between weapons, masculinity, and honor. Similar to the relationship between sticks as weapons of honor and as male domination over cattle among the Kunene was the use of the blade in some regions of Greater Kabinda.[244] Herbert Ward observed that in a Kongo ethnic group, being respected as a man required one to walk armed with a knife. An "unarmed man" was "treated with contempt" and told "to 'go and rear children.'"[245] While recourse to the stick was a Kunene man's primary response to a challenge to his reputation, knife fighting was the corresponding ritual weapon of vengeance in at least some parts of this equatorial region.[246] Analogous to the slapping of the face among Europeans, if a man from one of these northern Angolan societies was met with what he perceived to be a lack of proper respect, shown to him through word or action, masculine social discourse dictated that he respond. Although verbal sparring often preceded actual battle, a knife fight would inevitably follow. Regardless of the outcome of the resulting melee, by entering into combat the disrespected man restored or at least retained his honor.[247] Although violent, the ritual followed a tight script in which the combatants did not seek to kill each other but rather to shame the other with cuts, ideally to the face.[248] They "dueled over honor with knives inflicting 'dreadful gashes in the flesh,' such that the contest would end by 'one [combatant] generally falling from loss of blood or being disabled.' However, as intense as the battles might be, they carefully avoided 'dealing a mortal wound.'"[249]

The numerous cases of light wounding with blades reported in the Brazil police records suggest that African *capoeiras* may have drawn from a similar sense of honor.[250] Africans in particular were arrested in much larger numbers for woundings rather than murders.[251] Domingos Soares Calçada, a Brazilian-born black, appears to have been working under such understanding when he approached the bakery of Manuel Rodrigues dos Santos. He was followed by a group of young *caxingueles*, who began to provoke the employees. When dos Santos attempted to chase the youths away with a stick, Domingos cut him once with a *navalha* and then announced, "*este está pronto*" (this one is finished).[252] In some cases, then, it is likely that rather than trying to kill their victims, *capoeiras* went only as far as drawing blood to satisfy their impugned honor.

Similar ritual codes appear to have regulated conflicts between two groups of *capoeiras* that were settled in group battles or single combat. Some conflicts between societies were settled in general melees, but even these internecine conflicts seem to have followed a script. Filho notes that "the challenge between *capoeira* societies was announced by bell-rings in church towers."[253] Abreu describes their clashes as being preceded by a ritualized warning of lyrical dueling, with each society singing "in a country tune"; if taking advantage of musical bands during processions, *caxingueles* would advance, calling out the societies' slogans.[254] These battles were also marked by the ritual use of ribbons.

In other cases over contested respect between societies, the larger umbrella organization linking local *capoeira* societies would intervene, and such conflicts would be settled through ritual dueling between their respective chiefs: "If the bosses decided that a question was to be resolved in singular combat, while the two representatives of the red and white colors fought each other, the two societies maintained their distance and whatever the result, both sides broke out in praise of the winner."[255] The fact that both sides could cheer the outcome again highlights the fact that through the very act of showing bravery in single combat the two society leaders retained the honor of their respective societies.

Given the gender imbalances, a *capoeira*'s personal honor was likely extended to defending romantic interests from potential rivals. Studies of the honor systems of pastoral African males have shown that, relative to European honor systems, they were not focused on control over female sexuality.[256] However, with the crisis of masculinity implicit in enslavement in Brazil, African bondsmen and their descendants appear to have been concerned with securing their position with their female partners.[257] Much of the violence associated with *capoeiras* was linked to the subculture's establishment of honor and related notions of masculinity as being gauged not by responsibility but by sensitivity to insult, ability to fight, and coolness in the face of danger. With this strict sense of reflexive honor in place, any rival knew that to approach a female linked to a *capoeira* was to risk violent vengeance. Fighting over women and defending women were mentioned as the causes of numerous skirmishes.[258] Manuel Antonio used his position as the leader of a patrol to confront and slap the *senhor* of a bondswoman of whom he was fond.[259] At the same time, it is important to note that though *capoeiragem* was overwhelmingly a male practice, it was not exclusively so. Women more often pursued the achievement of status and some semblance of power under slavery through control over religious ceremonies or economic activities than through *capoeiragem*.[260] Yet, women also turned to violence in staking their claim over males, and some engaged specifically in *capoeiragem*.[261] In 1814 Paula Angola was arrested along with Paulo Congo and Jose Angola, "all three for *capoeira*."[262] Such women were awarded their place in the culture of honor. This was the case for Isabel and Ana, who demonstrated in a street fight before their arrest that "they were experts in *capoeiragem*. The citizens of the 10th district know them and were the first to say they deserve the title of courage."[263]

Organized Attack on White Supremacy

Not only did the *capoeiras* defend their own personal honor, but they also acted in many ways like African paramilitary societies that punished infractions against transgressors. Itier appears to be referring to them when he reports of closed societies among bondsmen linked with unsolved murders, which were "often led by free blacks, whose purpose was the protection of the slaves."[264] Melo Moraes Filho notes that many acts of vengeance, rather than being randomly improvised brutality, were predetermined at secret meetings in which groups of *capoeira* societies would decide how to punish transgressions against protected individuals. In the second half of the nineteenth century, for example, a coffee boom in the interior led to the relocation of numerous bondsmen from Rio into these rural plantations. However, if a bondsman who was protected by a malta was sold out of the city, the maltas would unite to avenge him. "When the circumstances demanded common revenge, they [*malta* leaders] disregarded questions of parish or neighborhood; for example, a master selling a slave affiliated with any *malta* to the plantations because of *capoeira*, they met and designated who would revenge him."[265]

Thus, if it had been decided at one of these clandestine meetings that a given person—enslaved African, free person of color, or white—had broken their codes, the *capoeiras* would then decide who would carry out the act of vengeance. Unlike cases of impugned personal honor, these individual transgressors might suffer at the hands of a complete stranger. This anonymity of communal justice was in keeping with African conceptions of retribution in which malefactors were punished by anonymous agents of the closed societies that enforced communal codes.[266] These acts of vengeance were often carried out at public festivals such as large Catholic processions or the *entrudo*, the precursor to the Brazilian Carnival. The large crowds at these public gatherings provided anonymity for the avenging *capoeira* and an easy escape from authorities. Thus, despite the fact that many *capoeira* victims were other bondsmen, and that the anonymity of the agents of justice may have made such strikes appear as random violence, the bonded community may have respected the role of the *capoeiras* in enforcing communal codes. Because *maltas* took it upon themselves to punish even whites, it seems that *capoeiras* did not internalize an automatic deference to landed whites. This conflict with racial and class structures was perhaps most apparent in the first half of the century before *maltas* were integrated into the political system of the city.

While available data do not indicate how the growing numbers of free people of color and white *capoeiras* in the later half of the century conceptualized their relationship to "whiteness" or the Brazilian power structure, it is clear that in the first half of the century the honor of bonded *capoeiras* was additionally connected to their defiance of racial hierarchies.[267] For this reason, many bondsmen may have looked up to the *capoeiras* as symbols of pride in relationship to their common oppressors. *Capoeiras* in Rio exhibited this pride through their brandishing of weapons, through their defiant words, and in their intimidation of white citizens. The use of knives by *capoeiras* was in direct defiance to being relegated to a lower status since the law allowed only white Brazilians to carry knives and other weapons.[268] Few European immigrants were brought in for this crime, although Portuguese often wore knives and dueled with them as badges of honor in Rio.[269] Thus, in their possession and frequent brandishing of knives the *capoeiras* of color were defying white pretensions to a monopoly on honor.

Capoeiras also denied white supremacy through their words and actions during the first half of the nineteenth century.[270] When the enslaved *capoeira* Graciano was arrested in 1836, police noted that he brazenly declared to his captors "various times that he was bent on taking away the boldness of whites."[271] Through such challenges and threats *capoeiras* verbally brought whites down from their pedestal of superiority and claimed the streets as their social space in which they were the masters. They physically enacted this mastery over the streets through their intimidation of the white citizenry. Well-known *capoeiras* could profit from their infamy, as depicted in the character of Chica-Juca, who gained a reputation as a hired tough who would avenge any imagined insults with violence. From "this he profited; there were no tavern owners that wouldn't extend him credit and didn't treat him well."[272] *Capoeiras* whose reputations were not enough to intimidate whites often turned to direct threats to frighten whites into subordination. Paulinho dos Santos went into a tavern, after receiving his drink got into a dispute, likely over his bill, and was arrested for threatening to head butt the owner. He was released from prison a month later and returned to the tavern, where he fulfilled his threat.[273] A more dramatic encounter occurred later in the century when "a group of more than 15 armed *capoeiras* attacked a tavern on Visconde de Sapucai Street, and beat the owner."[274]

Capoeiras went so far as to look down on and attack the very agents of white domination, the police and soldiers. They routinely resisted arrest. When the Bahian soldier José Raimundo de Souza attempted to arrest Celestino, "author of a great conflict on that street," he instead received a head butt that "caused his death almost instantly."[275] *Capoeiras* derogatorily referred to police as "morcegos" (bats), as in the case of João Benguela, who "entered into conflict with a patrol of the Guarda Real de Polica, calling them 'morcegos' besides other insults."[276] Similarly, Antonio de Vera Cruz, holding a folding blade, approached a patrolman calling him "morcego" and other "indecent words."[277] Although in this case he was arrested, his bold initiation of the conflict reflected a complete disrespect for the supposed superior status of the police.[278] In another case, an Angolan *capoeira* attempted to rob a soldier after attacking him with his devastating head butts.[279] Similarly, Luciano approached "a soldier standing guard at the General Headquarters, provoked him with insults and attacked him with head butts."[280]

Even entire patrols were not immune from attack, as when a *capoeira* society assaulted a body of soldiers of the Corpo de Permanentes. These *capoeiras*, "armed with knives[,] intended to take by the power of force from the jail guards" one of their arrested comrades.[281] Roberto Jorge Haddock Lobo, the police *subdelegado* of Engenho Velho parish, complained that when given only four military police to assist him in his patrol, he was "[w]ithout the force to make [himself] respected"; that is, despite his position as a white *senhor* and a *subdelegado*, without a vastly superior force of arms he could not expect the deference or submission of the blacks he sought to regulate.[282] One patrol had to struggle to arrest Bernardo Mina and Estanislau Crioulo, two *capoeiras* who resisted arrest with blows. After successfully arresting them, the patrol was surrounded by a *capoeira* society "that rained stones down on the aggressors."[283]

The municipal guard, which had an income requirement and was thus composed exclusively of men of status, was also a prime target for *capoeira* attacks. Although it is not clear what caused them to take action against the municipal guard patrol, particularly their chief, an attack on July 26, 1831, was clearly an example of a planned act of vengeance on the part of *capoeira* societies. The following day the justice of the peace of São José parish reported: "Last night a patrol of municipal guards brought before me two blacks and one mulatto.

The guards reported that the prisoners belonged to the two groups into which the blacks and mulattos divided themselves, numbering more than 200, to attack the civilian guards by throwing stones, which in fact they did, wounding the chief of the patrol on the head. This took place about seven in the evening, and the action showed coordination and premeditation, because one of the groups divided, the two parts going in opposite directions."[284] The following day the *capoeiras* again hurled both insults and stones at the municipal guard patrol and injured the patrol leader, suggesting that he may have been their primary target.

In these and numerous other assaults, *capoeiras* made powerful statements of their honor. Aniceto Borges single-handedly attacked a patrol "in reprisal for the arrest of two bondsmen by the same patrol."[285] Joaquim Benguela had the audacity to walk into police headquarters wearing his *capoeira* hat, presumably as a bold statement of his disregard for the police.[286] Among the most revealing of such attacks was the case of Manuel Pardo. On July 4, 1812, Manuel approached police headquarters and entered the building. In addition to verbally deriding his victims, he assaulted a police officer and a clerk with a whip, the very symbol of white domination over bondsmen.[287] Such attacks were symbolic slaps in the face of white patriarchal control of the society. In showing disrespect and intentionally challenging the very agents of the white coercive power that maintained the slave system, these verbal and physical assaults shattered the facade of white supremacy.

The practices of *capoeiras,* then, proved to be formidable means of claiming honor, and for bondsmen they were potential ways to resist the suppressive violence that underpinned the system. *Capoeiras* proclaimed their honor through initiation into a collective body, through their personal displays of regalia and agility, through their refusal to suffer the dishonor of random violence, through the enacting of vengeance against those who impugned their personal honor or collective codes, and at times through directly confronting the agents of state control. While free people of color and whites became initiated in the second half of the nineteenth century, the enslaved would remain the most powerful symbols of the pride manifested by *capoeiragem* as, even under the legal condition of slavery, they defied white supremacy and walked the streets with panache and pride.

The unique Central African martial art that utilized inverted kicks to ritually cross the *kalunga* was continued in Brazil by enslaved Africans and their descendants. Although they faced the painful consequences of whippings, imprisonment, and forced labor, it is clear that the life of a *capoeira* remained an attractive alternative to many African arrivals to the city and their progeny. As one journalist complained, "[t]here is no way to eliminate the *capoeiras*. As the number of those who go to jail increases, the number of those who are left outside to create work for the police also increases."[288] Young initiates were drawn by the dynamic movements and also by the prospect of joining a collective body that could offer the power of protection and would give them a sense of belonging and honor. Thus, *capoeira* societies, structurally reminiscent of African paramilitary societies, proved to be among the most indomitable and longest-lasting forms of empowerment exercised by bondsmen in Rio. This weapon was not aimed directly at toppling the slave system through force of arms but rather at claiming the dignity of honor within the social structure. There is little evidence of bonded *capoeiras* trying to escape the city, which suggests that their claim to honor and hard-fought battles to establish dominance over their social space prevented them from fleeing to *quilombos*. The example of Adão in the late eighteenth century highlights this. Although his master assumed that he had run away to a *quilombo,* in fact Adão had chosen to stay and live a life of urban maroonage as a *capoeira* on the streets of Rio.[289]

In their defiance of white authority through their mastery of the martial art of physical inversions, the *capoeiras* at times inverted the usual relationship of whites' domination over blacks in slavery. In their ongoing conflicts with state forces over control of the streets, *capoeiras* shattered the notion that Rio's bondsmen were willing to passively accept social and physical domination by whites. In their own societies Africans enslaved in Brazil often retained positions of authority over Brazilian-born blacks, *pardos,* and whites, thus completely inverting the racial hierarchy of the dominant society. While whites in the city frequently lived off their bondsmen's labor in a parasitic relationship, *capoeiras* at times lived off the wealth and labor of white tavern owners and shopkeepers whom they threatened into subordination. While most bondsmen in the Americas lived in fear of the random acts of brutality that perpetuated the slave system, *capoeiras* caused whites, even those in the Rio police force, to live under the constant fear of violence at their hands. Although this was a constant preoccupation, fear reached crisis proportions at various times, such as in the wake of the assassination of Jacinto José dos Reis in 1831 and the 1834 assassination of Joaquim Antonio Alves.[290] Jacques Arago, who visited Rio in 1818, describes the case of a bonded assassin who was sentenced to deportation to Angola.[291] Although not routine, this sentence was not uncommon.[292] While transfer to Angola was rife with new dangers, that such a sentence was carried out raises the remarkable possibility that through their mastery of this art of inversions some *capoeiras* in Brazil may have even managed to invert their physical passage across the Atlantic *kalunga.*[293]

Conclusion

Embodied Traditions

People brought to the Americas from the region of Angola understood passage across the Atlantic *kalunga* to be both a transformative process and a linking of two fundamentally connected worlds. This combination of change and continuity can be seen in the techniques of the *engolo* of southern Angola, which crossed the Atlantic and were used to meet the needs of bondsmen and contributed to a shared cultural tradition in many parts of the Atlantic world. This cultural influence did not travel only toward the Americas. The voyages of sailors and travelers back across the Atlantic *kalunga* may have taken elements of these combat traditions to Europe as well.

Maritime Connections

While previous chapters have addressed martial arts in separate regions of the Americas, the Atlantic *kalunga* that carried African captives to these places also offered the potential of further movement throughout the Atlantic world.[1] Therefore, we must consider these connections as routes for the further spread and interaction of martial arts traditions. This movement was perhaps most prevalent in the lives of Africans taken to the Caribbean. While a significant number of Africans died before leaving the sugar plantations to which they were confined, other Africans and their descendants involved in various maritime trades circulated widely throughout and beyond the region in numerous migrations that marked the Caribbean experience. The political alignment of Caribbean colonies shifted constantly, particularly during the French and British acquisition of Spanish-controlled islands in the seventeenth century, the Seven Years' War, the American Revolutionary War, and the French Revolution and Napoleonic Wars. In the Lesser Antilles, St. Lucia provided an extreme example of these conflicts as it was first colonized by the French and changed hands more than a dozen times before being annexed by the British in 1814.

Significant populations of Europeans relocated, with their enslaved Africans, as a result of some of these political shifts. Maroon groups crisscrossed the maritime routes that connected these individual islands into a larger social system.[2] In the eighteenth century maritime maroons often left the French Lesser Antilles for the perceived sanctuary of Trinidad and Puerto Rico.[3] These maritime movements likely played a role in the further dissemination of martial arts traditions. For example, the stick-fighting art called *kalenda* undoubtedly spread from the French Caribbean islands to Trinidad and New Orleans with the migration of enslaved peoples.[4] While such movements of people and cultural practices were more pervasive in the region, they were not limited to the Circum-Caribbean. Individuals also circulated widely in the various maritime-related trades that thrived in the coastal cities of the Americas. These included the lowcountry's Charles Town (now Charleston) and Savannah, Brazil's Salvador and Rio de Janeiro, Martinique's St. Pierre and Forte Royal (now Fort-de-France), Saint Domingue's Cap Français and Port au Prince, Jamaica's Port Royal and Kingston, Trinidad's Port of Spain, and Cuba's Havana. The port cities of the Americas required naval ships for defense and merchant ships to carry their goods abroad and bring in essential supplies from the metropole and other American ports.[5] These particular ocean voyages were intertwined with a more complex nexus of movement and sociocultural networks as smaller coastal and riverine vessels connected outlying areas with the ports. For instance, fishermen brought their produce to market, pilot boats guided incoming merchantmen to safe anchorages, open vessels ferried passengers and cargo from port to port, and itinerant black traders brought rural produce grown by bondsmen to trade with sailors and smugglers.[6]

On the eastern shores of the Atlantic, port cities such as Lisbon, Paris, Marseille, Nantes, Liverpool, London, Antwerp, and others provided their surrounding regions and hinterlands not only with trade goods but also with ideas and news from abroad. Similarly African ports such as Old Calabar were places where Africans from the interior and Europeans were incorporated into the sociocultural world of coastal communities. Some Europeans joined African closed societies such as *ekpe* in order to engage in trade.[7] These types of interactions highlight the fact that, in addition to goods and peoples, cultural practices and ideas were exchanged in the dynamic life of coastal cites and on the ships that connected them.[8] Thus, it is worthwhile to speculate briefly about the maritime world as a site for cultural interaction between the fighting systems of Africa and those of Europe and the Americas.

White sailors had frequent contact with Africans and their descendants in the Atlantic world. Seaman might wait for weeks or months on land for the holds of their ships to be filled with cargo for the return trip. Some waited longer to join the crews of other vessels, while others chose to remain on land indefinitely. In American ports sailors were present in large numbers. In the eighteenth century the population of sailors in Cap Français often outnumbered the populations of both the local whites and free people of color.[9] During the daytime sailors interacted with bonded stevedores, dockworkers, and porters. Many seamen traded their personal goods with black hucksters, who controlled the black-market economy of many port cities.[10] At night sailors interacted with blacks in boardinghouses, taverns, and areas of prostitution. Despite prohibitions, officials complained that seamen spent their time in "cabarets, in dark gambling houses, or among the slaves," and one observer in Cap Français in the 1770s counted more than fifteen hundred cabarets, rum shops, and gambling houses that catered to seafarers and urban blacks.[11] Such interactions between sailors and people of African descent were common throughout the Atlantic world.[12]

Given their shared social space with people of African descent, sailors were often exposed to African combat traditions. During their stays along the African coast, sailors often saw combat arts showcased, particularly those who united with Africans in acts of militancy or deserted to live with them.[13] As the governor of Cape Coast Castle complained in 1751, "White men are gone & daily going to live among the Negroes."[14] In the Caribbean sailors sought out bondsmen's gatherings to observe the dances and martial games exhibited there. In Trinidad and Brazil sailors of all ethnic backgrounds frequented many of the same taverns, restaurants, and brothels as did Trinidadian stick-fighting kings or Rio's *capoeiras*. Sailors often gained the reputation of being disorderly due to their engagements in street conflicts. Many white sailors may have gained experience of African combat traditions in street fights against people of color or as members of the working-class audiences who flocked to foot fights and other combative exhibitions.

Sailors may have gotten private viewings as black dockworkers in Martinique and Brazil's port areas were well known for entertaining themselves with *danmyé/ladja* and *jogo de capoeira* matches, respectively.[15] The wharves of Salvador, Brazil, and especially the Golden Warf (Cais do Ouro) were especially known to harbor *capoeiras*. Although detailed descriptions here are from the late nineteenth and early twentieth centuries, this zone that housed a high concentration of black day laborers had long been a site of conflict for bondsmen with each other and with the police. One *capoeira* who worked as a stevedore was famous on the wharves for his use of the *rabo de arraia* kick to knock police over and escape while they were down.[16] Antônio Vianna describes another fighter, who when caught by a police officer, knocked him and the rest of his patrol into the water with his head butts.[17] In Rio police reports from the early nineteenth century complained of "insults by blacks and capoeiragems" on Saco do Alferes beach, a well-known meeting place for sailors and fishermen.[18] Sailors and *capoeiras* also shared social space on the Cobra Island, which housed the naval armory where some ships were repaired and enslaved *capoeiras* and delinquent sailors were sent for forced labor. Away from these port areas, sailors were known to frequent Rio's *zungu* houses, and some were discovered in inland *quilombos*.[19]

White sailors also gained exposure to African fighting traditions while living at sea in close quarters with their black workmates. Blacks were present in large numbers as sailors on ships that linked the economic systems of the Atlantic world. Ship crews were often decimated by rampant disease and desertion when they reached Africa or the Caribbean.[20] African sailors called *grumetas* joined ships on the African coast, while in the Americas large numbers of free and bonded men of African heritage turned to sailing.[21] During wartimes seamen were conscripted by press gangs, and even during times of peace captains needing crews were not disposed to be overly concerned about the race or legal status of black potential crewmen with maritime experience. Aware of this, bondsmen often presented themselves as freemen willing to work on ships in a form of maroonage in the Caribbean.[22]

Sailing was in some ways a contemptible occupation for whites, who at times considered it close to slavery as it was characterized by forced conscriptions, cramped living quarters, low pay, and the power of captains to trade crew members to other ships against their will and discipline them with floggings. For men of African descent, however, sailing was one of the few social arenas in the Americas where people of color could compete as equals in terms of pay. Ships had their own subculture with a hierarchy of "boys," or ordinary seamen; "men," or able seamen; mates; pilots; and captains. As pay was by rank, an able black seaman received the same wages as a white of equal rank. For blacks the dangers of life at sea helped create a mutual respect with white colleagues that would have been exceedingly rare in plantation society. In addition, black sailors in the late eighteenth and nineteenth centuries seem to have dominated positions outside the hierarchy, such as those of steward, cook, and musician.[23] Olaudah Equiano, who began his maritime service as a steward, grew to act as a schooner captain on some occasions.[24] If this level of mobility was atypical, Equiano's ability to engage in petty trading to purchase his freedom was certainly common. Black sailors also participated in piracy in the Caribbean and along the coast of Africa. As pirates, many would enjoy better food, a more democratic sharing of wealth, and access to a common fund for those injured in the line of duty.[25] Such potentials drew many men of African descent from all regions of the Atlantic world to sailing in the eighteenth and nineteenth centuries. Around 18 percent of North American sailors were of African descent in 1802, while over 85 percent of the rank and file of Brazil's navy was composed of conscripted people of color.[26] As Jeffrey Bolster argues, these numerous seamen were culturally, economically, and politically influential in the black communities of the Americas.[27]

Sailors of African descent, enslaved or free, lived and fought in close proximity with sailors of European descent.[28] Therefore, they were exposed to European fighting styles such as English boxing. Equiano, for example, recalled that while he was on board the *Roebuck*, boxing matches were arranged to entertain some passengers of distinction: "[A]ll the boys were called on the quarter-deck, and were paired" by size, and after each match, "the gentlemen gave the combatants from five to nine shillings each." In this, his initial fight with a white youth, Equiano received his first bloody nose, which made Equiano fight "most desperately." The captain and company encouraged him in this pursuit, and he had "a great deal of this kind of sport" from then on.[29] Yet, such experiences were not indicative of the simple one-way "acculturation" assumed by many models of cultural interaction. Interestingly the tradition of English boxing often passed through African Americans to European Americans. The first seven American boxers to compete in England were blacks.[30] Black sailors confined to Dartmoor Prison during the War of 1812 ran a professional boxing school that taught white American sailors.[31] One former sailor, King Dick Crafus, continued to teach pugilism when he returned to Boston after the war.[32] If white sailors taught European combat techniques to blacks, the converse was also true; sailors of African descent maintained their own African combative traditions and introduced these to Europeans.

While some black and white sailors found a common ground in English-style boxing, the former also set themselves apart in the unique art of head butts, which appears to have been ubiquitous throughout the Americas.[33] Black sailors were well known by their white colleagues to have a separate combative culture.[34] On board the *Albert* a black steward in an altercation with one of the mates attempted to head butt his antagonist into submission.[35] William Butterworth, the sailor who sought out the performance rituals of Caribbean bondsmen, also took a keen interest in the head-butting ability of his ship's black cook.[36] Similarly, the black steward on board the *Ruthy* was "known as a champion of champions, having conquered a hero of his own colour by butting on all fours, like two rams, a mode of fighting common amongst blacks."[37] Thus, a unique fighting system was widespread among black sailors of the Americas, and many white sailors would have been quite familiar with Brazil's *jogo de capoeira* and Martinique's *danmyé/ladja*. This raises the question of the possible role of sailors, black and white, in spreading African-derived combat techniques to Europe.

Although this is yet to be confirmed by future research, it is possible that sailors who served in the Caribbean may have brought back to Marseille, France, kicking practices that became part of the martial art of *chausson Marseillaise*. This art was known for its high kicks, often "with a hand on the ground for balance."[38] As this French kicking art appears out of nowhere in the historical records, scholars have suggested that "it developed from contact with martial arts in the East."[39] Although there is not yet any written evidence to corroborate this hypothesis beyond the oblique evidence of kicking similarity, Jaques Komorn, the director of *la boxe française* in Guadeloupe, suggests that the *chausson*'s inverted kicks reflect the influence of the *wolo* kicks of *danmyé/ladja* in Martinique (or the infamous *rabo d'arraia* of the *jogo de capoeira*).[40] Given that such inverted kicks were much more prevalent in the African martial art traditions of the Americas than in Asian martial arts, and sailors' greater exposure to such arts in the Americas than in Asia, it would be at the very least equally plausible to consider that these inverted kicks were influenced by the African traditions of kicking.

If the *engolo* legacy's influence in Marseille remains speculative, its influence on the fighting style of Lisbon's rough *fadistas* is not. *Fado,* or in current slang *fadinho,* was a specific African Brazilian music and dance tradition derived from the *lundu* and other early black Atlantic music and dance forms.[41] Elements of these forms were brought to Lisbon by bondsmen returning from Brazil with their relocating *senhores* when the king moved his court back to the Portuguese mainland in 1821. Although the *lundu* and *fado* became popular dance forms among lower-class whites, José Ramos Tinhorão argues that the *fado* tradition was influenced by the variant dance forms of Africans and their descendants in Portugal. *Fado* had various modalities of dancing. One of them, called *fado batido,* was similar to Rio's *pernada,* a game in which one dancer used hip or leg attacks to try to knock down a rival who stood planted. Although it was a danced game, like the *jogo de capoeira,* the *fado batido* often ended in brawls. Such disorder led to an association between *fado* and members of Lisbon's lower classes, who enjoyed both the music and the conflict of the dance.[42] The connoisseurs of *fado* were known as *fadistas,* a term that came to imply either women involved in prostitution or men who were jobless, street-fighting, and disorderly.[43]

The danced forms of *fado* (*bailes do fado*) were later joined by predominantly sung forms of *fado.* Sailors were also significant players in both *fado* and the *fadista* street culture, as evidenced by the fact that the predominant "sung" form of *fado* before 1840 was *fado de marinheiro,* or "sailors' fado."[44] These sailors may have also played a role in bringing elements of the *jogo de capoeira* and *capoeiragem* to Lisbon. Certainly free *capoeiras* of European or African descent or even bondsmen returning from Brazil also could have introduced these fighting concepts to Lisbon. However, it is clear that sailors played a significant role in keeping Lisbon's communities of African descent in ongoing cultural and informational exchange with the latest trends in the communities of Luanda, Benguela, Cape Verde, Salvador, Recife, and Rio de Janeiro. A German traveler to Lisbon was struck by the number of people of African descent and commented, "there is a greater number here perhaps than in any other city of Europe, not excepting London," and that "[g]reat numbers of them are employed as sailors."[45]

These Portuguese mariners, black and white, occupied overlapping social spaces with *capoeiras* when they visited Brazil's ports. Like *capoeiras,* Portuguese sailors were known to be out at night frequenting taverns and brothels. Known for disorderly conduct, sailors were presumed to walk armed and ready to enter into street fights, often against *capoeiras*.[46] Attempts were made through a series of laws to curfew "sailors, nationals as well as foreigners, from walking on land at night, or face the penalty of eight days imprisonment."[47] Sailors were found in the presence of blacks on the beaches where bondsmen held their dances, in *zungu* houses, and even in *quilombos* in the interior.[48]

While naval officers came from elite families, the rank and file of Brazil's navy were filled by the forced conscription of the lowest members of society who were most vulnerable: vagrants, *capoeiras*, former bondsman, criminals, and other people of color without protection. Over 85 percent of sailors were of African descent.[49] Some of these sailors were *capoeiras*, such as Firmino, a sailor aboard the war schooner *Itaparica* who was arrested for "being with other blacks in *capoeiragem*."[50] Such tactics removed some *capoeiras*, who were considered socially dangerous or at least undesirable, from the city. An unintended consequence of such expulsions was that they allowed them to continue and carry their combative traditions to ports throughout the Atlantic world, particularly Lisbon.

This is not to suggest that the entire *jogo de capoeira* tradition was extended wholesale to Lisbon's *fadistas*. Lisbon street fighting was distinct as hand techniques were much more prevalent in the Portuguese combat arsenal.[51] Some of their leg attacks may have come from the fighting game of *fado batido*. Yet, an exchange of combative knowledge between *capoeiras* and *fadistas* was evidenced in their common slang and shared combat techniques. *Fadistas* utilized foot attacks like those of *capoeiras*, including the standing *cambapé* trip and dropping to the floor for a *rasteira* sweep (see appendix image 19). Beyond the fact that the use of such foot techniques appears to have been documented earlier among *capoeiras*, the shared term *ginga* directly confirms that the *fadistas* inherited some elements of their combat system from the *capoeiras*. *Ginga* was an Angolan term used in Brazil by *capoeiras* for the dancelike movement performed in front of an opponent in order to disguise one's attacks and stay prepared for acrobatic defenses.[52] *Fadistas* utilized the same Angolan term for the identical technique of "jumping in front of another person looking to hit the person."[53] Thus, it is clear that sailors and other migrants carried African diasporic fighting techniques with them throughout the greater Atlantic world, including to Europe, where they most clearly made a mark on the fighting system of the Portuguese *fadistas*.

African Combat Arts as Living Traditions

Because these arts spread throughout the Atlantic world, even to people with no biological connection to southern Angola, they are best understood as living traditions.[54] While it is not suggested that the African combat forms in the Americas continued as static replications of an unchanging martial art, these combat forms are extensions of a living tradition that adapts to new realities but does so in accordance with an enduring central paradigm. Jan Vansina outlines the properties of traditions in these terms: "Traditions are self-regulating processes. They consist of a changing, inherited, collective body of cognitive and physical representations shared by their members. The cognitive representations are the core. They inform the understanding of the physical world and develop innovations to give meaning to changing circumstances in the physical realm, and do so in terms of the guiding principles of the tradition."[55] In other words, traditions simultaneously embody continuity and change.[56] Traditions change in the face of new circumstances but may do so without compromising their continuity by adapting in ways that are harmonious with their fundamental principles. These properties accurately define the continuity and change in the martial arts of southern Angola and the diaspora.

In the Kunene region various unarmed combat systems were practiced. Youths performed slap boxing, but the more socially important variant was clearly *kandeka* stick fighting. At the core of unarmed combat of adult males were articulations of the head (in games imitating prized cattle) and the foot (in *engolo*). The latter was a tradition of foot fighting that can be examined as a living tradition emanating from core principles, one of which included an aesthetic appreciation for the use of inverted, circular, or push kicks. These kicks were not to be blocked, but avoided using low defensive positions, or defused by twisting or blending with the energy of the kick in any number of acrobatic movements emanating from a ready position of fluid swaying. Defense grew out of a danced ready position, and kicks were defended by dropping under them in low defensive positions, going over them with acrobatic maneuvers, or circling away with the energy of the kick (see appendix images 6, 8, 10, 12, 21). In close range, standing or low, circular foot sweeps were brought into play to fell an opponent.

Interactions within the Atlantic trade challenged the cognitive tradition of *engolo* first in Angola and then in the Americas. The trade brought many pugilists from the Kunene and neighboring regions to commercial entrepôts such as Benguela either as captives or as traders. Here, possibly for the first time, their cognitive assumptions about combat would have been in conflict with the physical reality they experienced as they became exposed to adepts of alternate combat traditions such as Chokwe wrestling or other African coastal grappling styles. A tension exists within traditions, and it is this tension that makes them dynamic and continually transforming. When the cognitive reality of the tradition becomes too far removed from the physical realities, then the tradition has to adjust. This adjustment might come in the form of adapting elements of an alternate tradition or developing innovations out of the cognitive core.[57] In the case of Martinique, although the data do not yet provide a conclusive reason why this occurred, it is clear that within the art of *ladja* the kicking legacy of *engolo* was combined with elements of alternate traditions.

The most prominent tradition incorporated was that of punches from the swinging-fist style of *kokoyé* boxing. However, the ritual practice of the style remained dominated by kicks in the early twentieth century.

Although the tradition was adapted in numerous ways in Brazil, the technical core of the *jogo de capoeira* remained close to the cognitive core of the *engolo* tradition. In more general melees, however, the use of weapons did present somewhat of a challenge to the centrality of the *jogo de capoeira* paradigm in street-fighting *capoeiragem*. The *jogo de capoeira* was a primary educational tool of the *caxinguele* initiates, who only later learned to train with combat movements using wooden and then metal blades. If the use of these and other skills integrated in these later stages of training and real brawls were outside the more specific tradition of *engolo*, they were certainly not far removed from principles of the wider Kunene tradition of applied combat. The historian Matthias Assunção argues correctly that by the late nineteenth century street-fighting *capoeiragem* "combined five complementary fighting techniques: head butts, foot kicks, open hand blows, knife and stick techniques"; however, Assunção erroneously concludes that "no source suggests that this kind of combination ever existed in Africa."[58] Quite to the contrary, this combination of techniques did indeed exist in Africa: in the bodies of numerous Kunene and Cimbebasian fighters, some of whom were brought to the Americas. Their primary dueling weapon was the stick, although stick techniques were adapted to knives in times of need. Their head butts were honed by contests imitating the battles of their cattle, their kicks through the dynamic *engolo*, and their open-hand slaps through *kandeka*. If these skills were ritually developed in separate training spheres, they were combined in the muscle memories of individual fighters during life and death conflicts.

If these culturally associated combat practices that coexisted with the *engolo*'s kicks for centuries did not provide new challenges to the kicking art's cognitive core, new physical realities of combat did emerge in Brazil in the form of the Portuguese staff and the folding blade. The sort of tension referred to above would have been experienced by *capoeiras* in their ongoing fights against Portuguese staff fighters. The arsenal of *capoeiragem* was predominantly shorter range, but in their rivalries with staff masters they countered a formidable long-range weapon. While this challenge certainly could have been met by adopting the staff, in this case the answer came from the existing tradition, with *capoeiras* staying safe through acrobatics until they saw openings to jump into close range to end the encounters with sweeps, kicks, or head butts. For more lethal encounters they developed a sharpened short stick rather than adding the staff or its techniques to their arsenal.

The *capoeira*'s street-fighting practices did incorporate the razor as an important weapon, but this process was not necessarily a "hybridization" marked by a wholesale integration of alternate traditions of razor fighting. Contrary to the

Figure C.6: A *lamparina,* by Calixto Cordeiro. *Revista Kosmos* 3 (March 1906)

model describing this art as the result of bricolage, mixing any and every martial input available, a longer historical view clearly reveals that instead the razor was integrated into the existing cognitive core informed by the kickboxing tradition of the *jogo de capoeira.* If an African or European with a background in razor fighting joined a *malta,* he undoubtedly would have continued to call upon that tradition in heated battle. The extent to which these razor-fighting traditions would have moved beyond individual fighters and been widely adopted into the tradition is another question. Details from nineteenth-century written sources are not sufficient to tell how the razor was actually used in combat. However, twentieth century blade usage clearly suggests that the technical use of the razor was an extension of the unarmed *jogo de capoiera* tradition.[59] According to Jair Moura, "The fight, with or without weapons, did not alter the form or the techniques."[60]

However, a slight discrepancy between the cognitive and physical realities may have remained in terms of the ascribed importance of the feet over the hands in ritual practice. This discrepancy was answered from the central core of the tradition. The razor, which was too important to drop from the arsenal, was instead grafted onto the core tradition in an even more harmonious way: the razor was held between the toes of the foot. This allowed *capoeiras* to maintain the added efficiency of the blade without sacrificing the feet as primary articulators of the tradition in the *jogo de capoeira.*[61] It is interesting to note that the creation of formal academies for the martial art in the 1930s effectively eliminated the use of the razor from the educational curriculum of trainees, and the art overwhelmingly reverted back to its ancestral, unarmed components of kickboxing with some use of the head.

Within the *jogo de capoeira* these precepts were the cognitive core of the tradition, which acted "as a touchstone for proposed innovations, whether from within or without."[62] These included judgments about the role of the feet in combat, aesthetics, and the use of acrobatics and dance as defense. If, on the contrary, the kicks of *engolo* were little more than one of many unrooted techniques to be sampled from a vast cultural buffet of martial bricolage created by the combat needs of bondsmen in Brazil, one would have expected to see the full integration of the techniques of Hausa or East African closed-fist punching, the deadly Senegambian joint-breaking techniques, or the combat-efficient techniques of the Nupe mixed martial arts. Practitioners of these and other African fighting styles were undoubtedly brought to the Americas from Hausaland, the Bight of Benin, Mozambique, and numerous other locations, yet such combat techniques were not integrated into the *jogo de capoeira*. Rather, the internal considerations of the *jogo de capoeira* precluded the systematic adoption of these other combat techniques. While some of these closed-fist or grappling techniques may have been called upon in street fights, they were not integrated into the logic, aesthetics, or ritual arsenal of the *jogo de capoeira.*

In Brazil the crystallization of the *engolo* kicking tradition into the *jogo de capoeira* took place in a relatively closed situation. The Portuguese had no prevalent unarmed form of fighting with which to hybridize the *jogo de capoeira*. Certainly other Africans brought rival African traditions, but none of these took hold over the long term, with the exception of the *semba*-like combat games such as *pernada,* which utilized leg sweeps and knockdowns, most of which were already part of the *engolo* tradition. The combative *semba* hip-bumping technique of this game may have been integrated into the *capoeiragem* of Rio.[63] The only other prevalent art was head butting. In Brazil these head butts constituted a separate ritual practice, as represented in the *jogo de cabeçadas*. Rugendas's description notwithstanding, head butting was by no means specifically linked to the *jogo de capoeira*. It was used by *capoeiras* and non-*capoeiras* alike and is thus best understood as part of the seemingly ubiquitous practice of head butting by people of African descent in the Americas. Although *capoeiras* used them frequently in real skirmishes, and possibly even ritual head-butting duels as per Rugendas's description, this did not represent a radical new cognitive reality since *engolo* masters had long been surrounded by Kunene head-butting games. Given their practicality, head butts became a prominent part of the street-fighting system of *capoeiragem*. At the same time, only a few butts remained in the regular ritual practice of the *jogo de capoeira,* and these did not alter the central position of foot attacks and acrobatic evasions of the art. In the mid-1930s the folklorist Edison Carneiro could note that within the *jogo de capoeira,* head-butts represented "not so much a technique as a recourse that served to keep at bay an opponent who is dangerously close."[64] Kicks, sweeps, and defensive agility remained solidly at the core of the art. New articulations of these leg and body movements were clearly developed by innovative individuals, but as Oliveira notes, these "creations" were always "faithful to the sacred precepts" of the *jogo de capoeira.*[65]

The kicking tradition existed in more heterogeneous conditions in North America than in Brazil. It was surrounded by other combat styles, including kicking a wrap, gouging, and collar-and-elbow wrestling. Even so, it appears that the fundamental paradigms of the Kunene people's unarmed martial arts remained unquestioned throughout most of the colonial and antebellum periods in North America as new needs were met through innovation rather than borrowing. As with the *jogo de capoeira,* the most prevalent techniques introduced into the system were "knocking" and "butting," which were married to the kicking art in name but often remained distinct approaches to unarmed combat, as they had with the Kunene people. In North America masters of the kicking tradition also practiced the more widespread games and ritual duels of head butting. In the ritual practice of drum circles, foot strikes and bodily acrobatics alone were highlighted. Yet, these distinct skills could be integrated, as in planter-inspired gladiatorial bouts or when practitioners were challenged by alternate traditions.

It is clear, then, that the Kunene unarmed martial art traditions of head butting and kickboxing were alive and well in the Atlantic world. While they often had to be adapted for unique challenges, these elaborations were usually in harmony with the fundamental paradigm of the tradition. Despite the alterations made to meet the specific conditions of each American community and countless innovations in style and technique by gifted adepts, these arts would have been fundamentally recognizable by adepts from different countries.[66] For example, knocking-and-kicking exponents would have felt equally at home in the circles of *danmyé* or *capoeira.* In fact, African Americans from North America had a long-term presence in the *capoeira* societies of Rio de Janeiro starting as early as 1812.[67] Head butting was even more ubiquitous and formed part of black culture across the Americas from New England to Rio de Janeiro. We can catch a glimpse of this familiarity in the narrative of William Butterworth. He recorded the encounter of his ship's cook, a knocking adept from Philadelphia named Tom Grace, with a similar art of "tupping" in the *bamboulas* of Guadeloupe. On witnessing the Guadeloupan ritual practice of head butting, Tom boasted: "'Now Darby, you will see me capsize one of these fellows in a crack!' 'You will crack your own head first,' said I, at the conceit of which Tom laughed pretty loudly. The person with whom our cook was to contend was a stout man, then master of the ring, elated with success. . . . As soon as they entered the circle, the jig tune commenced, and both began to dance: in which Tom, being unpracticed, appeared to great disadvantage. However, when the grand attack was made, he made good on his word, capsizing his antagonist with a vengeance, who fell, end over, and quietly withdrew, thereby acknowledging himself vanquished."[68]

This use of head butting to uphold one's honor in a duel was even adopted by some people of European descent in the Americas. In his novel *Warner Arundel: The Adventures of a Creole,* which is a composition of "a mixed nature of memoirs, a journal, an autobiography, and a collection of letters and essays," Edward Joseph describes a cotton planter on the Grenadine island of Bequia who forced his sole bondsman to fight with him.[69] The bondsman, who was at first reluctant to fight, eventually obeyed the planter's repeated commands to fight him after assurances by witnesses that they would testify that he was acting under orders if the matter went to court: "Fight they did, but not like men; they fought like enraged bulls. Each looked scowlingly at the other, and then walked back several paces, with their chins resting on their breasts; and then, at one and the same instant, both rushed forward encountering with a most violent shock. Dire and long was the conflict; the heads, knees, and unshod feet of the combatants were much used, but their hands very little; save when each tried to get hold of his opponent's ears; in order, as he expressed it, to 'butt his brains out!'"[70] This vivid description of head knocking, kicking, and butting highlights the familiarity of the author with these techniques and the potential for whites living in close proximity to bondsmen to adopt these techniques. Certainly some North American whites adopted African American head butting, Carribean whites learned the *kalenda* stick fight, and as we have seen, even white elites in Brazil became versed in the *jogo de capoeira.*

North American kicking was not the result of an ad hoc bricolage of numerous African combat traditions or of bondsmen creatively readapting elements of European combat traditions such as *gouging* or *jogo de pau.* Rather, kicking systems in this area were parallel derivations of the *engolo* tradition, just as the head butting with which they became associated also emerged out of African practices. It is important to note that Kunene foot fighting spread as a living tradition to places in the Americas, such as Virginia and Martinique, where Angolans in general were clearly represented in relatively small numbers. The fact that Central Africans did not numerically dominate in all these locations where Kunene pugilism continued clearly indicates that these arts were not the mere results of demographic clustering or of "retentions" or "survivals" doomed to disappear. Indeed, the *jogo de capoeira* underwent numerous adaptations, particularly in the early twentieth century, and is currently one of the fastest-growing martial arts in America and Europe. Accordingly these martial arts must be seen as living African traditions that have taken on unique indigenous forms in the Americas.

Embodying Honor

Bondsmen in the Americas utilized these living combat traditions in their struggle for reflexive honor even under the dehumanizing state of slavery.

Significantly their forbears across the *kalunga* in Africa had also utilized martial arts in search of honor. More than just forms of combat and recreation, the martial arts of *engolo, kandeka,* and *mgba* were expressions of deep-seated social values, and they were thus linked to the honor systems of their respective societies. The most honored members of Kunene communities were revered ancestors. The power of these forbears could be ritually called upon through circular kicks and physical inversions, a practice that helped inspire the unique martial art of *engolo*. This combat form served as entertainment and combat preparation. Yet, the highest respect was granted to those who mastered the art as a spiritual discipline by physically housing the force of a departed *engolo* master. The art of *kandeka* stick fighting was tied to the material source of community pride: cattle. Kunene males were expected to be able to dominate and defend their cattle from an early age. While in the pastures, boys earned the respect of their peers through their ability to fight bravely and dominate rivals in *kandeka* stick fighting. While community norms mandated that adult men learn self-restraint in daily life, a man's honor was never fully secure. Just as his prized cattle had to be vigilantly defended against raids, a man's claim to honor was also constantly at risk. Men had to be constantly prepared to defend their honor by resorting to stick duels to avenge insults or other affronts to their honor by peers.

In the Bight of Biafra, Igbos sought honor through individual achievement and the strict adherence to *omenani,* or proper custom. Because the spilling of blood could be an abomination against the Earth Mother, Igbos developed two distinct combative practices through which individuals could seek to achieve notoriety. The first was a grappling form, *mgba,* which was in many areas open to all members of society, female and male. One specific substyle focused on leg-wrapping techniques, but many other styles of *mgba* existed. All of them shared a "pacifist" approach to combat that sought to avoid bloodshed. *Mgba* played a crucial role in fertility rituals, life-cycle rites, conflict resolution, and distinguishing community aesthetics. Although *mgba* was used to establish honor rankings among individuals and communities, strict adherence to moral codes of conduct was necessary for a wrestler to attain the highest of all honors, becoming a transcendent hero. In contrast to this and other forms of "bloodless" combat in central Igboland, along Igbo frontiers in the north and west and among coastal Biafran groups a second combative tradition of "head-hunting" predominated. In times of peace the mastery of the machete to decapitate foes was taught to initiates of certain closed societies, and the most prestigious societies, such as *ekpe* and *ekpo,* required such a feat as a prerequisite for full initiation. When the ancestors sanctioned bloodshed, these lethal combat skills were called upon. During the widespread chaos that followed the spread of the Atlantic slave trade into the hinterland, young people from the borderland areas often traveled great distances in order to find an appropriate conflict to execute their skills and gain admittance to the honored class of warriors. Adepts of these were enslaved and forcibly relocated to the Americas, where these traditions continued to serve as potent tools in the quest for honor, albeit in radically new ways.

Because literate elites in the Americas overwhelmingly looked down on enslaved Africans as people without honor, many historians have overlooked the fact that even in the Americas these Africans and their descendants established honor communities among themselves. Orlando Patterson has pointed out that enslaved peoples everywhere experienced at least a generalized dishonor through the act of submission.[71] Ideally, bondsmen were understood by those above them as being without honor relative to their enslavers. European and European American elite males in the Americas often lived by a code of reflexive honor that was ritually displayed through duels. While they believed that they alone were honorable in their respective societies, poor whites also claimed honor within their honor communities. In Brazil poor Portuguese and their descendants reproduced similar patterns around knife fights. In the plantation and western frontier regions of North America poor whites defended their honor by engaging in gouging matches. Whether they won or lost, by virtue of putting their eyes, noses, and ears on the line in battle they proved their autonomy and status above those of enslaved Africans, who theoretically "could not jeopardize their value as property."[72] As we have seen, however, enslaved Africans and their progeny in turn also struggled among themselves to attain honor under the harshness of bondage.

Although many studies of bondsmen seek to establish the humanity of enslaved Africans by emphasizing their resistance to slavery, here we have taken a different view by focusing on their quest for honor. One of the greatest losses that Africans may have felt in their enslavement was attachment to a corporate body that could protect them. Thus, some Africans responded to their American bondage by seeking protection and attaching themselves to patrons or military units as gladiators, hired muscle, or soldiers. In the culture of coercion, gladiators faced the inherent dangers of the practice, particularly in the equivalent of Martinique's purported death matches. Yet, the role also brought the potential for elevated status to the position of driver and possibly even the honor of freedom. Many blacks gained their freedom via military service or were drawn into military service afterward. While black soldiers relied primarily on firearms when available, the martial arts skills of some could play celebrated roles. Such was the case of the bondsman Jack Sisson, who was immortalized in praise songs for his decisive use of head butting in the American Revolution, or the case of *capoeiras* who were popularly acknowledged for their role in the war against Paraguay. Zachary Molineaux's military service and fighting reputation allowed him to avoid charges of assault, and Rio's *capoeiras* gained some corporate protection against legal prosecution by joining the ranks of the national guard or working for private patrons as bodyguards and hired assassins.

Other Africans sought a very different form of protection against the harshness of slavery by joining closed societies in the Americas. Although legally powerless in the culture of coercion, these societies provided spiritual and physical protection, which was undoubtedly equally as important in the minds of enslaved Africans. While bondage threatened individuals with impoverishment, disease, physical beatings, and potential sale away from loved ones, these societies offered members some feeling of control over these dangers. Such groups often acted as mutual aid societies—for example, ensuring the financial resources to provide proper burial—and *maltas* offered alternative sources of income to its talented members through performances or employment by political elites.

Old Time Religion societies utilized knocking and kicking as a defense against random assault, and "tricking" power from across the *kalunga* provided an arsenal against disease and other misfortune. *Mayombe* societies in Saint Domingue promised participants spiritually enforced protection against witchcraft from within their communities and from the physical abuses of plantation owners. At times *capoeira* societies helped protect bondsmen from more subtle threats, such as concepts of white supremacy, while a few *maltas* inverted the domination by whites within their own societies when they had African chiefs leading local blacks, *pardos,* and even white members. More practically, members of *capoeira* societies were able to reestablish some power to protect themselves against sale out of Rio since *senhores* who dared sell a bondsman protected by a *malta* faced physical vengeance. A subtler, but no less important, danger that these societies protected against was alienation, which these collectives negated by providing members with a tangible sense of identity and belonging. Outside of these sodalities, bondsmen also endeavored to create a sense of community through their performance communities.

In their time away from the direct, controlling influence of whites, some bondsmen sought to establish themselves as separate honor communities, meeting most often during the evenings and on weekends and holidays. On rural plantations, these gatherings took place on the grounds or in secluded forests. Even in urban Brazil, where police forces patrolled constantly, bondsmen moved with relative ease through the city and found social spheres of their own, including *zungu* houses, church towers, and secluded beaches. In this culture of volition, martial arts could serve as informal entertainment for *ganhadores* awaiting customers or rice growers after a day's task was completed. More importantly, these arts served as community-affirming performances, as was the case with North American plays, urban *batuques,* and Caribbean *bamboulas.* Within these gatherings, different newly formed African nations often continued performance arts with distinctive variants while also affirming their participation in the wider bonded community through shared art forms, such as knocking and kicking, *danmyé, kalenda,* or the *jogo de capoeira.* Great performers could raise their status among the community, possibly leading to better chances in courting or attaining leadership positions. All who participated, whether as dancers, fighters, composers, drummers, or community choruses, established their group membership and respect. When such respected members died, these martial and other performance arts could be used to provide burial befitting a person of honor, thus helping spirits return to ancestral communities across the *kalunga.* These arts could also instill in their performers a sense of pride.

African men captured in war and who ended up suffering under racial slavery in the Americas did not necessarily forget their former sense of self-worth. Even for bondsmen born in the Americas, a profound sense of self-pride could result from the embodied inculcation of honor through combat mastery. In Africa the *engolo* and *mgba* had been used at times to connect living and past ancestral warriors. Even in the Americas, where this ritual understanding was forgotten, bonded people could forge a concept of themselves as proud fighters through the enactment of ritualized kicking or wrestling. Individuals' bodily experiences of enslavement affected their identities and worldviews at intimate levels, potentially making whippings as damaging on people's self-concept as they were on their physical bodies. Yet, African martial arts traditions could provide individuals with alternative models of identity that were independent of bondage. In this respect martial arts, like other forms of cultural performance, could help forge embodied identities distinct from those imposed by bondage. This role of martial arts as identity-altering instruments can be seen in the cases of Josiah Henson and Adão. Although Henson recalls that "[s]lavery did its best to make me wretched"—like other bondsmen, he witnessed his parents beaten and companions sold—his embodied identity as a champion wrestler and dancer prevailed in the formation of his self-concept. His physical virtuosity gained him the admiration of his community, and he "fully coincided in their opinion." He compared himself to Julius Caesar in his aspirations and described himself as a "black knight" in his valiant attempts to alleviate the sufferings of black women on the plantation. This bold identity, although originally cultivated in community performance contexts, extended to his service as the plantation owner's bodyguard. Perhaps most telling is the way he later described his repeated rescuing of this Maryland planter from brawls. He recalled that "in such affrays I carried it with a high hand, and would elbow my way among the whites[,] seize my master[,] and drag him out with the ease with which I would handle a bag of corn." Thus, despite the harshness of slavery, through his physical virtuosity as a wrestler Henson thought of himself not as a piece of property but as a black knight, a warrior who did for his master "what he could not do for himself." From his perspective, it was the master who was relegated to the status of a passive "bag of corn."[73] Similarly, in the case of Adão, the *jogo de capoeira* provided him with an alternative identity to the one imposed by slavery. Although he was "a robust type," he had always "been very obedient to his *senhor.*" However, when he began engaging in the practices of *capoeiras*, the "timid" Adão, who "before always lived humbly, became more self confident, independent," until he refused to return to his *senhor.*[74] Thus, while bondage imposed a generalized dishonor on people of African descent, individuals such as Henson and Adão established proud identities in part through their practice of martial arts.

As strong as this sense of inner pride could be, however, bonded communities had reflexive honor systems, meaning that social standing had to be validated by public opinion, which compelled men constantly and often physically to assert their standing among peers. This required men to be sensitive to the *point d'honneur,* and when they felt their honor impugned, they resorted to *code duello* through martial rituals, including wrestling, kicking, and head butting. Honor inhered in distinct subcommunities as well as in individuals. When the accusation of witchcraft was aimed at bondsmen of Father Labat's sugar plantation, they rose up en masse to uphold their group prestige in a drawn-out feud fought with sticks.[75] The victorious individuals or group thus socially established their claim over rivals. Yet, even the vanquished retained their sense of status and validated anew their claims to honor by boldly entering into such conflicts. Usually reflexive honor required a response through combat only when the affront came from a relative peer. That is, an elite man need not challenge a poor white or bondsman to a duel over what he perceived as a lack of respect since they were part of separate honor communities. At times, however, some bondsmen refused to be beaten by poor white overseers or wealthy planters without fighting.

The coercive power of the state was poised to punish any bondsmen who were not physically submissive to whites. Yet amazingly, some bondsmen still chose to defend themselves and fight back. In some cases the martial art skills developed in performance contexts and honed through dueling among bondsmen were turned against individuals as well as the coercive arms of the state. In the early stages of the Haitian Revolution, enslaved Africans and their progeny aimed their martial mastery with the stick and the machete at directly toppling the oppression of the slave regime. Unarmed fighting ability could also be used to seek honor in more subtle ways.

If a central feature of slavery was the loss of honor and its relation to the inability of bondsmen to defend themselves, as Patterson suggests, then the individuals who turned their fighting skills against their enslavers undercut the ideology of bondage and at the same time claimed honor. Julian Pitt-Rivers argues that "the claim to honor depends always in the last resort, upon the ability of the claimant to impose himself. Might is the basis of right to precedence, which goes to the man who is bold enough to enforce his claim, regardless of what may be thought of his merits."[76] Frederick Douglass, following his triumphant confrontation with Covey, echoes this sentiment, writing that "a man without force is without the essential dignity of humanity."[77] Thus, fighting ability under the right circumstances provided exceptional individuals with the force to demand dignity. Even the less fortunate who were killed in their attempts to defend their honor died fighting as proud women and men. Both they and the more successful claimed their bodies as their own. Those who resisted the dishonor of whippings disarmed their oppressors of the central means of physical discipline. Their resistance ideologically rejected their status as mere chattel objects and proclaimed their authority over their own bodies and their will above that that of their enslavers. As seen through the experience of Frederick Douglass, this could lead to a profound psychological empowerment and affirmation of their human dignity.[78] *Capoeiras* outwardly displayed a similar inner pride through their distinctive dress and bold rocking swagger. The people of Rio knew these signs to be loud proclamations by *capoeiras* that they were their own masters and would proudly defend such mastery with kicks, head butts, and blades. They boldly fought for control of the streets and offensively turned the fear of physical violence against white *senhores* and even their agents of domination, the police and national guards.

The legacy of African martial arts traditions in the Americas provided bondsmen with potent weapons for physical and ideological defense. These martial arts can be read as a logos of diasporic culture that was subjected to bondage but ultimately, in cultural terms, was not bound by it. Examining the history of fighting styles and their purposes in shifting demographic and political circumstances offers particular insight into modes of individual and group agency under bondage. However, understanding these combat techniques as a living African tradition is perhaps an equally important insight of this study since it reveals a process of cultural transference that would otherwise be overlooked. Indeed, the modern co-optation and reconfiguration of the *jogo de capoeira* as devoid of African content threaten to erase this history and deny the enduring strength of living African traditions in the diaspora. Regaining a sense of the historical continuities in African traditions—in this case literally embodied in fighting moves such as head butts and inverted kicks—assures that the honor fought for and hard-won in the state of bondage will not be lost in their historical legacy.

Appendix

Engolo Techniques

All images in the appendix were drawn by Albano Neves e Sousa in southern Angola in the 1950s. While this is a representative list of techniques utilized in the *engolo*, it is by no means exhaustive. There are numerous variants of many of these movements. All these images are copyrighted © 2007 by Maria Luisa Neves e Sousa and not to be reproduced without consent, and all are courtesy of Maria Luisa Neves e Sousa.

1. Lunge with hand on ground

2. Handstand

3. Headstand

4. Cartwheel

5. Circular kick

6. Low defensive squat

7. Circular kick

8. Spinning *away* from kick

9. Full-body kick from inverted position

10. Falling back defensively

11. Cartwheel kick (from inverted position)

12. Angling away from kick

13. Kicking from handstand with one leg (from inverted position)

14. Circular kick (from inverted body position)

15. Kicking from inverted position

16. Push kicks to the back (from inverted position)

17. Straight push kicks to front

18. Standing foot sweep

19. Sweep from defensive crouch

20. Circular kick with body supported by hands

21. Hip checking sweep

22. Lateral movements out of low defensive postures

Notes

Introduction

1. I am using the term "tradition" in the way that we speak of a Judeo-Christian tradition, not as a static unchanging practice.

2. Lydia Parish, *Slave Songs of the Georgia Sea Islands* (Hatboro, Pa.: Folklore Associates, 1965), 20. See also Patricia Jones-Jackson, *When Roots Die: Endangered Traditions on the Sea Islands* (Athens, Ga.: University of Georgia Press, 1987).

3. I had originally hoped to develop my analysis of the martial traditions in Congo and what was then Zaire in a separate chapter. However, my trip was interrupted after one month in Zaire by the heavy fighting between the forces of Laurent Kabila and Mobuto Sese Seko. After a harrowing experience of being trapped between these groups, I made my way across to Congo-Brazaville, but the cultural material was nowhere as rich as what I had encountered in Zaire, and again political turmoil eventually led me to conclude my fieldwork prematurely. In southern Angola, however, I was fortunate enough to time many of my multiple fieldwork trips between 1994 and 1998 during relatively moderate periods of the Angolan civil war, which flared up and dissipated in waves.

4. By this I mean kicks delivered from a position with the upper torso bending down, often with the hands assisting in supporting the body weight. See Appendix 1: Engolo Techniques (hereafter ET), nos. 9, 11, 13–16.

5. T. J. Desch-Obi, "Divining History: Historical Linguistics and African Divination in Historical Reconstruction," paper presented at the African Studies Association Conference, Washington, D.C., December 2002.

6. I am using the term "Angola" here in its wider conception denoting the area from north of the Ogooué River to south of the Kunene River, making it synonymous with West Central Africa here. Similarly the terms "Angolans" and "Central Africans" are used here to denote the Bantu-speaking population of this region, and the terms "Kongo" and "Kongolese" refer to all KiKongo-speaking peoples, rather than specifically to the kingdom of Kongo.

7. By Biafran here, I am referring to the Bight of Biafra and its hinterland.

8. The term "European" will be used to refer to European natives, and "European American" refers to American-born people of strictly European descent. The term "white" will be used to encompass both Europeans and European Americans. The term "African" will be used to denote African natives, and "African American" refers to people of African descent born anywhere in the Americas (as opposed to strictly North American). The terms "black" and "people of color" will be used here to denote both African-born and their descendants, including their progeny with some European ancestry.

9. Joseph C. Miller, *Way of Death: Merchant Capitalism and the Angolan Slave Trade, 1730–1830* (Madison: University of Wisconsin Press, 1988), 4–5.

10. Olaudah Equiano, *The Interesting Narrative of the Life of Olaudah Equiano,* ed. Robert Allison (Boston: Bedford Books of St. Martin's Press, 1995), 53–54. Despite recent questions about Equiano's exact place of birth, I will treat his descriptions as representative of Igbo experiences. See Vincent Carretta, "Olaudah Equiano or Gustavua Vassa? New Light on an Eighteen Century Question of Identity," *Slavery and Abolition* 20, no. 3 (1999), 96–104.

11. See, for example, Marquetta L. Goodwine, ed., *The Legacy of Ibo Landing: Gullah Roots of African American Culture* (Atlanta, Ga.: Clarity Press, 1998).

12. Ras Michael L. B. Brown, "Crossing Kalunga: West-Central Africans and Their Cultural Influence in the South Carolina–Georgia Lowcountry" (Ph.D. diss., University of Georgia, 2004), 263–77. In Brazil the term continues to be used in reference to spiritual forces linked to the sea and grave objects. Some Brazilians at times distinguished between the related *kalunga grande* ("the big sea") and *kalunga pequeno* (a cemetery, literally "the little realm of the dead"). See John T. Schneider, *Dictionary of African Borrowings in Brazilian Portuguese* (Hamburg: Buske, 1991), 82–84.

13. Elizabeth Fenn, "Honoring the Ancestors: Kongo-American Graves in the American South," *Southern Exposure* 13, no. 5 (1985): 42–47; Robert Farris Thompson, *Flash of the Spirit: African and Afro-American Art and Philosophy* (New York: Random House, 1983), 132–42.

14. These regions have received less attention than others by African historians as well. A. E. Afigbo notes that "it can be claimed with much cogency, that of all African ethnic nationalities of about their numeric size and general dynamism, the Igbo are the least studied"; see A. E. Afigbo, *Ropes of Sand: Studies in Igbo History and Culture* (Ibadan: Published for University Press in association with Oxford University Press, 1981), 2. An even stronger statement on the lack of scholarship dealing with Southern Angola could be made.

15. This trend is now beginning to be corrected in the recent work of Douglas Chambers.

16. Linda Marinda Heywood, ed., *Central Africans and Cultural Transformations in the American Diaspora* (Cambridge: Cambridge University Press, 2002).

17. Gerhard Kubik notes the presence of cultural forms and musical instruments in Brazil with origins from the southern region of Angola. See Gerhard Kubik, *Angolan Traits in Black Music, Games and Dances of Brazil: A Study of African Cultural Extensions Overseas* (Lisboa: Junta de Investigações Científicas do Ultramar, 1979).

18. I am intentionally focusing my attention on the martial art technologies themselves. Although at times they are as invisible in my citations as they have been to Western scholarship, I hope that it becomes clear through the text that the martial arts have been a central source for my analysis. Most of Western writing on African history has been based on the written records of upper-class Africans or the writings of Europeans visiting Africa, and I have used these wherever I could find references to martial arts. However, the movement of the body was the text of the common African. As John McCall has cogently argued, African history is danced. Africans wrote their beliefs and experiences into their dances, gestures, and movements. See John C. McCall, *Dancing Histories: Heuristic Ethnography with the Ohafia Igbo* (Ann Arbor: University of Michigan Press, 2000).

19. I am exploring the historical spread and indigenization of combat traditions that took on unique local forms in the Americas but will do so without using the problematic term "creole." The use of the term by anthropologists and historians has become increasingly imprecise and continues to be used in racialized ways. In addition to its more theoretical problems, the term is practically difficult to sever from its use in relation to local group identities in places as disparate as Louisiana, Cape Verde, and Mauritius. As Richard Price suggests, in the last two decades the term has "recently been appropriated and watered down, perhaps to the point of meaninglessness." Furthermore, the linguist Victor Manfredi has highlighted the fact that linguists have not been able to define or point to any specific distinctness of creole languages, and he has raised serious doubt about the theory of "creolization" and its inherent ties to racial ideology. Thus, while acknowledging the insights gained by "creolization"-inspired studies, this study will avoid the term beyond making reference to "French Creole" languages or engaging the literature. See Richard Price, "African Diaspora and Anthropology," paper presented to the "African Diaspora Studies and Disciplines Conference," Madison, Wis., March 23–26, 2006; and Victor Manfredi, "Philological Perspectives on the Southeastern Nigeria Diaspora," *Contours* 2, no. 2 (2004): 239–87; T. J. Desch-Obi, "Combat and Creolization," paper presented to the "Rethinking Boundries" Conference, New York University, February 9–10, 2007.

20. Douglas Brent Chambers, "'He Gwine Sing He Country': Africans, Afro-Virginians, and the Development of Slave Culture in Virginia, 1690–1810," Ph.D. diss., University of Virginia, 1996.

21. Saidiya V. Hartman, *Scenes of Subjection: Terror, Slavery, and Self Making in the 19th Century America* (New York: Oxford University Press, 1997), 11.

22. Elliott J. Gorn, "'Gouge and Bite, Pull Hair and Scratch': The Social Significance of Fighting in the Southern Backcountry," *American Historical Review* 90 (1985): 18.

23. *Kata* in this sense is often used to describe the prearranged sets of movements that must be performed by the student in exact imitation of the master. The literal meaning of *kata* is "to form in the sense of molding wet sand in a bucket to make sand castles." It should be pointed out, however, that beyond *kusanku/kanku-dai* and possibly *sanchin,* the antiquity of most contemporary Japanese *kata* known in the Americas may actually be less than a century old. See Fred Greitzer, "Ancient Training Methods or Mere Modern Creations? The Real History of Karate Kata," *Black Belt* 37 (February 1999): 128–33.

24. Michael Poliakoff, *Combat Sports in the Ancient World: Competition, Violence, and Culture* (New Haven, Conn.: Yale University Press, 1987), chap. 4.

25. Raymond Quevedo (Atilla the Hun), *Atilla's Kaiso: A Short History of Trinidad Calypso* (St. Augustine: University of the West Indies, 1983); Carsten Nieguhr, *Reisebeschreibung I* (Copenhagen, 1774), 169–70; and Scott T. Carroll, "Wrestling in Ancient Nubia," *Journal of Sport History* 15, no. 2 (1988): 121–37.

26. Jan Vansina, *Paths in the Rainforests: Toward a History of Political Tradition in Equatorial Africa* (Madison: University of Wisconsin Press, 1990).

27. This is not to suggest that the rhythms or lyrics that accompanied them in ritual practice were not also important aspects of arts. They certainly were, but that would be another study. Some scholars of Trinidadian cultural history have taken such an approach by tracing the songs of the stick-fighting *kalenda* and their continued

legacy in the later genre of *calypso*. A detailed analysis of the lyrics of the *jogo de capoeira* remains to be undertaken. In the meantime Gerhard Kubik has done a fine outline on the African inputs on the instrumentation, and Waldeloir Rego recorded a compilation of songs from the 1960s. See Jacob Delworth Elder, "Evolution of the Traditional Calypso of Trinidad and Tobago: A Socio-Historical Analysis of Song-Change" (Ph.D. diss., University of Pennsylvania, 1966); John Cowerly, *Carnival, Canboulay and Calypso Traditions in the Making* (Cambridge: Cambridge University Press, 1996); Raymond (Atilla Hun) Quevedo, *Atilla's Kaiso: A Short History of Trinidad Calypso,* (St. Augustine: University of the West Indies, 1983); Hollis "Chalkdust" Liverpool, *Rituals of Power and Rebellion: The Carnival Tradition in Trainidad and Tobago, 1763–1962* (Chicago: Research Associates School Times Publications, 2001); Gerhard Kubik, *Angolan Traits in Black Music, Games and Dances of Brazil* (Lisbon: Junta de Ivestigações Científicas do Ultramar, 1979); Waldeloir Rego, *Capoeira Angola Ensaio Sócio-Etnográfico* (Rio de Janeiro: Gráf. Lux, 1968).

28. The latter three terms relate to contemporary Korean and Japanese classification of combative practices. It should be noted that the use of these terms to distinguish between these different categories is relatively recent. For the historical context in which Japanese fighting skills were conceptualized in two competing approaches equivalent to combat sports and martial ways, see G. Cameron Hurst III, "Sports and Spirituality in Japanese Martial Arts," paper presented to Baruch College, May 9, 2002.

29. See, for example, Everett L. Wheeler, "*Hoplomachia* and Greek Dances in Arms," *Greek, Roman and Byzantine Studies* 23 (1982): 223–33.

30. For more on this, see William Hardy McNeill, *Keeping Together in Time: Dance and Drill in Human History* (Cambridge, Mass.: Harvard University Press, 1995).

31. United States Marines, *Close-Quarters Combat Manual* (Boulder, Colo.: Paladin Press, 1996); Ian Knight, *Brave Men's Blood: The Epic of the Zulu War, 1879* (London: Greenhill, 1990); John Laband, *Fight Us in the Open: The Anglo-Zulu War through Zulu Eyes* (Pietermaritzburg: Shuter & Shooter, 1985).

32. Wenshan Huang, *Fundamentals of Tai Chi Ch'uan: An Exposition of Its History, Philosophy, Technique, Practice, and Application* (Hong Kong: South Sky Book Co., 1973).

33. In my own fieldwork I have documented over seventy-five martial art styles in some seven countries of Western Africa, not including those I encountered in Southern Africa, Eastern Africa, and its archipelago.

34. There are, however, enclaves of pugilism within this largely grappling zone, and there are some combat traditions, such as *ekocheche,* that combine striking and grappling.

35. A more violent and less common variant of this wrestling integrated the use of fighting bracelets in a percussive manner.

36. Chinua Achebe, *Things Fall Apart* (New York: Anchor Books, 1994), 46–51.

37. This leg-wrapping style may have cognates in other parts of West or Central Africa. Futher research will be necessary to verify. Certainly individual leg-wrapping techniques were widespread in West and Central Africa but predominantly as a defensive technique against a host of other techniques in their grappling systems.

38. This region contained three distinct major ports of Malembo, Cabinda, and Loango and numerous distinct ethnic groups. For simplicity I will use the term

"Greater Loango Coast" to refer to the entire region from the Zaire to Oguoué Rivers. Although the Kikongo and Vili languages were spoken only in parts of this region, the kingdoms of Kongo and Loango influenced, at least politically, the entire region. See Vansina, *Paths in the Rainforests,* 159.

39. João José Reis, *Slave Rebellion in Brazil: The Muslim Uprising of 1835 in Bahia,* trans. Arthur Brakel (Baltimore: Johns Hopkins University Press, 1993), 92.

40. Arquivo Nacional, Rio de Janeiro, Brazil, Ij6-217, January 20, 1854, p. 55.

41. Eduardo Theodoro Bösche, *Quadros alternados: Impressões do Brasil de D. Pedro I,* trans. Vincente de Sousa Queirós (São Paulo: Tip. da Casa Garraux, 1929), 193–94.

Chapter 1: From across the *Kalunga*

1. The best-watered central plateau allowed the Ovimbundu to reach the highest population densities of the region, perhaps followed in size by the Kunene floodplains. See Joseph C. Miller, "Central and Southern Angola to ca 1840," published as "Angola central e sul por volta de 1840," *Estudos Afro-Asiáticos* 32 (December 1997): 8.

2. Miller, *Way of Death.*

3. Cimbebasia is used here to describe the region from the southern section of the central highlands to just north of the Etosha pan, roughly the area where the Cimbebasian subblock of Bantu languages were spoken. Seventeenth-century maps placed Cimbebasia east of the escarpment around latitude 15°S, roughly near the center of this region. The term "Cimbebasian" here replaces the previous usage of the term "Southwest-Bantu" languages. The languages of Cimbebasia are standardly divided into three large branches: Ambo languages, Kunene languages (see below), and the group of languages often lumped under the umbrella term "Herero." While this standard division is still useful in many regards, it is important to note that Anita Pfouts has suggested a subdivision of these languages into five branches: Ngumbi, Ngambwe, Hakaona, Themba-Herero, and Kwanyama-Ambo. See Jill Kinahan, "The Etymology and Historical Use of the Term Cimbebasia," *Cimbebasia: Journal of the State Museum, Windhoek* 10 (1988): 5–18; and Anita Pfouts, "Economy and Society in Northern Namibia 500 BCE to 1800 CE: A Linguistic Approach," Ph.D. diss., University of California, Los Angeles, 2003.

4. I am using the term "Kunene peoples" or "Kunenes" to refer to the peoples living within the curve of the Kunene River and just beyond it—in particular the Handa de Mupa, Handa de Kipungu, Mutano, Mulondo, Kiteve, Kamba, Kilenges-Humbe, Kilengues-Muso, Ngambwe, Mwila (Nyaneka), and Kipungu. This use of the term replaces my earlier use of the term "Bangala," by which these people are known to their southern neighbors because it can be taken as pejorative in current practice. Likewise the term "Nyaneka-Humbe" is not used because it was imposed during colonialism on the erroneous assumption that Handa and Kipungu were "Nyaneka" (Mwila). Anita Pfouts suggests that Ngambwe and Humbe are equidistantly related branches of Cimbebasian, which calls into question their being lumped together, and raises questions about the classification of the other languages in the group. Lexical analysis shows that Handa is more distinct from Nyaneka than it is from Mulondo, and even Nyaneka (Mwila) and Ngambwe are quite distinct. I have intentionally not included the Ndongona, Hinga, and Kwankwa, which may more accurately belong with the Ambo branch of Cimbebasian languages. Thus the use of the term "Kunene"

languages will be much less unwieldy and neutral until the linguistic details of these linguistic relationships have been worked out. For my linguistic breakdown with language samples, see T. J. Desch-Obi, "Divining History: Historical Linguistics and African Divination in Historical Reconstruction," paper presented at the African Studies Association Conference, Washington, D.C., December 2002. On the conflation of Handa, Kipungu, Mwila, and Ngambwe, see W. G. Clarence-Smith, "Capitalist Penetration among the Nyaneka of Southern Angola, 1760s to 1920s," *African Studies* 37, no. 2 (1978): 163.

5. Note, for example, the somewhat similar techniques documented by Robert F. Thompson among KiKongo-speaking peoples. However, the various techniques mentioned were not part of a single combat form, at least based on available evidence. There certainly are indications that further research in the Greater Loango region might reveal a complete cognate art. See Robert F. Thompson, "Tough Guys Do Dance," *Rolling Stone,* March 24, 1988, 135–40.

6. Although I am artificially separating the impact of Imbangalas and Europeans for analysis, they were in fact related to each other in some important ways and often affected societies in the same decades.

7. Christopher Ehret, "Spread of Food Production to Southern Africa," in *The Archeological and Linguistic Reconstruction of African History,* ed. C. Ehret and M. Posnansky (Berkeley: University of California Press, 1982).

8. These Njila languages are alternatively known as "Western Savannah Bantu" languages. This discussion is drawn from the following works, which should be consulted for a more detailed description of the early settlement of the region: Pfouts, "Economy and Society"; Desch-Obi, "Divining History"; and Jan Vansina, *How Societies Are Born: Governance in West Central Africa before 1600* (Charlottesville: University Press of Virginia, 2004).

9. Pfouts, "Economy and Society," 72–73.

10. W. G. Clarence-Smith, *Slaves, Peasants, and Capitalists in Southern Angola, 1840–1926* (Cambridge: Cambridge University Press, 1979), 76.

11. For Luba political centralization via public works, see Thomas Q. Reefe, *The Rainbow and the Kings: A History of the Luba Empire to 1891* (Berkeley: University of California Press, 1981), 70–71.

12. Smith, *Slaves,* 76.

13. Our fuller knowledge of these institutions comes from recent centuries, but the historical roots of these developments lie in still earlier times. The development of territorial chieftaincies, marked by the coining of the term *ohamba* for territorial chief, was already under way before the divergence of the dialect chains by 1300. An additional impetus to the spreading of people and languages during the brief wet phase beginning in the thirteenth century may have been the response of peoples seeking to avoid falling under such emerging political impositions along the Kunene.

14. Miller, "Central and Southern Angola," 5. Among the Luchazi people to the east of Kunene, warriors were redistributed with interest. See Gerhard Kubik and Moses Yotamu, *The Luchazi People: Their History & Chieftancy, Angola, Congo, Namibia, Zambia* (Lusaka: Central African Oral History Research Project, 1998), 209.

15. In later centuries the king was awarded half the cattle and captives taken during such raids. For ritual practice of cattle raids, see Märta Salockoski, "On the

Dynamics of Pre-colonial Society in Northern Namibia" (unpublished paper, National Archives of Namibia, Windhoek, 1985), 15–18.

16. Joseph C. Miller, "Angola," in *Encyclopedia of Africa South of the Sahara,* ed. John Middleton (New York: C. Scribner's Sons, 1997), 41; Märta Salockoski, "Symbolic Power of Kings in Pre-colonial Ambo Societies" (these de licenciatura, University of Helsinki, Franzeninkatu, 1992), 168. When this process first began will not be clear without further linguistic and archaeological research. It likely evolved over centuries following the introduction of cattle into the region in the first millennium of the Common Era. Vansina dates this adoption roughly around the seventh century based on archaeological evidence from areas far to the southeast, while Pfouts's linguistic evidence dates the adoption of cattle some centuries earlier.

17. James Denbow suggests that the two critical nodes controlled by elites were trade and cattle. Possession of the latter "was the currency of political authority, reflecting an owner's ability to mobilize commodity production, people and spiritual power to his own ends." See James Denbow, "Material Culture and the Dialectics of Identity in the Kalahari: AD 700–1700," in *Beyond Chiefdoms: Pathways to Complexity in Africa,* ed. Susan McIntosh (Cambridge: Cambridge University Press, 1999), 121.

18. Carlos Estermann, *The Ethnography of Southwestern Angola: The Nyaneka-Nkumbi Ethnic Grou,p* ed. Gordon Gibson, vol. 2 (New York: Africana Publishing, 1979), 154–59.

19. Filippo Pigafetta, *A Report of the Kingdom of Congo and of the Surrounding Countries: Drawn Out of the Writings and Discoveries of the Portuguese, Duarte Lopez,* trans. Margarite Hutchinson (London: F. Cass, 1969), 43–44.

20. This polity was also later written as Mataman. See Kinahan, "Etymology." On the monumental stone architecture, see António Almeida and Franca Camarate, "Recintos mulharados de Angola," *Estudos sobre a Pré-histoória do Ultramar Português* 16 (1960): 109–24.

21. Miller, "Central and Southern Angola," 21. At the very least they may have been influential enough to impact the political imaginations in the highlands. In the oral history of the Bie people, as collected by Serpa Pinto, Tucker, and Childs, the name Bie is attributed to a Humbe mythic hunter from the Kunene floodplain. This is one of three oral traditions. One of the other variants comes from the Ngalangi peoples, while the last is actually a Songo or Lunda tradition, according to Childs. See Alexandre Alberto da Rocha de Serpa Pinto, *How I Crossed Africa: From the Atlantic to the Indian Ocean, through Unknown Countries; Discovery of the Great Zambesi Affluents, &c.* 2 vols. (London: Sampson Low, Marsten, Searle, & Rivington, 1881), 1:156; John T. Tucker, *Drums in the Darkness* (New York: George H. Doran Co., 1927), 34; Gladwyn Murray Childs, *Umbundu Kinship & Character: Being a Description of Social Structure and Individual Development of the Ovimbundu of Angola, with Observations Concerning the Bearing on the Enterprise of Christian Missions of Certain Phases of the Life and Culture Described* (London: Published for the International African Institute by Oxford University Press, 1949), 172–73. See also António Francisco Ferreira da Silva Porto, *Viagens e apontamentos du um portuense em Africa* (Lisboa: Divisão de Publicações e Biblioteca, Agência Geral das Colónias, 1942), 165–71.

22. Miller, "Central and Southern Angola," 6–7. Vansina (*How Societies Are Born,* 200–201) suggests that this development may have also been a social revolution of

the poor, who had been exploited by the rich but then turned on their former lords with the prospect of the Atlantic slave trade.

23. Although the origin and spread of Imbangala *kilombos* remain a point of debate in the historiography of Angola, there is evidence that suggests that the Imbangala *kilombo* first emerged from Kunene societies. Joseph Miller traces the tradition to circumcision camps that he places among the proto-Ovimbundo. However, Ovimbundu peoples who were not Imbangala were not known to circumcise in later centuries; nor does the linguistic evidence suggest that they did earlier. Rather, these early *kilombos,* along with the term *kilombo,* seem to have emerged among Cimbebasians. In his first manuscript based on his years of service in Angola from 1654 to 1667, the Capuchin missionary Giovanni Antonio Cavazzi da Montecúccolo recorded an oral tradition linking the kingdom of Mataman with the genesis of the Imbangala *kilombo.* According to Cavazzi, the founder of the Imbangala military codes was personified in the oral tradition as Zimbo, a barbarous soldier who decided to leave his homeland in the "mountains of the lion" and lead an ever-mobile army that defeated and incorporated soldiers from every kingdom they encountered. Zimbo eventually settled down, founding his kingdom on the banks of the Kunene River. (Could Zimbo be a personification of the kingdom of Muzumbu a Kalunga? Zimbo's founding of a kingdom on the Kunene River connects with Portuguese knowledge of this title from the 1620s.) Thus, while the *kilombo* may have further developed in the central highlands particularly in the adoption of a military cult called *maji a samba,* the oral tradition links the *kilombo*'s early genesis to a powerful kingdom on the banks on the Kunene. Vansina also places the Imbangala origins in northern Cimbebasia, particularly the Kilengues region. He cites as evidence first the fact that the term recorded as Chimbangala was a Humbe term for vagrants that was not used in Ovimbundu. Second, he notes that for Cavazzi, "nguri" meant "lion" in the language of the Imbangala, and nguri means "lion" in Mwila (Nyaneka). See Giovanni Antonio Cavazzi de Montecúccolo, *Missione Evangelica al regno del Congo,* trans. John Thornton trans. (forthcoming), chaps. 1 and 2; Cavazzi, *Missione evangelica al regno del Congo, et altri circonvicini, siti nell Ethiopia interiore parte dell Africa meridionalae, fata dalla religione capuccina, con il racconto di varii successi seguiti* (1667; repr., 1977), 57n21, 122; Vansina, *How Societies Are Born,* 197. See also António de Oliveira de Cadornega, *História geral das guerras angolanas,* 3 vols., ed. Alves da Cunha and José Delgado (Lisboa: Agência-Geral das Colónias, Divisão de Publicaçoes e Biblioteca, 1940–42), 3:175–78. On the more general debate about the political origins of the Imbangala titles and the *kilombo,* see Joseph C. Miller, "Requiem for the Jaga," *Cahiers d' études Africaines* 13 (1973): 121–49; John Thornton, "A Resurrection for the Jaga," *Cahiers d' études Africaines* 19 (1979): 223–38; Joseph C. Miller, "Thanatopsis," *Cahiers d' études Africaines* 19 (1979): 229–31; François Bontinck, "Un mausolée pour les Jaga," *Cahiers d' études Africaines* 20 (1980): 387–89; and Anne Hilton, "The Jaga Reconsidered," *Journal of African History* 22 (1981): 191–202.

24. Cavazzi, *Evangelical Missions to the Kong,o* chap. 5. The Zulu equivalent was the battle formation known as "chest-and-horns" divided into three units: the central unit (*isi fuba*) and two outer horns (*upondo*). See R. Summers and C. W. Pagden, *The Warriors* (Cape Town: Books of Africa, 1970), 55–57. However, the Imbangala did not hold their divisions in tight formations as the Zulu but rather spread out openly. See Cavazzi, *Missione evangelica,* 48.

25. Cavazzi, *Missione evangelica,* chap.14.

26. Joseph Calder Miller, *Kings and Kinsmen: Early Mbundu States in Angola* (Oxford: Clarendon Press, 1976), 239. A possibly unrelated emphasis on war clubs/ axes was documented in the nineteenth century. Peter Möller found that the Kunene descendants of the southernmost *kilombo* continued to be experts in the techniques of the war hatchets when he visited Mutano in the late 1800s. See Peter August Möller, *Journey in Africa through Angola, Ovampoland and Damaraland,* trans. Ione and Jalmar Rudner (Cape Town: C. Struik, 1974), 90.

27. John K. Thornton, "The Art of War in Angola, 1575–1680," *Comparative Studies in Society and History* 30, no. 2 (1988): 362–63.

28. Lorenzo da Lucca, *Relations sur le Congo du père Laurent de Lucques, 1700–1717,* ed. and trans. J. Cuvelier (Brussels: Institut Royal Colonial Belgeã 1953), 47.

29. Giovanni Antonio Cavazzi de Montecúccolo, *Descrição histórica dos três reinos do Congo, Matamba e Angola,* 2 vols., ed. and trans. Graziano de Leguzzano (Lisboa: Junta de Investigações do Ultramar, 1965), 109.

30. This often rose beyond the level of friendly rivalries. Some individuals took this opportunity to settle personal grudges, and Cavazzi notes that such events usually ended with at least a dozen murders having been committed in the frenzy of the dance. See Cavazzi, *Descricão,* 152; Ras Michael Brown, personal communication, June 8, 2000.

31. Cavazzi de Montecúccolo saw such large-scale ritual combat primarily as a form of loyalty. He defines *sangamento,* the Portuguese derivative of *nsanga,* as "to have faith" (*ter fé*) or "to show oneself faithful" (*mostrar-se fiel*). See Cavazzi, *Descricão,* 151.

32. In some cases war dances were seen as omens of bravery and success, while in other cases they could be a form of breaking the effects of an enemy's charms. See, for example, Miller, *Kings and Kinsmen,* 245–46; and John H. Weeks, *Among the Primitive Bakongo: A Record of Thirty Years' Close Intercourse with the Bakongo and Other Tribes of Equatorial Africa* (London: Seeley, Service & Co., 1914), 192–93.

33. Miller, *Kings and Kinsmen,* 237.

34. Ibid.

35. Ibid., 233, 237.

36. Andrew Battell, who lived among the Imbangala for twenty-one months, notes that the child would wear a collar as a symbol of disgrace until he proved himself by killing an enemy and returning with his head. See Ernest George Ravenstein, *The Strange Adventures of Andrew Battell, of Leigh, in Angola and the Adjoining Regions* (1901; repr., Nendeln: Liechtenstein Kraus Reprint, 1967), 32, 33, 85.

37. Miller, *Kings and Kinsmen,* 237.

38. Ibid.,177n6, 233.

39. Ibid., 234–35.

40. Ibid., 235.

41. Reports of actual cannibalism must be taken with some reservation. While the ideology of cannibalism was central to the *kilombos,* actual cannibalism would probably have been limited to ritual practice if it existed at all. Cavazzi gives eyewitness accounts in *Missione evangelica,* 53, and yet he also admits a bias toward exaggerating his negative impressions of these Africans to make it appear that his "escaping from their hands . . . be attributed to nothing less than a miracle." See Cavazzi, *Missione*

evangelica, 63. Moreover, it was not uncommon for an African group to describe unrelated peoples as cannibals, and this to be erroneously taken literally by Europeans. For a fuller discussion of the European tendency to project the stigma of cannibalism onto Africans, see W. Arens, *The Man Eating Myth* (Oxford: Oxford University Press, 1979).

42. Miller, *Kings and Kinsmen,* 226, 245–47.

43. Wyatt MacGaffey, *Astonishment and Power* (Washington, D.C.: Published for the National Museum of African Art by the Smithsonian Institution Press, 1993), 98.

44. Cavazzi, *Missione evangelica,* 63.

45. Miller, *Kings and Kinsmen,* 248.

46. Ravenstein, *Strange Adventures of Andrew Battell,* 30; Miller, *Kings and Kinsmen,* 242.

47. R. Avelot, "Les Grands mouvements des peuples en Afrique-Jaga et Zimba," *Bulletin de géographie historique et descriptive* 27 (1912): 164–66.

48. Estermann sees the attack of the Imbangala soldier bands in the oral history of the clans in Mutano as well. He further supports his identification of the Ovakwaluwo with the Imbangala by cultural similarities between the Ovakwaluwo chiefs and the Imbangala as recorded by Cavazzi, particularly their rain-making ceremonies. Other evidence supporting this relationship includes the Imbangala titles such as Humbe and Ngonga, which were passed down among the ruling clan of Mutano, and reports of cannibalism. See Estermann, *Nyaneka-NKumbi,* 16–17, 24–25. Imbangala attacks in the Kunene floodplain region related to may have been the impetus for later Ambo and Herero migrations across the Kunene into what is now Northern Namibia. Particularly the ruling clans of some Ambo groups likely crossed the river only around this time. See Frieda Nela Williams, *Precolonial Communities of Southwestern Africa: A History of Ovambo Kingdoms 1600–1920* (1991; repr., Windhoek: National Archives of Namibia, 1994), 51–67.

49. Cited in Childs, *Umbundu Kinship,* 188.

50. They were referred to informally as "Omalyangolo," or "great eaters of zebra meat," since the other Bantu-speaking peoples did not eat zebra meat. Estermann refers to them as "Black Khoisan" and suggests that they were a group of Bantu who lived as and possibly spoke the language of the Khoisan peoples. They were more likely, however, the descendants of the Khoe groups such as the Kwadi or Ju, who were very dark skinned in contrast to the stereotypical image of "yellow" Khoisan peoples. Urquhart describes one related Khoe subgroup, the Cuisse, as being "extremely black in color." See Alvin W. Urquhart, *Patterns of Settlement and Subsistence in Southwestern Angola* (Washington, D.C.: National Academy of Sciences–National Research Council, 1963), 13.

51. Avelot, "Les Grands mouvements," 165; translation cited in Estermann, *Nyaneka-NKumbi,* 14–15.

52. The Ambo are a group of seven ethnic groups to the east and south of Humbe Inene: Ondonga, Uukwanyama, Uukwambi, Ongandjera, Ombalantu, Uukwaluudhi, and Uukolonkadhi. Of these, the Uukwaluudhi and Ondonga kingdoms alone include no mention in the oral histories of direct influence by Kunene peoples. Yet, most of the Ambo groups migrated into the present Amboland from the region of Humbe Inene. The Ondonga, for example, according to Kampungu's study of Okavango

migrations, comigrated from the Handa province of Humbe Inene as a result of the southern advance of the Imbangala. Yet, this departure did not take place before the Imbangala left their mark on the group. According to Frieda Williams, the legendary figure of Andonga, who led his people to set up his kingdom at their present location, was the bearer of the title Andonga, one of three titles to reach Amboland in their original form and that were also found among the Lunda, perhaps by Imbangala influence in both regions. Such migrations, however, likely refer to a small ruling group. Larger population shifts would have been completed before 1300.

The oral histories of the majority of Ambo kingdoms show that they may have developed as satellite states to Humbe Inene. For example, the origin story of the Kwanyama kingdom notes that the first royal blood arrived from Ondonga while hunting and found it so bountiful decided to stay in this land of meat (*onyama*). The eldest of the Ondonga princes was made king, but a group of people from Mutano arrived and would not accept the king. The Mutano people won the ensuing battle and frightened the king out of his court. Eventually the ex-king asked to rule over a small group in his immediate vicinity, and the Mutano agreed under the stipulation that he never erect an *ombala* (court). The Kunene peoples from Mutano erected an *ombala,* and their descendants continued to rule Kwanyama.

Other Ambo traditions acknowledge Humbe Inene as being the origin of the progenitors of the Kwambi, Mbalantu, and Ngandjera kingdoms, as well as the Askwaneyuma ruling clan of the Mbanja kingdom. The Kwanyama kings, descendants from Kunene stock, remained vassal to Mutano until the reign of King Hambili ja Haufiku, a Mutano prince who separated from direct vassalage in the first half of the nineteenth century and founded the first Kwanyama *ombala* (palace). Yet, even after declaring their independence, Mutano continued to be seen by many of the Ovambo groups as the source of political legitimacy. For example, according to the Mbalantu oral traditions, their sacred fire was collected every year from Mutano. Likewise, among the Kwanyama kings' ceremonial objects to be received at installation was an iron throne given by the king in Mutano. King Ueyulu ya Hedimbi, who ruled from 1884 to 1904, was the last Kwanyama king to receive this iron throne from the lords of Mutano. See Romanus Kampungu, "Okavango Marriage Customs" (Ph.D. diss., Pontifical University, Rome, 1965), 1:240–43; Herman Tonjes, *Ovamboland: Country, People, Mission,* trans. Peter Reiner (1911; repr., Windhoek: Namibia Scientific Society, 1996), 35–38; Edwin M. Loeb, *In Feudal Africa* (Bloomington: Indiana University Research Center in Anthropology Folklore and Linguistics, 1962), 23; Williams, *Precolonial Communities,* 84; and Dowie Fourie, *Oshiwambo: Past, Present, and Future* (Windhoek: University of Namibia, 1992), 5.

53. There are numerous differences in vocabulary and social practice in each of these Kunene societies. However, in an effort not to overwhelm readers who do not have a background in this area, I will be painting with broad strokes in this entire section.

54. Nephews and unmarried sons often remained after marriage, bringing their wives and children into the social unit.

55. These included rituals invoking the ancestors, the ritual distribution of provisions, and blessings before journeys such as seasonal relocations or military, trade, and salt-seeking expeditions. See Williams, *Precolonial Communities,* 49; and Möller, *Journey,* 84.

56. Loeb (*In Feudal Africa*), in his illustration of an Ambo homestead's central meeting place, includes the image of two individuals sparring *kandeka,* which will be discussed below.

57. Eduardo Cruz Carvalho and Jorge Vieira da Silva, "The Cunene Region: Ecological Analysis of an African Agropastoral System," in Franz-Wilhelm Heimer ed., *Social Change in Angola* (Munich: Weltforum Verlag, 1973), 145–92.

58. Clan influence, which had dominated social relations from an earlier age, was far-reaching, and members of a clan could seek the assistance of their maternal clan members in distant regions. Members of a clan saw themselves as distantly related to one another and bound by a "totemic" plant or animal only eaten under ritual conditions. Each individual was related by birth to the clan of his father and the clan of his mother. It is the father's clan that was invoked in oaths and praised in song, but it is the maternal clan that predominated in most social and economic relations. When a woman married, she joined the homestead of her husband. However, inheritance was distributed along matrilineal lines, which acted against the accumulation of wealth in any given localized decent group as an *eumbo* owner's matriclan members were spread out widely throughout the region. Members of the same clan or an allied clan could claim possession of certain items in times of need. This acted to promote communal balance and equality among clans. See Clarence-Smith, "Underdevelopment and Class Formation in Ovamboland 1845–1915," *Journal of African Histor,y* 16, no. 3 (1975): 365–381; and Estermann, *Nyaneka-NKumbi,* 122, 126–31.

59. Women voluntarily joined forces for fishing, hoeing, and weeding. In addition to the public works demanded in areas near the floodplains, men from various *eumbos* united for joint ventures. During the dry season the men linked their herds for transhumant seasonal migration. They also united for hunting, salt seeking, cattle raiding, and trading expeditions under the direction of chiefs and headmen. Long-distance trade involved iron ore from the region of the Kassinga mines. This iron was worked by Kunene and Kwanyama smiths and traded to the east (Kavango) and south (Herero), while salt from Ambo tributaries of Humbe Inene was traded for tobacco. See Williams, *Precolonial Communities,* 49–50; Carvalho and Silva, "Cunene Region," 134, 154; Estermann, *Nyaneka-NKumbi,* 111; and Clarence-Smith, "Underdevelopment," 371.

60. Gerhard Kubik, *Muziek van de Humbi en de Handa uit Angola* (Tervuren: Musée royal de l'Afrique centrale, 1973), 73.

61. Again reflecting numerous regional variations that I am glossing over here.

62. Salockoski, "Symbolic Power of Kings," 168; Maria de Fátima, "Relexões Sobre o Casamento na Sociedade Tradicional Nyaneka-Nkumby" Tese de licenciatura, Universidade Agostinho Neto (Lubango, 1997).

63. Tomas Segundo, interview at farm outside Lubango, September 8, 1997. Note that all interview were conducted by the author unless otherwise specified.

64. See, for example, Carlos Estermann, "La fête de Puberté dans quelques tribus de L'Angola Méridionale," *Portugal in África: Revista de Cultura Missionária* 1 (November/December 1944): 340–55.

65. Some Kunene groups would later in the twentieth century extend the term to refer to marriage ceremonies in general. See Estermann, *Nyaneka-NKumbi,* 74.

66. Ricardino Ferreira, "Aspectos da vida indígena, material, espiritual e social e história do actual sobado "Bula" no posto do Mulondo (Alto Cunene)," 30, article in possession of AH.

67. My ethnographic work did not turn up any direct references to this special competition, and therefore I cannot confirm the existence of such a tournament apart from the regular *engolo* exhibitions held in such festivals. However, according to Neves e Sousa, who had been in the region half a century earlier, in this *engolo* contest the object of the dance was to kick an opponent's face, and the winner "has the right to choose a wife from among the newly initiated without paying a dowry." See Albano Neves e Sousa, *Da Minha África e do Brasil que eu vi* (Luanda, n.d.); Luis da Camara Cascudo, *Folclore do Brasil: Pesquisas e notas* (Rio de Janeiro: Editôra Fundo de Cultura, 1967), 184–85; and letter from Albano Neves e Sousa to Luís de Camâra Cascudo referenced in Cascudo, *Folclore do Brasil,* 239. On the nature of this dowry, see T. J. Desch-Obi, "Combat Traditions in African and African Diaspora History" Ph.D. diss., University of California, Los Angeles, 2000, 46–47n103.

68. C. S. Tastevevin, "Le Nyaneka: Tribu Bantu de l'Angola Meridionale," undated manuscript draft in the archive of the Holy Spirit Fathers, Chevilly-Larue, France.

69. The two largest Kunene kingdoms were divided into provinces (*omikunda*) led by *ovipundi,* provincial leaders personally chosen by the king. Below each *ovipundi* were local chiefdoms led by *nambalu,* chiefs. In turn, each ward of a chiefdom was led by a headman who bore the title *mwene-pembe* or *mukunda.* See Doming Muendakonhomy, interview, Mutano, Angola, August 23, 1997.

70. The council was composed of special agents who passed royal commands to provincial leaders and oversaw the *efico* and *ekwendje,* elders from the nonroyal clans who served as an advisory board for the king and various ministers. The four major ministers included the *mwene makesongo,* the minister of war; the *mwene-mphela,* or "the owner of words" in charge of judicial functions and pronouncements; the *mwene-mphemba,* who was in charge of royal rituals and offerings including *ekwendje;* and the *mwene-hambo,* "the owner of cattle," who managed the king's herds and sacred cattle, whose vitality represented the health and prosperity of the people. See Maria Gomes, "A autoridade da ombala nos Nyaneka-NKumbi: Estrutura, funcionamento, e influência na vida deste povo no passado e no presente" (these de licenciatura, Agostinho Neto University, Lubango, 1993); and Estermann, *Nyaneka-NKumbi,* 154–59.

71. This fortress may have been developed in response to instability and raids associated with droughts and the expansionist phases of the Ovimbundu kingdoms. For archaeological descriptions, see "Recinto Muralhado do Eleu," *Boletim da Câmara Municipal de Sá da Bandeira* 38 (1974): 33–44.

72. Gomes, "A autoridade da ombala nos Nyaneka-NKumbi," 33–34.

73. Regional trade consisted of items of specialized production such as dried fish, agricultural products, cattle products, or goods collected by hunting and gathering Khoisan groups. Longer distance trade rested on three staples: salt, copper, and iron. Salt was produced in several areas, but its principal sources were the coastal salt mines in the west and the Etosha pan to the south. Copper came from the Ndonga mines near what is now Tsumeb in northern Namibia. Iron ore was drawn from mines near modern-day Cassinga, and was worked by Kunene and Ambo smiths.

Valuable animal products, such as ivory and ostrich eggs, were obtained predominantly from Khoisan groups and were initially less significant commodities in this long-distance trade, although ivory grew to a dominant position after the linking of these trade routes with the Atlantic system in the early 1700s. For precolonial trade, see Harry Siiskonen, "Ovamboland and Economic Change in Southwestern Africa" (paper presented at "Studying the Northern Namibia Past," research seminar in Tvarminne, December 1985); and Clarence-Smith, "Underdevelopment," 368–69.

74. The king's right to seize potential wives and to demand labor for his fields ensured that he had the largest fields in the territory. More central to his wealth in Kunene terms was the size of his herd. Gerald J. Bender's research among the Humbe in 1960 revealed that the royal herd numbered over half a million (Gerald J. Bender, personal communication, January 18, 1997).

75. Clarence-Smith, "Underdevelopment," 370.

76. Prior to this trade the Kunene region may have been linked to trade networks that connected the regions just to the south with commerce from the Indian Ocean as early as 1000 C.E. See Vansina, *How Societies Are Born,* 108–16.

77. See, for example, the experience of José Brochado. Traders of Luso-Atlantic (and Luso-Indian) goods could be European, *pardo* (of dual African and European ancestry), or Africans who spoke some Portuguese. Important trade goods included firearms, alcohol, and Indian textiles. José Brochado, "Descripção das terras do Humbe, Camba, Mulondo, Quanhamae, outras, contendo uma idéa da sua população, seus costumes, vestuarios, etc.," *Annaes do Conselho Ultramarino,* unofficial part, 1st series (November 1855): 188. On alcohol, see José Curto, "Alcohol and Slaves: The Luso Brazilian Alcohol Commerce at Mpinda, Luanda, and Benguela during the Atlantic Slave Trade c. 1480–1830 and Its Impact on the Societies of West Central Africa" (Ph.D. diss., University of California, Los Angeles, 1996). On Indian textiles, see Roquinaldo Amaral Ferreira, "Transforming Atlantic Slaving: Trade, Warfare and Territorial Control in Angola, 1650–1800" (Ph.D. diss., University of California, Los Angeles, 2003).

78. While Tams does not mention the name of the group he is describing, it was likely Cimbebasians, given that his contemporaries who visited the Kunene regions all remarked that they were the ones most famous for their stick fighting. See George Tams, *Visit to the Portuguese Possessions in South-Western Africa* (New York: Negro University Press, 1969), 136.

79. Tams, *Visit,* 142–43.

80. Even as late as the 1980s it was not uncommon for fighters in Southern Africa to take "a detachable axe head which is carried in the pocket and fixed to a suitable stick should the need arise, thus converting the stick into a war axe." See Liam Keeley, "Zulu Stick Fighting: Weapons and Training," *Martial Arts Legend* (February 1998): 107.

81. José Brochado, "Notícia de alguns territórios, e dos povos que os habitam, situados na parte meridional da provincial de Angola," *Annaes do Conselho Ultramarino,* unofficial part, 1st series (December 1855): 190.

82. Möller, *Journey,* 90.

83. Unlike Zulu stick fighting, however, when a person was using two sticks both were used simultaneously for attack and defense.

84. Tams, *Visit,* 143.

85. Loeb (*In Feudal Africa,* 198) found that among their Ambo neighbors, different ethnic groups were distinguished by the fashioning of the heads of their fighting sticks.

86. Among their southern neighbors, the Kwanyama, one of the markers of *omasenge* (homosexuals) is that they are "seen walking about without a stick, without even a knobkerrie stick, which is the phallic symbol of manhood" (Loeb, *In Feudal Africa,* 239).

87. African herding cultures of honor appear to have been much less concerned with the control of female sexuality than the Mediterranean honor cultures were. The former appear to have been much focused on the relationship between men and their cattle. See Mark Moritz, "Honor Psychology and Pastoral Personality: An Ecocultural Analysis of Herding Routines and Socialization into the Culture of Honor among Nomadic Fulbe in West Africa" (unpublished article), 9.

88. Dale Lott and Benjamin Hart, "Aggressive Domination of Cattle by Fulani Herdsmen and Its Relation to Aggression in Fulani Culture and Personality," *Ethos* 5 (Summer 1977): 177.

89. Although many of the following examples are drawn from other pastoral peoples in West Africa, similar patterns were found among the Kunene. See Moritz, "Honor Psychology," 9–10.

90. A. F. Fraser, "The State of Fight or Flight in the Bull," *British Journal of Animal Behavior* 5 (1957): 48–49.

91. Lott and Hart, "Aggressive Domination," 180.

92. Josefino Djolele, interview, Lubango, Angola, October 28, 1997.

93. Monica Hunter Wilson, *Reaction to Conquest: Effects of contact with Europeans on the Pondo of South Africa* (London: H. Milford, 1936). Although socially similar, the Kunene style of fighting was different from that of the southern Nguni, who used a stave in the left for defense and a knobkerrie in the right for attack. Some individual Kunene used a parrying stick with a protective arch where the stick would be held, but overall Kunene stick fighting was more free in form, and attacks could come from either stick.

94. Loeb, *In Feudal Africa,* 81.

95. Thomas Segundo, interview, Lubango, Angola, October 17, 1997.

96. Kubik, *Muziek,* 73.

97. A. F. Nogueira, *A Raça Negra: Sob o ponto de vista da civilisacão da Africa: Usos e costumes de alguns povos gentîlicos do interior de Mossamedes e as colonias portuguezas* (Lisbon: Typ. Nova Minerva, 1880), 269.

98. Vertical honor means the right to special respect enjoyed by those of superior class/rank; internal honor, the self-respect one has for oneself; and horizontal or reflexive honor, the right to respect from one's peers that must be achieved through demonstrations of one's prowess. See Frank Henderson Stewart, *Honor* (Chicago: University of Chicago Press, 1994).

99. Brochado, "Notícia de alguns territórios," 191.

100. Moritz, "Honor Psychology," 3, 6, 8.

101. Ibid., 8.

102. T. E. Tirronen, *Ndonga-English Dictionary* (Ondangwa: ELCIN, 1986).

103. Loeb, *In Feudal Africa,* 337.

104. At least in more recent years these free-fighting matches could include the recourse to head butts and elbow strikes at close range, particularly as a counter to

hand-trapping techniques. See Hendrik Wangushu, interview, Enana, Namibia, January 12, 1998; Wangushu, taped interview, Windhoek, Namibia, January 15, 2006.

105. Although I did not notice a direct connection beyond shared ritual space and the practice of *kandeka* in dance circles to *engolo* songs, Neves e Sousa, whose fieldwork was done decades earlier, described the slap-fighting art (which he erroneously called *liveta* [literally "slap"]) that acted as the preliminary phase of the *engolo*. See Neves e Sousa, *Da Minha África,* 57.

106. Interestingly the distinctive hand position of the *kandeka* challenge-and-ready position directly parallels the hand position used by older men dancing in imitation of their cattle's horns.

107. Neves e Sousa, *Da Minha África.* Again, while I did not find *kimbandas* at the center of most performances, they were present at some.

108. The following description is based on my own ethnographic fieldwork in the 1990s.

109. Brochado, "Descripção," 188; Möller, *Journey,* 66.

110. International Capoeira Angola Foundation, *Capoeira Angola* (Washington, D.C., n.d.), 58–59.

111. Carlos Estermann, "Os Ba-nhaneca e os Ban-kumbi no Deserto de Moçâmedes: Comentário a um artigo de A. F. Nogueira," *Museu de Angola-Boletim Cultural* 2 (1960): 17.

112. Dareck Joubert, producer, National Geographic Explorer, *Zebras: Patterns in the Grass* (videotape, 1991).

113. Neves e Sousa, *Da Minha Africa,* 57; Jaime Thomé, interview, Mulondo, Angola, August 23, 1997.

114. This term can be dated to the time before the Cimbebasian languages diverged based on its being an innovation and its noncontiguous distribution. These pugilistic arts were quite widespread among Cimbebasian peoples and even present to a limited degree among neighboring language-speaking groups. For example, the kicking art was practiced in Kilenges in the northwestern-most extent of Kunene peoples, and it was also present under the name *engolo* among some Ambo groups more than five hundred kilometers to the southeast. Likewise the slap-boxing game of *kandeka* was practiced among the most northeastern Kunene-speaking group, the Handa, and was also practiced under the same name by Herero speakers far to the southwest. See T. J. Desch-Obi, "Divining History: Historical Linguistics and African Divination in Historical Reconstruction," paper presented at the African Studies Association Conference, Washington, D.C., December 2002; and Desch-Obi, "Divining History: The Development of Combative Culture in Southern Angola," paper presented at the African Studies Association Conference, New Orleans, La., November 2004.

115. Patrick McNaughton quoted in "Bamana: The Art of Existence in Mali," exhibition at the Museum for African Art, New York City (September 13, 2001–May 19, 2002), curated by Jean-Paul Colleyn and Catherine De Clippel; Patrick R. McNaughton, *Secret Sculptures of Komo: Art and Power in Bamana Initiation Associations* (Philadelphia: ISHI, 1979).

116. Guthrie's CS 709 and CS 711, respectively. Malcolm Guthrie, *Comparative Bantu,* 4 vols. (Farnborough, Gregg Press, 1967–71).

117. Guthrie's CS 715.

118. Christopher Ehret, personal communication, 1994 and 2005. Estermann also links the term to the word for "sentient" or "intelligent." See Carlos Estermann and Gordon D. Gibson, *The Ethnography of Southwestern Angola: The Nyaneka-Nkumbi Ethnic Group,* ed. and trans. Gordon Gibson (New York: Africana Publ. Co., 1979), 2:190; Estermann, *Nyaneka-Nkumbi,* 190; Carlos Estermann, *The Ethnography of Southwestern Angola: The Non-Bantu Peoples. The Ambo Ethnic Grou,p* ed. and trans. Gordon Gibson (New York: Africana Pub. Co., 1976), 181.

119. Z. S. Strother, *Inventing Masks: Agency and History in the Art of the Central Pende* (Chicago: University of Chicago Press, 1997), 94.

120. Cavazzi, *Descrição,* 1:93; translation of quotation by James Sweet; James Sweet, personal communication, October 31, 2000.

121. The use of head butting, like inversions, was primarily associated with dueling ritual specialists.

122. Cimbebasians did correlate the lower half of their cosmograms with the spiritual realm, but further research is necessary to uncover if they, like some other Angolan groups, specifically associated the legs with defensive spiritual forces. For example, among the Kongo, sacred medicines (*biteke/minkisi*) intended to attack were associated with the upper body, while those that served protective purposes were conceptually related to the lower body. Similarly the Pende example also conceptually linked semicircular kicks with the defensive medicines that protect a village. See Hein Vanhee, "Agents of Order and Disorder: Kongo Minkisi," in *Re-Visions: New Perspectives on the African Collections of the Horniman Museum,* ed. Karel Arnaut (London: Horniman Museum and Gardens, 2000), 97; Wyatt MacGaffey, *Kongo Political Culture: The Conceptual Challenge of the Particular* (Bloomington: Indiana University Press, 2000), 81–82; and Strother, *Inventing Masks,* 94.

123. Brochado, "Descripção," 191.

124. Domingo Muendakonhomy, interview, Mutano, Angola, August 23, 1997.

125. Female professions included potters and hairdressers. See Estermann, *Nyaneka-NKumbi,* 202–12..

126. Vansina, *How Societies Are Born,* 153–54.

127. At least according to twentieth-century practice, the clear delineations of acceptable techniques were often crossed in real fights, bringing in the potential for these close-quarters blows. While we are using the term *engolo* here to distinguish the martial art, the term also referred to joints, such as knees and elbows generally, and to strikes with these joints. For example, among many Cimbebasians, elbowing was called *kandula (a) nongolo,* and the term *engolo* was also used to refer to knee strikes. Thus, beyond the use of kicking, Kunene fighters in a general melee might also rely on slap boxing, kneeing, elbowing, or head butting.

128. Pero Rodrigues, "História da residência dos Padres da Companhia de Jesus em Angola, e cousas tocantes ao Reino e conquista," in António Brasio, ed., *Monumenta Missionaria Africana,* vol. 4 (Lisbon: Agência Geral do Ultramar, Divisão de Publicações e Biblioteca, 1954), 563.

129. A. Ngongolo and Justo Pedro, taped interviews, November 3, 1997; August 21, 2006.

130. At least according to twentieth-century practice, straight kicks with the toe or snap kicks were considered "ugly" by Kunene aesthetics and were often prohibited.

131. For a fuller description, see Thornton, "Art of War," 363–64; and John Kelly Thornton, *Warfare in Atlantic Africa, 1500–1800* (London: UCL Press, 1999).

132. This skill was also known as *vanga* or *okuyepa.*

133. Rodrigues, "História," 563. This technique of *sanguar* was also noted by Cavazzi, *Missione evangelica,* 48.

134. Rodrigues, "História," 563.

135. Loeb, *In Feudal Africa,* 82.

136. Unlabeled manuscript in Archives Generales Congregation du Saint-Esprit, Chivilly-Larue, France, 477 B; also published in Alphonse Lang and Constant Tastevin, *La tribu des Va-nyaneka* (Corbeil: Impr. Crété, 1937). Lang and Tastevin's book was based in large part on the observations gathered by Father Dekindt in the 1880s.

137. According to Möller (*Journey,* 90–91), arrows were often prepared "with a mixture of snake, ant, and vegetable poisons."

138. Even in the last decades of the nineteenth century Möller could add to his list of Kunene weapons only that "occasionally one sees a gun." Father Wunenberger noted that although the rich had guns and they were gaining esteem in the 1880s, "*Leur arme favorite est l'arme blanche. Les blancs á bóut de munitions leur sont de beaucoup inférieurs en xe genre de combat.*" (Their favorite weapons are *arme blanche.* The whites without their munitions are very inferior in this genre of combat.) See Möller, *Journey,* 90–91; Charles Wunenberger, "La mission et le royaume de Cunène sur les bords de Cunène," *Les Missions Catholiques* 20 (1888): 263.

139. See Wunenberger, "La mission," 263–64. Other group tactics developed to aid in cattle raiding and defending included *kowa,* the Kunene system of cries to communicate over long distances.

140. Miller, *Way of Death,* 222.

141. The relationship between warfare and enslavement is a complex issue. The number of captives, soldiers or civilians, acquired through war was certainly variable from insignificant to dominant. As a whole, however, there can be no doubt that warfare and raiding were significant in procuring captives as spikes in exports from various regions of Western Africa were often the result of warfare. Thornton argues that African military service was the means by which many if not most of the Africans found themselves enslaved prior to the Haitian Revolution; see John K. Thornton, "African Soldiers in the Haitian Revolution," *Journal of Caribbean History* 25, nos. 1 & 2 (1991): 59. For a less military-oriented description of the slaving system in Angola, see Miller, *Way of Death.* Ferreira ("Transforming Atlantic Slaving," 1) notes that even when the number of captives was low, "warfare constituted a central dimension of seventeenth century Angolan slaving because military operations were used to coerce African rulers into signing commercial agreements and prevent the development of independent trading networks."

142. Miller, "Central and Southern Angola," 13.

143. Ralph Delgado, *Ao sul do Cuanza: Ocupação e aproveitamento do antigo reino de Benguela* (Lisboa, 1944), 137; Ralph Delgado, *História de Angola* (Lisbon: Edição do Banco de Angola, 1970), 2:125–26.

144. It was probably following the initial growth of this trade that a subordinate lord from the Handa province named Tyipa traveled westward to resettle in Kipungu. Following their migration these emigrants, later known as the Handa of Kipungu,

thrived on the trade and operated a trading network carrying trade goods by pack-oxen between Kilenges and the lower Kunene that continued into the nineteenth century. Control of the trade along this route was most likely the main factor in an invasion of Kilenges led by a sublord from Humbe Inene who must have moved to control the growing trade from Kipungu to Benguela via Kilenges. He established his *ombala* at the foot of the Bonga or Chivela Mountain and established a nominal overlordship over the Kilenge-Muso *ombalas* to the north. See Leonel Cosme, "A expansão ultramarina Portuguesa no contexto do colonialísmo Europeu," *Boletim da Câmara Municipal de Sá de Bandeira* 38 (October 1974–March 1975).

145. In the sixteenth and early seventeenth centuries the European battles were being won with infantry utilizing the pike. Firearm technology was relatively stable over the eighteenth century, with the standard arm being the flintlock musket until the mid nineteenth century. On the one hand, these weapons were a challenge to Kunene tactics in that individual bullets could not be dodged in the same way that other weapons could. On the other hand, these guns took up to a minute to reload (powder and shot had to be rammed down their wrought iron barrels) and were inaccurate at ranges beyond fifty yards. Africans armed with bows and crossbows had a higher rate of fire and equal accuracy at this close range. Firearms led to carnage in Europe because European troops tried to make up for the inadequacy of their weapons by standing directly in front of each other in tight ranks and firing together in volleys. Highland armies fought in spread-out formations, nullifying the effects of focused volleys. See Andrew Uffindell, "The Closed Ranks and Close Ranges of Napoleonic Warfare," *Military History* 61 (October 1997): 75.

146. Thus the real importance of cavalrymen was to optimize the performance of African soldiers. For an excellent analysis of European warfare in Angola and the trade and use of horses, see Roquinaldo Amaral Ferreira, "Transforming Atlantic Slaving: Trade, Warfare and Territorial Control in Angola, 1650–1800," Ph.D. diss., 2003.

147. The Portuguese often served as a heavily armored infantry but could not win large battles without these African soldiers "and were regularly massacred when they tried to do so." See John Thornton, *Africa and Africans in the Making of the Atlantic World: 1400–1800* (New York: Cambridge University Press, 1998), 116; and Thornton, "Art of War."

148. See n. 138 for Wunenberger's quote.

149. Arquivo Histórico Nacional de Luanda (hereafter AHNL), "Rellação de João Pilarte da Silva, hoje falecido ao Captain mor José Vierra de Araujo da viage que fez ao Cabo Negro por terra no anno de 1770 em compania de José dos Santos hoje captain mor de Caconda."

150. On the Brazilian influence in southern Angola, see Ferreira, "Transforming Atlantic Slaving."

151. Delgado, *Ao sul,* 282.

152. Miller, "Central and Southern Angola."

153. Curto, "Alcohol and Slaves," 368, 373.

154. Ibid., 26.

155. Cosme, "A expansão ultramarina Portuguesa," 18; Albino Sá, "A Portugalização do sul de Angola," *Boletim da Câmara Municipal de Sá da Bandeira* 20 (January 1968): 23.

156. AHNL, *Rellação de João Pilarte da Silva.*

157. Joseph C. Miller, "The Numbers, Origins, and Destinations of Slaves in the Eighteenth-Century Angolan Slave Trade," in *The Atlantic Slave Trade,* ed. Joseph Inikori and Stanly Engerman (Durham: Duke University Press, 1992), 82.

158. Ibid., 84.

159. Ibid., 109, fig. 4.

160. Miller, *Way of Death,* 222.

161. Ferreira ("Transforming Atlantic Slaving," 8) points out that Brazilians in Benguela also had access to Asian textiles.

162. These routes reached far to the east of these regions. See Miller, *Way of Death,* 11.

163. Within a year this led to the capture of sixty-five slavers, and the traffic fell to thirty-three thousand in 1840 and twenty-three thousand in 1841. See Mary C. Karasch, "The Brazilian Slavers and the Illegal Slave Trade, 1836–1851" (M.A. thesis, University of Wisconsin, 1967), 4. On illegal trade, see also Roquinaldo Amaral Ferreira, "Dos Sertões ao Atântico: Tráfico ilegal de Escravos e Comércio Lícito em Angola, 1830–1860" (M.A. thesis, Universidade Federal do Rio de Janeiro, 1996).

164. Ships flying the United States flag were immune to search by the British following the War of 1812. See Karasch, "Brazilian Slavers," 6.

165. Manuel Júlio de Mendonça Torres, *O districto de Moçâmedes: Nas fases da origem e da primeira organização, 1485–1859* (Lisboa: Divisão de Publicações e Biblioteca, Agência Geral das Colónias, 1950), 27.

166. Even after this the Mutano trade routes continued to provide cattle and captives as one of the major suppliers of the legal trade to São Tomé.

167. AHNL, *Rellação de João Pilarte da Silva.*

168. These skills were certainly utilized in the urban cities and may have been linked to the use of weapons by bondsmen held in the large port cities. Kunene martial traditions in general were undoubtedly utilized as well in the banditry that swept over both urban Benguela and the hinterland in the nineteenth century. Another form of resistance by enslaved Kunene people would have been the forming of maroon communities that will be discussed in the context of North America. Captives sold out of Benguela were taken to Luanda in large numbers in the 1720s. Many of these escaped and established maroon communities. See Police Inspector DaCosta, interview, Benguela, Angola, September 15, 1997; Neves e Sousa cited in Cascudo, *Folclore do Brasil,* 185–86; Francisco de Salles Ferreira, Chefe de Policia servindo de Administrador do Conselho, *Repartição de Policia em Loanda 30 de Março de 185;4* Brochado, "Notícia de alguns territórios," 204; Clarence-Smith, *Slaves, Peasants, and Capitalists,* 79; W. G. Clarence-Smith, "Runaway Slaves and Social Bandits in Southern Angola, 1875–1913," in *Out of the House of Bondage: Runaways, Resistance and Maroonage in Africa and the New World,* ed. Gad Heuman (London: F. Cass, 1986), 23–33; and Ferreira, *Transforming Atlantic Slaving,* 209.

Chapter 2: Bloodless Duels

1. There has been some unresolved debate over whether an identity named "Igbo" emerged prior to or only as a result of the transatlantic slave trade. On the one hand, there is evidence that the use of the term, or at least a certain consciousness

regarding that term, was altered by the process of enslavement and forced migration. On the other hand, the term was not unknown prior to the Atlantic trade, given its use in place names such as Igbo-Ukwo and Amaigo ("the abode of the Igbo"). At present, I will apply the term here to describe the ancestors of the people who would eventually apply that term to themselves primarily to avoid the cumbersomeness of using terms such as "pre-Igbo," "proto-Igbo," or "the people who would later come to be known as Igbo." Similarly I will use the term "Yoruba" in distinguishing an ethnic group to the west, whose collective identity and collective nomenclature are also the subject of debate. See Chambers, "He Gwine Sing He Country," 141–42; Michael Gomez, *Exchanging Our Country Marks: The Transformation of African Identities in the Colonial and Antebellum South* (Chapel Hill: University of North Carolina Press, 1998), 125–26; David Northrup, "Igbo and Myth Igbo: Culture and Ethnicity in the Atlantic World, 1600–1850," *Slavery and Abolition* 21 (2000): 1–20; Douglas B. Chambers, "The Significance of Igbo in the Bight of Biafra Slave-Trade: A Rejoinder to Northrup's 'Myth Igbo,'" *Slavery & Abolition* 23 (April 2002): 101–20; Gwendolyn Midlo Hall, *Slavery and African Ethnicities in the Americas: Restoring the Links* (Chapel Hill: University of North Carolina Press, 2005), 126–43; and Robin Law, "Ethnicity and the Slave Trade: 'Lucumi' and 'Nago' as Ethnonyms in West Africa," *History in Africa* 24 (1997): 205–219.

2. Elizabeth Allo Isichei, *A History of the Igbo People* (London: Macmillan, 1976), 3.

3. A cuesta is a highland with a cliff on one side and a gentle slope on the other. See Afigbo, *Ropes of Sand,* 6–7.

4. John E. Flint, *Nigeria and Ghana* (Englewood Cliffs, N.J.: Prentice-Hall, 1966), 63.

5. Afigbo, *Ropes of Sand,* 10–11.

6. Isichei, *History,* 32.

7. The earliest currency in Igboland was earthen jars from Uburu, which were later replaced by copper and brass horseshoe-shaped bars, iron money minted in the northern plateau known as *umumu,* and possibly cowrie shells. See Isichei, *History,* 33; and Afigbo, *Ropes of Sand,* 139.

8. David Northrup, "The Growth of Trade among the Igbo before 1800," *Journal of African History* 13, no. 2 (1972): 217–36; Afigbo, *Ropes of Sand,* 132–33.

9. Thurstan Shaw, *Igbo-Ukwu: An Account of Archaeological Discoveries in Eastern Nigeria* (Evanston, Ill.: Northwestern University Press, 1970).

10. Some villages or village groups in contact with Ibibio peoples incorporated closed societies into their political structure, while age sets played a significant political role among some societies in contact with other Cross River peoples. Significantly some communities that interacted with the Edo people to the west developed more centralized polities, but even these were rarely much larger in scale than large village groups. See Toyin Falola, ed., *Igbo History and Society: The Essays of Adiele Afigbo* (Trenton, N.J.: Africa World Press, 2005), 155–65.

11. A. E. Afigbo, *The Warrant Chiefs: Indirect Rule in Southeastern Nigeria, 1891–1929* (London: Longman, 1972), 20.

12. Ibid., 21.

13. Nwando Achebe, *Farmers, Traders, Warriors, and Kings: Female Power and*

Authority in Northern Igboland, 1900–1960 (Portsmouth, N.H.: Heinemann, 2005), 170–71.

14. Richard Henderson, *King in Every Man* (New Haven, Conn.: Yale University Press, 1972), 106–7.

15. Victor Chikezie Uchendu, *The Igbo of Southeast Nigeria* (New York: Holt, Rinehart and Winston, 1965), 20.

16. Ibid., 19.

17. Herbert M. Cole, *Mbari, Art and Life among the Owerri Igbo* (Bloomington: Indiana University Press, 1982), 58.

18. This is just one of a few variations of the Earth Mother's name, including Ala, Ani, Ajala, or Ajana.

19. Henderson, *King,* 115.

20. Ibid., 115–16.

21. Cole, *Mbari,* 54–55.

22. Afigbo, *Ropes of Sand,* 9–10.

23. Chambers, "He Gwine Sing He Country," 116.

24. Uchendu, *Igbo,* 81–82; McCall, *Dancing Histories,* 21–50.

25. Afigbo, *Warrant Chiefs,* 25.

26. K. Onwuka Dike and Felicia Ifeoma Ekejiuba, *The Aro of South-Eastern Nigeria, 1650–1980: A Study of Socio-Economic Formation and Transformation in Nigeria* (Ibadan: University Press, 1990), 286–89.

27. On the importance of "wearing one's identity" through society hats, see McCall, *Dancing Histories,* 23–25. On *nsibidi,* see Ute M. Roschenthaler, "Honoring Ejagham Women," *African Arts* 1 (Spring 1998): 38–50; and Simon P. X. Battestini, "Reading Signs of Identity and Alterity: History, Semiotics, and the Nigerian Case," *African Studies Review* 34 (April 1991): 99–116.

28. Among the Efik towns of Old Calabar, for example, *ekpe* was the sociopolitical institution enforcing conformity on the individual towns. See, for example, David Northrup, *Trade without Rulers: Pre-Colonial Economic Development in South-Eastern Nigeria* (Oxford: Clarendon Press, 1978), 108–10.

29. Don Ohadike, "Igbo-Benin Wars," in *Warfare and Diplomacy in Precolonial Nigeria: Essays in Honor of Robert Smith,* ed. Robert Sydney Smith, Toyin Falola, and Robin Law (Madison: African Studies Program, University of Wisconsin at Madison, 1992), 166.

30. Afigbo, *Ropes of Sand,* 63.

31. Ibid., 158. Priests of Ana had to be consulted for permission before engaging in war. See Uchendu, *Igbo,* 96.

32. Ohadike, "Igbo-Benin Wars," 167.

33. Falola, *Igbo History and Society,* 314.

34. M. D. W. Jeffreys, "Ibo Warfare," *Man* 56 (June 1956): 77–79.

35. U. D. Anyanwu, "Kinship and Warfare in Igbo Society," in *Warfare and Diplomacy,* ed. Smith, Falola, and Law, 163.

36. Jeffreys, "Ibo Warfare," 77–79.

37. Falola, *Igbo History and Society,* 314.

38. Their martial culture was also reflected in their village planning. Communities built their houses in unbroken rows along each side of narrow streets running

radially out from a central village square, which housed a war drum that would draw warriors together. An invading force that tried to enter the village down one of these narrow streets would find lateral movement almost impossible and could be trapped by even a handful of skilled warriors at both ends of the street. See Anyanwu, "Kinship and Warfare," 20–21.

39. Isichei, *History,* 82.

40. Chukwuma Azuonye, "The Heroic Age of the Ohafia Igbo: Its Evolution and Socio-Cultural Consequences," *Genève-Afrique* 28 (1990): 7–35; John C. McCall, *Dancing Histories: Heuristic Ethnography with the Ohafia Igbo* (Ann Arbor: University of Michigan Press, 2000), 37.

41. On the achievement of women in these categories, see Achebe, *Farmers, Traders, Warriors, and Kings.*

42. In Ohafia these women were called *dike nwami* (heroines, warrior women, or brave women). See McCall, *Ohafia War Dance,* 117–36.

43. Chukwuma Azuone, "The Heroic Age of the Ohafia Igbo," *Geneva Africa* 28, no.1 (1990): 15.

44. The term "secret society" is so loaded with unspoken connotations that the anthropologist Evans-Pritchard moved to replace it with the more neutral and accurate term "closed association." See E. E. Evans-Pritchard, *Witchcraft, Oracles, and Magic among the Azande* (Oxford: Clarendon Press, 1937), 511.

45. Canon Udobata Onunwa, *Studies in Igbo Traditional Religion* (Uruowulu-Obosi: Pacific Publishers, 1990), 24–26.

46. Dike and Ekejiuba, *Aro,* 286–89.

47. Cf. Malcolm Ruel, *Leopards and Leaders: Constitutional Politics among Cross River People* (New York: Tavistock Publications, 1969), 201–51.

48. Leopard societies often had special techniques to kill their victims while making it look like an animal attack. See, for example, K. J. Beatty, *Human Leopards* (London: H. Rees, 1915); Malcom Ruel, *Leopards and Leaders: Constitutional Politics among a Cross River People* (New York: Tavistock Publications, 1969); and Wade Davis, *Passage of Darkness: The Ethnobiology of the Haitian Zombie* (Chapel Hill: University of North Carolina Press, 1988), 105.

49. These societies are linked to head-hunting, a trait that may have been part of the ancestral Igbo culture or learned from other Cross River peoples. See Onunwa, *Studies,* 25; and M. M. Green, *Igbo Village Affairs* (London: Frank Cass, 1964), 66–67; Falola, *Igbo History and Society,* 118.

50. These fighters also formed the "inner circle" of other societies. See Percy Amaury Talbot, *The Peoples of Southern Nigeria: A Sketch of Their History, Ethnology and Languages, with an Abstract of the 1921 Census* (London: F. Cass, 1969), 828–29.

51. Dike and Ekejiuba, *Aro,* 171.

52. Jill Salmons, "Martial Arts of the Annang," *African Arts* 19 (November 1985): 60.

53. Boniface Obichere, personal communication and letter to author, September 1994.

54. Salmons, "Martial Arts," 60.

55. Dike and Ekejiuba, *Aro,* 171.

56. Afigbo, *Ropes of Sand,* 22.

57. Although often described as mercenaries in some texts, these warriors fought not for money but for the chance to become full citizens in their natal societies. See Isichei, *History,* 52.

58. Unrelated neighbors often made peace through oaths that in effect made them putative kinsman, ideally to preclude full-scale war in the future. See Anyanwu, "Kinship and Warfare," 160–165.

59. Hoplology is "the science of arms and weapons of offense and defense, human and bestial." Burton opined that hoplology's study of combative behavior "plays the most important part in the annals of the world." See Richard F. Burton, *The Book of the Sword* (1984; repr., London: Chatto and Windus, 1987), 6, 1.

60. Nijel Binns, *Nuba Wrestling: The Original Art* (Los Angeles: Trans-Continental Network Productions, 1990), 9.

61. Equiano, *Life,* 11; G. T. Basden, "Notes on Ibo Country," *Geographical Journal* 19 (1912): 246–47; M. D. W. Jeffreys, "Dual Organization in Africa," *African Studies* 5, nos. 2 & 3 (1946): 82–85; Ambrose M. Chukwudum, *Know Thy Root* (Onitsha: Uni-world Educational Publishers, 1995).

62. Manfredi explores the larger meaning of these claims in "Philological Perspectives."

63. D. D. Hartle, "Archeology in Eastern Nigeria," *Nigeria Magazine* 93 (1967): 134–143; Afigbo, *Ropes of Sand,* 11.

64. Rems Nna Umeasiegbu, *Words Are Sweet* (Leiden: Brill, 1982), 122–23. See also "Why Ghost Offerings Are Made before Towns," in Perry Amaury Talbot, *In the Shadow of the Bush* (London: Heinemann, 1912), 7–9.

65. Celestine Ugbome, head wrestling coach of Benin City, Nigeria, interview, November 15, 1990.

66. Winifred Gallaway contends that Gambian wrestling "appears to have evolved as a modified version of real combat." See B. K. Sidibe and Winifred Gallaway, "Wrestling in the Gambia," *Gambia Museum Bulletin* 1 (February 1981), 29; and Josy Michalon, *Le Ladjia: Origine at practiques* (Paris: Editions caribéennes, 1987), 42–43.

67. The following details have to be drawn from late nineteenth- and twentieth-century ethnographic reports. However, given their interrelationship with the ancestral Igbo cultural patterns, it is quite probable that many of these social functions, if not particular details, are of some antiquity.

68. Sigrid Paul, "The Wrestling Tradition and Its Social Functions," in *Sport in Africa: Essays in Social History,* ed. William Baker and James Mangen (New York and London: Africana Publishing Co., 1987), 32.

69. Frank A. Salamone, "Gungawa Wrestling as an Ethnic Boundary Marker," *Afrika und Übersee* 57, no. 3 (1973–74): 193–202.

70. An ankle pick is a technique by which a grappler seizes an opponent's upper body as in a side hold position and then reaches across to grab the opponent's ankle and pull it out from under him while leaning his body weight over that leg.

71. G. T. Basden, *Among the Ibos of Nigeria* (London: Frank Cass, 1966), 129.

72. Ken Pfrenger, "Irish Collar and Elbow Wrestling," *Hop-Lite* 6 (1998): 6.

73. Talbot, *In the Shadow,* 285. In the sense that what is referred to in the British tradition as Greco-Roman relies more on locking the upper body for throws and excludes groundwork, Talbot seems more accurate.

74. Although it does not preclude the possibility of Edo cultural influence in the Americas, it should be noted that the Edo were rarely taken to the Americas. The Benin kingdom of the Edo refused to sell captives to Europeans for much of the era of the slave trade. Even in Hall's broad scouring of African ethnic groups in American documents, she reported, "Only one Edo—in Trinidad—was found in all the other lists of slaves studied in this book" (Hall, *Slavery and African Ethnicities,* 105).

75. For example, *itu eko* (leg wrapping). Michael J. C. Echeruo, *Igbo-English Dictionary* (New Haven, Conn.: Yale University Press, 1998) also adds *uge* in addition to two variations on leg wrapping (*ege* and *nge*), but it is not clear from the description to which specific technique it refers.

76. For a fictional but informative picture of how these regional techniques are perpetuated, see Buchi Emecheta, *The Wrestling Match* (New York: G. Braziller, 1983, 1983).

77. Edward Powe, *Combat Games of Northern Nigeria* (Madison, Wis.: D. Aiki Publications, 1994), 65.

78. Frank Salamone, "Persistence and Change in Ethnic and Religious Identity" (Ph.D. diss., State University of New York, Buffalo, 1973).

79. Paul, "Wrestling Tradition," 38.

80. Francis Arinze, *Sacrifice in Ibo Religion* (Ibadan: Ibadan University Press, 1970), 16, 27, 106.

81. C. K. Meek, *Law and Authority in a Nigerian Tribe* (New York: Barnes & Noble, 1970), 26.

82. P. Amaury Talbot, *Tribes of the Niger Delta* (London: Barnes & Noble, 1967), 317–18.

83. Emmanuel N. Akwaranwa, *A Politico-Cultural History of Nigeria and Ukwa People of Imo State of Nigeria* (Owerri: Government Printer, 1988), 41.

84. Marius Nkwoh, *Igbo Cultural Heritage* (Onitsha: University Publishing Co., 1984), 211.

85. Ibid., 211–13.

86. Talbot, *Peoples of Southern Nigeria,* 817.

87. R. F. Adams, "Ibo Texts," *Africa* 7, no. 4 (1934): 453–54.

88. Meek, *Law and Authority,* 197–99.

89. Paul, "Wrestling Tradition," 29.

90. *Ikpo* means "bells," which these wrestlers wore to show their confidence in not being thrown.

91. Simon Ottenberg, *Boyhood Rituals in an African Society: An Interpretation* (Seattle: University of Washington Press, 1989), 82–87.

92. Ugbome interview.

93. Northrup, *Trade without Rulers,* 93.

94. Azuka A. Dike, *The Resilience of Igbo Culture: A Case Study of Awka Town* (Enugu, Nigeria: Fourth Dimension Publishers, 1985), 31.

95. Paul, "Wrestling Tradition," 41.

96. Ibid.; Ugbome interview; Alyce Taylor Cheska, *Traditional Games and Dances in West African Nations* (Schorndorf: K. Hofmannã 1987), 58.

97. G. T. Basden, *Niger Ibos* (London: Cass, 1966), 348.

98. Veena Sharma, "'Leisure' in a Traditional West African Society," *Africana* 2 (October 1989): 9–10.

99. Other means of attaining heroic status included bravery in war, agricultural mastery, oratorical skill, and judicial honesty. All but the former would be marked by different masquerades. See Emeka Nwabueze, "The Masquerade as Hero in Igbo Traditional Society," *Frankfurter Afrikanistische Blätter* 1 (1989): 95–107.

100. Afigbo, *Ropes of Sand,* 158.

101. Anyanwu, "Kinship and Warfare," 163.

102. Chambers, "He Gwine Sing He Country," 147; M. Angulu Onwuejeogwu, *An Igbo Civilization: Nri Kingdom & Hegemony* (London: Ethnographica / Benin City, Nigeria: Ethiope, 1981), 21–22, 31–50; Afigbo, *Ropes of Sand,* 8–9; Dike and Ekejiuba, *Aro,* 109–4.

103. For an example of wrestling to settle matters of honor and personal offenses, see Meek, *Law and Authority,* 230; Macarthy Olufemi, interview, Benin City, Nigeria, November 17, 1990, and letter to author, February 21, 1993.

104. Olufemi interview.

105. Arthur Leonard, *The Lower Niger and Its Tribes* (London: Frank Cass, 1968 [1906]), 17–19.

106. Meek, *Law and Authority,* 8; Chambers, "He Gwine Sing He Country," 169.

107. Northrup, *Trade without Rulers,* 102.

108. Afigbo, *Warrant Chiefs,* 16.

109. Chambers, "He Gwine Sing He Country," 149.

110. The Aro were not alone in supplementing their agricultural endeavors with other specializations. The Awka, Nkwerre, and Abiriba became famous as traveling blacksmiths, while the Awka also became agents of an oracle called Agbala. See Afigbo, *Ropes of Sand,* 17–18, 131–35.

111. The other specialist groups conducted their business by "periodic occupational wanderings" known as *iga uzo ije, iga mbia,* or *iga n'uzu.* In this system the specialists wandered about the country, stopping at strategic locations temporarily to conduct their business. See Afigbo, *Ropes of Sand,* 24.

112. In some regions the society developed strong political power as well.

113. J. N. Oriji, "A Re-Assessment of the Organization and Benefits of the Slave and Palm Produce Trade amongst the Ngwa-Igbo," *Canadian Journal of African Studies* 16, no. 3 (1982): 523–48.

114. Dike and Ekejiuba, *Aro,* 171.

115. Herman Kölar, reproduced in Elizabeth Isichei, *Igbo Worlds: An Anthology of Oral Histories and Historical Descriptions* (Philadelphia: Institute for the Study of Human Issues, 1978), 201–3.

116. *Bulletin de la Congregation* (December 1891–March 1892), 358, reproduced in Isichei, *Igbo Worlds,* 201–3.

117. There were, however, numerous cases of villages that effectively resisted Aro military domination. See J. N. Oriji, "Strategies and Weapons of Warfare and Defense in Igbo Society during Slavery," paper presented at African Studies Association meeting, December 6, 2002.

118. It is difficult to separate and quantify methods of enslavement, but kidnapping appears to have been the most common form, followed by warfare and, to a lesser degree, sale by family or as a criminal punishment. Northrup, *Trade without Rulers,* 65–80.

119. Equiano, *Life,* 9.

120. James Barbot, *A Description of the Coasts of North and South Guinea; and of Ethiopia Inferior, vulgarly Angola* (1678–82), in Awnsham and John Churchill, *A collection of voyages and travels some now first printed from original manuscripts, others now first published in English* (London: J. Walthoe, 1732) 1:381, 461. For further discussion of Barbot as a source, see P. E. H Hair, Adam Jones, and Robin Law *Barbot on Guinea: The Writings of Jean Barbot on West Africa, 1678–1712* (London: Hakluyt Society, 1992).

121. John Adams, *Sketches Taken during Ten Voyages to Africa between the Years 1786 and 1800 . . .* (1822; repr., New York: Johnson Reprint Corp., 1970), 39.

122. Northrup estimates the Igbo percentage at 60 percent, while Chambers follows the trader John Adams and estimates the percentage at 80 percent. See Northrup, *Trade without Rulers*, 62; Adams, *Sketches*, 116, 129; and Chambers, "He Gwine Sing He Country,"160. For wider perspectives, see Paul Lovejoy, "The Impact of the Atlantic Slave Trade on Africa: A Review of the Literature," *Journal of African History* 30 (1989): 375; E. J. Alagoa, "The Slave Trade in the Niger Delta: Oral Traditions and History," in *Africans in Bondage: Studies in Slavery and the Slave Trade*, ed. Paul Lovejoy (Madison: African Studies Program, University of Wisconsin–Madison, 1986), 127; and Hall, *Slavery and African Ethnicities*, 126–43.

123. Preferences by American planters for or against enslaved Biafrans also helped to funnel Biafrans into specific areas of the Americas in large numbers. See Hall, *Slavery and African Ethnicities*, 55–79, 126–43.

124. These figures are drawn from David Eltis, Stephen D. Behrendt, David Richardson, and Herbert S. Klein, *The Trans-Atlantic Slave Trade: A Database on CD-ROM* (Cambridge: Cambridge University Press, 1999).

125. Monica Schuler, *"Alas, Alas, Kongo": A Social History of Indentured African Immigration into Jamaica, 1841–1865* (Baltimore: Johns Hopkins University Press, 1980), 93–96.

126. For a description of the violence and uncertainty that plagued these regions during the slave trade, see Isichei, *History;* and Miller, *Way of Death.*

Chapter 3: Enslaved Honor

1. Even in North America, Gen. William Moultrie of South Carolina found out when he returned to his plantation during the War for American Independence. As he approached, "old Africans joined in a war-song in their own language, of 'welcome the war home.'" See William Moultrie, *Memoirs of the American Revolution, so far as it related to the states of North and South Carolina, and Georgia compiled from the most authentic materials, the author's personal knowledge of the various events, and including an epistolary correspondence on public affairs, with civil and military officers, at that period*, 2 vols. (New York: David Longworth, 1802), 2:356. Special thanks to Ras Michael Brown for this reference. For Igbo war dance in Trinidad, see Andrew Pearse Collection, Court of Criminal Inquiry, Port of Spain, November 21, 1823.

2. See, for example, Thornton, "African Soldiers in the Haitian Revolution," 58–80; John K. Thornton, "African Dimension of the Stono Rebellion," *American Historical Review* 96, no. 4 (1991): 1101–13; John K. Thornton, "'I Am the Subject of the King of Congo': African Political Ideology and the Haitian Revolution," *Journal of World History* 4, no. 2 (1993): 181–214.

3. Eltis et al., *Trans-Atlantic Slave Trad;e* David Eltis and David Richardson, eds., *Routes to Slavery: Direction, Ethnicity and Mortality in the Transatlantic Slave Trade* (Portland, Oreg.: Frank Cass, 1997).

4. Joseph E. Holloway, *Africanisms in American Culture* (Bloomington: Indiana University Press, 1991); Peter H. Wood, *Black Majority: Negros in Colonial South Carolina from 1670 through the Stono Rebellion* (New York: W. W. Norton & Company, 1975); Chambers, "He Gwine Sing He Country"; Gwendolyn Midlo Hall, *Africans in Colonial Louisiana: The Development of Afro-Creole Culture in the Eighteenth Century* (Baton Rouge: Louisiana State University Press, 1992); Mary C. Karasch, *Slave Life in Rio de Janeiro, 1808–1850* (Princeton, N.J.: Princeton University Press, 1987); William D. Piersen, *Black Yankees: The Development of an Afro-American Subculture in Eighteenth-Century New England* (Amherst: University of Massachusetts Press, 1988); John Thornton, *Africa and Africans in the Making of the Atlantic World: 1400–1800* (New York: Cambridge University Press, 1998); Gomez, *Exchanging Our Country Marks;* Reis, *Slave Rebellion in Brazil;* Manuel Raymundo Querino, *Costumes africanos no Brasil* (Rio de Janeiro: Civilização brasileira s.a., 1938); Raymundo Nina Rodrigues and Homero Pires, *Os Africanos no Brasil,* 3rd ed. (São Paulo: Companhia Editora Nacional, 1945); Maya Deren, *Divine Horsemen: The Living Gods of Haiti* (London and New York: Thames and Hudson, 1953); Martha Warren Beckwith, *Black Roadways: A Study of Jamaican Folk Life* (New York: Negro Universities Press, 1969).

5. Equiano, *Life,* 52.

6. For a detailed study on the role of wrestling as an ethnic marker, see Salamone, "Gungawa Wrestling," 193–201.

7. Thus, while enslaved Senegambians, for example, would have continued to distinguish themselves in the bonded community through their particular grappling style, they also would have been keenly aware of its overarching similarities to *mgba* and other West African styles in contrast to the radically divergent form of Euro-Americans, who wrestled on the ground looking to maim an opponent.

8. The English art of boxing emerged as a combat sport with at least a generalized set of rules under James Figg in the late seventeenth century and became relatively more refined with the promulgation of Jack Broughton's rules in 1743. See John Ford, *Prizefighting: The Age of Regency Boximania* (Newton Abbot: David and Charles, 1971); and Tom Parramore, "Gouging in Early North Carolina," *North Carolina Folklore Journal* 22 (1974): 58.

9. Gorn, "Gouge and Bite," 20.

10. Thomas Anburey, *Travels through the Interior Parts of America,* 2 vols. (1789; repr., New York: New York Times, 1969), 2:349; Rhys Isaac, *The Transformation of Virginia, 1740–1790* (Chapel Hill: University of North Carolina Press, 1982), 98.

11. Gorn, "Gouge and Bite," 19–22.

12. William Oliver Stevens, *Pistols at Ten Paces* (Boston: Houghton Mifflin, 1940), 33–37.

13. Gorn, "Gouge and Bite," 22.

14. Ibid., 41–42.

15. Elliott Gorn, *The Manly Art* (Ithaca, N.Y.: Cornell University Press, 1986), 35.

16. David Hackett Fischer, *Albion's Seed: Four British Folkways in America* (New York: Oxford University Press, 1989), 735–37.

17. Allen Guttman, "English Sports Spectators: The Restoration to the Early Nineteenth Century," *Journal of Sport History* 12, no. 1 (1985): 103–25. See also Milton Sherman, "Traditional Wrestling Styles: A Survey and Analysis" (M.A. thesis, East Carolina University, 1979).

18. This style was also known at various times as scuffing, Irish-style scuffing, New Cornish, Square Hold, and Box wrestling. The style not only was practiced in Ireland but also had variations in Scotland and northern England. See Charles M. Wilson, *The Magnificent Scufflers: Revealing the Days When America Wrestled the World* (Brattleboro, Vt.: Stephen Greene Press, 1959).

19. Edward MacLysaght, *Irish Life in the Seventeenth Century* (Cork: University Press, 1950 [1939]), 152.

20. Wilson, *Magnificent Scufflers,* 5.

21. David K. Wiggins, "Sport and Popular Pastimes in the Plantation Community: The Slave Experience" (Ph.D. diss., University of Maryland, 1979), 94.

22. At age eighteen George Washington held a countywide and possibly colony-wide championship. Later as leader of the Continental army he demonstrated his favorite technique, throwing seven Massachusetts volunteers with his "flying mare." Other collar-and-elbow wrestling presidents included Zachary Taylor, William Taft, Chester Arthur, and Calvin Coolidge, while Abe Lincoln was a championship "catch-as-catch-can" wrestler. See Wilson, *Magnificent Scufflers,* 6–7.

23. Wilson, *Magnificent Scufflers,* 6–7.

24. Gomez (*Exchanging Our Country Marks*) argues that the timing of this demographic transition also marked the transition of perspective from specific African ethnicities to a black identity.

25. Other West African regions besides Biafra may have had similar substyles. For example, the *even* style of the Edo just to the west of Biafra contains a similar substyle, as may numerous other ethnic groups between the Niger and Kwanza rivers. The side-hold position was a common defensive strategy in many West African wrestling styles but was apparently not central to all of them. For example, Balandier lists the major techniques of Senegambian wrestling, and there is no mention of leg wrapping. See G. Balandier and P. Mercier, *Particularism et évolution: Les Pêcheurs Lebou du Senegal* (Saint Louis, Sénégal: Centre IFAN, 1952), 59–60.

26. Another parallel was the use of wrestling as a form of conflict resolution. In twentieth-century practice in the lowcountry, when two youths were caught fighting, the black elders would separate them and make them wrestle. They consciously tried to limit the feelings of anger and envy surrounding such communally sanctioned bouts so that the wrestling could be used to keep peace in the community. Under bondage, as we shall see shortly, wrestling was also used as a form of conflict resolution, such as in disputes between rivals in romance. Wrestling was used, as in Biafra and likely other areas of Africa, to limit conflicts. In cases of actual fighting, bondsmen often turned instead to the male-dominated striking art of knocking and kicking. See Margaret Smalls and Sam Toomer, taped interview, Beaufort, S.C., July 14, 1992.

27. R. F. Adams, "Igbo Texts," *Africa* 7, no. 4 (1934): 453–54; Sigrid Paul, "The Wrestling Tradition and Its Social Functions," in *Sport in Africa,* ed. Baker and Mangen, 38.

28. Ottenberg, *Boyhood Rituals,* 89–90.

29. See the story of Sarah Fitzpatrick, who wrestled against whites as a child, in John W. Blassingame, *Slave Testimony: Two Centuries of Letters, Speeches, Interviews, and Autobiographies* (Baton Rouge: Louisiana State University Press, 1977), 641.

30. Margaret Smalls and Sam Toomer, taped interview, Beaufort, S.C., July 14, 1992.

31. South Carolina planters, possibly due to some stereotypes, often purchased Biafran women but rejected Biafran males (Holloway, *Africanisms,* 10).

32. Although British ships also called along the coast of Benguela and at the mouth of the Kunene River, most of the Angolans taken to North America were purchased along the Greater Loango Coast. Robert F. Thompson notes that people taken from the Greater Loango region also had an elaborate system of butting. Thus, while the art of inverted kicking (and possibly "knocking" head butts, which will be described shortly) appears to have been derived primarily from southern Angola, head butting had at least one additional African source from northern Angola. While some other African groups practiced the equivalent of "butting" at close quarters (such as in northern Angola or urban Sierra Leone), I am not yet aware of anyplace other than Cimbebasia where people charged each other like rams. Certainly there may have been other African sources of butting as well, but at present detailed studies of African martial arts are lacking. On butting along the Greater Loango Coast, see Robert Farris Thompson, "Foreword," in J. Lowell Lewis, *Ring of Liberation: Deceptive Discourse in Brazilian Capoeira* (Chicago: University of Chicago Press, 1992), xiii.

33. Rather than being spread directly from Africa, head butting may have been spread rhizomatically across the Americas by black sailors, as we shall explore in the last chapter.

34. W. Faux, *Memorable Days in America: Being a Journal of a Tour to the United States, Principally Undertaken to Ascertain, by Positive Evidence, the Condition and Probable Prospects of British Emigrants; Including Accounts of Mr. Birkbeck's Settlement in Illinois* (1823; repr., New York: AMS Press, 1969), 10.

35. Emory Cambell, interview, Beaufort, S.C., March 11, 1994.

36. Mike Cohen, interview, Hilton Head, S.C., July 13, 1992; Perry White, interview, Beaufort, S.C., July 13, 1992.

37. Sam Toomer, interview, Beaufort, S.C., July 14, 1992.

38. Sam Toomer, interview, Beaufort, S.C., July 18, 1992.

39. Herman Carter, interview, Beaufort, S.C., March 26, 1994.

40. John Anerum, interview, Beaufort, S.C., March 10, 1993.

41. Eric Murray, personal communication, July 2002.

42. Al Alston, interview, Charleston, S.C., March 12, 1992; Zora Dance, Petersburg, Va., March 11, 1994.

43. Sam Toomer, interview, Beaufort, S.C., March 9, 1994; Peter Smalls, interview, Beaufort, S.C., July 13, 1992.

44. Ira Berlin, *Many Thousands Gone: The First Two Centuries of Slavery in North America* (Cambridge, Mass.: Belknap Press of Harvard University Press, 1998), 64–76.

45. Graham Russel Hodges, *Root & Branch: African Americans in New York and East Jersey, 1613–1863* (Chapel Hill: University of North Carolina Press, 1999), 41–43; Berlin, *Many Thousands Gone,* 195–215.

46. For a detailed synchronic and diachronic analysis of bondage in these regions, see Ira Berlin, "Time, Space, and the Evolution of Afro-American Society on British Mainland North America," *American Historical Review* 85 (1980): 44–78; and Philip D. Morgan, *Slave Counterpoint: Black Culture in the Eighteenth-Century Chesapeake & Lowcountry* (Williamsburg: North Carolina Press, 1998).

47. On South Carolina, rice production, and African rice technologies, see Wood, *Black Majority;* Daniel Littlefield, *Rice and Slaves: Ethnicity and the Slave Trade in Colonial South Carolina* (Urbana: University of Illinois Press, 1981); and Judith A. Carney, *Black Rice* (Cambridge, Mass.: Harvard University Press, 2001).

48. Piersen notes the place of stick fighting and other combat sports in black election day festivities of New England. A *kalenda* stick-fighting tradition was practiced in Louisiana and possibly South Carolina. Head butting, kicking, and a boxing style called cutting remain part of the legacy of the lower Mississippi Valley. See Piersen, *Black Yankees,* 124. See also Lewis, *Ring of Liberation,* 227n6; Earl White, personal communication, July 1989; field notes from Bogalusa, La., and Normal, Ala., Spring 1993.

49. This section is deeply indebted to the work and wisdom of Christopher Kouri, whom I met when we were both in South Carolina researching the subject. I gained many insights from our discussions and his thesis. One of these was that the art was also called *yuna onse* or *hana onse,* terms that I had not been aware of up to then. See Kouri cited in C. Daniel Dawson, *Capoeira Angola and Mestre João Grande: The Saga of a Tradition; The Development of a Master* (New York, 1993), 7; and Christopher Henry Kouri, "The Search for Knocking and Kicking: Notes toward a Definition and Historical Understanding of the Old Time Slave Derived Martial Art and Related Fighting Techniques of the Gullah" (B.A. thesis, Yale University, 1990). On gouging spreading from the Chesapeake and lowcountry across the south, see Gorn, "Gouge and Bite."

50. In the case of stick fighting, the *kalenda* form may well have spread from the French Caribbean, but early scattered references to stick dances among bondsmen in Iberia and continued practice in places such as the Cape Verde Islands make it possible to postulate that some ritual stick fighting in the Americas may have been part of the cultural legacy tied to the early Atlantic Africans of Iberia.

51. As a result of code switching between these two realms, Gomez (*Exchanging Our Country Marks,* 8–10) concludes that African Americans "engaged in polycultural rather than syncretic life-styles."

52. Gomez, *Exchanging Our Country Marks,* 10.

53. A fourth context, but one that I explore elsewhere, is the use and transmission of combat arts in prisons across the Atlantic world. See T. J. Desch-Obi, "Masculinity and the 52 Combat Aesthetic," paper presented at the Black Masculinities Conference, Graduate Center, City University of New York, February 2005.

54. C. Daniel Dawson appropriately rejects labeling maroons with the oxymoron "runaway slaves" and describes them as self-liberated Africans. See Dawson, "The Culture of Freedom: Quilombos, Palenques and Maroon Societies in the Americas," lecture presented at New York University, April 2, 2003.

55. See Richard Price and Maroon societies, *Maroon Societies: Rebel Slave Communities in the Americas,* 2nd ed. (Baltimore: Johns Hopkins University Press, 1979).

56. I am eagerly awaiting the thesis of Kenyatta Gedegbevi, who is documenting the role of African martial traditions among maroon groups in the lowcountry.

57. Prince Edward Court Order Book, 1754–58, 78, cited in Morgan, *Slave Counterpoint,* 439.

58. Morgan, *Slave Counterpoint,* 450.

59. Thornton, "African Dimension," 1112.

60. Dawson, *Capoeira Angola,* 7–8; C. Daniel Dawson, personal communication, February 26, 1994.

61. Y. N. Kly, "The Gullah War: 1739–1858," in Marquetta L.Goodwine ed. *The Legacy of Ibo Landing,* 19–53.

62. For descriptions of maroons and this swamp, see Frederick Law Olmsted, *A Journey in the Seaboard Slave States with Remarks on Their Economy* (New York: Dix & Edwards, 1856), 146–63; Portsmouth Library, *Readings in Black and White: Lower Tidewater Virginia* (Portsmouth, Va.: by the author, 1993).

63. James Mellon, ed., *Bullwhip Days: The Slaves Remember, an Oral History* (New York: Weidenfeld & Nicolson, 1988), 140–41.

64. Austin Steward, *Twenty-Two Years a Slave and Forty Years a Freeman* (1857; repr., New York, 1968), 58–59.

65. Literally weevils, or snout beetles. See Charles L. Perdue Jr., Thomas E. Barden, and Robert K. Phillips, eds., *Weevils in the Wheat: Interviews with Virginia Ex-Slaves* (Bloomington: Indiana University Press, 1980), 297, 299.

66. Ira Berlin, Marc Favreau, and Steven Miller, eds., *Remembering Slavery: African Americans Talk about Their Personal Experiences of Slavery and Freedom* (New York: New Press, 1998), 55.

67. Frederick Douglass, *My Bondage and My Freedom* (1855; repr., New York: Miller, Orton & Mulligan, 1994), 292–93. See also George P. Rawick, *The American Slave: A Composite Autobiography,* 19 vols. (Westport, Conn.: Greenwood Press, 1972), 15:pt. 2, p. 132.

68. Rawick, *American Slave,* 6:418.

69. Willie Lee Rose, *A Documentary History of Slavery in North America* (New York: Oxford University Press, 1976), 276–82.

70. Petition of John Rose, Richland District, 1831, Slavery Files, South Carolina Archives, Columbia, cited in Charles Joyner, "The World of Plantation Slaves," in *Before Freedom Came: African-American Life in the Antebellum South,* ed. Edward D. C. Campbell and Kym Rice (Charlottesville: University Press of Virginia, 1991).

71. David Wiggins, "Leisure Time on the Southern Plantation: The Slaves' Respite from Constant Toil 1810–1860," in *Sport in America,* ed. Donald Spivey (Westport, Conn.: Greenwood Press, 1985), 25–50.

72. Anonymous, *American Museum* 1, no. 3 (1787): 215.

73. John Adams, *Travels of Four Years and a Half in the United States of America: During 1798, 1799, 1800, 1801, and 1802* (London, 1803), 385.

74. Obviously there were some skilled bondsmen for whom the distinction was less clear, but even some of these would have been aware that their talents were profiting their enslavers.

75. Roger D. Abrahams and John F. Szwed, eds., *After Africa: Extracts from British Travel Accounts and Journals of the Seventeenth, Eighteenth and Nineteenth Centuries*

Concerning the Slaves, Their Manners and Customs in the British West Indies (New Haven, Conn.: Yale University Press, 1983), 1–48.

76. John Blassingame, *The Slave Community* (New York: Oxford University Press, 1979), 39–40. There was more variation during the eighteenth century, but by the nineteenth century the half-day Saturday was widely established. See Wiggins, "Leisure Time," 39; and Chambers, "He Gwine Sing He Country," 439.

77. Wiggins, "Leisure Time," 39. Furthermore, these "days off" were actually essential workdays as well. Planters often provided the enslaved with provision gardens or "kitchen gardens," from which the enslaved were expected to grow much for their own sustenance. This allowed some planters to purchase less food and provided some bondsmen the hope of gaining income of their own by selling their surplus at a local market.

78. Douglass, *My Bondage,* 253–54.

79. Wiggins, "Leisure Time," 39.

80. Allen Kulikof, *Tobacco and Slaves* (Chapel Hill: University of North Carolina Press, 1986), 271.

81. Georgia Writers Project, *Drums and Shadows: Survival Studies among the Georgia Coastal Negroes* (Athens: University of Georgia Press, 1940).

82. Sterling Stuckey, *Slave Culture* (New York: Oxford University Press, 1987).

83. Jurretta Jordan Heckscher, "All the Mazes of the Dance: Black Dancing, Culture, and Identity in the Greater Chesapeake World from the Early Eighteenth Century to the Civil War" (Ph.D. diss., George Washington University, 2000), 59.

84. See the descriptions of shouts, conjure dance, and voodoo dancing in Lawrence R. Murphy, *The Slave Narratives of Texas* (Austin, Tex.: Encino Press, 1974), 81–95.

85. These new nations were not fixed equivalents of African ethnic groups or nationalities but constantly changing negotiations between specific African ethnicities and larger collective identities. Changing membership in these new nations reflected place of birth, port of emigration from Africa, sociopolitical changes in Africa, and flexible redefinitions based on solidarity, ideology, spirituality, and prestige. Although these nations were once dismissed by some scholars as merely port names imposed by European traders, Gwendolyn Hall has shown that these were often self-identifications in many parts of the Americas. Smaller, more specific ethnic identities were not forgotten, and if significant number emerged in a social context, they could break off as their own group. Olabiyi Yai has highlighted the fact that many Africans in Africa and the Diaspora held multiple nationalities without contradiction. Ivor Miller has shown that these self-identifications with certain nation and African locations could spread spiritually to those (Africans, African Americans, or even Europeans) without previous biological, political, or cultural links to these regions. These new nations were often transnational as highlighted by Lorand Matory. See Russell Lohse, "Slave-Trade Nomenclature and African Ethnicities in the Americas: Evidence from Early Eighteenth-Century Costa Rica," *Slavery & Abolition* 23, no. 3 (1980):73–92; Douglas B. B. Chambers, "Ethnicity in the Diaspora: The Slave-Trade and the Creation of African 'Nations' in the Americas," *Slavery & Abolition* 22 (December 2001): 27–29; Paul E. Lovejoy, "Ethnic Designations of the Slave Trade and the Reconstruction of the History of Trans-Atlantic Slavery," in Paul E. Lovejoy

and David Vincent Trotman, *Trans-Atlantic Dimensions of Ethnicity in the African Diaspora* (London and New York: Continuum, 2003); Hall, *Slavery and African Ethnicities;* and Ivor L. Miller, "The Formation of African Identities in the Americas: Spiritual 'Ethnicity,'" *Contours* 2, no. 2 (2004): 193–202.

86. John F. Watson, *Annals of Philadelphia, being a collection of memoirs, anecdotes, & incidents of the city and its inhabitants, from the days of the Pilgrim founders: To which is added an appendix, containing olden time researches and reminiscences of New York City* (Philadelphia: E. L. Carey & A. Hart, 1830), 351–52.

87. Verbal duels by the late nineteenth century would take the form later called "signifying," "sounding," or "playing the dozens." See Roger D. Abrahams, "Playing the Dozens," *Journal of American Folklore* 75 (July–September 1962): 209–20, particularly 219n1 on the antiquity of the practice that may have African prototypes. On dancing competitions, see Heckscher, "All the Mazes." For an excellent discussion of this complex in the Caribbean, see Roger D. Abrahams, *The Man-of-Words in the West Indies: Performance and the Emergence of Creole Culture* (Baltimore: Johns Hopkins University Press, 1983); and Elizabeth A. McAlister, *Rara! Vodou, Power, and Performance in Haiti and Its Diaspora* (Berkeley: University of California Press, 2002).

88. For discussion of centrality of dance to African combat traditions, see Judith L. Hanna, "African Dance and the Warrior Tradition," *Journal of Asian and African Studies* 12, nos. 1–2 (1977): 111–33; and Earl White, "Martial Arts and African Dance: The Hidden Connection," *Inside Kung Fu* 25 (May 1998): 96–104.

89. Ron Daise, personal communication, Beaufort, S.C., March 11, 1994. The art was also performed covertly in Christian dance circles. See T. J. Desch-Obi, "Combat and the Crossing of the Kalunga," in *Central Africans and Cultural Transformations,* ed. Heywood, 366–67.

90. John Pierpont, journal, 10–13, Pierpont Morgan Library, New York, N.Y., quoted in Dena J. Epstein, *Sinful Tunes and Spirituals: Black Folk Music to the Civil War* (Urbana: University of Illinois Press, 1977), 84.

91. South Carolina begins in many ways as an offshoot of Barbados. See, for example, Wood, *Black Majority,* 13–34.

92. Richard Ligon, *A true & exact history of the island of Barbados illustrated with a mapp of the island, as also the principall trees and plants there, set forth in their due proportions and shapes, drawne out by their severall and respective scales: Together with the ingenio that makes the sugar, with the plots of the severall houses, roomes, and other places that are used in the whole processe of sugar-making* (London: Humphrey Moseley, 1657), 50.

93. Douglass, *My Bondage,* 253–54.

94. Wiggins, "Leisure Time," 69, 156–57.

95. Paul, "Wrestling Tradition," 23–46. For example, Salamone notes of Gungawa intervillage matches, "Its aim was to hurt the opponent, with or without the dangerous wrestling bracelet" (in ibid., 29).

96. Piersen, *Black Yankees,* 117–40.

97. Ibid., 129–31.

98. W. Jeffrey Bolster, *Black Jacks: African American Seamen in the Age of Sail* (Cambridge, Mass.: Harvard University Press, 1997), 110–19.

99. Even when enslaved males were fighting each other, women of the community often provided music accompaniment or verbal encouragement as spectators.

100. Douglass, *My Bondage*, 253.

101. Among Igbo, see Rems Nna Umeasiegbu, *The Way We Lived: Ibo Customs and Stories* (London: Heinemann Educational, 1969), 37–38.

102. O. K. Armstrong, *Old Massa's People: The Old Slaves Tell Their Story* (Indianapolis: Bobbs-Merrill, 1931), 160–63. Figure 3.4 also depicts a duel in Venezuela between two rival suitors, but the weapon of choice for this duel was obviously a local variant on knocking.

103. Winthrop Jordan, "American Chiaroscuro: The Status and Definition of Mulattoes in the British Colonies," *William and Mary Quarterly*, 3rd ser., 19 (1962): 183–200; Morgan, *Slave Counterpoint*, 81–83.

104. Many Indigenous American groups also had blacks among their ranks fighting against these militias. See William Katz, *Black Indians: A Hidden Heritage* (New York, 1986); and Jack D. Forbes, *Africans and Native Americans: The Language of Race and the Evolution of Red-Black Peoples* (Urbana: University of Illinois Press, 1993).

105. Quoted in Nat Fleischer, *Black Dynamite: Story of the Negro in Boxing* (New York: C. J. O'Brien, 1938), 19–20.

106. Sidney Kaplan, *The Black Presence in the Era of the American Revolution 1770–1800* (Washington, D.C.: Smithsonian Institution, 1973), 50–51.

107. Roger D. Abrahams, *Singing the Master: The Emergence of African-American Culture in the Plantation South* (New York: Pantheon Books, 1992), 65.

108. Eugene Genovese, David Wiggins, and Andrew Kaye question the regular existence of such planter-inspired contests on the basis that "intra-communal fighting was inimical to the need for self-preservation and group consensus that was important in captivity." See Eugene Genovese, *Roll, Jordan, Roll: The World the Slaves Made* (New York: Pantheon Books, 1974), 569, 784n20; David K. Wiggins, "Slave and Popular Pastimes in the Plantation Community: The Slave Experience" (Ph.D. diss., University of Maryland, 1979), 69; and Andrew M. Kaye, "A Tiger in the Ring and a Pussycat Outside: American Attitudes towards Black Prizefighters, 1810–1938" (M.A. thesis, Emory University, 1998), 16.

109. Gorn, *Manly Art*, 35.

110. Henry Bibb, *Narrative of the Life and Adventures of Henry Bibb, an American Slave*, in *Puttin' on Ole Massa: The Slave Narratives of Henry Bibb, William Wells Brown and Solomon Northrup*, ed. Gilbert Osofsky (New York: Harper & Row, 1969), 68.

111. Douglass, *My Bondage*, 253–54.

112. Bibb, *Narrative*, 68.

113. William Faulkner, *Absalom, Absalom!* (New York: Vintage Books, 1936; repr., 1990), 20–21.

114. While "their betting habits seem irrational even by the more prudential standards of their own day," Breen explains that gambling in Virginia was a ritual activity that brought together planters' realities and beliefs about competitiveness, honor, independence, materialism, and chance. See Timothy H. Breen, "Horses and Gentlemen: The Cultural Significance of Gambling among the Gentry of Virginia," *William and Mary Quarterly* 34 (April 1977): 329–47.

115. Charles Brown in Richard M. Dorson, ed., *American Negro Folktales* (Greenwich, Conn.: Fawcett Publications, 1967), 134.

116. Perdue et al., *Weevils in the Wheat*, 317.

117. Jeptha Choice in Mellon, *Bullwhip Days*, 138.

118. Fleischer, *Black Dynamite,* 34–35. For another version of the same combat, see Louis Golding, *The Bare-Knuckle Breed* (New York: Barnes, 1954), 121–27. Unfortunately neither author discloses his source, leaving the historic validity of either account tenuous.

119. There are various versions of black folktales in which the hero, who embodies the trickster hero, is pitted against a rival fighter of much greater strength and size. However, before the contest he prepares a trick and intimidates his adversary to win the fight and gain his freedom. See Dorson, *American Negro Folktales,* 132–35; and James Brewer, *Worser Days and Better Times* (Chicago: Quadrangle Books, 1965), 108–10. For a fuller exploration of the trickster-hero among African Americans, see Lawrence Levine, *Black Culture and Black Consciousness: Afro-American Folk Thought from Slavery to Freedom* (New York: Oxford University Press, 1977).

120. Some of these enforcers may have been chosen solely for their size, but certainly others would have been chosen for their fighting skills or a combination of both. This pattern was paralleled in Brazil, where, as we shall see, expert martial artists were hired as bodyguards and assassins.

121. Wood, *Black Majority,* 230–31.

122. Perdue et al., *Weevils in the Wheat,* 280.

123. Ibid.

124. William Craft, *Running a Thousand Miles for Freedom: Or the Escape of William and Ellen Craft from Slavery* (London: William Tweedle, 1860), 14–15.

125. Lowndes quoted in Wood, *Black Majority,* 231.

126. Ibid., 231–32.

127. Josiah Henson, "Josiah Henson (1789–1883)," in *Slavery in the South: First-Hand Accounts of the Ante-Bellum American South from Northern and Southern Whites, Negroes, and Foreign Observers,* ed. Harvey Wish (New York: Noonday Press, 1968), 32–33.

128. Again, I am using the term "closed society" here in place of the older and misleading term "secret society." See chapter 2, note 44.

129. Jill Salmons, "Martial Arts of the Annang," *African Arts* 19 (November 1985): 60; Boniface Obichere, personal communication and letter to author, September 1994. Note, for example, the case of the well-documented leopard societies in Sierra Leone and West Central Africa. See Birger Lindskog, *African Leopard Men* (Uppsala, 1954); and K. J. Beatty, *Human Leopards* (London: H. Rees, 1915).

130. Betty Kuyk, "The African Derivation of Black Fraternal Orders in the United States," *Comparative Studies in Society and History* 25 (October 1983): 559–92; Betty M. Kuyk, *African Voices in the African American Heritage* (Bloomington: Indiana University Press, 2003), 52–69.

131. Archival sources show the occasional mention of other Biafran ethnic groups such as the Moko, but on the whole most Biafrans would have been joined together into the new nation called "Ibo" or "Carabaree." See Douglas Chambers, "'My Own Nation': Igbo Exiles in the Diaspora," *Slavery & Abolition* 18 (1997): 72–97. Ras Micheal Brown has documented the link between the terms "Gullah" and "Angola"; see Brown, "Crossing Kalunga," 220, 259–60.

132. Piersen, *Black Yankees.*

133. As David Geggus has pointed out, only a small percentage of Africans brought to Saint Domingue were Senegambians, and yet their Mandingo society of King

Mohammad lasted into the twentieth century. See David P. Geggus, "The French Slave Trade: An Overview," *William and Mary Quarterly* 58, no. 1 (2001): 136.

134. Brown, "Crossing Kalunga," 199.

135. For references to Igbo Landing, see Georgia Writers Project, *Drums and Shadows*. For Mozambique influence, see the possible origin of Brazilian *cachaça* from East African *kachasu* in Kubik, *Angolan Traits in Black Music* (1979), 12–13.

136. Herbert Klein, *The Atlantic Slave Trade* (New York: Cambridge University Press, 1999), 208–9.

137. For an oral testimony of a family of Biafran Americans brought after 1808, see Sam Gadsden, *An Oral History of Edisto Island: Sam Gadsden Tells the Story,* 2nd ed. (Goshen, Ind.: Goshen College, 1975). For an alternate reading of this story that convincingly ties this story to Central Africa, see Kuyk, *African Voices,* 3–6.

138. This number is based on importation figures comes from Phillip Morgan, while Ras Michael Brown's analysis of probate inventories found that almost 26 percent of Africans with named origins were identified as "Eboe." See Phillip D. Morgan, "African Migration," in *Encyclopedia of American Social History,* vol. 2, ed. Mary Kupiec Cayton, Eliott J. Gorn, and Peter W. Williams (New York: Maxwell Macmillan International, 1993), 803; and Brown, "Crossing Kalunga," 186–88.

139. Wood, *Black Majority,* 325.

140. Note the trade in enslaved Igbos during the illegal trade and the possible resultant Igbo community in Gadsden, *Oral History.*

141. For a detailed study of the formation of the "African Lowcountry," see Brown, "Crossing Kalunga."

142. Holloway, *Africanisms,* 12–13; Gomez, *Exchanging Our Country Marks,* 226–27.

143. Littlefield, *Rice and Slaves,* 150; Brown, "Crossing Kalunga," 189–90.

144. Manfredi, "Philological Perspectives," 239–86.

145. This highlighted place in counterhegemonic activities may have given Biafrans a positive reputation among other bondsmen as resisters, which may explain their prominence in oral testimonies.

146. Note not only the numerous references to Igbo Landing in the interviews of former bondsmen but also its place (along with Biafran-derived terms such as *bukra* for overbearing whites) among contemporary lowcountry peoples. See Georgia Writers Project, *Drums and Shadows;* Goodwine, *Legacy of Ibo Landing;* and Cornelia Bailey and Christena Bledsoe, *God, Dr. Buzzard, and the Bolito Man: A Saltwater Geechee Talks about Life on Sapelo Island* (New York: Anchor Books, a Division of Random House, 2001).

147. Gomez, *Exchanging Our Country Marks,* 3; Edward A. Pearson, *Designs against Charleston: The Trial Record of the Denmark Vessey Slave Conspiracy of 1822* (Chapel Hill: University of North Carolina Press, 1999), 62.

148. Wood, *Black Majority,* 250.

149. Littlefield, *Rice and Slaves,* 145.

150. Margaret Washington Creel, *"A Peculiar People": Slave Religion and Community-Culture among the Gullahs* (New York: New York University Press, 1988).

151. Brown, "Crossing Kalunga," 317–18.

152. Carter G. Woodson, *The African Background Outlined: Handbook for the Study of the Negro* (Washington, D.C.: Association for the Study of Negro Life and History, 1936), 169–70.

153. Thompson, *Flash of the Spirit,* 132.

154. Joyner, "World of Plantation Slaves," 82; Gomez, *Exchanging Our Country Marks,* 9.

155. "American Freedman's Inquiry Commission Interviews, 1863," 377, cited in Pearson, *Designs,* 16, 62.

156. Cited in Charles W. Joyner, *Down by the Riverside: A South Carolina Slave Community* (Urbana: University of Illinois Press, 1984), 132–33.

157. *South Carolina Gazette,* September 17, 1772.

158. Pearson, *Designs,* 62–63.

159. Chambers, "He Gwine Sing He Country," 442–44.

160. Kenneth Bilby, "Gumbay, Myal, and the Great House: New Evidence of the Religious Backgroud of Jonkonnu in Jamaica," *AJIC Research Review* 4 (1999): 47–70.

161. Rawick, *American Slave,* 9:459.

162. Gomez, *Exchanging Our Country Marks,* 101.

163. Blassingame, *Slave Community,* 40.

164. Again, this is not to suggest that the old-time-religion societies or these practices were of Biafran origin. The use of the ritual staves was widespread in Africa and the African diaspora.

165. On *ikenga,* see Adiele Afigbo, "Ikenga, the State of Our Knowledge," in *Igbo History and Society,* ed. Falola, 447–57.

166. John L. Gwaltney, "Afro-American Ritual Carving," *Transforming Anthopology* 7, no. 2 (1998): 70.

167. Zola Jefferson, interview, Beaufort, S.C., March 12, 1994.

168. Although this term was also applied to early forms of Christianity as practiced by African-derived peoples, I will use it here in reference to what John Gwaltney calls the "old time core black religion," which perpetuated many African-derived beliefs and practices along with Christianity in closed community circles. I remain grateful to the late John Gwaltney for introducing me to "deacons" and families in these communities in Surry County, Virginia, and the lowcountry.

169. Root doctoring was the art of utilizing herbal knowledge and/or spiritual power for various purposes such as healing, harming, or self-defense. For an excellent discussion of root doctoring in North America, see William Dillon Piersen, *Black Legacy: America's Hidden Heritage* (Amherst: University of Massachusetts Press, 1993), 99–117.

170. Although a fictional account, Arna Bontemps's use of the term "fighting hand" for these sacred medicines reflects oral tradition. "Hand" appears to be derived from the Bantu term *handa.* See Arna Bontemps, *Black Thunder* (Boston: Beacon Press 1968), 79; John M. Janzen, *Lemba, 1650–1930: A Drum of Affliction in Africa and the New World* (New York: Garland, 1982), 101; and Brown, "Crossing Kalunga," 254.

171. While not all trick doctors were members of Old Time Religion societies, all elders of these societies were versed in the tradition of tricking.

172. John Gwaltney quoted in Kouri, "Search for Knocking," 3.

173. Willie Nelson, interview, Beaufort, S.C., March 10, 1994.

174. Herman Carter, interview, Beaufort, S.C., March 26, 1994.

175. John Langston Gwaltney, *Drylongso: A Self-Portrait of Black America* (New York: Random House, 1980), xvi.

176. Johnathan C. David, "On One Accord: Community, Musicality, and Spirit among the Singing and Praying Bands of Tidewater Maryland and Delaware" (Ph.D. diss., University of Pennsylvania, 1994), 325.

177. Wood carving was sacred when used to make the *dala,* or ritual staffs of the Old Time Religion. See Gwaltney, "Afro-American Ritual Carving," 70. For a wider discussion of wood carving not tied to closed societies, see John Michael Vlach, *The Afro-American Tradition in Decorative Arts* (Athens: University of Georgia Press, 1990), 27–43.

178. John Gwaltney cited in Kouri, "Search for Knocking," 9.

179. Gomez, *Exchanging Our Country Marks,* 199–208; Piersen, *Black Legacy,* 42–50.

180. John Thornton, "Cannibals, Witches, and Slave Traders in the Atlantic World," *William and Mary Quarterly* 60, no. 2 (2003): 1–16.

181. Part of this worldview held "that Africans had a natural right to be free, that they had the right to defend themselves against any attempt to deny them that basic right and that they, themselves, individually and collectively, would have to secure their own liberation" (Ella Forbes, "'By My Own Right Arm': Redemptive Violence and the 1851 Christiana, Pennsylvania Resistance," *Journal of Negro History* 83 [Summer 1998]: 159–67).

182. Dawson (*Capoeira Angola,* 14) notes that in North America the art of trickery and deception was known as "tricknology" or "oky doke." I am adopting the term here to refer to the entire philosophical, physical, and spiritual trickery complex.

183. For the importance of trickiness in the wider context of African and African-American culture, see Levine, *Black Culture.*

184. Bibb, *Narratives of the Life and Adventures of Henry Bib,b* 17.

185. In its complete form it was recorded among Georgia bondsmen as "kum buba yali kum buba tambe, kum kunka yali kum kunka tambe." The original Central African proverb was recorded as "Ku mbuba yandi, ku mbuba ntambe, ku nkoku yandi, ku nkonku ntambe," meaning "he is tricky, so I will win by being tricky too! He asks clever questions, so I will win by using clever questions too!" See Winifred K. Vass, *The Bantu Speaking Heritage of the United States* (Los Angeles: Center for Afro-American Studies, University of California, 1979), 70–71. In both cases this social proverb was acknowledged as a powerful incantation among bondsmen. See Virginia Hamilton, *The People Could Fly: American Black Folktales* (New York: Alfred A. Knopf, 1985), 170; and Georgia Writers Project, *Drums and Shadows,* 79.

186. For a detailed description of "flying Africans," see Jason Randolph Young, "Rituals of Resistance: The Making of an African-Atlantic Religious Complex in Kongo and along the Sea Islands of the Slave South" (Ph.D. diss., University of California, Riverside, 2002), 231–51. For descriptions of the ability being passed down to American-born, see John Bennet, *Doctor to the Dead: Grotesque Legends & Folktales of Old Charleston* (New York: Rinehart & Company, 1943), 140.

187. Even in Central Africa this use of the surprise head butt was called upon in self-defense conditions (Benina Kinaudi, personal communication, April 13, 1993).

188. Jack White, interview, Beaufort, S.C., July 18, 1992.

189. "There are communities of Negroes in the tobacco belt of Virginia to-day that so far resemble an African tribe as to have a professional trick doctor, a man whose only employment, and therefore whose only means of making a living, lies in the practice of the art of witchcraft" (Philip Alexander Bruce, *The Plantation Negro as a*

Freeman: Observations on His Character, Condition, and Prospects in Virginia [1889; repr., Williamstown, Mass.: Corner House, 1970], 115).

190. I am drawing distinction between conjure (root doctoring) traditions and voodoo traditions as practiced in New Orleans and Texas, a distinction some bondsmen made, although currently many scholars conflate the two. Abram Sells notes, "The conjure doctor, old Dr. Jones . . . He didn't cast spells like the voodoo doctor, but used roots for smallpox" (in Murphy, *Slave Narratives,* 88). On *mojo* as a Biafran term, see Chambers, "He Gwine Sing He Country," 412. On obeah (and obr [presumably *obeah*]) being derived from the Igbo term *dibia* (*ndi obia*), see Jerome S. Handler and Kenneth M. Bilby, "On the Early Use and Origin of the Term 'Obeah' in Barbados and the Anglophone Caribbean," *Slavery and Abolition* 22, no. 2 (2001): 87–100. On *hand,* see Janzen, *Lemba,* 101; and Kuyk, *African Voices,* xxiv. On *wanga* as Angolan spiritual weaponry, see McAlister, *Rara,* 153. On *gopher* and its Central African antecedents, see Thompson, *Flash of the Spirit,* 105. The African term *gris gris* was also common in Louisiana; see Hall, *Africans in Colonial Louisiana,* 38, 163.

191. W. E. B. Du Bois, *Souls of Black Folk,* ed. Natalie Zemon Davis, Ernest R. May, Lynn Hunt, and David W. Blight (Boston: Bedford/St. Martin's, 1997), 152.

192. On the timing of Christianity into the black community, see Gomez, *Exchanging Our Country Marks,* 245–63. Wilder highlights that African associations often gave rise to the early African churches; see Craig Steven Wilder, *In the Company of Black Men: The African Influence on African American Culture in New York City* (New York and London: New York University Press, 2001).

193. Yvonne Patricia Chireau, *Black Magic: Religion and the African American Conjuring Tradition* (Berkeley: University of California Press, 2003), 16–17.

194. Du Bois, *Souls of Black Folk,* 152.

195. For the profits made by trick doctors, see Chireau, *Black Magic,* 24–25. For examples of bondsmen using roots to feign illness and avoid labor, see Jean W. Robinson, "Black Healers during the Colonial Period and Early Nineteenth-Century America" (Ph.D. diss., Southern Illinois University, Carbondale, 1979), 64–65. For an example of a bondsman using root doctoring to injure his master covertly, see the testimony of Clara Walker in Rawick, *American Slave,* 2:21. For an example of slave masters fearing excesses due to poison use, see Hall, *Africans in Colonial Louisiana,* 162–65.

196. Cited in Chireau, *Black Magic,* 13.

197. W. H. Councill, "Synopsis of Three Addresses" (1900), repr. in *After Africa,* ed. Abrahams and Szwed, 37.

198. Hellen Catterall, *Judicial Cases Concerning American Slavery and the Negro* (New York: Octagon Books, 1968), 2:414, 521.

199. William Wells Brown, *My Southern Home; or, the South and Its People* (1880; repr., Upper Saddle River, N.J.: Gregg Press, 1968), 75.

200. Henry Clay Bruce, *The New Man: Twenty-Nine Years a Slave, Twenty-Nine Years a Free Man; Recollections of H. C. Bruce* (1985; repr., Lincoln: University of Nebraska Press, 1996), 54; Charles Jones, *The Religious Instruction of the Negroes in the United States* (1842; repr., New York: Negro Universities Press, 1969), 128; Blassingame, *Slave Community,* 110.

201. Henry Bibb was so convinced that the root-doctoring bag he procured would keep him from being whipped that he intentionally sassed his enslaver. See Henry

Bibb, "Narrative of the Life and Adventures of Henry Bibb, an American Slave," in *I Was Born a Slave: An Anthology of Classic Slave Narratives,* ed. Yuval Taylor (Edinburgh: Payback Press, 1999). See also Armstrong, *Old Massa's People,* 245–54; and Chireau, *Black Magic,* 15–18.

202. "He told me . . . where there was a certain root, which if I would take some of it with me, carrying it always on my right side, would render it impossible for Mr. Covey, or any other white man, to whip me" (Frederick Douglass, *Narrative of the Life of Frederick Douglass: An American Slave, Written by Himself,* ed. David W. Blight [Boston: Bedford/St. Martin's, 1993], 78).

203. The introduction of Christian moral honor into the bonded community is a complex one that likely followed different patterns in various regions of North America. Christianity may have been first introduced by Kongolese peoples whose adoption and indigenization of Christianity predated the slave trade to North America by over a century. In the lowcountry and Chesapeake regions, only a minority of bondsmen adopted European-style Christianity before the Civil War. Those who did (primarily individuals in their older years) tended to adopt a distinct form of moral honor that was quite distinct from the honor code of the majority. See John K. Thornton, "Religious and Ceremonial Life in the Kongo and Mbundu Area, 1500–1700," in *Central Africans and Cultural Transformations,* ed. L. Heywood (Cambridge: Cambridge University Press, 2002), 71–90; Gomez, *Exchanging Our Country Marks,* 245–61; and John C. Willis, "From the Dictates of Pride to the Paths of Righteousness: Slave Honor and Christianity in Antebellum Virginia," in *The Edge of the South: Life in Nineteenth-Century Virginia,* ed. Edward L. Ayers and John C. Willis (Charlottesville: University Press of Virginia, 1991).

204. Obviously bondsmen who paraded their honor too openly ran the risk of becoming targets for the collective retribution of European American society. Therefore, the honor system of the enslaved was often masked or cloaked in secrecy. See John Charles Willis, "Behind 'Their Black Masks': Slave Honor in Antebellum Virginia" (M.A. thesis, Baylor University, 1987), 6–7. According to Wyatt-Brown, males of the planter class made claims of honor and respect through conviviality, oath taking, competitive display, and the perceived willingness and ability to enact violence on any who would deny their claim; see Bertram Wyatt-Brown, *Southern Honor: Ethics and Behavior in the Old South* (New York: Oxford University Press, 1982), 25–61.

205. Willis, "Behind 'Their Black Masks,'" 22–23.

206. The enslaved used the song "Steal Away Jesus" to advise of an upcoming secret meeting and the phrase "weevils in the wheat" to warn each other that whites had learned of a planned meeting and it was postponed (Perdue et al., *Weevils in the Wheat*), 297.

207. John Brown, *John Brown: Slave Life in Georgia,* in *I Was Born a Slave,* ed. Yuval Taylor (Edinburgh: Payback Press, 1999), 72,

208. Wyatt-Brown, *Southern Honor,* 90–91.

209. Shane White and Graham White, *Stylin': African American Expressive Culture from Its Beginnings to the Zoot Suit* (Ithaca, N.Y.: Cornell University Press, 1998), 5–84; Willis, "From the Dictates of Pride"; Willis, "Behind 'Their Black Masks,'" 28–29.

210. For more on these verbal skills and their place in African diaspora culture, see Abrahams, *Man-of-Words.*

211. Samuel Crowther and John Taylor, *The Gospel on the Banks of the Niger: Journals and Notices of the Native Missionaries Accompanying the Niger Expedition of 1857–1859* (London: Church Missionary House, 1859), 430.

212. Meek, *Law and Authority,* 230–31.

213. Wrestling was also used in this way in the early twentieth century. Jacob Drewson of Hilton Head Island explained that in his youth he would deal with affronts to his reputation by using his wrestling skills to throw people (Jacob Drewson, interview, Beaufort, S.C., February 26, 1994).

214. Lewis Clarke quoted in Blassingame, *Slave Testimony,* 157.

215. Charles C. Jones, *Religious Instruction of the Negroes* (Savannah, Ga.: T. Purse, 1842), 130–31.

216. Daniel Hundley and William Cooper, *Social Relations in Our Southern States* (Baton Rouge: Louisiana State University Press, 1979), 332.

217. Pehr Kalm, *Peter Kalm's Travels in North America,* trans. John Forster (Barre, Mass.: Imprint Society, 1972), 202.

218. Hartman, *Scenes of Subjection.*

219. The reader should note the example of a bondsman named Congo Sam, who had attacked Thomas Thislewood with a machete and yet was later acquitted. See Diana Paton, "Punishment, Crime, and the Bodies of Slaves in Eighteenth-Century Jamaica," *Journal of Social History* 34, no. 4 (2001): 923–54; and Douglas Hall, *In Miserable Slavery: Thomas Thistlewood in Jamaica, 1750–86* (London: Macmillan, 1989), 54–56.

220. Note the case of Josiah Henson, who was physically deformed in an attack by a white man seeking revenge (Henson, "Josiah Henson," 34).

221. *Taqiya* is a doctrine that taught that "it was permissible, or even obligatory" to use outward dissimulation while inwardly holding onto the truth when threatened by possible violence.

The Shi'is, often a persecuted minority in the Sunni world, are best known for employing this principle at times to avoid unnecessary confrontations. See Juan R. I. Cole and Nikki R. Keddie, *Shi'ism and Social Protest* (New Haven, Conn.: Yale University Press, 1986), 28–29; and Michael M. J. Fischer, *Iran: From Religious Dispute to Revolution* (Cambridge, Mass.: Harvard University Press, 1980), 66–70.

222. Kouri, "Search for Knocking," 8–10.

223. Joyner, "World of Plantation Slaves," 92.

224. Phillip J. Schwartz, *Twice Condemned: Slaves and the Criminal Laws of Virginia, 1705–1865* (Union, N.J.: Lawbook Exchange, 1988), 230–41. Many of these received a death penalty or were sold out of the colony.

For those pushed to this level and assured of a spiritual return to mother Africa, such lethal ramifications certainly were not always an effective deterrent when the dictates of honor required vengeance.

225. Willis, "Behind 'Their Black Masks,'" 33–52.

226. Perdue et al., *Weevils in the Wheat,* 317.

227. Some resisted this dishonor through temporary or permanent maroonage. John Brown, for example, when faced with a beating, ran away and was fed by his steadfast fellow bondsmen at night. He returned to the plantation only when he was granted immunity from the beating in exchange for his return. See Brown, "John Brown."

228. Perdue et al., *Weevils in the Wheat,* 156.

229. In the case of Biafran woman, see Nwando Achebe, *Farmers, Traders, Warriors, and Kings: Female Power and Authority in Northern Igboland, 1900–1960* (Portsmouth, N.H.: Heinemann, 2005). Equiano points out that "All are taught the use of these weapons; even our women are warriors, and march boldly to fight along with the men." Olaudah Equiano, *The Interesting Narrative of the Life of Olaudah Equiano* Robert Allison ed. (Boston: Bedford Books of St. Martin's Press, 1995), 40. For assertive marketeering by women in South Carolina see Robert Olwell, "Loose, Idle and Disorderly: Slave Women in the Eighteenth Century Charleston Marketplace" in David Barry Gaspar and Darlene Clark Hine ed. *More Than Chattel: Black Women and Slavery in the Americas* (Indiana University Press, 1996), 97–110. In Angola, note the military example of Queen Nzinga, who remained a figure of female power throughout the African diaspora, in John K. Thornton, "Legitimacy and Political Power: Queen Njinga, 1624–1663," *Journal of African History* 32, no. 1 (1991): 25–40; and Linda Heywood, "Memory through Space and Time: Queen Njinga and Remembrance in Angola and Brazil," paper presented to New York University Atlantic World Series, October 28, 2003.

230. James Oliver Horton and Lois E. Horton, "Violence, Protest, and Identity: Black Manhood in Antebellum America," in *A Question of Manhood: A Reader in US Black Men's History and Masculinity,* ed. Darlene Clark Hine and Earnest Jenkins, vol. 1: *"Manhood Rights": The Construction of Black Male History and Manhood, 1750–1870* (Bloomington: Indiana University Press, 1999–2001), 393–95.

231. Frederick Douglass, *The Life and Times of Frederick Douglass* (New York: Gramercy Books, 1993), 123.

232. Rawick, *American Slave,* 8:807.

233. Silvia Dubois, "Silvia Dubois," in *Black Women in Nineteenth Century American Life,* ed. Bert James Loewenburg and Ruth Bogin (University Park: Pennsylvania State University Press, 1976), 39–47.

234. Perdue et al., *Weevils in the Wheat,* 48–49.

235. Ibid., 36, 280.

236. Ibid., 117. Francis Henderson in Benjamin Drew, *A North-Side View of Slavery: The Refugee; or, The Narratives of Fugitive Slaves in Canada Related by Themselves; With an Account of the History and Condition of the Colored Population of Upper Canada* (New York: Negro Universities Press, 1968), 158–59.

237. J. D. Green, *Narrative of the Life of J. D. Green, A Runaway from Kentucky* (Huddersfield: Henry Fielding, 1864), 19.

238. Perdue et al., *Weevils in the Wheat,* 84.

239. Ibid.

240. Genovese, *Roll, Jordan, Roll,* 619.

241. *New York Times,* January 14, 1862, quoted in Blassingame, *Slave Testimony,* 170.

242. Berlin et al., *Remembering Slavery,* 18–19.

243. Perdue et al., *Weevils in the Wheat,* 26–27.

244. Jermain Wesley Loguen, *The Rev. J. W. Loguen as a Slave and as a Freedman* (Syracuse: J. G. K. Truair & Co., 1859), 230–43.

245. Blassingame, *Slave Community,* 319.

246. Elijah Marrs, *Life and History* (Louisville, Ky.: Bradley & Gilbert, 1885), 249.

247. Douglass, *My Bondage;* William Green, *Narrative of Events in the Life of William Green* (Springfield, Mass.: L. M. Guernsey, Printer, 1853), 13; Perdue et al., *Weevils in the Wheat,* 84.

248. Perdue et al., *Weevils in the Wheat,* 255.

249. Mellon, *Bullwhip Days,* 140–41.

250. Douglass was surprised that he got off without punishment after fighting the overseer Covey despite the law of Maryland, which could have him hanged. His only explanation was "that Covey was, probably, ashamed to have it known and confessed that he had been mastered" by Douglass. "Mr. Covey enjoyed the unbounded and very valuable reputation of being a first rate overseer and Negro breaker. . . . His interest and his pride mutually suggested the wisdom of passing the matter by, in silence." Subsequently, Douglass even tried to provoke him into another fight, but without success. See Douglass, *My Bondage,* 247–49.

251. Douglass, *My Bondage,* 246–47. It is also worth noting that Douglass equates this action on his part with manhood. Ideologically the patriarchal slave system kept black males in a perpetual state of infancy. "Every man [was] called a boy till he [was] very old," recalled William Craft (*Running a Thousand Miles,* 14–15). By taking a stand against a white man, black men simultaneously asserted their manhood against such ideological paradigms.

252. Perdue et al., *Weevils in the Wheat,* 194.

253. Mellon, *Bullwhip Days,* 140–41.

254. "I watched my chance and gave him a heavy kick close under the ribs. This kick fairly sickened Hughes, so that he left me in the hands of Mr. Covey. This kick had the effect of not only weakening Hughes, but Covey also. When he saw Hughes bending over with pain, his courage quailed" (Douglass, *Narrative,* 78).

255. Perdue et al., *Weevils in the Wheat,* 155.

256. William Grimes, *Life of William Grimes,* in *Five Black Lives,* ed. Arna Bontemps (Middletown, Conn.: Wesleyan University Press, 1971), 92.

257. Steward, *Twenty-Two Years,* 276–77.

258. Orlando Patterson, *Slavery and Social Death: A Comparative Study* (Cambridge, Mass.: Harvard University Press, 1982), 13.

Chapter 4: Return Passages

1. While agricultural production was the backbone of wealth of the French Caribbean, it should be pointed out that the economies and ranges of slave labor were actually quite diverse. For a detailed study of this complexity, see Verene Shepherd, *Slavery without Sugar: Diversity in Caribbean Economy and Society since the 17th Century* (Gainesville: University Press of Florida, 2002).

2. Although much of the historical and anthropological literature still treats African ethnic groups along tribal models, Igor Kopytoff's work suggests rather that African societies grew out of and continued to produce a series of frontier communities in which small groups from various established societies came together to form the nucleus of new societies. In this process, as outlined by Kopytoff, different groups came together in these frontier areas and filled the institutional vacuum by modifying aspects of preexisting social models and adopting newcomers as kinsmen. Ideological duality allowed room for first-comers' claims to legitimacy and late-comers' roles in creating the legitimacy of the former. See Igor Kopytoff, *The African Frontier:*

The Reproduction of Traditional African Societies (Bloomington: Indiana University Press, 1987).

3. Other islands of the French Caribbean that remained in French control for significant periods of the eighteenth and early nineteenth centuries included Grenada, Saint Lucia, Dominique, Tobago, and Saint Croix.

4. Herbert Klein, *The Atlantic Slave Trade* (New York: Cambridge University Press, 1999), 28–29, 79.

5. Geggus, "French Slave Trade," 119–38.

6. An earthquake in 1727 devastated the cocoa industry, leading to the widespread exodus of many of these poorer planters while others turned to coffee, which suffered at the time as an export crop because the Company of the Indies had a monopoly to supply coffee to France from its plantations in the Levant. See Robert W. Harms, *The Diligent: A Voyage through the Worlds of the Slave Trade* (New York: Basic Books, 2002), 341–46; and Michael-Rolph Trouillot, "Coffee Planters and Coffee Slaves in the Antilles: The Impact of a Secondary Crop," in *Cultivation and Culture,* ed. Berlin and Morgan, 124–37.

7. Seeds of the rocou plant were crushed and boiled into paste that was sold to prime white cloth to receive dyes. See Harms, *Diligent,* 372–73.

8. The Caribs who survived the European diseases that ravaged their populations were expelled, and many made their way to islands that had not been colonized, such as St. Vincent. See Robin Blackburn, *The Making of New World Slavery: From the Baroque to the Modern, 1492–1800* (London / New York: Verso, 1997), 283.

9. These often changing stereotypes were based on factors such as purported strength, health, cultural and technical background, as well as fanciful myths romanticizing some groups and demonizing others. See Darold D. Wax, "Preferences for Slaves in Colonial America," *Journal of Negro History* 58, no. 4 (1973): 371–401; David P. Geggus, "Sugar and Coffee Cultivation in Saint Domingue and the Shaping of the Slave Labor Force," in *Cultivation and Culture,* ed. Berlin and Morgan, 79–88; and Hall, *Slavery and African Ethnicities,* 66–70.

10. Eltis et al., *Trans-Atlantic Slave Trade.*

11. In the case of Biafrans, their more even gender ratios may have been appealing to planters in Guadeloupe seeking to promote natural population growth. See Geggus, "French Slave Trade," 119–38. The numerous delta inlets made it popular among smugglers as well during the illegal phase of the trade. The slave trade was legally abolished in the French colonies in 1815, but the law was largely ignored, and large-scale trading continued until 1833. During this phase the ports of Bonny and Old Calabar appear to have been major suppliers. See Françoise Thésee, *Les Ibos de l'Amélie: Destinée d' une cargaison de la traite clandestine à la Martinique 1822–1838* (Paris: Editions Caribéenees, 1986).

12. David Eltis, personal communication, October 14, 1999. The slave trade data suggest that Africans from the Bight of Benin may have been most numerous at 37 percent, followed by Angolans representing about 20 percent and dominating in the earliest phases of the trade, and people taken from Biafra forming the third largest group at around 14 percent and being the largest during the last phase of imports and particularly during the illegal trade. To what extent reexportation affected these numbers remains to be addressed. See Eltis et al., *Trans-Atlantic Slave Trade.*

13. Some scholars have already made use of local evidence to get a sense of the African origins of the bondsmen for certain years. Abbé Bernard David, for example, was able to substantiate the large Biafran presence late in the trade using manumission records in Martinique between 1833 and 1839, writing, "Out of 191 African-born freemen listed, 112 were Ibo (Biafrans), 25 Caplahous (from Ivory Coast), 17 Congo (Angolan), 15 Arada (from Bight of Benin), and 8 Cape Verte/Senegal"; see Abbé Bernard David, *Les origines de la population Martiniquaise au fil des ans 1635–1902* (Fort-de-France: Mémoires de la Société d'histoire de la Martinique, 1973), 100. For Guadeloupe, Vanony-Frisch analyzed existent probate inventories dating between 1770 and 1789 for ethnic patterns; see Nicole Vanony-Frisch, "Les esclaves de la Guadeloupe à la fin de l'ancien régime," *Bulletin de la Societé de la Guadeloupe* 62–63 (1985): 32–36. See also Gabriel Debien, *Les esclaves aux Antilles Françaises, XVIIe–XVIIIe siècles* (Basse-Terre: Société d'histoire de la Guadeloupe, 1974).

14. Julius Sherrard Scott, "The Common Wind: Currents of Afro-American Communication in the Era of the Haitian Revolution" (Ph.D. diss., Duke University, 1986), 13.

15. Herbert S. Klein, *African Slavery in Latin America and the Caribbean* (New York: Oxford University Press, 1986), 45–58.

16. Geggus, "Sugar and Coffee Cultivation," 74–75.

17. Trouillot, "Coffee Planters," 124–25.

18. *Vodun* was the name for a spiritual entity, roughly the equivalent to the Yoruba *orisha*. While the term *vodun* was most associated with Saint Domingue's West Province, it also appears to have been widely used by some observers as an umbrella term for all African-derived religious practices. Yet, in the eighteenth century Central African, Biafran, Senegambian, and other religious traditions were also practiced separately in the colony. In many areas these traditions remained distinct, while in some urban and other areas there was a merger into interrelated practices of Rada and Petro, although the dating of this is unclear. The Angolan contributions, including African Catholicism, to Haitian religious practices are only now receiving balanced scholarly attention. See David P. Geggus, "Haitian Voodoo in the Eighteenth Century: Language, Culture, Resistance," *Jahrbuch für Geschichte von Staat, Wirtschaft, und Gesellschaft Lateinamerikas* 28 (1991): 21–51; Hein Vanhee, "Central African Popular Christianity and the Making of Haitian Vodou Religion," in *Central Africans and Cultural Transformations*, ed. Heywood, 243–64; Thompson, *Flash of the Spirit*, 161–91; and Wyatt MacGaffey, "Twins, Simbi Spirits, and Lwas in Kongo and Haiti," in *Central Africans and Cultural Transformation*, ed. Heywoo,d 211–26. Although beyond the scope of this study, these Fon, Aja, Ewe, and Yoruba peoples also carried other martial traditions to Saint Domingue, including those of Dahomey and Oyo explored by Olayinka Fadahunsi in "Dahomey and 'The Real National Weapon' in the Shadow of Oyo and Egba, 1727–1890," paper presented at "Perspectives on Yoruba History and Culture," University of Texas at Austin, March 26–28, 2004.

19. Eltis et al., *Trans-Atlantic Slave Trade*.

20. Gabriel Debien (*Les esclaves aux Antilles Françaises*, 49–52) highlights that despite the use of blanket terms in trade inventories, newspaper advertisements for runaways in Saint Domingue listed more nations, such as Loangos, Mayombés, Mondomgues, and Benguélas. Given the limited access that French ships had to the formal port of Benguela and the thriving rival trade between Humbe merchants and

French ships at the mouth of the Kunene River, many of these Benguélas were likely drawn from the Kunene trade. Given that some 47 percent of enslaved Africans working with livestock were of the umbrella Congo nation, it is possible that some Cimbebasians and other Angolan pastoralists made their way into this specialization as few other "Congos" would have had equivalent pastoral experience. Certainly pastoral Fulani and Nupe were similarly likely to advance into these positions. See Geggus, "Sugar and Coffee Cultivation," 88.

21. Geggus, "French Slave Trade" 128.

22. Ibid.

23. Carolyn E. Fick, *The Making of Haiti: The Saint Domingue Revolution from Below* (Knoxville: University of Tennessee Press, 1990), 25.

24. Urban-style bondage will be addressed in the following chapter.

25. Debien, *Les esclaves aux Antilles Françaises,* 85.

26. This unwittingly also provided bondsmen with a source for poison, which was a widely feared form of resistance in the Francophone Caribbean. See E. Rufz, *Recherches sur les empoisonnemens pratiqués par les nègres a la Martinique* (Paris: J.-B. Baillière, 1844), 103–20.

27. Jean Baptiste Labat, *Nouveau voyage aux isles de l'Amérique,* 6 vols. (Paris: T. Le Gras, 1722), 4:148. At the time of Labat's plantation these Aradas would have been primarly Aja peoples, but the Arada nation in the French Caribbean would also include other Gbe speakers and neighboring peoples from the region of the Bight of Benin. See Hall, *Slavery and African Ethnicities,* 123.

28. Labat, *Nouveau voyage,* 4:148–49.

29. Labat (3:202–6) suggested that a "wise and intelligent" bondswomen should be selected to run the infirmary.

30. Harms, *Diligent,* 357.

31. Labat's mill, however, was powered by water, and others were driven by wind power. On the role of African technical background in determining labor tasks, see Geggus, "Sugar and Coffee Cultivation," 79–88.

32. Labat (*Nouveau voyage,* 3:205–6) notes that since overtired bondsmen would often get their hands cut and be pulled into the crushers, a machete was kept at hand to cut off a limb before an entire person was crushed. The famous Makandal in Saint Dominque, who went on to lead a large closed society that utilized ritual medicine and poison against the whites of the island, had lost his arm while working in a sugar mill. See Laurent Dubois, *Avengers of the New World* (Cambridge, Mass.: Harvard University Press, 2004), 51.

33. He believed that a woman would be less likely to drink up the brandy than a man would and thus should be in charge of the distillery. Geggus's analysis of mill specialists in late eighteenth-century Saint Domingue shows that they were typically male. See Labat, *Nouveau voyage,* 3:202–6; and Geggus, "Sugar and Coffee Cultivation," 87.

34. Harms, *Diligent,* 355.

35. Debien, *Les esclaves aux Antilles Françaises,* 85, 135, 145.

36. In the nineteenth century a third group called the "grass gang" was made up of the children from around five years old to the age they were deemed ready to join one of the adult gangs. The grass gang cut grass to feed the livestock, weeded the cane, and helped the *grand atelier* during planting by putting manure into the cane

holes. See Dale W. Tomich, *Slavery in the Circuit of Sugar: Martinique and the World Economy, 1830–1848* (Baltimore: Johns Hopkins University Press, 1990), 221.

37. Harms, *Diligent,* 352.

38. Reproduced in ibid., 359.

39. Geggus, "Sugar and Coffee Cultivation," 89–90. On mortality on the Lamentine plantations in Martinique, see Myriam Cottias, "Mortalité et créolisation sur les habitations martiniquaises du XVIIIe au XIXe siècle," *Population* 44 (January–February 1989): 55–84. On mortality in Guadeloupe, see Vanony-Frisch, "Les esclaves de la Guadeloupe," 59–67.

40. As Trouillot ("Coffee Planters," 128) opines, "To put it bluntly, the underdog among the free achieved success and survival at the slave's expense." In eighteenth-century Guadeloupe, for example, small coffee and cotton growers with twelve to fifteen bondsmen rented them out to sugar plantations, where their labor was likely extremely exploited. The initial clearing of the trees was hazardous, and the highland climate claimed the lives of some Africans unaccustomed to it.

41. Laurent Dubois, *A Colony of Citizens: Revolution & Slave Emancipation in the French Caribbean, 1787–1804* (Chapel Hill: University of North Carolina Press, 2004), 50–51.

42. Stewart R. King, *Blue Coat or Powdered Wig: Free People of Color in Pre-Revolutionary Saint Domingue* (Athens: University of Georgia Press, 2001).

43. Officers of African descent were much more common in Saint Domingue than in the Lesser Antilles, but an English sailor described a colored commissioned officer in Guadeloupe who was able to draw on such institutional support for his private enterprise. See William Butterworth [Henry Schroeder], *3 Years Adventures of a Minor in England, Africa, the West Indies, South-Carolina, and Georgia* (1823; repr., Leeds: Thomas Inchbold, 1831), 312–13; and Dubois, *Colony of Citizens,* 55–56.

44. King, *Blue Coat,* 55–56. Plantation owners who did not wish to pay the taxes to free bondswomen, who could not serve in the military, were often simply released from service without legal manumission. See Bernard Moitt, "In the Shadow of the Plantation: Women of Color and the *Libres de fait* of Martinique and Guadeloupe, 1685–1848," in *More than Chattel,* ed. Gaspar and Hine, 40.

45. Some of these colored units served in the American Revolution, particularly the battle of Savannah.

46. On arming the of bondsmen during the revolution, see David Geggus, "The Arming of Slaves during the Haitian Revolution," paper presented to the Gilder-Lehrman Center's "Arming of Slaves from the Ancient World to the American Civil War," in *Arming Slaves: From Classical Times to the Modern Age,* eds. Christopher Leslie Brown and Philip Morgan (New Haven: Yale University Press, 2006), 209–32.

47. In other ways, of course, their being treated as equals in the military inherently undermined the racial order on which the plantation system was built.

48. Tomich, *Slavery,* 259–80.

49. Dale Tomich, "Une Petite Guinée: Provision Ground and Plantation in Martinique, 1830–1848," in *Cultivation and Culture,* ed. Berlin and Morgan, 221–242.

50. Scott, "Common Wind."

51. Yvon Debbasch, "Le maroonnage: Essai sur la désertopm de l'esclave antillais," *L'Année Sociologique* (1961–62): 1–112, 117–95; Debien, *Les esclaves aux Antilles Françaises,* 411–69; M. L. E. Moreau de Saint-Méry, Blanche Maurel, and Étienne

Taillemite, eds., *Description topographique, physique, civile, politique et historique de la partie française de l'isle Saint Domingue* (Paris: Société de l'histoire des colonies françaises, 1958), 2:497–503; Clarence J. Munford, *The Black Ordeal of Slavery and Slave Trading in the French West Indies, 1625–1715,* vol. 3 (Lewiston/Queenston/Lampeter: Edwin Mellon Press), 933–77.

52. Scott, "Common Wind"; Jorge Chinea, "A Quest for Freedom: The Immigration of Maritime Maroons in Puerto Rico, 1656–1800," *Journal of Caribbean History* 31, nos. 1 & 2 (1997): 51–87; N. A. T. Hall, "Maritime Maroons: Grand Marronage from the Danish West Indies," *William and Mary Quarterly* 42 (October 1985): 476–98.

53. The nomenclature relating to drum circles in the Francophone Caribbean is a complex one deserving its own study. One of the reasons for this complexity is that European observers often conflated the words for the drum, the rhythm, its accompanying song, the dance performed to this music, and the gatherings around these dances. As we shall see shortly, Father Jean-Baptiste Labat described a *calenda* line dance in northern Martinique in the 1690s, while Moreau de Saint-Méry depicted a very different *calenda* couples dance in Saint Domingue a century later. The exact original meaning of *kalenda* is unclear, although Alfred Métraux suggested that it was the term for religious dances. Eighteenth-century prohibitions against gatherings of bondsmen in 1758 and 1772 both specify these gatherings as *kalendas.* Thus, the term was used throughout the Francophone Caribbean, and places influenced by it, to describe either specific dances, songs, or the entire event. At times the terms *bamboula* and *kalenda* were used to describe different dances; yet, in many cases they were used synonymously to describe the event as a whole. Thus, these two terms overlapped in time and space, although the term *kalenda* was likely older and in wider use in terms of describing dances and dance events. However, the term *kalenda* was also applied to a popular form of stick fighting, which will be discussed shortly. Thus, while acknowledging that the term *kalenda* may be a better choice in other discussions, here I will use the term *bamboula* in its wider sense of "drum dance event" so as not to confuse the reader when discussing *kalenda* as a form of stick fighting. See Alfred Métraux, *Voodoo in Haiti,* trans. Hugo Charteris (New York: Schocken Books, 1972), 32–33. For a detailed chronology of the use of these terms, see John Houlston Cowley, "Kalenda: A Sample of the Complex Development of African-Derived Culture in the Americas" (unpub. manuscript); and John Houlston Cowley, "Music and Migration: Aspects of Black Music in the British Caribbean, the United States, and Britain, before the Independence of Jamaica and Trinidad & Tobago" (Ph.D. diss., University of Warwick, 1992), 60–90, 555–58. For an interpretive attempt to deal with these terms, see Julian Gerstin, "Tangled Roots: Kalenda and Other Neo-African Dances in the Circum-Caribbean," *New West Indies Guide* 78, nos. 1 & 2 (2004): 5–41.

54. Labat, *Nouveau voyage,* 4:153–54.

55. Julian Harris Gerstin, "Traditional Music in a New Social Movement: The Renewal of Bèlè in Martinique" (Ph.D. diss., University of California, Berkeley, 1996), 15.

56. Gerstin, "Traditional Music," 118.

57. Marie-Céline Lafontaine, "Musique et société aux Antilles," *Présence Africaine* 121–22 (1982): 89–90; "Article de la Fête Dieu à la Martinique en 1753," reproduced

in Jacqueline Rosemain, *La musique dans la société antillaise* (Paris: L'Harmattan, 1986), 57–58. Note the similarity to African Brazilian brotherhoods with their "Kings and Queens." See Elizabeth Kiddy, "The Kings of Kongo in Brazilian Religious Festivals, Popular Pageants, and Armed Rebellions, 1700–1888," paper presented at "Bantu into Black: Central Africans in the Atlantic Diaspora," Howard University, September 1999.

58. Liliane Chauleau, *La vie quotidienne aux antilles françaises au temps de Victor Schoelcher: XIXe siècle* (Paris: Hachette littérature, 1979), 179.

59. There is clear evidence for the religious implications of *bamboulas* in the context of funeral practices, as we shall see below. Documentation for the religious context of dances is much richer for Saint Domingue, where participants often swore oaths not to reveal the activities of nocturnal assemblies. See Gabriel Debien, "Assemblées nocturnes d'esclaves á Saint-Domingue (La Marmelade, 1786)," *Annales Historiques de la Révolution* 44 (1972): 273–84; and Geggus, "Haitian Voodoo," 21–51.

60. Rosemain, *La musique,* 21, 69. Unfortunately Rosemain does not provide a source, so this claim must be treated as tenuous until corroborated by further evidence.

61. Alex Uri and Françoise Uri, *Musiques & musiciens de la Guadeloupe: Le chant de Karukéra* (Paris: Con brio, 1991), 52. In twentieth-century Guadeloupe the *bamboulas* were also called "soirée la rose" or "Lo Rose society evenings," shortened to *léwòz*. See Gerstin, "Traditional Music," 116.

62. Moitt suggests that many of these were led by women; see Bernard Moitt, *Women and Slavery in the French Antilles, 1635–1848* (Bloomington: Indiana University Press, 2001), 149–50.

63. Debien, *Les esclaves aux Antilles Françaises,* 154. Allowing bondsmen to have provision gardens became an important policy during wartimes, when importation of food supplies to feed the large bonded population became exceedingly difficult. By the nineteenth century bondsmen were commonly given an additional half-day off on Saturday. See Tomich, *Slavery,* 81–83.

64. Labat, *Nouveau voyage,* 4:153–54.

65. Although Labat attributes this dance to the Aradas (possibly related to the fact that this was the nation with which he could speak), numerous scholars have linked these practices to Angolan models. Kubik compares them to the Kunene *musakalunga* and the Ngangela/Mbwela *kamundonda* dances of southern Angola, although here a male danced up to a female of his choice and made the pelvic thrusting bounce stop action without actually making physical contact. The actual bouncing of midsections, along with these other features, appears to be particular to the northern regions of Angola, while the term *semba* is most specifically Kimbundu. Gerstin concludes that the contact included "everything from bellies through thighs, but Labat comes very close for someone who in all likelihood never tried the dance himself." See Gerhard Kubik, "Drum Patterns in the 'Batuque' of Benedito Caxias," *Latin American Music Review* 11, no. 2 (1990): 159–61; Dominique Cyrille, "Sa Ki Ta Nou (This Belongs to Us): Creole Dances of the French Caribbean," in *Caribbean Dance from Abakuá to Zouk: How Movement Shapes Identity,* ed. Susanna Sloat (Gainesville: University Press of Florida, 2002); and Gerstin, "Tangled Roots," 7.

66. Labat felt that "this dance is opposed to decency" but also points out, "The Spanish have taken it from the blacks, and dance it in all America in the same

manner as the blacks" (Labat, *Nouveau voyage,* 4:154). Variants drawing on similar dance components spread throughout the Atlantic world, including the *chica, congo,* fandango, fado, and *lundu.* The latter three even became a rage in Europe. See Peter Fryer, *Rhythms of Resistance: African Musical Heritage in Brazil* (Middletown, Conn.: Wesleyan University Press, 2000), 109–33.

67. Labat, *Nouveau voyage,* 4:153–58.

68. Vanony-Frisch ("Les esclaves de la Guadeloupe," 39) calculates that from 1770 to 1789, 60–70 percent of bondsmen were locally born in Guadeloupe, but this demographic trend may have happened earlier in Martinique, with its older plantation communities.

69. Cited in David, *Les origins de la population Martiniquaise,* 81.

70. The equivalent of these nations or the closed societies that sponsored these dances were referred to as "regiments" by Francophone bondsmen in early nineteenth-century Trinidad. In 1823, after an Igbo war dance was mistaken as a call for rebellion, an inquiry reported that "Societies or meetings of slaves for dancing, both in country and Town are referred to in the said declaration, under the military designation of 'Regiment'; by which words appears . . . to be used by French negroes . . . on the occasion of Dances on Holy days to denote different parties, tribes or nations such as Regiment Congo, Ibo etc." (West Indiana & Special Collections Dept. (hereafter WIS), University of the West Indies, St. Augustine, Trinidad, Andrew Pearse Collection, box 1, folder 4, Court of Criminal Inquiry, Port of Spain, November 21, 1823).

71. M. R. Max-Radiguet, "Une bamboula à la Martinique," *La France-Maritime* (1838), cited in Chauleau, *La vie quotidienne,* 176–77.

72. The following description is taken from Butterworth, *3 Years Adventures,* 300–305. Laurent Dubois (*Colony of Citizens,* 56) suggests that William Butterworth may have been a pen name for Henry Schroeder.

73. Jurretta Heckscher, synthesizing the scholarship on movement systems as vehicles for collective memory and identity, writes that "cultural patterns of bodily movement are particularly potent instruments of identity and social values because they are transmitted and configured largely unconsciously in the earliest stages of life, through example and imitation . . . and thereafter become so habitual as to appear wholly and exclusively 'natural' to those who obey their ordering unawares" (Heckscher, "All the Mazes," 296–97). Pierre Bourdieu suggests that culture "entrusts to bodily automatisms those principles most basic to it and most indispensable to its conversation" (Pierre Bourdieu, *Outline of a Theory of Practice,* trans. Richard Nice [Cambridge: Cambridge University Press, 1977], 94, 218n44). In this sense, through exposure to the kinetic systems of dance and martial art, children at these *bamboulas* were absorbing fundamental elements of the cosmologies, social values, and the embodied identities of their predecessors.

74. In urban bondage, as will become clearer in the next chapter, while some tasks were more valued than others, there was not an equivalent to the rural discrepancies of large numbers of field laborers and relatively few domestics and skilled laborers.

75. Moitt, *Women and Slavery,* 149–50.

76. Outside of this performative context, some women resorted to these pugilistic forms in settling issues of honor, at least in eighteenth-century Saint Domingue, according to Moreau de Saint-Méry, as we will see below.

77. Winners of the competition carried the flags back with them after the *bamboulas,* announcing to the even wider community their exploits.

78. This type of wrestling was also known as *lévé-fessé* in Martinique. See Raoul Grivalliers, interview, Martinique, July 15, 1993; and David Alexandre, personal communication, May 13, 2000. *Sové* means "to save," and *vayan* means "valiant or strength." See Henry Tourneux and Maurice Barbotin, *Dictionnaire pratique du créole de Guadeloupe: Marie-Galante* (Paris: Karthala, 1986), 383, 414.

79. Butterworth, *3 Years Adventures,* 303–4.

80. I was unable to work in the Centre des Archives d'outre Mer while in France, beyond the Fonds de St. Méry, which were available in microfilm at the National Archive. Perhaps this archive would contain references that might help flesh out the historical evolution of these arts in the future.

81. E. Rufz, *Chronologie des maladies de la ville de Saint-Pierre (Martinique) depuis l'année 1837 jusqu'à l'année 1856* (Paris: Baillière, 1869), 120.

82. For example, there is a possibility that these later practices were influenced by the large immigration of African indentured "Congos" in the nineteenth century. Some elder living masters of *ladja/danmyé* are children of these immigrants. See Jean-Claude Blanche, "L'immigration Congo en Guadeloupe," in *L'historial Antillais,* 6 vols., ed. Tony Djian, Jacques Sabatier, and Daniel Rouche (Pointe-'a-Pitre: Dajani éditions, 1981), 4:149–171.

83. This form of boxing was prevalent in Martinique. See Daniel Georges Bardury, interview, Fort-de-France, Martinique, July 19, 2002.

84. Fernando Ortiz, *Los bailes y el teatro de los negros en el folklore de Cuba* (Havana: Editorial Letras Cubanas, 1993).

85. This was, however, a stick fight, but the term appears related to the "French Creole" terms *kou* (strike) or *koko makak* (fighting stick). See Tato Conrad, interview, San Juan, Puerto Rico, July 21, 2003; Modesto Cepeda, taped interview by author, Santurce, Puerto Rico, December 7, 2003.

86. Lubangi Munienya, interview, New York City, September 19, 1996; field notes from Zaire, 1996. These may have also been influenced by English pugilism in the Regency period, when boxers stood toe to toe.

87. Tio Raul, interview, Benguela, Angola, October 16, 1997; "Fronfrons" Lebau, taped interview, Saint Anne, Guadeloupe, July 11, 2002.

88. Literally meaning "circle fist."

89. The practice of *bèrnaden* was limited to Guadeloupe in the twentieth century, but given the connections between the islands, fighters of Martinique would have been aware of this style. See David Alexandre, personal communication, February 9, 2002.

90. A gentler variant called for trying to knock the other's hat off. See Fronfrons Lebau, taped interview, Saint Anne, Martinique, November 7, 2002.

91. Although the terms *danmyé* and *ladja* are often conflated currently, they will be used distinctly here to distinguish between the earlier ritual form dominated by foot fighting and the composite combat-oriented fight that mixed various styles, including the kicks of *danmyé.* My use here is, however, somewhat artificial in that there is much debate and possibly regional and temporal changes in the meaning of these terms over time. The cultural group AM4, which is reviving the art, often uses the term *danmyé* to denote the composite art, but most of the elders I interviewed

were quite clear in suggesting the opposite. There also seem to have been some regional distinctions with northern fighters more known for kicking and southern fighters more known for arm techniques. As such, it is possible that there were regional variations in nomenclature making *ladja* and *danmyé* roughly equivalent, while the terms *ladja lan mò (ladja de la mort)* referred to their more hybrid, combative variants. Again, nineteenth-century documentation would be necessary to be sure. The term *danmyé* may well have come to the fight from the drumming technique called *danmyé,* through which the drummer communicates with the fighters and directs the ritual combat. According to Dominique Cyrille, the technique may date back to a tradition of *laura danmyé,* which was used to set the pace for the transportation of sugarcane to the carts. See Dominique Cyrille, personal communication, December 28, 2005; AM4 (Association Mi Mes Manmay Matnik), *Asou chimen danmyé: Propositions sur le danmyé, art martial martiniquaises* (Fort-de-France: Association Mi Mes Manmay Matnik, 1992); multiple interviews in Martinique in 1993, 2000, 2002, with Raoul Grivalliers, Georges Oranger, Michele Sousou, George La Venture, Gerard Harpan, Ysmyn Cachacou Mememiel, Stephan Laviolette, George Nolbas, Daniel Georges Bardury, Sully Cally, and others.

92. Gerstin, "Traditional Music," 335–36.

93. Edward L. Powe, *Danmyé, Ladjia, Wonpwen* (Madison, Wis.: Dan Aiki Publications, 2003), 33; Pierre Dru, taped interview, Fort-de France, Martinique, May 12, 2002; Nacinimo Deodee, taped interview, Bed-sty, New York, July 4, 2006. Stedman may have witnessed a variant in Suriname; see John Gabriel Stedman, *Stedman's Surinam: Life in an Eighteenth-Century Slave Society,* ed. Richard Price and Sally Price (Baltimore: Johns Hopkins University Press, 1992).

94. This term appears in some sources with the orthography *ladja, laghia,* and *l'ag'ya.*

95. Joseph Zobel, *Laghia de la mort: Nouvelles Antillaises* (Fort-de-France: Impr. A. Bezaudin, 1946).

96. Sully Cally-Lézin, *Musiques et danses Afro-Caraîbes: Martinique* (Gros Morne: Sully-Cally/Lezin, 1990), 60; Stephen Laviolette, interview, Fort-de-France, Martinique, July 7, 1993.

97. Gerstin, "Traditional Music," 336.

98. Stephan Laviolette, interview, Fort-de-France, Martinique, January 1, 1993.

99. As there is no written evidence to corroborate such tales, it is difficult to be sure if Zobel based his novel on stories he heard or if he invented the story himself and his novel is responsible for the existence of such popular stories today. Therefore, the role of such death matches in the hybridization of *ladja* remains at best a tentative hypothesis.

100. Cally-Lézin, *Musiques,* 60. Again, such claims are difficult to validate, given the lack of written documentation, but razors and other weapons were apparently held in the feet in other combative contests as well.

101. Vidiadhar Surajprasad Naipaul, *The Middle Passage: Impressions of Five Societies—British, French, and Dutch—in the West Indies and South America* (New York: Vintage Books, 1981), 222–23; Powe, *Danmyé,* 24.

102. Although dating is difficult, this clearly took place well before the early twentieth century when Katherine Dunham filmed *ladja* matches, presumably in the 1930s. The contest she filmed in her first location included some punches but was

still dominated by ritual foot fighting with inverted kicks much like those of the *engolo*, knocking and kicking, or *jogo de capoeira*. The contests she filmed at the docks contained foot strikes, but in comparison the use of *kokoyé*-style punches was much more pronounced.

103. Gerstin, "Traditional Music," 336.

104. AM4, *Asou chimen danmyé*, 17.

105. Alternative orthographies include *kouri la ronde, Alé la wonn,* and *kouri*. Unfortunately Dunham's footage cuts off the beginning of the eight matches, making it difficult to compare recent practice to that in the first half of the twentieth century.

106. Josy Michalon (*Ladjia*) argues that the *ladja* is a derivative of Benin wrestling. She traces it to the arts of *kadjia* and *kokoule* wrestling forms of the Basantché and Kotokoli people, respectively. Given the large numbers of captives brought to Martinique from the Bight of Benin, it is tempting to accept her etymology of *ladja* and *cocoyé* as deriving from the Basantché and Kotokoli names for wrestling, *kadjia* and *kokoule*. As *cocoyé* was historically used to describe a pugilistic art, this is not a likely derivation. The case for *ladja* is more compelling, given that a grappling element does exist in *ladja*. However, as with the origin of the term *capoeira*, there are equally compelling hypotheses using Bantu and French etymologies, none of which has documented support. See also Cally-Lézin, *Musiques*, 59.

107. Cally-Lezin, *Musiques*, 69. Note that the name for this combat art was likely drawn from the name of the drumming as we had seen in the case of the *bamboula*.

108. Kubik, "Drum Patterns," 115–81; Gerstin, "Traditional Music," 113–14; Kenneth Bilby, "The Caribbean as a Musical Region," in *Caribbean Contours*, ed. Sidney Mintz and Sally Price (Baltimore, 1985), 187; John F. Szwed and Morton Marks, "The Afro-American Transformation of European Set Dances and Dance Suites," *Dance Research Journal* 20, no. 1 (1988): 30.

109. Johann Moritz Rugendas, *Viagem pitoresca através do Brasil*, trans. Sérgio Milliet (São Paulo: Livraria Martins, 1940). Charles Ribeyrolles also describes the *jogo de capoeira* as being accompanied by a "Congolese drum" (*tambor do Congo*), thereby identifying it as Central African; see Charles Ribeyrolles, *Brasil pitoresco: História, descrições-viagens-colonização instituições* (São Paulo: Livraria Martins, 1941), 37. Kubik notes that in the *batuque* dances in which the *jogo de capoeira* was practiced, this drum (called *tambu*) was accompanied by another transverse drum called *quinjenge* and musical sticks like the *tibwa* called *matraca*. He notes the use of musical sticks on the back of a drum to be a widespread West Central African pattern. While the drums were also common of a wide Bantu pattern, he traces the names directly to the Kongo *ntambu* and the Cimbembasian *kenjengo*. See Kubik, "Drum Patterns," 148–53.

110. Argeliers León, *Del canto y el tempo* (Havana: Editorial Letras Cubanas, 1984), 71–72. See also T. J. Desch-Obi, "The Surprising Success of Early Black Boxers," paper presented at the African Activists Association Conference, University of California, Los Angeles, May 1995.

111. Thompson, *Dancing*, 7.

112. Ibid, 5.

113. Stuckey, *Slave Culture*, 11, 12.

114. Raoul Grivalliers, interview, Martinique, July 15, 1993.

115. The above is spelled with contemporary orthography, while the original source is "Gardez ca Mukla, Comme il cavaye pie." See Katherine Dunham [under

pseudonym Kaye Dunn], "L'Ag'ya of Martinique," *Esquire* 12, no. 5 (1939): 84–85, 126.

116. Ibid., 86.

117. Stephen Laviolette, interview, Fort-de-France, Martinique, July 20, 1993.

118. It is clear that as a combat system, *ladja* shows no documentable influence from *kadjia* as suggested by Michalon. The first of two dominant techniques include lifting the opponent to throw, which could have been drawn from any and all West and Central African wrestling styles. The second grappling technique, *sote-kaï,* involves falling to one's back with a foot in the adversary's abdomen to throw him over. This technique violates the rules and aesthetics of *kadjia* and other forms of West African wrestling in which a fighter who fell to his back would immediately forfeit the match. In addition, it is clear that wrestling was not a central component of the *ladja* in the matches filmed by Katherine Dunham in the 1930s. The dominant techniques utilized were kicks, many of them inverted, a significant number of hand strikes from *kokoyé*. In terms of grappling techniques, there was one leg grab and a push, but no *kadjia*-like throws or takedowns. As she explained to me in a personal interview, "L'agya is more footwork and not like wrestling" (Katherine Dunham, interview, New York City, May 19, 2002). It appears that her association of *ladja* with wrestling was due to her sense that it was an African practice, and she had been exposed to wrestling only in her trips to Gambia and Nigeria. The heavier wrestling element in modern *ladja* comes in part from some of the trainers of AM4 who learned judo and aikido before their attempts to revive *ladja.*

119. Although both British boxing and French kick boxing were popular in Martinique, none of the toe kicks of *savate* or the actual boxing hand blows seem to have left any mark on the art, according to AM4, *Asou chimen danmyé,* 18. As we shall see in the last chapter, however, the Central African martial art tradition may have influenced the creation of French boxing.

120. Further research is needed on the numerous boxing styles of the Atlantic and Indian Ocean regions that may have influenced these.

121. Debien, *Les esclaves aux Antilles Françaises,* 345.

122. Monica Schuler, "Liberated Central Africans in Nineteenth-Century Guyana," in *Central Africans and Cultural Transformations,* ed. Heywood, 319–352.

123. Esteban Montejo, *The Autobiography of a Runaway Slave* ed. Miguel Barnet (London: Macmillan, 1993), 63–64. See T. J. Desch-Obi, "Combat and the Crossing of the Kalunga," in *Central Africans and Cultural Transformations,* ed. Heywood, 353–70.

124. Priscilla McCullough cited in Harold Courlander, *A Treasury of American Folklore* (New York: Crown Publishers, 1976), 286.

125. While Rosa's mother was not able to fly, it was generally believed that even those who were American-born could attain the gift of flight if the connection to Africa was maintained in some format. One folk tradition recalls the case of a young woman who, with the blessings of her father, flew back to Africa when a driver was about to beat her. Other oral traditions maintain that an American-born person could reclaim this ability to fly back from Africans who ritually reawaken their forgotten connection to their past. See Georgia Writers Project, *Drums and Shadows,* 145; John Bennet, *Doctor to the Dead: Grotesque Legends & Folktales of Old Charleston* (New York: Rinehart & Company, 1943), 140; and Young, "Rituals of Resistance," 250.

126. Jean-Claude Annezer, Danielle Begot, and Jack Manluis, "L'universe magico-religieux," in *L'historial Antillais,* ed. Djian, Sabatier, and Rouche, 1:469.

127. Works that trace the Central African traditions of burial in the Americas are, for example, Elizabeth Fenn, "Honoring the Ancestors: Kongo-American Graves in the American South," *Southern Exposure* 13, no. 5 (1985): 42–47; Thompson, *Flash of the Spirit,* 132–42; and James Denbow, "Heart and Soul: Glimpses of Ideology and Cosmology in the Iconography of Tombstones from the Loango Coast of Central Africa," *Journal of American Folklore* 112, no. 445 (1999): 404–23.

128. Charles Ball, *Slavery in the United States: A Narrative of the Life and Adventures of Charles Ball, a Black Man* (1837; repr., Detroit: American Library, 1969), 265.

129. *Abstract of the Evidence Delivered before a Select Committee of the House of Commons in the Years 1790 and 1791 on the Part of the Petitioners for the Abolition of the Slave Trade* (Cincinnati: American Reform Tract and Book Society, 1855), 115–16.

130. Michel-René Hilliard d'Auberteuil, *Considerations sur l'etat present de la colonies francaise de Sainte-Domingue,* 2 vols. (Paris, 1776–1777), 1:141; Moreau de Saint-Méry et al., *Description,* 1:51.

131. Moreau de Saint-Méry et al., *Description,* 1:31; Everild Young and Kjeld Helweg-Larsen, *The Pirates' Priest: The Life of Père Labat in the West Indies, 1693–1705* ([London:] Jarrolds, 1965), 41–42.

132. In Brazil, too, funerals were a common context for the *jogo de capoeira.* See Adolfo Moarales de Los Reis Filho, *O Rio de Janeiro imperial* (Rio de Janeiro: A Noite, 1946), 52.

133. Félix Longin, *Voyage à la Guadeloupe* (Le Mains, 1848), 203–5; Abbé Dugoujon, *Lettres sur l'esclavage dans les colonies françaises* (Paris: Pagnerre, 1845), 73.

134. Huguette Bellemare, "Survivances africaines," in *L'historial Antillais,* ed. Djian, Sabatier, and Rouche, 280.

135. If the home was not big enough for the event, the men would construct a make-shift, open-air canopy for the occasion. See Diana Ramassamy, *Guide de la veillée mortuaire* (Petit-Bourg: Ibis Rouge, 2002), 29.

136. For examples of such word games, which began with the call "krik" and response "krak," see Roger Fortuné, "Folklore de la Guadeloupe: La veillée mortuaire," *Parallèls* 10 (1965): 16–17. For an in-depth discussion of men of words, see Abrahams, *The Man-of-Words in the West Indies.*

137. Anca Bertrand, "Le cercle de culture ansois," *Parallèls* 14 (1966): 19–21.

138. Such discontented souls in Angola or the Americas often had to be dealt with by ritual specialists to prevent them from harming the living. For an overview of the *zombie* cosmology in Angola and the Americas, see Hans-W. Ackerman and Jeanine Gauthier, "The Ways and Nature of the Zombi," *Journal of American Folklore* 104 (Autumn 1991): 466–94. In both Imbangala and Brazilian *kilombos,* the office of ritualist who specialized in this hazard was the *nganga a nzumbi* (Imbangala) and presumably the Ganga Zumba (Brazil), who played central roles in their respective societies. In Brazil the holder of this priestly title came to lead the *kilombo* of Palmares. In Barbados, Entiope Holt noted funeral ritual among bondsmen to help prevent the soul from returning. See Stuart B. Schwartz, *Slaves, Peasants, and Rebels* (Urbana: University of Illionois Press, 1992), 122–28; and letter of Arthur Holt in 1729, cited in Jerome S. Handler and Frederick W. Lange, *Plantation Slavery in*

Barbados: An Archeological and Historical Investigation (Cambridge, Mass.: Harvard University Press, 1978), 204.

139. John Storm Roberts, *Black Music of Two Worlds* (New York: Praeger, 1972), 48. On *zonbi* (*zombie*) belief in Guadeloupe, see Longin, *Voyage à la Guadeloupe*, 202–7.

140. This is no longer a common context for modern *ladja/danmyé* although listed as such by Ralph Ludwig, *Dictionnaire Créole français (Guadeloupe): avec un abrégé de grammaire créole, un lexique français/créole, les comparaisons courantes, les locutions et plus de 1000 proverbes* (Paris: Servedit/Editions Jasor, 1990), 195.

141. Françoise Montreuil, "Rites mortuaires et représentation collective de la mort à la Martinique," M.A. thesis, Université R. Descartes, 1973, 33.

142. Although Trinidad was not a French colony politically, the bondsmen there were part of the Francophone world, most of them speaking "French Creole" as their primary language through the nineteenth century. See Kenneth M. Bilby and Fu-Kiau kia Bunseki, *Kumina: A Kongo-Based Tradition in the New World* (Brussels: Centre d'Etude et de Documentation Africaines-Cedaf, 1983), 71.

143. Georges Oranger, taped interview, Saint Esprit, Martinique, May 11, 2002.

144. Grenada was a French colony to 1783 (although captured by the British in the Seven Years' War), and "French Creole" remained the *lingua franca* of bondsmen even after the British took control of the island in that year. See *Grenada, Carriacou, Petit Martinique: Spice Island of the Caribbean* (London: Hansib, 1994), 156.

145. WIS, Andrew Pearse Collection, box 1, folder 4, item 8.

146. Wyatt MacGaffey, *Religion and Society in Central Africa: The Bakongo of Lower Zaire* (Chicago: University of Chicago Press, 1986), 43–51.

147. Kuyk, *African Voices*, 13.

148. This section draws on material primarily from Saint Dominque and Martinique, along with Guadeloupe, Trinidad, and Grenada. Yet, in the words of Gabriel Debien, "Il est encore prématuré de presenter une vue d'ensemble sur les esclaves de nos Antilles" (Debien, *Les esclaves aux Antilles Françaises*, 7). This combination is not to suggest that they shared historical trajectories but that, due to a scarcity of data on any one island, I am combining them. Unlike these other islands, Trinidad was not formally French, but French-based creole was dominant among bondsmen there.

149. Rugendas, *Viagem*, 155.

150. Marcos Turio Colmenarez, interview, Lara, Venezuela, March 5, 1995; Eduardo Sanoja, interview, Lara, Venezuela, July 5, 1995; Eduardo Sanoja, *Juego de garrote larense: El método venezolano de defensa personal* (Caracas: Federación Nacional de la Cultura Popular, 1984).

151. *City Gazette* (Charleston), March 20, 1798.

152. Piersen, *Black Yankees*, 117–28.

153. Labat, *Nouveau voyage*, 63–64; English translations from Jean Baptiste Labat, *The Memoirs of Père Labat, 1693–1705*, trans. John Eaden (London: Frank Cass, 1970).

154. Note that rock throwing, one of the five Kunene arts of war, was also widespread among bondsmen in the Caribbean. In Saint Croix, which was held by the French from 1650 to 1733, stone throwing served an auxiliary martial function to "the stick-fighting duels dearly cherished" by bondsmen. This skill "was acquired in childhood, the slave child's first amusement as soon as it began to creep being stone

throwing. It persisted into adult life, and stones were used not only for chasing dogs, pigs, goats and other animals but were also employed against each other in moments of irritation or during disputes." In nearby St. Thomas, bondsmen hailed down stones on houses in the cover of night as acts of defiance. See Neville A. T. Hall, *Slave Society in the Danish West Indies: St. Thomas, St. John and St. Croix* (Baltimore: Johns Hopkins University Press, 1992), 119–20.

155. Moritz, "Honor Psychology," 13.

156. William Bosman, *A New and Accurate Description of the Coast of Guinea* (London / New York: Frank Cass / Barnes and Noble, 1967), 396. See also Fadahunsi, "Dahomey."

157. For example, Moreau de Saint-Méry referred to stick-fighting games in eighteenth-century Martinique under the term *jankouliba,* while in the nineteenth century Lafcadio Hearn used the term *kalenda* for stick fighting in Martinique. In contemporary practice, while the earlier term *jankouliba* is still known, stick fighting is more generally referred to as *komba baton,* although it uses the same fighting postures and techniques called *kalenda/kalinda* elsewhere. Similarly in Haiti the art is still known in some contexts as *kalenda* but also as *tiré baton, tire bwa,* and other names. In contemporary practice in Guadeloupe, stick fighting is most commonly known as *mayole.* See Daniel Georges Bardury, interview, Fort-de-France, Martinique, July 19, 2002; Mr. Rapsode, interview, Moule, Guadeloupe, April 20, 2000; Harold Courlander, *The Drum and the Hoe: Life and Lore of the Haitian People* (Berkeley: University of California Press, 1960); and Petit Jolibois, interview, Segu, Haiti, May 20, 2003.

158. The term was often used synonymously with *bambula* and was used in the twentieth century to describe particular drum rhythms on many islands as well. It will be used here, however, exclusively in reference to the stick-fighting style also called *kalenda.*

159. The technical aspect of this stick-fighting style may not be traceable to any one particular ethnic group's style; however, ritual use of these sticks points most specifically to the influence of Angolans and particularly Kikongo-speaking peoples. Even as late as the nineteenth and early twentieth centuries in Trinidad, ritually prepared fighting sticks were called by the Bantu term *wanga.* In Jamaica, according to one of Maureen Lewis-Warner's informants, stick fighting was carried out only by "Congo descendants at Seaforth." In Cuba it was the Congo "nation" that came out on festival days brandishing their wooden weapons. See Alan Lomax, *Trinidad Carnival Roots* (Rounder CD, 2000); Maureen Lewis-Warner, *Guinea's Other Suns: The African Dynamic in Trinidad Culture* (Dover, Mass.: Majority Press, 1991), 151–52; Judith Bettelheim, *Cuban Festivals: An Illustrated Anthology* (New York: Garland, 1993); and Fernando Ortiz, *Los instrumentos de la musica Afrocubana,* vol. 4 (Havana: Cardenas y Cia, 1954).

160. Lafcadio Hearn, *Two Years in the French West Indies* (New York: Harper & Brothers, 1923), 173.

161. In the twentieth century Courlander encountered a danced stick fight named Mousondi, after a specific ethnic group from Kongo. It was practiced to a war song, "Mousundi, na fè la guè, Eya eya eya, Nou ce' nanchon la gu, Ou pa tendé canon-m tire?," or in Courlander's orthography, "Mousondi, na fai la guè, Eya eya eya, Nous c'est anchon la gué, Ou pas tendé canon'm tire" (Mousondi, we will make war, Eya,

eya, eye, We are a nation of war, Don't you hear my cannon shouting?). The fact that such a song still linked stick fighting to a particular African ethnicity even after the Haitian Revolution is fascinating since much of the memory of such arts now looks to the revolution itself. See Courlander, *Drum*, 131–32.

162. Melville Herskovitz, *Rebel Destiny: Among the Bush Negroes of Dutch Guiana* (New York: McGraw-Hill and Company, Inc., 1934), 277.

163. Moreau de Saint-Méry et al., *Description*, 1:275. Debien published the documents regarding this case in "Assemblées nocturnes," 273–84. Geggus ("Haitian Voodoo," 33–36) outlines the Kongo precedents of these items and adds that *mayombe* referred to the pouch containing the medicines rather than the stick itself.

164. On these distinctive postures, see Robert Ferris Thompson, "Gestuelle des Arts Martiaux" in Christine Falgayrettes-Leveau ed., *Le Geste Kôngo* (Paris: Musée Dapper, 2002), 127–29; and Félix Bárbaro Martínez Ruiz, "Kongo Machinery: Graphic Writing and Other Narratives of the Sign" (Ph.D. diss., Yale University, 2004). We anxiously await the upcoming work of Bárbaro Martínez Ruiz based on his current fieldwork that includes Cimbebasia.

165. Lennox Honychurch, "Chatoyer's Artist: Agostino Brunias and the Depiction of St Vincent," *Journal of the Barbados Museum and Historical Society* 50 (2004): 104–28.

166. Julian Pitt-Rivers, "Honor," in *International Encyclopedia of the Social Sciences*, ed. David Sills (New York: Macmillan, 1968), 6:503–10.

167. Geneviève Leti, *Sante et societe esclavagiste a la Martinique: 1802–1848* (Montreal: L'Harmattan, Inc., 1998), 38–40.

168. Pierre-François-Régis Dessalles, *Annales du conseil souverain de la Martinique, ou tableau historique du gouvernement de cette colonie, depuis son premier établissement jusqu'à à nos jours* (1786; repr., A Bergerac, Chex J. B. Puynesge, 1977), 1:258.

169. Geggus, "Haitian Voodoo," 33–35. Compare with the use of nails to activate Kongo *nkisi*. See MacGaffey, *Kongo Political Culture*, 104–6.

170. Moreau de Saint-Méry et al., *Description*, 51:3–54. These sticks were also referred to as *bâtons ferrés*.

171. Dessalles, *Annales*, 1:248.

172. "*Gros batons*," cited in Antoine Gisler, *L'esclavage aux antilles françaises (17e–19e siècle): Contribution au problème de l'esclavage* (Fribourg: Éditions Universitaires, 1965); Lucien Pierre Peytraud, *L'esclavage aux antilles françaises avant 1789, d'après des documents inédits des Archives Coloniales* (Paris: Hachette et cie, 1897), 21. Note also the later law of July 4, 1758, outlawing just the *bangalas* with metal heads (AN Col. Série L, vol. 4, 227).

173. Cited in Gisler, *L'esclavage*, 80–81.

174. Labat describes such a snakebite problem in *Nouveau voyage*, 1:161.

175. For a description of such ornamented sticks as symbols of status in Biafra and the Americas, see Hugh Crow, *Memoirs of the Late Captain Hugh Crow of Liverpool, Comprising a Narrative of His Life Together with Descriptive Sketches of the Western Coast of Africa, Particularly of Bonny, the Manners and Customs of the Inhabitants, the Production of the Soil and the Trade of the Country to Which Are Added Anecdotes and Observations Illustrative of the Negro Character* (1830; repr., [London:] F. Cass, 1970), 217; Piersen, *Black Yankees*, 136; and Abrahams and Szwed, *After Africa*, 265, 306.

176. Dessalles, *Annales*, 1:248.

177. Geggus, "Haitian Voodoo," 33–36; Bercy de Drouin, *De Saint-Domingue: De ses guerres, de ses révolutions, de ses resources, et de moyens a prendre pour y rétabilir la paix et l'industrie* (Paris: Chez Hocquet, 1814). As Geggus notes, sticks had also been a marker of participation in some Kongolese closed societies.

178. These *mayombe* ceremonies were held in a region of recently established coffee plantations; thus Congo nation bondsmen were likely present in large numbers. Mayombe was the name of a port along the northern Angola coast, named after a forested Kikongo-speaking region in its hinterland.

179. Vanhee, "Central African Popular Christianity," 252.

180. Debien, "Assemblées nocturnes," 273–84 (based on the notes of Gressier de la Jaloussière, May 26, 1786).

181. AN Col. C 8 A20, January 11, 1715, reproduced in Munford, *Black Ordeal,* 907.

182. "Sometimes the dance was aimed at retracing the image of combats" ("*Quelquefois la danse était destinée à retracer l'image des combats, afin que jusques dans ses plaisirs, le guerir pût nonrrir son ame des sentimens qui le faisent voler à la glorie*"); see M. L. E. Moreau de Saint-Méry, *De la danse* (Parme: Imprimé par Bodoni, 1801), 5.

183. Butterworth, *3 Years Adventures,* 303–4.

184. While bondsmen in Guadeloupe may have been influenced by dueling norms, local whites on many islands of the Caribbean later also took up these danced combat forms of bondsmen. In a fictional account in 1838, E. Joseph described local-born whites of Bequia (near St. Vincent) performing a stick-fighting dance to the sound of "negro drums." In Trinidad even upper-class whites in the nineteenth century were drawn to *kalenda* stick fighting. See E. L. Joseph, *Warner Arundel: The Adventures of a Creole* (London: Saunders and Otley, 1837), 51; and Liverpool, *Rituals of Power,* 160–64.

185. *Collection Moreau de Saint-Méry,* Série F, vol. 133, p. 588.

186. This clear-cut gender division may have been overstated. While it is impossible to extrapolate backward and from another island, it should be noted that in the following century in Trinidad there were well-known female stick fighters. See WIS, Andrew Pearse Collection, box 1, folder 4, item 4.

187. Moreau de Saint-Méry et al., *Description,* 1:53–54.

188. Sandra Barnes, ed., *Africa's Ogun* (Bloomington: Indiana University Press, 1989).

189. Luca da Caltanisetta, *Diaire congolais, 1690–1701,* ed. François Bontinck (Louvain: Éditions Nauwelaerts, 1970), 6.

190. Although it is not possible to date the beginning of such a connection, these stick/machete–fighting skills were linked to Haitian closed societies in the twentieth century. Like many closed societies, these societies inflicted punishments on fallen insiders and external enemies. Perhaps the most striking example of the latter was the closed society of the maroon leader François Makandal, who had an extensive network that, according to one account, covered the entire colony of Saint Domingue and utilized such poisons to terrorize the white population in the 1750s. In the twentieth century the use of poisons was one of three types of vengeance brought by these societies. The first was *coup poudre* (the use of powders to bring illness, death, or

worse, living zombification). The next was *coup l'air* (a spiritual punishment that brings misfortune), a tactic that was certainly present during the revolution in the form of *wanga,* a Bantu-derived term for war medicines. Last, the machete was used to bring a physical *coup* for those who resisted the society's executives. At least by the twentieth century the use of sticks and machetes was formally perpetuated in closed societies in certain regions of Haiti. One report depicts the formal brandishing of these weapons in honor of a king of the Sanpwel. See Fick, *Making of Haiti,* 59–73; Davis, *Passage of Darkness,* 272; Jean Yves Blot, interview, Port-au-Prince, Haiti, May 25, 2003; and Molly Ahye, *Golden Heritage* (Petit Valley: Moonan Printers, Ltd., 1978), 118.

191. Among blacks in many places in the Americas, including Colombia, Venezuela, and Haiti, stick fighting is still used as a training tool in learning how to fight with machetes.

192. All the above cases are cited in Leti, *Sante,* 42.

193. Hearn, *Two Years,* 141.

194. Ibid., 147.

195. David Geggus, "Yellow Fever in the 1790s: The British Army in Occupied Saint Domingue," *Medical History* 23 (1979): 38–58; Wenda Parkinson, *This Gilded African: Toussaint L'Ouverture* (London and New York: Quartet Books, 1978).

196. Moreau de Saint-Méry et al., *Description,* 1:55.

197. Although it is impossible to give a precise dating of when this began, the fighting art was divided into three interrelated levels: *tiré baton,* using stick fighting in various substyles; *tiré machet,* which, like the Biafran art, used the machete in strikes at angles designed to dismember an opponent; and a transitional training style used when the *tiré machet* strikes were learned using the safety of sticks. See multiple interviews, taped interviews, and participant observation during training and initiation in Segu, Haiti, with Damas Galant, Necker Patanace, Joseph Estimé, Saint Pha, Demosthenes Dechalex, Petit Jolibois, Ti-Jean, Ti-Po, and others in 2002, 2003, and 2004.

198. Moreau de Saint-Méry et al., *Description,* 1:57.

199. African religious beliefs, such as their assured return to Africa if killed in battle, may have encouraged some revolutionaries, while the morales of others were undoubtedly raised by the use of defensive charms and medical treatment. Oath taking and divination were important elements of early meetings, such as the feast of August 14, 1791, and the Bois Csiman ceremony. The many leaders described as employing ritual specialists during the revolution may have continued to make use of divination. Certainly there are numerous references to the use of offensive *wanga* and of poison. I treat this subject in more detail in "A Machete Will Do for Me: African Combative Traditions and the Independence Struggles of Haiti and Cuba," paper presented to Mellon Seminar on Violence, City University of New York, March 12, 2005.

200. AN DXXV 22, 223, 224; Claudine B. Auguste, "Les Congos dans la revolution haitienne," *Bulletin du Bureau National d'Ethnologie* 1 & 2 (1986): 57–90. The Moko nation was associated with peoples from the coastal region of Biafra, particularly Ibibio and surrounding peoples.

201. Fick, *Making of Haiti,* 97.

202. Althéa de Puech Parham ed., *My Odyssey: Experiences of a Young Refugee from Two Revolutions* (Baton Rouge: Louisiana State University Press, 1959), 64.

203. Fick, *Making of Haiti,* 98.

204. I am drawing here on the pioneering work of John Thornton, who has done detailed studies on the role of African soldiers in the Haitian Revolution. For an overview of his work on African military traditions, see Thornton, *Warfare in Atlantic Africa.*

205. I am not suggesting here that these tactics were utilized exclusively by these two groups, as variations on this theme were widespread in Central Africa at least. Cf. Thornton, "Art of War," 360–78. Félix Carteau, *Soirées Bermudiennes, ou, Entretiens sur les événemens qui ont opéré la ruine de la partie française de l'isle Saint-Domingue* (Bordeaux: Chez Pellier-Lawalle, 1802), 100.

206. Parham, *Odyssey,* 51.

207. Fick, *Making of Haiti,* 110.

208. Thornton, "African Soldiers," 71.

209. Andrew Uffindell, "The Closed Ranks and Close Ranges of Napoleonic Warfare," *Military History* 61 (October 1997): 75.

210. Bryan Edwards, *The History, Civil and Commercial, of the British West Indies; With a Continuation to the Present Time,* 5 vols. (1819; repr., New York: AMS Press, 1966), 72–75.

211. Ibid.

212. Public Records Office (hereafter PRO), HCA 30 393, 78; Bricaud to M. Bernard, Les Cayes, December 12, 1792, cited in Bernard Foubert, "Les volontaires nationaux de la Seine-Inferieur a Saint-Domingue," *Bulletin de la Société d'histoire de la Guadeloupe* 51 (1982): 29.

213. *Boston Independent Chronicle and Universal Advertiser,* September 29, 1791, F110.

214. By knives, he clearly means machetes, as becomes clear in his illustration of the event on p. 88. See Parham, *Odyssey,* 91.

215. Although he was discovered and almost dismembered, one of the leaders spared him (Parham, *Odyssey,* 129–34).

216. Even years into the war, *l'arme blanche* could play a decisive role, as in the battle at the small fort La Crete à Pierrot. This was a critical moment in the defense of the country after a large French force under Leclerc's command landed on the island in January 1802. Although he inflicted heavy casualties, Toussaint-Louverture was being pushed back on all fronts. Twelve hundred men under the command of Jean-Jacques Dessalines and Lamartinière were pinned down in the small fort, while the French attacking army amounted to twelve thousand men, according to Gen. Pamphile La Croix. Despite their lack of munitions, the blacks repelled wave after wave of assaults. Even with all their ammunition wasted, they were able to repel bayonet charges with their mastery of *l'arme blanche.* Dessalines and later Lamartinière led their men, armed only with their blades, into the superior French forces. Although they lost nearly half their men, the rest literally cut their way through the French to safety. Although Leclerc took the fort, it proved an indecisive and costly victory, remembered as a decisive turning point in the war. See Thomas O. Ott, *The Haitian Revolution, 1789–1804* (Knoxville: University of Tennessee Press, 1973), 155–58; and Mark Bird, *The Black Man* (New York, 1869), 42–44.

Chapter 5: Urban Inversions

1. Klein, *African Slavery,* 72; Eltis et al., *Trans-Atlantic Slave Trade.*

2. For a comprehensive treatment of slave life in the city, including the epidemics that ravaged the city raising the mortality rates of urban bondsmen beyond those in rural areas, see Karasch's seminal work, *Slave Life in Rio de Janeiro.*

3. James Henderson, *A History of the Brazil: Comprising Its Geography, Commerce, Colonization, Aboriginal Inhabitants, &c.* (London: Longman, Hurst, Rees, Orme, and Brown, 1821), 72. A large percentage of this black majority was held in bondage. In 1834 over 56 percent of the city residents were enslaved Africans; see Karasch, *Slave Life in Rio de Janeiro,* 61–62.

4. Miller, *Kings and Kinsmen,* 55–56. For a detailed analysis of the implications of this term in Brazil and its related meanings in other languages of northern and southern Angola, see Robert W. Slenes, *"Malungu, Ngoma vem!" África encoberta e descoberta no Brasil* (Luanda: Ministério da Cultura, 1995), 9–11.

5. Joseph C. Miller, "Central Africa during the Era of the Slave Trade, c. 1490s–1850s," in *Central Africans and Cultural Transformations,* ed. Heywood, 51.

6. Miller, "Central Africa," 51.

7. Karasch, *Slave Life in Rio de Janeiro,* 20–21.

8. Of West Africans, Biafrans were brought to this region of Brazil in the largest numbers but numbered only about 1 percent, while those from the Gold Coast and Bight of Benin comprised less than half of 1 percent each. Yet, "Minas" were certainly visible and influential in the city. While the term "Mina" was most associated with Africans from the Gold Coast elsewhere, it at times included peoples from the Bight of Benin when used in Brazil. See Eltis et al., *Trans-Atlantic Slave Trade;* Hall, *Slavery and African Ethnicities,* 101–25; and Robin Law, "Ethnicities of Enslaved Africans in the Diaspora: On the Meanings of 'Mina' (Again)," *History in Africa* 32 (2005): 247–67.

9. Other Angolan foods common in Rio were *pirão*—which, like *angú,* was similar to *fufu*—and *muqueca,* a seafood ragout with palm oil, peppers, and tomatoes. Often owned by free black women, *zungu* houses at times rented rooms to Africans and their progeny as well as selling their preferred foods to wage-laboring bondsmen. Early in the nineteenth century they were at times referred to as *casas de quilombos* in police records as they were thought to harbor urban maroons. See Karasch, *Slave Life in Rio de Janeiro,* 230–32; Leila Mezan Algranti, *O feitor ausente: Estudo sobre a escravidão urbana no Rio de Janeiro* (Petrópolis: Vozes, 1988), 209; and Carlos Eugênio Líbano Soares, *Zungú: Rumor de muitas vozes* (Rio de Janeiro: Arquivo Publico de Rio de Janeiro, 1998).

10. *Kulundus* were by no means the only African religion introduced to Rio. Islam and West African religious practices were also brought to Rio by enslaved Africans. In addition to the Christianity imposed by the Brazilian authorities, Angolan Catholics brought their own form of Christianity to Brazil. See James H. Sweet, *Recreating Africa: Culture, Kinship, and Religion in the African-Portuguese World, 1441–1770* (Chapel Hill: University of North Carolina Press, 2003).

11. As in North America, the term *kalunga* was adopted into the general vocabulary of African-derived peoples in reference to the sea, things of the sea, and ancestral spirits related to the sea. Some Brazilians would at times distinguish between the related *kalunga grande* ("the big sea") and *kalunga pequeno* (a cemetery;

literally "the little realm of the dead"). See Schneider, *Dictionary of African Borrowings*, 82–84.

12. The etymology of the term *capoeira* is uncertain. Numerous possibilities have been put forward, but without historical evidence to support them, they remain conjectural. One popular theory is that it derives from a combination of two Tupi words: *caá* (forest) and *puêra* (that which has disappeared), together referring to a cleared area in a forest, with the idea that that is where the martial art was practiced. *Capoeira* was also the name for a woven basket used by bondsmen to transport items. Given the link between bonded day laborers and *capoeiragem,* this etymology seems especially promising. The term *capoeira,* meaning "chicken cage," was also given to thieves who stole from them and was applied by extension to all petty thieves. It has also been suggested that the term derives from the Portuguese *capão,* for "male chicken," from a supposed resemblance between *jogo de capoeira* and cockfighting. Another possibility is that the term *capoeira* refers to a native Brazilian bird known to attack rivals and whose distinctive call might be compared to the practice of whistling unique to *capoeiras* in Rio. C. Daniel Dawson and Fu-Kiau Bunseki have presented an African derivation from the Kikongo term *kipura/kipula,* from the root *pura,* meaning "to struggle, to fight, to flog." In many Cimbebasian languages *kipura* means "to/a slap or strike," although the most interesting Bantu possibility may be Umbundo *kupwila,* meaning "to rush headlong into; to cause to fall." For a detailed historiography of this discourse, see Thomas H. Holloway, "'A Healthy Terror': Police Repression of *Capoeiras* in Nineteenth-Century Rio de Janeiro," *Hispanic American Historical Review* 69, no. 4 (1989): 643n12; Carlos Eugênio Líbano Soares, *A Negregada Instituição: Os capoeiras no Rio de Janeiro* (Rio de Janeiro: Prefeitura da Cidade do Rio de Janeiro Secretaria Municipal de Cultura Departamento Geral de Documentação e Informação Cultural Divisão de Editoração, 1994), 19–23; Carlos Eugênio Líbano Soares, *A capoeira escrava e outras tradições rebeldes no Rio de Janeiro, 1808–1850* (Campinas: Editora da UNICAMP CECULT, 2001), 49–53; and Kubik, *Angolan Traits in Black Music,* 29; Dr. K. Kia Bunseki Fu-Kiao is cited in Dawson, *Capoeira Angola,* 10–11.

13. Given the highly polemic debates surrounding this issue, the competing theories of the *jogo de capoeira*'s origins should be outlined briefly. In this text I propose that the *jogo de capoeira* is both derived from an Angolan pugilistic tradition and also a uniquely Brazilian expression of this tradition. Just as the version of jiujitsu developed by the Gracie family in Brazil can be accurately termed "Brazilian Jiu Jitsu" without the need to deny its direct evolution from Japanese Jiu Jitsu, so too can the *jogo de capoeira* be described as uniquely Brazilian without denying that it emerged from an Angolan tradition. Unfortunately, however, some writers have felt the need to deny its African provenance in order to accept the *jogo de capoeira* as Brazilian.

These vehement denials have been based on political stances rather than any serious research. Indeed, their arguments seem to hinge on their own ignorance of African practices. The first author to promote the Brazilian origin thesis was Plácido de Abreu, who wrote: "Some attribute it to the black Africans, which I personally think is a mistake for the simple fact that in Africa our *capoeiragem* is not known, merely some forms of head-butting. To our natives [Indigenous Americans] we also cannot attribute this, because even though they have the agility that characterizes *capoeiras,* they don't know the methods that *capoeiras* use for attack and defense. The most rational [explanation] is that *capoeiragem* was created, developed, and perfected among us." Note here that the basis of his conclusion for denying the widespread notion of an African genesis was simply his ignorance of any dynamic kicking art akin to the *jogo de capoeira* in Africa. In more current decades Mária Jardim and countless others have repeated this same logic—without having done any research on the subject—in order to deny any African origin: "no cultural manifestation similar to *capoeira* was found in Africa and therefore the conclusion can be drawn that the expression '*capoeira* Angola' is a Brazilian creation without any cultural connotation with Africa." A more-recent Eurocentric version of this denial, by Matthias Assunção, rests on his erroneous conviction that the writings of the ethnographer Carlos Estermann prove that there was no pugilism in southern Angola, but only wrestling. Assunção clearly missed the fact that Estermann, like many other ethnographers, was not interested in the details of martial arts and used the term "wrestling" to denote any agonistic activity, including the pugilistic arts he witnessed. Note, for example, the twentieth-century description of the *jogo de capoeira* by Ruth Landers as a "competition of wrestlers of a West African type called capoeira." In light of the detailed ethnographies that Landers wrote on the subject, her use of the term "wrestling" here should not be taken to mean that *capoeira* was a form of grappling. We can be sure that this was true in the case of Estermann in his passing reference to "wrestling" among the Kunene. Had Assunção read the source closely, he would have noticed plate 243, entitled "Nyaneka boys wrestling," which is unequivocally a photograph of slap-boxing *kandeka*! As we see, then, an ignorance or misunderstanding of African martial art traditions lies at the heart of these arguments. In place of any connection to African traditions, these writers have put forward origin myths based on racial mixture or Afro-Brazilian creation.

At the same time, these scholars have not been successful at documenting a tenable hypothesis of how the *jogo de capoeira* came into being in Brazil without an African precedent. Some such as Penna Marinho, moved by their political motivations to use *capoeira* as a tool to promote the myth of lusotropicalism, suggested that *capoeira* emerged out of the racial mixing of Africans, Europeans, and Indigenous Americans. This position is incompatible with available data from the first half of the nineteenth century. Prison records in Rio for the early nineteenth century reveal that *capoeiragem* was predominantly linked to enslaved Africans. European participation picked up only in the second half of the century, and I have not yet seen any documentation of Indigenous American participation. While this lusotropical origin myth is still recycled, most writers have held one of three variations of an African-Brazilian origin thesis, with *capoeira* being created in situ out of the combative needs of bondsmen.

The first suggests that bondsmen created the *jogo de capoeira* in Brazil by merging some African dance styles into a makeshift fighting art. The immediate problem with this argument is that it is predicated on and promotes the erroneous stereotype of a tabula rasa state among enslaved Africans. This deficit model assumes that Africans had no martial arts to draw on for them to have to combine dance movements to defend themselves. As this is clearly not the case, this theory begs the question: If enslaved peoples were to create a hybrid fighting system under the oppression of bondage, why did they not take only the most deadly techniques of the lethal form of West African grappling found throughout most of Western Africa or *dambe*'s powerful punches that could be learned much faster than inverted kicks? While

Assunção acknowledges the existence of African martial arts, his argument falls into this general category as he ultimately suggests that *capoeira* was a result of the mixture of some martial dances. He concludes that the problem with my work "is that there are so many possible ancestors for *capoeira,*" but the only other possibilities he mentions are two dances: the Lunda *cufuiha,* a knife-wielding war dance with no kicks or head butts; and the *ómudinhu,* a Kunene dance that has no combative techniques. Another dance-related myth is that the dance elements of the art were added in Brazil to camouflage the martial art, with Africans disguising it as a dance so that the masters would not understand what they were actually practicing. The historical record, however, is clear that police, journalists, and even European visitors had no difficulty distinguishing the *jogo de capoeira* from seemingly innocuous dances. Further, the practice of the *jogo de capoeira,* "even with the purpose of entertainment," was expressly forbidden by the decree of July 27, 1831. As we shall see, the police could pick out *capoeiras* by their dress, and even the possession of the musical instruments used in the *jogo de capoeira* would lead to arrest.

The final two African Brazilian origin paradigms suggest that the *jogo de capoeia* was first conceptualized in *quilombos* or urban bondage. Annibal Burlamaqui, an early twentieth-century practitioner-writer, claimed that *jogo de capoeia* was born in the *quilombos* of Palmares, out of the need of Africans to defend themselves. The fighting art may well have been used there as a form of training, but *quilombolas* fought with weapons, and there is no evidence to show that the *jogo de capoeira* was used in Palmares, let alone created there. In addition, unaware of the Angolan pugilistic tradition, another popular explanation for *jogo de capoeira*'s arsenal of kicks from an inverted position is that enslaved Africans created the art in Brazil as a way to defend themselves when their hands were chained together. This is not historically plausible for two reasons. First, most bondsmen were often chained by the legs or neck rather than the hands since a bondsman chained by the legs could still work and not run away. Kidder and Fletcher note that in Rio the most common forms of physical bondage were logs chained to the legs, neck collars, or iron masks. The only illustration of a *capoeira* in chains clearly shows a chain on his leg. Second, bondsmen were chained only under limited conditions, making it extremely unlikely that they would develop a martial art around being chained.

In contrast to these inventive mythological origins, there is a long-standing tradition of evidence linking the *jogo de capoeira* to Angola. While the enslaved Africans who dominated this art in Brazil obviously did not have opportunities to publish their understanding of the art's origins, they clearly memorialized their art's Angolan legacy in the ritual practice of the art. This is most clear in the Bahian tradition of the art, which came to dominate its practice throughout Brazil in the twentieth century. In Bahia, West Africans dominated demographically, particularly those known as Nagô (Yoruba), Jeje (Aja- Fon-Ewe), and Hausas. According to João José Reis, in 1835 the majority of Bahian bondsmen were African born, and "Nagô represented two-thirds of the African community in the 1850s, which meant that old ethnic divisions slowly declined to be replaced by a kind of Nagô cultural hegemony." Given this context, it is certainly meaningful that the names of the major rhythms of the art all relate to Angola (Angola, Benguela, and Sao Bento—the patron saint of Angola), and African references in the songs of the art overwhelmingly refer to Angola. As Kubik has shown, both the nineteenth-century drum and the later musical bow with its style of play were clearly of Angolan provenance. Plácido de Abreu, when making his argument, had to acknowledge a widespread understanding in the nineteenth century that the art was African. His contemporary Pires de Almeida states that the art was brought from Angola to Rio ("from the lands of Congo"). João do Rio (Paulo Barreto) similarly records that it was brought from Angola. In Bahia, Manuel Raymundo Querino, an African Brazilian born in the mid-nineteenth century, also attributes it to Angolans.

In light of the current study, scholars can no longer claim the argument that there was no kicking art akin to the *jogo de capoeira* in Africa as a basis for their denial of the *emic* understanding of Angolan provenance within the art. I encourage scholars who still wish to contend that the *jogo de capoeira* was born in Brazil without an African martial art precedent to do so by producing a rational and substantiated argument of how and why the *jogo de capoeira* emerged ex nihilo or out of numerous dances in Brazil. Regardless of whatever weaknesses may exist in my scholarship, the fundamental, undebatable fact is that these kicking techniques did exist together in one art in southern Angola. The same region funneled more captive Africans to Rio de Janeiro than any other region of Africa, such that none can doubt that Kunene and Cimbebasian captives sold through Benguela were most often destined for Rio, the epicenter of the *jogo de capoeira* by available records. No martial art in the world shares a more common technical base of kicking with the *jogo de capoeira* than *engolo* (leaving aside knocking and kicking and other related arts). Thus, while it is within the realm of remote possibility that this similarity in kicking methods is a mere coincidence, at present the clearest and most parsimonious explanation for this otherwise amazing similarity is that this singular kicking art that developed in southern Angola was brought to Brazil, where it was adapted by enslaved Africans into a uniquely African Brazilian expression of this ancestral tradition. I deal with this material in much more depth in three as yet unpublished papers: "Angola and the 'Luta Brasileira': A Question of Origins," presented at the York University / UNESCO Conference "Enslaving Connections: Africa and Brazil during the Era of the Slave Trade," October 2000; "Historical Linguistics and African Divination in Historical Reconstruction," presented to the African Studies Association, Washington, D.C., December 2002; and "Divining History: The Development of Combative Culture in Southern Angola," presented to the African Studies Association, New Orleans, La., November 2004. Citations to material in this note include Plácido de Abreu, cited in Soares, *A capoeira escrava,* 40; Mária Público de Sousa Veiga Jardim, *Capoeira* (São Paulo, 1976), 1; Matthias Röhrig Assunção, *Capoeira: A History of an Afro-Brazilian Martial Art* (New York: Routledge, 2005); Anne Dimock, "*Capoeira Angola,*" in *Black People and Their Culture: Selected Writings from the African Diaspora,* ed. Lynn Shapiro (Washington, D.C.: Festival of American Folklife, 1976), 123; Ruth Landes, "Fetish Worship in Brazil," *Journal of American Folklore* 53 (October–December 1940): 262; Daniel P. Kidder, James C. Fletcher, et al., *Brazil and the Brazilians Portrayed in Historical and Descriptive Sketches* (Philadelphia: Childs & Peterson, 1857); I. A. Rosen, "*Capoeira* Deceit and Trickery: The Development and Incorporation of a Habitus in a Brazilian Martial Art" (M.A. thesis, University of Amsterdam, 1994); João José Reis, "Batuque: African Drumming and Dance between Repression and Concession, Bahia, 1808–1855," *Bulletin of Latin American Research* 24 (2005): 207; Pires and José Ricardo de Almeida, *Brazil-Album* (Rio de Janeiro: Typographia leuzinger, 1908); João do Rio, *A Alma Encantadora das Ruas* (Rio de Janeiro: H. Garnier, 1910); and Manuel Raymundo Querino, *Bahia de Outrora: Vultos e factos populares* (Bahia: Livraria Economica, 1916).

14. *Macombo,* an Mbundu word for "hideout," was the common term for maroon communities prior to the rise of the *quilombo* of Palmares in the 1600s. Schwartz (*Slaves, Peasants, and Rebels,* 122–28) links Palmares to the Angolan *kilombos.*

15. Karasch notes that *quilombolas* were often the chiefs of *capoeira* societies. Maciel de Aguilar claims to have interviewed in 1978 a 104-year-old *capoeiragem* master, who was raised in a *quilombo* and learned *capoeiragem* from Africans (and noted specifically that it was "Cabindans" and "Benguellas" who taught other Africans). In Maranhão the combat art of *punga* is primarily practiced by *quilombolas. Punga* is a variant on the art of sweeps and knock-downs called *pernada* in Rio and described as being dominated by Angolans by Carneiro. See Karasch, *Slave Life in Rio de Janeiro,* 299; Maciel de Aguilar, *Teodorinho Trinca-Ferro* (Centro Cultural Porto de São Matteus: Editora Brasil-Cultura, 1995); and Edison Carneiro, *Negros Bantus: Notas de ethnographia religiosa e de folk-lore* (Rio de Janeiro: Civilização brasileira, 1937).

16. Arquivo Nacional, Rio de Janeiro (hereafter ANRJ), codex 327, vol. 1, April 17, 1824.

17. Reis, "Batuque," 201–214; Nina Rodrigues, *Os Africanos no Brasil* (Brasília: Editora Universidade de Brasília, 2004 [1932]), 253; Stuart B. Schwartz, *Sugar Plantations in the Formation of Brazilian Society: Bahia 1550–1835* (Cambridge: Cambridge University Press, 1985), 483–84.

18. Karash, *Slave Life,* 242. Again these new nations were not fixed equivalents of African continental nationalities. Igbos in Rio, for example, may have come together with other Biafrans under the nation of "Carabari," named after their port(s) of emigration, often Old or New Calabar. Many Kunene speakers might have chosen to identify with other peoples from southern Angola in the Benguela nation in Rio. However, individuals of either group may have felt compelled by prestige or religious calling to identify with other nations in Rio, and many Africans would have held multiple loyalties to various nations in Rio as well as communities in Africa. See chap. 3, endnote 85.

19. The latter was called *semba/samba* among some Kikongo and Kimbundu speakers and was utilized in dances of bondsmen around the Atlantic world. See Kubik, "Drum Patterns," 115–81; and Fryer, *Rhythms of Resistance,* 109–33.

20. While they may not have had these elements combined with inverted kicking in a single ritual art form, it is likely that Kongolese and other northern Angolan peoples in Brazil would have found many of the elements of the *jogo de capoeira* familiar, particularly the use of sweeps and defensive postures in combat. Thus, Cimbebasia was not necessarily the only source for some individual techniques, but this does not make the *jogo de capoeira* a technical hybrid as all these techniques were also already found in *engolo.* Northern Angolans' adoption of the entire system of *jogo de capoeira* may have been one of many primary divisions that were broken down between various Central African groups that would have seen themselves as separate groups in Africa but eventually came together to form what Robert Slenes describes as a "pan-Bantu" ethnicity in Brazil. It went on, however, to be adopted by other people of African descent as well. On the martial techniques of Kongo peoples, see Thompson, "Gestuelle des arts Martiaux," 128–29; and Slenes, *Malungu, Ngoma vem!*

21. Ribeyrolles, *Brasil pitoresco,* 37–38.

22. Elysio de Araujo, *Estudo histórico sobre a polícia da capital federal, 1808–1831* (Rio de Janeiro: Imprensa Nacional, 1898), 57.

23. The document uses the term *mulatto,* but I will be using the term *pardo* through the rest of this chapter to refer to people with both African and other ancestries.

24. ANRJ, Tribunal de Relação, codex 24, book 10, July 25, 1789.

25. The *jogo de capoeira* was never formally criminalized in law until the penal code of October 11, 1891. However, it was considered an act of resistance in all its forms. The decree of July 17, 1831, reinforced what was already common practice by calling for the arrest not only of initiated *capoeiras* but also anyone who practiced the art, "even with the purpose of entertainment." See Decisões, no. 205, July 27, 1831, in *Collecção das Leis do Império do Brazil em 1831* (Rio de Janeiro: Typ. Nacional, 1875), 152–53.

26. This factor limiting the punitive abilities of the city would not be resolved before abolition as the pressure on *senhores* would only increase in the nineteenth century after the 1821 policy requiring *senhores* to pay for their bondsmen's maintenance while in prison. See ANRJ, codex 330 (Ordens e ofícios expedidos aos juízes do crime dos barrios de São José, Santa Rita, Sé e Candelária, 1819–31), vol. 3, May 11, 1821; and Algranti, *O feitor ausente,* 170.

27. For a description of a beating leading to death, see Jacques Arago, *Narrative of a Voyage round the World, in the Uraine and Physicienne Corvettes, Commanded by Captain Freycinet, during the Years 1817, 1818, 1819, and 1820* (London: Treuttel & Wurtz, Treuttal, jun. & Richter, 1823), 67.

28. Cf. Zephyr L. Frank, *Dutra's World: Wealth and Family in Nineteenth-Century Rio de Janeiro* (Albuquerque: University of New Mexico Press, 2004).

29. In 1857 the *ganhadores* of Salvador went on strike to protest increased regulation via licensing. They effectively shut the city's transport for a week. See João José Reis, "'The Revolution of the Ganhadores': Urban Labour, Ethnicity and the African Strike of 1857 in Bahia, Brazil," *Journal of Latin American Studies* 29 (May 1997): 355–93.

30. As Karasch (*Slave Life in Rio de Janeiro,* 55–91) points out in detail, urban bondsmen still encountered numerous physical and social boundaries.

31. There were laws that theoretically required them to carry passes signed by their *senhores,* but these were systematically ignored. See Reis, "Revolution of the Ganhadores," 356.

32. A *confraria* is literally a brotherhood like the religious brotherhoods popular among the bondsmen of Rio. For use of the term *confrarias,* see Karasch, *Slave Life in Rio de Janeiro,* 298–99. *Badernas* may possibly derive from the light rigging used on ships to connote unifying connection. According to Holloway ("Healthy Terror," 643–44n12), the term *malta* "may be related to old Lisbon slang for itinerant laborers and street rowdies, who stereotypically were migrants from the island of Malta, or may denote the members' sticking together like the wax and tar sealing mixture of the same name."

33. June E. Hahner, *Poverty and Politics: The Urban Poor in Brazil, 1870–1920* (Albuquerque: University of New Mexico Press, 1986), 59; R. Walsh, *Notices of Brazil* (London, 1830), 1:330.

34. Soares, *A capoeira escrava,* 81.

35. For more on these brotherhoods, called *confrarias,* see Karasch, *Slave Life in Rio de Janeiro,* 82–86; A. J. R. Russell-Wood, "Black and Mulatto Brotherhoods in Colonial Brazil: A Study in Collective Behavior," *Hispanic American Historical Review* 54 (1974): 567–602; and Elizabeth Kiddy, "Brotherhoods of Our Lady of the Rosary of the Blacks: Community and Devotion in Minas Gerais, Brazil" (Ph.D. diss., University of New Mexico, 1998).

36. Reis, "Revolution of the Ganhadores," 368–69.

37. In addition to Edward Evans-Pritchard's call to replace the term "secret" with "closed," Michael Gomez has more recently argued that these societies should be labeled by their raison d'être and not their clandestine nature. See E. E. Evans-Pritchard, "Mani, Azande Secret Society," *Sudan Notes and Records* 14 (1931): 105–48; E. E. Evans-Pritchard, *Witchcraft, Oracles, and Magic among the Azande* (Oxford: Clarendon Press, 1937), 511; and Gomez, *Exchanging Our Country Marks,* 94–95.

38. The term "gang" is loaded with unspoken connotations that may not be helpful in fully understanding the social world of *maltas,* particularly since drug trafficking transformed the nature of many modern street gangs in the late twentieth century. Although *maltas* often fought in street battles, not all groups that fought rivals would be best understood just as street gangs. For example, nineteenth-century fire brigades in New York also fought over turfs, and "all sought tough men who were willing to battle it out with opposing brigades, sometimes while a building burned to the ground." In Rio free people formed competing social groups called *folias,* which often entered into violent conflicts with rival groups of other neighborhoods. *Capoeira* societies, like fire brigades or *folias,* were socially distinct in many ways from modern street gangs. Scholars who label maltas as gangs become complicit in the criminalization of these cultural practices and tend to obscure rather than elucidate their inner workings. Therefore, we will frame them as closed societies. See Ruth Horowitz, "Sociological Perspectives on Gangs" in *Gangs in America,* ed. C. Ronald Huff (New York: Sage Publications, 1990); Elliott J. Gorn, "The Meaning of Prizefighting," in *The New American Sport History,* ed. S. W. Pope (Urbana: University of Illinois Press, 1997), 231; and Soares, *A capoeira escrava,* 171, 233n10.

39. For a broad definition of "secret" society as a voluntary association that possessed an esoteric knowledge, see Davis, *Passage of Darkness,* 244. Davis, for example, uses five markers to set apart "secret" societies: the existence of an esoteric body of knowledge; rituals that reinforce the solidarity of the collective; recognized sanctions against those who transgress the codes of the societies; periodic public displays that demonstrate the authority and independence of the group; and a dialectic relationship with the institutions of the dominant society. See Davis, *Passage of Darkness,* 241–49; and Lau-Fong Mak, *The Sociology of Secret Societies: A Study of Chinese Secret Societies in Singapore and Peninsular Malaysia* (Kuala Lumpur: Oxford University Press, 1981).

40. *Ekpe* was a male society but perhaps more specifically a society of warriors and former warriors since, at least among the Ohafia, women who had proved themselves as warriors were also allowed to join. See McCall, *Dancing Histories,* 117–36.

41. Among the Efik towns of Old Calabar, for example, *ekpe* was the sociopolitical institution enforcing conformity on the individual towns. See, for example, Northrup, *Trade without Rulers,* 108–10.

42. The relationship between these predatory cats and human authority is widespread in West and Central Africa and generally is associated with the leopard's ability to take human life. Two distinct traditions of leopard metaphors exist: the association of the leopard with kingship; and its association with the power of closed societies that normally operated outside the control of monarchs. See McCall, *Dancing Histories,* 66–68.

43. On the importance of "wearing one's identity" through society hats, see McCall, *Dancing Histories,* 23–25. On literacy in the written and gestural scripts of *nsibidi,* see Ute M. Roschenthaler, "Honoring Ejagham Women," *African Arts* 1 (Spring 1998): 38–50; and Simon P. X. Battestini, "Reading Signs of Identity and Alterity: History, Semiotics, and the Nigerian Case," *African Studies Review* 34 (April 1991): 99–116.

44. Thompson, *Flash of the Spirit,* 27–28.

45. Leopard societies often had special techniques to kill their victims while making it look like an animal attack. See, for example, K. J. Beatty, *Human Leopards* (London, 1915), 147; D. Burrows, "The Human Leopard Society of Sierra Leone," *Journal of the Royal African Society* 13 (January 1914): 143–51; Geoffrey Nwaka, "The 'Leopard' Killings of Southern Annang, Nigeria, 1943–48," *Africa* 56 (1986): 417–40; Jeremy Rich, "'Leopard Men,' Slaves, and Social Conflict In Libreville (Gabon), 1860–1879," *International Journal of African Historical Studies* 34 (2001): 619–39; and Davis, *Passage of Darkness,* 105.

46. On their paramilitary enforcement of laws, see Canon Udobata Onunwa, *Studies in Igbo Traditional Religion* (Uruowulu-Obosi: Pacific Publishers, 1990), 24–26. For examples of the use of leopard and related closed societies striking out against colonialism, see Philip A. Igbafe, "West Ibo Society and Its Resistance to British Rule: The Ekumeku Movement," *Journal of African History* 12 (1971): 441–59; and R. E. Dennett, "The Ogboni and Other Secret Societies in Nigeria," *Journal of the Royal African Society* 16 (October 1916): 16–29.

47. Joseph Miller uses demographics to suggest that the initiation schools for adolescents east of the Kwango, Kasai, and Kunene rivers would be likely prototypes on which the *maltas* were based. In the Kasai closed associations were at times linked to a warrior culture and played paramilitary roles such as execution. Yet, the potential influence of the initiation societies such as *Lemba, Kinkomba,* and *Kimpasi* from the Kongo and Greater Loango regions cannot be overlooked. Margaret Washington outlines a similar framework in North American Gullah culture that she traces to the *Poro* and *Sande* societies of modern-day Sierra Leone, Liberia, and Guinea. For a broad survey of the numerous West and Central African types of closed societies but lacking historical specificity, see Frederick William Butt-Thompson, *West African Secret Societies, Their Organisations, Officials and Teaching* (London: H. F. & G. Witherby, 1929). See also Joseph C. Miller, "Struggling for Identity through Enslavement in Angola and under Slavery in Brazil" (paper presented at "Enslaving Connection: Africa and Brazil during the Era of the Slave Trade," York University, Toronto, Canada, October 5, 2000); Janzen, *Lemb;a* Karl Laman, *The Kongo,* 4 vols. (Uppsala: Studia Ethnographia Upsaliensa, 1953–68) 3:244–56; and Creel, *"Peculiar People."*

48. Variations of the term such as *molecão* and *molecote* were used to describe more mature captives than the youth specifically designated by *moleque.* The term

was later applied derogatorily in Brazil to mean something akin to "street urchin." See Miller, *Way of Death,* 68, 388.

49. Soares, *A Negregada Instituição,* 85.

50. The term was used more widely in Brazil to denote a squirrel or an intrusive individual. The use here may relate to either of these meanings. On the etymology of the term, see Schneider, *Dictionary of African Borrowings,* 115.

51. "*Capoeiras,*" *Diário do Rio de Janeiro,* March 11, 1872.

52. A decree of July 27, 1831, called for the arrest of "black *capoeiras,* as well as those who practice it, even with the purpose of entertainment" (Decisões, no. 205, July 27, 1831, in *Collecção das Leis do Império do Brazil em 1831* [Rio de Janeiro: Typ. Nacional, 1875], 152–53).

53. Plácido de Abreu, *Os capoeiras* (Rio de Janeiro: Tip. da Escola Serafim Alves de Brito, 1886), 2.

54. Melo Moraes Filho (1843–1919), *Festas e tradições populares do Brasil* (São Paulo: Editora da Universidade de São Paulo, 1979), 260.

55. Gabriela Tigges, "The History of *Capoeira* in Brazil" (Ph.D. diss., Brigham Young University, 1990), 39.

56. For a description of the *cantos* and the inauguration of their leaders, see Reis, "Revolution of the Ganhadores," 368–69.

57. Filho, *Festas,* 258.

58. "There is a singular secret society among the Negroes in which the highest rank is assigned to the man who has taken the most lives" (in Kidder et al., *Brazil,* 137).

59. Soares, *A Negregada Instituição,* 117–18.

60. Abreu, *Os capoeiras,* 6.

61. Filho, *Festas,* 258.

62. According to DeCramer, Vansina, and Fox, the Central African religious complex was centered around providing *ngolo,* or force, for a community. This force could be divided into three component constellations: fecundity, status, and protection ("invulnerability and impunity"). While there is not enough data to describe the religious knowledge of nineteenth-century *capoeiras,* it is clear that early twentieth-century *capoeiras* were masters of specific esoteric knowledge surrounding invulnerability and impunity. This was enacted through a series of ritual prayers, medicines, and taboos designed to *fechar o corpo,* or close the body from attack by blows, blades, or even bullets. One of the most prominent of twentieth-century practices of *capoeiras* followed the Central African tradition of inserting sacred medicines under one's skin to close off the body from harm. It is most likely that nineteenth-century *capoeiras* dominated a similar constellation of knowledge. See Willy DeCramer, Jan Vansina, and Renee Fox, "Religious Movements in Central Africa: A Theoretical Study," *Comparative Studies in Society and History* 18 (1976): 458–75. For a discussion of *corpo fechado* among early twentieth-century fighters, see the DVD *Besouro Preto (Black Beetle),* directed by Salim Rollins (New York: Griot Films, 2003).

63. ANRJ, codex 403, vol. 1, September 26, 1811.

64. This ritual understanding of these hats acknowledges that they would have also doubled as physical weapons. The fact that the pins were pointing out rather than inward suggests their dual function as weapons that increased the potency of head butts. For a ritual reading of these hats, see Soares, *A capoeira escrava,* 81.

65. Maya Talmon Chvaicer, "The Criminalization of *Capoeira* in Nineteenth Century Brazil," *Hispanic American Historical Review* 82 (August 2002): 538.

66. Arquivo Nacional da Torre do Tombe, Lisbon (hereafter ANTT), Inquisição de Lisboa, Cadernos, Processos, 3641. I am indebted to James Sweet for alerting me to the existence of Inquisition cases in Brazil, where this physical inversion remained linked to African religious practices (James Sweet, personal communication, October 31, 2000). For a fuller analysis of these practices and their association with the ritual specialists of both Central Africa and Brazil, see James H. Sweet, "Recreating Africa: Race, Religion, and Sexuality in the African-Portuguese World, 1441–1770" (Ph.D. diss., City University of New York, 1999), 119–37.

67. Ritual specialists in Brazil could often attain freedom through their practices. See ANTT, Inquisição de Lisboa, Cadernos do Promotor, no. 85, livro 278, 132–49, cited in Sweet, *Recreating Africa,* 142.

68. The terms "house" and "province" are mentioned in the late nineteenth century by Abreu, *Os capoeiras,* 7.

69. *Relatório do Chefe de Policía da Corte, 1878,* cited in Holloway, "Healthy Terror," 669.

70. For elements of African power systems in insignia, see Soares, *A Negregada Instituição,* 29; and Tigges, "History of *Capoeira,*" 27.

71. Apparently some bondsmen applied themselves solely as bell ringers. See ANRJ, codex 323 (Registro da correspondência da Polícia, 1809–42), vol. 15, January 15, 1841, cited in Soares, *A capoeira escrava,* 240n77, 298.

72. Filho, *O Rio de Janeiro,* 52; Tigges, "History of *Capoeira,*" 17–18.

73. Holloway, "Healthy Terror," 668. At times these church towers may have afforded *capoeiras* some protection since Henderson notes that criminals who fled to churches were "privileged from capture till an order was obtained from the bishop for his arrest" (Henderson, *History of the Brazil,* 80).

74. Holloway, "Healthy Terror," 644; Karasch, *Slave Life in Rio de Janeiro,* 299.

75. Abreu, *Os capoeiras,* 5.

76. Coincidentally the colors red and white, along with yellow, were also prominent in Biafran *ekpe* and had powerful connotations for Central Africans. Red was the color of the leopard, and only those Biafrans who had killed in battle were allowed to wear the color red in their hats, as the hat/ribbon was said to be dyed with the blood of human victims. Leopard hats were red, white, and black, while yellow also marked some lodges of *ekpe* (see n. 82 below). Of course, these colors had ritual significance for other Africans as well. For example, note the Central African implications of these colors in Anita Jacobson-Widding, *Red-White-Black as a Mode of Thought: A Study of Triadic Classification by Colours in the Ritual Symbolism and Cognitive Thought of the Peoples of the Lower Congo* (Stockholm: Uppsala, 1979).

77. ANRJ, cód 403 (Relação de presos feitos pela Polícia, 1810–21, 3 vols.), vol.1, May 17, 1815, f.248.

78. "*Andar por capoeiras*" (ANRJ, cód 403, vol. 2, December 29, 1819; November 22, 1819).

79. At the beginning of the nineteenth century these colors marked the African nations of the given societies. However, in the second half of the century the societies gradually lost the association with specific African ethnicities, although the two

major umbrella organizations of Nagoas and Guaiamos may have been most associated with Africans and *pardos* respectively. See Filho, *Festas,* 258.

80. ANRJ, cód 403, vol.1, May 15, 1818.

81. ANRJ, cód 403, vol.1, December 13, 1814; November 21, 1815.

82. It is interesting to note a similar practice among leopard societies. For example, "A piece of yellow cotton nailed on any one's door implied the protection of" *ekpe* in the town of Brass. See H. P. Fitzgerald Mariott, "The Secret Societies of West Africa," *Journal of the Anthropological Institute of Great Britain and Ireland* 29, no. 1 (1899): 22; and ANRJ, codex 403, vol. 2, May 14, 1818.

83. Soares, *A capoeira escrava,* 80.

84. ANRJ, codex 403, vol. 2, May 14, 1819.

85. ANRJ, codex 403, vol. 2, November 12, 1819.

86. Burrows, "Human Leopard Society," 147.

87. Émile Allain, *Rio-de-Janeiro: Quelques données sur la capitale et sur l'administration du Brésil* (Paris: L. Frinzine, 1886), 272.

88. "Aprendis *capoeira,*" *Diário do Rio de Janeiro,* January 17, 1872.

89. Soares, *A capoeira escrava,* 197.

90. Filho, *Festas,* 259.

91. Jules Itier, *Journal d'un voyage en Chine en 1843, 1844, 1845, 1846,* 3 vols. (Paris: Dauvin et Fontaine, 1843–53), 1:49–50.

92. Filho, *Festas,* 259.

93. *Bizango* members also meted out vengeance for misconduct through "cuts" with physical blades or spiritual weapons. In case of *bizango,* such retribution was only a last resort after perpetrators had been warned of their infraction but refused to make a move toward restitution. See Davis, *Passage of Darkness,* 241–84.

94. Douglas H. Johnson, "Criminal Secrecy: The Case of the Zande 'Secret Societies,'" *Past and Present* 130 (February 1991): 170–71.

95. Georg Simmel, *The Sociology of Georg Simmel,* trans. Kurt Wolff (Glencoe, Ill.: Free Press, 1950), 472.

96. Clearly some closed societies were contrary to the state only at certain times of their existence—such as the Freemasons or the Ku Klux Klan, which was at one time outlawed—but at other times were in rough harmony with local and state governments. See Johnson, "Criminal Secrecy," 170–200. Also, in some African examples there were no centralized states for closed societies to react against.

97. For a thorough historical treatment of the police forces of Rio, see Thomas H. Holloway, *Policing Rio de Janeiro: Repression and Resistance in a 19th-Century City* (Stanford, Calif.: Stanford University Press, 1993).

98. Karasch, *Slave Life in Rio de Janeiro,* 123.

99. Gilberto Freyre, *The Mansions and the Shanties: The Making of Modern Brazil* (New York, Knopf, 1963). Certainly the continued fear inspired by the Haitian Revolution may also have played a role in this suppression.

100. Adèle Toussaint-Samson, *A Parisian in Brazil* (Boston: James Earle, 1891), 97.

101. Soares, *A capoeira escrava,* 85.

102. Thomas Holloway recounts an example of an envoy sent by the police *subdelegado* of Engenho Vellho to investigate a *batuque*. The *batuque* participants turned en masse on the police with an assortment of weapons, freeing their arrested companions

and forcing the small patrol to flee with injuries. See Holloway, *Policing Rio de Janeiro,* 220–21.

103. Barreto Filho and Lima cited in Rego, *Capoeira Angola,* 295.

104. Letter of Dom Pedro I to Carlos Frederico Bernardo de Caula, Febuary 6, 1822, reprinted in Almeida Prado, *Tomas Ender: Pintor austriáco na côrte de D. João V.I. no Rio de Janeiro, um episódio da formação da classe dirigente brasileira 1817/1818* (São Paulo: Companhia Editôra Nacional, 1955), 300–301.

105. "An expedient was resorted to . . . that was a licence to the Moleques, or blacks, and the rest of the rabble to take up arms . . . such slaves in a high state of excitement, armed with knives and daggers, let loose on a city. . . . A regular warfare soon ensued between them [German rebelling troops] and the armed Moleques" (Walsh, *Notices,* 1:287–94).

106. Edmundo Teodoro Bösche, "Quadros alternados de viagems," *Revista do Instituto Histórico e Geográphico Brasileiro* 83 (1918): 193–94.

107. As Jules Itier opines, these closed societies established a network and organization for an uprising. "The only thing these bondsmen are missing is a Spartacus, and a war with England would surely produce one" (Itier, *Journal,* 1:62).

108. While on the whole the police system was repressive of the enslaved and supported by the property owners, these relationships could also be ambiguous. It was not unheard of for bondsmen to flee to the police, to complain of exceedingly cruel treatment by their enslavers, or for police to be forced to intervene on behalf of bondsmen against cruel enslavers. See Karasch, *Slave Life in Rio de Janeiro,* 124.

109. Karasch, *Slave Life in Rio de Janeiro,* 122, 124. It is interesting to note that both of these were "crimes" in that they offered an alternative lifestyle and society.

110. This complaint was specifically against the policies of the new criminal codes passed in 1830 and 1832 (quoted in Holloway, "Healthy Terror," 651).

111. Cited in Robert Edgar Conrad, *Children of God's Fire: A Documentary History of Black Slavery in Brazil* (Princeton, N.J.: Princeton University Press, 1983) 110. See also Luiz dos Santos Vilhena, *Reopilação de notícias soteroplitanas e brasílicas: 1802* (Salvador, Bahia, 1821), 1:185; and Algranti, *O feitor ausente,* 165.

112. Patricia Aufderheide, "Order and Violence: Social Deviance and Social Control in Brazil 1780–1840" (Ph.D. diss., University of Minnesota, 1976), 96.

113. Henderson, *History of the Brazil,* 74.

114. Reis ("Revolution of the Ganhadores," 362) notes that *ganhadores* "often earned money from several clandestine sources, such as drumming, *capoeira,* and divination."

115. Karasch notes the case of Col. Felipe Neri de Carvalho, who was killed by his bondsman Camilo. Camilo confessed to the murder because his enslaver was a "bad man"; yet, "it was public opinion that Camilo had been hired to kill him by a very important person he refused to name." See Karasch, *Slave Life in Rio de Janeiro,* 329.

116. ANRJ, codex 402, January 4, 1817. While this may have been an individual case of a free *capoeira* chief "having seduced" (*ter seduzido*) this bondsmen for personal gain, it also raises the possibility that *maltas,* like many African closed societies, charged fees for initiation into higher grades of the society.

117. Fernando Bastos Ribeiro, *Cronicas da policia e da vida do Rio de Janeiro* (Rio de Janeiro: Departamento de Imprensa Nacional, 1958), 41.

118. Allain, *Rio-de-Janeiro,* 142–43, 271–72.

119. Holloway, "Healthy Terror," 654–61; Soares, *A Negregada Instituição,* 156.
120. Soares, *A Negregada Instituição,* 77.
121. *Correio Mercantil,* December 14, 1855, 1.
122. ANRJ, IJ6-484, OCP-C, January 19, 1859, cited in Holloway, "Healthy Terror," 665.
123. Most rank-and-file soldiers were of African descent, and some six thousand bondsmen were freed through participation in the war (on enlistment they were given a provisional manumission that stipulated that they serve on the front). See Peter M. Beattie, "Measures of Manhood: Honor, Enlisted Army Service, and Slavery's Decline in Brazil, 1850–1890," in *Changing Men and Masculinities in Latin America,* ed. Matthew C. Gutmann (Durham, N.C.: Duke University Press, 2003), 233–55.
124. Soares, *A Negregada Instituição,* 32.
125. Ibid., 107.
126. Holloway, "Healthy Terror," 658.
127. Angenor Lopes de Oliveira, *Os capoeiras,* cited in Soares, *A Negregada Instituição,* 189. Also see Querino, *Costumes,* 275–77. Kraay notes the use of *capoeira* skills by the commander of an all-black Zoavo company from Bahia in a hand-to-hand struggle over the enemy's flag in the battle of Curuzú; see Hendrik Kraay, "Patriotic Mobilization in Brazil: The Zuavos and Other Black Companies," in Hendrik Kraay and Thomas Whigham, *I Die with My Country: Perspectives on the Paraguayan War, 1864–1870* (Lincoln: University of Nebraska Press, 2004), 72–73, 77–78.
128. Soares, *A Negregada Instituição,* 193, 117.
129. The Nagoas included the *capoeiras* of the parish areas of Gloria, Lapa, Santana, Santa Luzia, São José, Moura, Boltinha da Prata, and many other small *capoeira* societies. Guaiamos were the combined *capoeira* societies of São Francisco, Candelaria, Santa Rita, Sacramento, Ouro Preto, São Domingos de Gusmão, and numerous smaller affiliates.
130. This is not unlike the black soldiers who fought in the North American Civil War or soldiers from African colonies who fought in the world wars and returned with widened visions of themselves and their role in society. See Nelson Werneck Sodré, *A história military do Brasil* (Rio de Janeiro: Civilização Brasileira, 1979), 143. Kraay ("Patriotic Mobilization," 79–80) notes, however, that the nation offered these soldiers scant opportunities for active participation in the nation.
131. Tigges, "History of *Capoeira,*" 34.
132. Filho, *Festas,* 258.
133. Hahner, *Poverty,* 59.
134. Ibid.; Sam Adamo, "The Broken Promise: Race, Health, and Justice in Rio de Janeiro, 1890–1940" (Ph.D. diss., University of New Mexico, 1983), 249.
135. Ibid., 220.
136. James Wetherell, *Brazil: Stray Notes from Bahia* (Liverpool: Webb and Hunt, 1860), 119.
137. Filho, *Festas,* 259.
138. Abreu, *Os capoeiras,* 7–8. Other writers have reversed the names of these two kicks.
139. Although the term *ginga* likely derives primarily from the languages of northern Angola, it is interesting to note that in many Cimbebasian languages *njenga* meant "to joke or play," and *ndjinga* repeated meant "to remain in motion shaking,

undulating, or rocking." Another term in Brazil for swaying back and forth or a lazy walk was *calungagem*, derived from the motions of the *kalunga*. For a detailed treatment of *ginga* in Angolan and Brazilian culture, see Julio Cesar de Souza Tavares, "Gingando and Cooling Out: The Embodied Philosophies of the African Diaspora" (Ph.D. diss., University of Texas at Austin, 1998); and Schneider, *Dictionary of African Borrowings*, 84.

140. Rugendas, *Viagem*, 155.

141. On *jogo de cabeçadas*, see ANRJ, codex 403, vol. 2, August 25, 1819. Rugendas's first visit to Rio began in 1821, just two years later. Rugendas's famous picture *Jogar Capoëra: Ou Danse de la Guerre* is not helpful on this issue as it depicts the two adepts neither head butting as described in his written description nor kicking. The bent legs of one of the players may reflect them being in a *ginga* sway between attacks, but the postures also seem reminiscent of the genre of engravings of British boxers of his era, particularly John Young's "Molineaux" and Richard Dighton's "A Striking View of Richmond." Rugendas's works went beyond mere "documentary accuracy." He was influenced by the English traveler Henry Koster and had his own artistic and intellectual agenda of defending the moral character of Africans. He intentionally associated Africans with biblical and classical heroines in other illustrations. Thus, it is possible that he was making an allusion to the popular portraits and caricatures of classical prizefighters in England, at their height just before Rugendas's voyage. If one were inspired to point to heights to which blacks could rise, there is clearly no more striking example than that of Tom Molineaux, who had fought for the world boxing championship twice and was arguably the most famous black in all of Christendom. For a general discussion of Rugendas's social agenda, use of allusion, and the influence of Koster, see Robert Slenes, "African Abrahams, Lucretias and Men of Sorrows: Allegory and Allusion in the Brazilian Anti-Slavery Lithographs (1827–1835) of Johann Moritz Rugendas," *Slavery and Abolition* 23 (2002): 147–68.

142. This would have been akin to the way the term "football" was used in nineteenth-century North America for both the ball-kicking sport akin to soccer in some colleges and a rugby-style game that carried the ball in the hands in other colleges. See Elliott J. Gorn and Warren Jay Goldstein, *A Brief History of American Sports* (Urbana: University of Illinois Press, 2004), 129–31.

143. ANRJ, codex 324 (Registro de ofícios expedidos pela Polícia à Secretaria de Estado dos Negócios da Justiça, 1827–41), vol. 1, p. 19, December 22, 1829.

144. ANRJ, codex 403, vol. 1, December 21, 1815.

145. A.P.D.G., *Sketches of Portuguese Life, Manners, Costume, and Character* (London: G. B. Whittaker, 1826), 304.

146. As in the case of North America, widespread use of head butts may have also reflected a wider Kongo-Njila legacy since head butting was practiced in many areas of West Central Africa. Note the parallel categorization of head butts in the northern region of Angola in the work of Thompson. Head butts were occasionally used among some West African groups, but in none of the West African combat systems I have documented thus far were these techniques as systematic or socially integrated as those of Central Africa. Of course, much more work is still needed in studying African combatives, and future research may well find some West African systems of head butting. See Robert Farris Thompson, "Foreword," in Lewis, *Ring of Liberation*, xiii.

147. Primary among these were the *lamparina,* a slap that could have come from *kandeka.* A few closed-fist blows used in *capoeiragem* may have come from combatants influenced directly or indirectly by African traditions such as slap-boxing *kandeka, dambe,* or by British boxing.

148. "This blow is unique and terrible because if the enemy is armed with a punhal or knife, he unfailingly kills himself" (*Este golpe é original e terrivel, porque se o inimigo estiver armado de punhal ou faca suicida-se infallivelmente*) (Annabal Burlamaqui, *Gymnastica nacional (capoeiragem): Methodisada e regrada* [Rio de Janeiro, 1928], 41–42).

149. Holloway, *Policing Rio de Janeiro,* 35.

150. Araujo, *Estudo histórico,* 55.

151. Freyre, *Mansions,* 326.

152. Algranti, *O feitor ausente,* 199.

153. Araujo, *Estudo histórico,* 58. Although this paragraph outlines academic writing on the subject, it is important to note that these and other calculations throughout this chapter that are based on police records cannot be taken as conclusive. The problem with arrest records is that the data may reflect the level and effectiveness of police efforts to arrest bondsmen with weapons rather than a true increase in the use of weapons.

154. Of the five combat arts Kunene men in Angola were trained in (archery, stone throwing, stick fighting, hand-to-hand combat, and head-butt dueling), only archery was not practiced in urban Brazil, and for obvious reasons. I am not suggesting, however, that the use of these weapons in Brazil was a direct continuation of Kunene traditions. There were many areas of West and Central Africa with martial traditions of stick use and perhaps also of rock use that may have influenced *capoeiras* in Rio.

155. "It is important to also mention a type of military dance: two groups armed with sticks line up in front of each other and the talent consist in avoiding the powerful blows of the adversary" (*É preciso mencionar, também, uma espécie de dança militar: dois groupos armadas de paus colocam-se um en frente do outro e o talento consiste em evitar os golpes de ponta do adversário*) (Rugendas, *Viagem,* 155).

156. ANRJ, codex 403, vol.1, January 21, 1814.

157. ANRJ, codex 403, vol. 1, April 18, 1816, f. 300

158. ANRJ, codex 403, vol. 2, November 12, 1818.

159. Razor use may have been influenced by Iberian traditions of razor/dagger dueling or even the Fon use of the feared *ananun wa hwisu* razor, the "cutting-badly blade." More detailed descriptions of razor use would be necessary to move past merely listing possibilities. Below we will look at a knife-fighting practice from an extremely northern area of Angola. Certainly some *ladinos,* or bondsmen who spent time in Portugal, may have learned the details of Portuguese blade work in earlier centuries. In seventeenth-century Barbados, Richard Ligon noted that some bondsmen

> who have been bred up amongst the Portugalls, have some extraordinary qualities, which the others have not; as singing and fencing. I have seen some of these *Portugal Negres,* at Collonell *James Draxes,* play at Rapier and Dagger very skillfully, with their Stookados, their Imbrocados, and their Passes: And at single Rapier too, after the manner of *Charanza,* with such comelinesse; as, if the skill had been wanting, the motions would have pleased you; but they were skillful

> too, which I perceived by their binding with their points, and nimble and subtle avoidings with their bodies, and the advantages the strongest man had in the close, which the other avoided by the nimbleness and skillfulness of his motion. For, in this Science, I had bin so well versed in my youth, as I was now able to be a competent Judge. Upon their first appearance upon the Stage, they march towards one another, with a slow majestic pace, and a bold commanding look, as if they meant both to conquer; and coming neer together, they shake hands, and embrace one another, with a cheerful look. But their retreat is much quicker than their advance, and being at first distance, change their countenance, and put themselves into their posture; and so after a passe or two, retire, and then to 't again: And when they have done their play, they embrace, shake hands, and putting on their smoother countenances, give their respects to their Master, and so go off. (Ligon, *True & exact history,* 52)

160. "In cases of quarrels amongst themselves they frequently use them, and quickly fold the capote [cape] around the left arm, which serves as a sort of shield" (Henderson, *History of the Brazil,* 77).

161. Holloway, "Healthy Terror," 647n17.

162. Walsh, *Notices,* 1:331.

163. ANRJ, Ij6-163, September 4, 1824. Because bondsmen were responsible for these activities, he suggested that the knives be replaced by handsaws.

164. Thomas Cabinda was arrested, "For *Capoeira* with others who escaped, having in his hand a knife, which he threw away in the process of being arrested" (ANRJ, codex 403, vol. 2, December 23, 1819).

165. Soares, *A capoeira escrava,* 94.

166. Soares, *A Negregada Instituição,* 180. Numerous political cartoons in the second half of the nineteenth century utilized the razor as a symbol for *capoeiragem.* This use of the symbol may have been influenced by the elite perception in Portugal of the *fadistas* as street ruffians who fought with razors. The *fadistas,* as we shall see in the next chapter, represented a dangerous subculture that was looked down on by many elites, who represented them with the caricatures of the female *fadista* as prostitute and the male *fadista* as razor-wielding disorderly. This imagery of the male *fadista,* certainly well-known to literate elites in Brazil, may have influenced their image of *capoeiragem.*

167. It would be hasty to conclude, as Matthias Assunção does, that because the use of *navalhas* increased in the second half of the century when new Portuguese immigrants also entered *capoeira maltas,* "one can safely assume that [*capoeiras*'] specific skills in its handling" came from these immigrants. Certainly in terms of a direct influence of specifically *fadista navalha* techniques on *capoeiragem,* there is little evidence beyond this general overlap of increase in immigrant Portuguese representations in *maltas* and increased association of the art with the razor in the second half of the century. A closer look at the data casts doubt over Assunção's assumption. First, both Araújo and Algranti document that the most dramatic increase in the use of *navalhas* by Rio's bondsmen clearly came between the years 1812 and 1814, when razor use increased from fewer than five cases in 1812 to around forty in 1814, where it seemed to plateau for some time. The increase in *navalha* use in the second half of the century appears much less pronounced. Second, the epicenter of Portuguese *fadista* street-fighting culture was Lisbon. Yet, few of the immigrants who entered

into Rio's *maltas* were from Lisbon. Soares's data shows that in the years 1861–68, when Portuguese first entered *capoeiragem* in significant numbers, only 17 percent of the Portuguese with identifiable origin were from Lisbon. However, this was based on a sample size of six Portuguese with identifiable origins (i.e., only one could be identified as coming from Lisbon). From 1870 to 1879 Lisbon was not represented among a larger sample size of sixteen, and between 1881 and 1888 only 2 percent of a sample of thirty-six Portuguese in Rio's *maltas* hailed from Lisbon. Thus, available data on Portuguese *capoeiras* clearly reinforce the data on immigration in general, which show that the vast majority of immigrants came from northern Portugal and the Portuguese Atlantic islands. These were areas where the stick-fighting art of *jogo de pau,* not razor fighting, predominated. Assunção's assumption begs the question of why Rio's *capoeiras,* who had utilized their own *navalha* techniques since the beginning of the century, would suddenly discard these half a century later in favor of those of Portuguese immigrants, particularly immigrants who were much better fighting with staves than razors. Certainly *capoeiras* may have incorporated some aspects of a longer-standing Iberian tradition of knife and razor fighting, although there are no clear data to support this. Caution must be exercised in hypotheses regarding stylistic borrowings, particularly given that, in contrast to the upright Iberian tradition being marked by a cloak-and-dagger style, *capoeiras* at least by the late nineteenth century were using it from their own unique body positions. They likely would have been aware of these Iberian skills and possibly incorporated some technical aspects or perhaps adopted defenses to them as they were publicly exhibited on the streets of Rio in blade duels. But bondsmen were exposed to Iberian blade systems from earlier decades if not centuries, so there is no reason to date any possible technical adaptation to the second half of the century, especially given alternate explanations for the increased use of the razor in the second half of the century.

Soares notes that in the beginning of the first half of the century, African-born *capoeiras* were more likely to be found with knives and Brazilian-born with *navalhas.* By extension, the demographic domination of Brazilian-born *capoeiras* over African-born would be an equally strong explanation for the rise of razors in the second half of the century. However, this does not need to be understood as a cultural discrepancy between African- and Brazilian-born. The fact that some Africans did use *navalhas* early in the century clearly does not support that interpretation. Rather, given the practical advantages of the weapon, beginning with the sharpness of its blade and its compactness when folded, it was more likely a widely preferred weapon among most bondsmen; thus, the distinction in weapon use more likely reflects the social/material capital of Brazilian-born bondsmen providing them with greater access to these more expensive implements. This perspective is certainly supported by an Atlantic-wide perspective. For example, the razor was also the preferred weapon of the plantations of North America where Iberian influence was negligible. Kouri points out that in North America the use of razors was also ancillary to knocking and kicking. In the nineteenth-century United States the razor emerged as a symbol for people of African descent through black dandy characters that were developed under the minstrel tradition and later popularized through song. Philip Bruce in the nineteenth century described blacks' affinity for razors over guns or knives as arising from practical and aesthetic considerations, in addition to "it being an admirable means of attack or defense." Given the need for blacks to conceal their weapons, the razor's ability to be wielded at speeds that made it a mere glimmer to the opponent, and the visually dramatic wounds it inflicted, it is no wonder that it was the preferred weapon of urban fighters across the Atlantic world. See Assunção, *Capoeira,* 84–87; Soares, *A Negregada Instituição,* 167–200; José Ramos Tinhorão, *Fado, dança do Brasil, cantar de Lisboa: O fim de um mito* (Lisboa: Editorial Caminho, 1994); Kouri, "Search for Knocking"; Bruce, *Plantation Negro;* and Marcy S. Sacks, "'A Razor Properly Handled': The Image and Reality of Violence in New York City's Black Population before World War I," paper presented to the Organization of American Historians, San Jose, Calif., April 1, 2005.

168. Soares, *A Negregada Instituição,* 263–64.

169. Renato Almeida, "O brinquedo da capoeira," *Biblioteca Nacional* 84, no.7 (1942): 157; Cobrinha Verde and Marcelino dos Santos, *Capoeira e mandingas* (Salvador: Editora Rasteira, 1990), 50.

170. Although his rendition is fictional, Abreu was himself a *capoeira,* and thus his rendition, while adapted for dramatic effect, was likely extrapolated from his accurate awareness of contemporary *capoeiragem.* See Abreu, *Os capoeiras,* 19–22.

171. Soares, *A capoeira escrava,* 88.

172. ANRJ, Ij6-166, June 9, 1833, "Extrato das partes." Not limited to Rio, the battles between Portuguese immigrants and *capoeiras* were especially prominent in northern areas such as Pernambuco.

173. Despite their shared squalor, as whites the Portuguese could advance socially and economically, forcing blacks out of housing and job opportunities. Although it addresses these issues for a slightly later period, see Adamo, "Broken Promise."

174. Holloway, "Healthy Terror," 657.

175. Gastão Cruls, *Aparência do Rio de Janeiro* (Rio de Janeiro: J. Olympio, 1965), 1:417.

176. Ibid.; Valdemar de Oliveira, *Frevo, capoeira e "passo"* (Recife: Companhia Editôra de Pernambuco, 1971), 76.

177. Cascudo (*Folclore do Brasil,* 187) erroneously suggests that the use of clubs by *capoeiras* was the influence of Portuguese *jogadores de pau,* but in fact the Portuguese weapon was a staff roughly equal to the wielder's height, while the stick of the *capoeiras* was "never longer than fifty centimeters." See also Filho, *Festas,* 258. The use of the staff in western Iberia was possibly first noted in the second century B.C.E. when the Roman forces met stiff resistance from a group in the region of Montes Herminios (Serra da Estrela) fighting with stones and staves. However, some scholars believe that the techniques utilized since the seventeenth century have their origin in the Malabari staff fighting of Kerala in India, which was brought back by sailors. See Ian L. Crocker, "Jogo do Pau," *Hoplos* 3, no. 3 (1981): 1. Luis Preto, *Jogo do Pau: The Ancient Art and Modern Science of Portuguese Stick Fighting,* trans. Guy Windsor (Highland Village, Tex.: Chivalry Bookshelf, 2005).

178. Ibid., 2.

179. Cruls, *Aparência do Rio de Janeiro,* 1:407.

180. Filho, *Festas,* 263.

181. Cited in Ruy Duarte, *História social do Frevo* (Rio de Janeiro: Ed. Leitura, 1968), 20n1.

182. Cf. Jocélio Teles dos Santos, "A Mixed-Race Nation: Afro-Brazilians and Cultural Policy in Bahia, 1970–1990," in *Afro-Brazilian Culture and Politics: Bahia 1790s*

to 1990s, ed. Hendrick Kraay (Armonk, N.Y.: M.E. Sharpe, 1998), 125–33; Luís Renato Vieira, "Da vadiação à capoeira regional: Uma interpretação da modedrnização cultural no Brasil" (M.A. diss., Universidade de Brasília, 1990).

183. Michael R. Trochim, "The Brazilian Black Guard: Racial Conflict in Post-Abolition Brazil," *Americas* 44, no. 3 (1988): 285–301.

184. Arquivo Público do Estado do Rio de Janeiro (AP), livro (book) 1890, 104, January 10, 1890.

185. Hahner, *Poverty*, 60.

186. This was an early phase of a larger trend by elites to co-opt African Brazilian cultural practices for promotion of a national character. See Alison Raphael, "Samba and Social Control: Popular Culture and Racial Democracy in Rio de Janeiro" (Ph.D. diss., Columbia University, 1980); and Diana D. Brown, *Umbanda: Religion and Politics in Urban Brazil* (Ann Arbor, Mich.: UMI Research Press, 1986).

187. *Careta* (Rio de Janeiro), May 29, 1909; *O Malho* (Rio de Janeiro), October 13–20, 1910; *Journal do Brasil* (Rio de Janeiro), May 9, 1912; Jair Moura, "Evolução, apogou, e declíno da *capoeiragem* no Rio de Janeiro," *Cadernos Rioarte* 3 (1985): 87, 93.

188. Oliveira, *Frevo*, 85–87.

189. Ibid., 88.

190. Ibid., 94–102.

191. For a detailed description of *capoeiragem* in this period, see Adriana Albert Dias, "Os 'fiéis' da Navalha: Pedro Mineiro, *capoeiras*, marinheiros e policias em Salvador na Rupública Velha," *Afro-Ásia* 32 (2005): 271–303.

192. Vieira, "Da vadiação," 120.

193. Ibid., 28.

194. Ribeyrolles, *Brasil pitoresco*, 37–38.

195. Kubik, *Angolan Traits in Black Music*, 34. For a detailed historical evolution of this instrument, see Richard Graham, "Technology and Culture Change: The Development of the 'Berimbau' in Colonial Brazil," *Latin American Music Review* 12, no. 1 (1991): 1–20.

196. Rego, *Capoeira Angola*, 71–76; Jean-Baptiste Debret, *Voyage pittoeresque et historique au Brésil, ou séjour d'un artiste francais au Brésil dépuis 1816 jusqu'en 1831 inclusivement* (Paris: Firmin Didot Frères, 1834), 39, 129; Jair Moura, *A luta regional Baiana* (Salvador: Divisão de Folclore, Departamento de Assuntos Culturais, Secretaria Municipal de Educação e Cultura, Prefeitura Municipal do Salvador, 1979), 9.

197. Kubik, *Angolan Traits in Black Music*, 28; Graham, "Technology," 1–20.

198. The *agôgo* clearly derives from the Yoruba instrument of the same name, and the *caxixi* basket rattle may have derived from a Biafran prototype. See Kubik, *Angolan Traits in Black Music*, 35–36. Not all *bambas*, however, incorporated these instruments into their orchestras for their *jogo de capoeira*, and the combinations varied from *bamba* to *bamba*. See Vieira, "Da vadiação."

199. Kubick, *Angolan Traits in Black Music*, 31.

200. Reis, *Slave Rebellion in Brazil*, 150–51. Due to trading relationships, the destruction of the kingdom of Oyo, and the expansion of the Dahomey kingdom, the Yoruba and the Aja-Fon-Ewe formed a majority among the enslaved Africans brought to Bahia in the nineteenth century. See Reis, *Slave Rebellion in Brazil;* and Pierre

Verger, *Trade Relations between the Bight of Benin and Bahia from the 17th to 19th Centuries*, trans. Evelyn Crawford (Ibadan, 1976).

201. Daniel Coutinho, *O ABC da capoeira de Angola: Os manuscritos do Mestre Noronha* (Brasília: Centro de Documentação e Informação Sobre a Capoeira, 1993), 42.

202. It was most associated with Cachoeira, Santo Amaro, and Salador, Bahia.

203. On the history of this form, one anticipates the upcoming work of Frederico José de Abreu on the subject.

204. Edison Carneiro, *A sabedoria popular* (Rio de Janeiro: Ministério da Educacão e Cultura Instituto Nacional do Livro, 1957), 207–10; Carneiro, *Negros Bantus*, 164. The poet Manuel Rozentino describes the *capoeira* figure as "the terror of the batuque" in "O capadócio," *Revista Popular* 1 (November 1897).

205. Another technique that may have been added to the tradition in Brazil was the *tesoura*, or scissors sweep using both legs. While this genre of sweeps may have come from Biafran *ntele ukwu*, which specialized in scissors techniques, it most likely was developed locally in Brazil as a natural extension of earlier leg sweeps.

206. Rego, *Capoeira Angola*, 315. The final watershed that would alter the practice of the martial art was its codification in formal academies in the 1940s, which would again transform the context of the *jogo de capoeira*. For a detailed discussion of this transitory period, see Vieira, "Da vadiação"; and Maria Angela Borgres Salvdori, "Capoeiras e malandros: Pedaços de uma sonora tradição popular (1870–1980)" (M.A. thesis, Universidade Estadual de Campinas, 1990).

207. The use of the term "honor" is not intended to glorify the *capoeiras*. In the popular media the term is often applied to valiant soldiers or romanticized knights fighting for love. The honor that is being discussed here is quite distinct from these or Christian moral honor. This reflexive honor of *capoeiras* shared more in common with the honor of feuding or the demand for "respect" that currently leads to tragic violence in urban America. See Richard E. Nisbett and Dov Cohen, *Culture of Honor: The Psychology of Violence in the South* (Boulder, Colo.: Westview Press, 1996); Fox Butterfield, *All God's Children: The Bosket Family and the American Tradition of Violence* (New York: Alfred A. Knopf, 1995); and Frank Henderson Stewart, *Honor* (Chicago: University of Chicago Press, 1994).

208. Kidder et al., *Brazil*, 126; Holloway, "Healthy Terror," 662–63.

209. ANRJ, *Relatório do Chefe da Polícia da Corte*, 1878, pp. 31–32.

210. ANRJ, Ij6-217, January 20, 1854, p. 55.

211. Filho, *Festas*, 260.

212. At least some of these attacks may have been directed at people of African descent who were perceived as collaborating with the agents of oppression, such as the *capoeira* attack on the African Demiciano who worked for the police. See Holloway, "Healthy Terror," 663.

213. Soares (*A capoeira escrava*, 94) calculates that for the first half of the century the physical attacks of bondsmen were directed at other bondsmen in about 38 percent of cases, while about 29 percent were directed at free people.

214. *Diário do Rio de Janeiro*, July 17, 1849, 4.

215. "*Capoeiras*," *Diário do Rio de Janeiro*, March 5, 1872, 1.

216. As a French visitor noted, "It sometimes happens that their victims are innocent passersby, against whom they have no reason for animosity," but usually their

weapons were used "among themselves, against their enemies, or against those at whom they direct their revenge" (Allain, *Rio-de-Janeiro,* 271–72).

217. Some of these seemingly random attacks may have in reality reflected the political savvy of *capoeiras.* Police chief Antônio Simões da Silva accused the *maltas* of attacking people "intentionally to provoke the authorities into using extreme measures, which in turn are always criticized and often rebuked" (ANRJ, Ij6-212, November 13, 1849).

218. The following discussion is drawn from Suzanne Miers and Igor Kopytoff, eds., *Slavery in Africa: Historical and Anthropological Perspectives* (Madison: University of Wisconsin Press, 1977).

219. Ibid., 12.

220. Orlando Patterson, *Freedom in the Making of Western Culture* (New York: Basic Books, 1991).

221. Miers and Kopytoff, *Slavery in Africa,* 17.

222. Joseph C. Miller, "Retention, Re-Invention, and Remembering: Restoring Identities through Enslavement in Angola and under Slavery in Brazil," in *Enslaving Connections: Changing Cultures of Africa and Brazil during the Era of Slavery,* ed. José C. Curto and Paul E. Lovejoy (Amherst: Humanity Books, 2004).

223. Manuel Antônio de Almeida, *Memórias de um sargento de milícias* (Rio de Janeiro: Livros Técnicos e Cientificos, 1978), 68.

224. If certain *capoeiras* did not have the financial means to attain this style, some may have sought it through illegal means, such as Victoriano Crioulu, who was arrested for stealing the clothes of an Englishman, or Joao Benguela, who used a head butt to rob a freedman of his hat (ANRJ, codex 403, vol. 1, November 14, 1811; vol. 2, December 10, 1819).

225. Soares, *A capoeira escrava,* 83.

226. "*Seu andar é oscilante, gingando*" (Filho, *Festas,* 258).

227. Allain, *Rio-de-Janeiro,* 271–72. In addition to *jogo de capoeira* exhibitions, these festivals were also sites for *capoeiragem*-related violence. According to Alexandre José de Mello Moraes Filho, "*capoeiras* form groups of 20 to 100 in front of troops, carnival processions, national and holy days, and provoke disorder, they run, wound." Similarly, Minister of Justice José Thomas Nabuco d'Araujo reported, "The *capoeiras* make use of festive days for their 'runs,' commit crimes and intentionally frighten the peaceful citizens." See Filho, *Festas,* 258; and ANRJ, Ij6-484, January 19, 1859.

228. ANRJ, codex 403, vol. 2, December 16, 1818.

229. Soares, *A capoeira escrava,* 197.

230. Filho, *O Rio de Janeiro imperial,* 53.

231. As one officer reported, "I have the honor to report to his Excellency that this morning a freed black fell from the tower of the church Our Lady Mother of Mankind, where he landed dead" (ANRJ, Ij6-165, November 2, 1831).

232. Chvaicer, "Criminalization of *Capoeira,*" 546.

233. Henderson, *History of the Brazil,* 73.

234. Note the Bahian example of resisting illegal recruitment by a national guardsman against two police officers. After his declaration that his status as a national guardsman made their actions illegal proved fruitless, the guardsman "adept in *capoeira,* raised a foot (*calçou o pé*) and planted a head butt in one, throwing him to

the floor." See *Alabama,* September 4, 1867, quoted in Frederico José de Abreu, *Capoeiras: Bahia, século XIX* (Salvador: Instituto Jair Moura, 2005).

235. A.P.D.G., *Sketches,* 304–6.

236. ANRJ, codex 403, vol. 2, April 11, 1821. In New England bondsmen drew on the reputations of their enslavers to help them gain influence in elections. See Piersen, *Black Yankees,* 129–30.

237. Adolfo Morales Rios Filho, "Os *Capoeiras,*" in *O Rio de Janeiro imperial* (Rio de Janeiro: A. Noite, 1946), 51–54 (reprint of earlier article published in *Vamos Ler* 4 [January 19, 1939]).

238. Filho, *O Rio de Janeiro imperial,* 51–54. His reputation was also widened for being hired by Princess Carlota Joaquina as an assassin. See n. 294 below.

239. The initiation process of *capoeira* societies out of the *moleque* stage of "childhood" into the manhood represented by *capoeiras* symbolically worked against the perpetual infancy imposed by a patriarchy and augmented their sense of themselves as respected men.

240. On sex ratios, see Sweet, "Recreating Africa," 101–2; and David Eltis and David Richardson, "West Africa and the Transatlantic Slave Trade: New Evidence of Long-Run Trends," *Slavery and Abolition* 18 (April 1997): 16–35.

241. Not merely a question of demographic numbers, African gender constructs often conflicted with the demands of slavery in subtle but significant ways. Notions of gender in Africa were also tied to a division of economic activities. Among agropastoral Kunene, manhood was linked to pastoralism, while agriculture and local trade were associated with womanhood; yet, on a Brazilian plantation a Kunene man might be forced to take up agriculture. Similarly in urban Rio, African men forced to carry water for households as *ganhadores* may have perceived this as a subtle threat to their manhood, as water-carrying was a task associated with women and especially young girls in their natal societies.

242. ANRJ, codex 403, vol. 2, August 25, 1819. Another possible modality may have been the *jogo de pancadas,* although it is not clear exactly what type of pugilism it entailed. The brief references to it are too vague to rule out the possibility that the combat game utilized punches or slaps. It may have been the stick-fighting contest that Rugendas witnessed but did not name. The term *pancada* in this volume of the records could be applied to the blows of sticks, as when Mariano Pardo was arrested for "giving *pancadas* with a stick." Alternately, it may have been another expression for the *jogo de capoeira,* as implied by records of João Thompson and Pedro Cabrete, North American blacks arrested for "*jogando capoeira, digo pancadas.*" See ANRJ, codex 403, vol. 1, October 21, 1812; November 16, 1812; October 28, 1812; August 26, 1814; and Rugendas, *Viagem,* 155.

243. On European honor and dueling, see Stewart, *Honor;* Ute Frevert, *Men of Honour: A Social and Cultural History of the Duel* (Cambridge, Mass.: Polity Press, 1995); and Petrus Cornelis Spierenburg, *Men and Violence: Gender, Honor, and Rituals in Modern Europe and America* (Columbus: Ohio State University Press, 1998).

244. I am not suggesting that this was the origin of the technical use of the knife by *capoeiras* or that northern Angola was the only place that blades held this significance in Africa. I am simply pointing out that the connection between masculinity and blade dueling (paralleling the use of the stick in Kunene societies) was part of the heritage that at least some Africans carried with them to Brazil.

245. Herbert Ward, "Ethnographical Notes Relating to the Congo Tribes," *Journal of the Anthropological Institute of Great Britain and Ireland* 24 (1895): 285–99.

246. Cimbebasian men usually carried knives with them, and in a pinch they would apply their stick-fighting techniques to their use of knives in duels. Although knives could at times serve the purpose, sticks were clearly the socially dictated preferred weapon of vengeance. Note the same approach among pastoral Fulbe. See Hendrick Wangushu, interview, Enena, Namibia, January 15, 2006; and Moritz, "Honor Psychology," 8–10.

247. Thomas Gallant found that among Greek knife fighters, "The one who was cut did not suffer shame but rather, as the Greeks put it, *systoli*—a word whose root meaning is 'diminuition.' In other words, losing a knife duel did not *dis*honor a man. He kept his honor, but his reputation was diminished." By not responding violently, however, men from this region of Greater Loango or Greece would lose their honor and be treated with contempt by their peers from then on. See Thomas W. Gallant, "Honor, Masculinity, and Ritual Knife Fighting in Nineteenth-Century Greece," *American Historical Review* 105, no. 2 (2000): 359–82.

248. This emphasis on the importance of shaming through mutilation of an opponent's face paralleled the gouging of North American whites. See Gorn, "Gouge and Bite," 18–43.

249. W. F. Owen and Heaton Bowstead Robinson, eds., *Narrative of Voyages to Explore the Shores of Africa, Arabia, and Madagascar* (New York: J. & J. Harper, 1833), 2:183.

250. White Brazilians also fought in knife duels, but it is unclear if these were intended to stop short of lethal effect. Henderson recounts a British officer who "suddenly received a *facada* by a person who drew a knife from under a capote, or cloak (which the Brazilians are in the habit of wearing), concealed for the purpose, and which terminated his existence. It is said that this wretch had unjustly encouraged a feeling of jealousy against the British officer in regard to his wife, or some part of his family" (Henderson, *History of the Brazil,* 77).

251. Soares, *A capoeira escrava,* 93.

252. Literally, "this one is ready" (Arquivo Judiciário do Estado do Rio de Janeiro, "Domingos Soares Calçado," caixa [box] 23, processo [process] 17).

253. Filho, *Festas,* 326.

254. Abreu, *Os capoeiras,* 6.

255. Ibid.

256. Moritz, "Honor Psychology," 9.

257. What was the role of women in relation to the subculture of *capoeiras*? It is clear that *capoeiras* often hung out at *zungu* houses, which were often owned by free black women and, given the shared social spaces, likely developed relationships with female *ganhadores* and prostitutes. While the data are extremely limited, it is possible that there were some parallels to the world of Trinidadian stick fighters. In nineteenth-century Trinidad women played both supportive and active roles in the violence associated with stick fighters. They provided songs to accompany stick-fighting matches, and women who made money as prostitutes or hucksters helped provide for their men financially as well. (This latter relationship can be seen in the Brazilian case detailed by Sandra Graham.) David Trotman's study of conflict in Trinidad concluded that, "Just as the scarcity of females prompted violence in the

urban community, it often led the unemployed or marginally employed women to resort to violence to secure and maintain the companionship of males." One exemplary case is that of a woman named Boadicea who defeated Alice Sugar in an hour-long battle for the right to the sexual favors of a renowned stick fighter named Cutaway Rimbeau. Boadicea on a later date also had to beat Rimbeau with his own fighting stick for daring to have extended his sexual favors to the sister of Alice Sugar! See Sandra Lauderdale Graham, "Honor among Slaves," in *The Faces of Honor: Sex, Shame, and Violence in Colonial Latin America,* ed. Lyman L. Johnson and Sonya Lipsett-Rivera (Albuquerque: University of New Mexico Press, 1998); and David Vincent Trotman, *Crime in Trinidad Conflict and Control in a Plantation Society 1838–1900* (Knoxville: University of Tennessee Press, 1986), 180–82.

258. Cruls, *Aparência do Rio de Janeiro,* 1:406; Oliveira, *Frevo,* 76. Again, these conflicts over women were likely more often tied to reflexive honor than to a sense of chivalry, although the case of Josiah Henson in North America suggests that such sentiments were not necessarily absent among bondsmen.

259. ANRJ, 323, vol. 2, December 5, 1810, 9–10.

260. While the contemporary dominance of women and homosexual males in Candomblé houses may be a postslavery development, there were certainly many female ritual specialists who organized *kalundus* and other Angolan-derived religious practices during the slave regime. Note, for example, the bondswoman Rosa, who in late eighteenth-century Rio had "public fame for being a *feiticeira* who killed various slaves and cattle" (cited in Sweet, *Recreating Africa,* 172). On honor among women of color in relation to their economic success relative to male counterparts in Brazil, see Graham, "Honor among Slaves," 201–28.

261. Women who were not experienced fighters themselves called on the skills of the *capoeiras* surrounding them to avenge what they perceived as infidelity. One anonymous observer from the early nineteenth century noted, "The women of color in Rio de Janeiro are remarkable for their jealous and vindictive temper; and death alone is capable of glutting their revenge for the infidelity of those with whom they have cohabitated. Murders are therefore exceedingly frequent; and although, in the absence of an active periodical press, few of these occurrences are made public, I have known even thirty to have been committed in the space of a month, most of them from motives of jealousy, and at the instigation of mulatto women" (A.P. D.G., *Sketches,* 303–4).

262. ANRJ, codex 403, vol. 1, March 28, 1814, p. 194.

263. "Ate na bella sexo," *Journal do Commercio,* January 29, 1873.

264. Itier, *Journal,* 1:62.

265. Filho, *Festas,* 259.

266. For a rich ethnography dealing with the administering of communal justice in both Biafra and Haiti through closed societies, see Davis, *Passage of Darkness.*

267. Might white *capoeiras,* through their initiation into a historically African and bonded institution, have been inculcated into a counterhegemonic stance toward the power structure of elite whites? Holloway implies that white *capoeiras* may have viewed their clashes with authorities in terms of class divisions: "A clear way for the slave, black, brown, and poor people [i.e., poor whites] to express the resentment of have-nots against the haves, then, was to engage in street battles with municipal guard patrols" (Holloway, *Policing Rio de Janeiro,* 80).

268. An exception was of course made for blacks and *pardos* serving as police or soldiers.

269. On few being arrested for this crime, see Holloway, *Policing Rio de Janeiro,* 42, 198. Arago, who was in Rio in 1818, notes that Portuguese and Brazilians were allowed to duel with knives (Arago, *Narrative of a Voyage,* 74).

270. A late nineteenth-century poem by Manuel Rozentino relates his admiration for *capoeiras,* but while watching a *jogo de capoeira* he was warned to "get away white man!" (*afomente-se branco!*). While published after the abolition of slavery, this idea on the part of *capoeiras* that they dominated their social space was clearly a long-standing belief. See Rozentino, "O capadócio," reproduced in Abreu, *Capoeiras,* 116.

271. "*Dizia algumas vezes que havia de tirar as teimas dos broncos*" (cited in Holloway, "Healthy Terror," 637).

272. Almeida, *Memórias,* 66.

273. ANRJ, codex 403, vol. 1, August 13, 1811. Influence over taverns also provided access to hide-out spots and possible gambling in the form of *jogo de casquinhas* (peel games). On the latter game, see Soares, *A capoeira escrava,* 178–81.

274. *Relatório do Ministério da Justiça, 1887* (cited in Holloway, "Healthy Terror," 670).

275. Quoted in Oséas Morais de Araujo, *Notícias sobre a polícia militar da Bahia no século XIX* (Salvador: Claudiomar Gonçlaves, 1997), 117.

276. ANRJ, codex 403, vol. 1, July 17, 1810.

277. ANRJ, codex 403, vol. 1, November 21, 1812.

278. Ibid.

279. One observer later in the century even described the police as being "intimidated" by *capoeiras:* "*A polcia, amedrontada e sem força, fazia constar que perseguia os desordeiros, acontecendo raríssimas vezes ser preso este or aquele, que respondia a processo*" (Filho, *Festas,* 260).

280. ANRJ, codex 403, vol. 1, (?) 10, 1812.

281. ANRJ, codex 403, vol. 1, December 13, 1811.

282. *Diário do Rio de Janeiro,* June 16, 1849, 2.

283. ANRJ, Ij6-212, June 13–15, 1849; Holloway, *Policing Rio de Janeiro,* 221.

284. ANRJ, codex 403, vol. 2, March 7, 1820.

285. Cited in Holloway, *Policing Rio de Janeiro,* 221.

286. This bold attack demonstrated not only his defense of his society's honor but likely also his confidence in the spiritual items that he carried (ANRJ, codex 403, vol. 1, September 26, 1811).

287. ANRJ, codex 398 (Relação de prisões no Rio de Janeiro), December 24, 1849.

288. ANRJ, codex 403, vol. 1, July 4, 1812.

289. *Gazeta de Noticias* (Rio de Janeiro), February 26, 1878, 1.

290. Many *capoeiras* may have chosen to keep up some economic or social relations with their respective *senhores* for, among other reasons, a measure of legal protection. Yet, in other ways many of them lived lifestyles paralleling urban maroons. Adão, at least temporarily, actually became an urban maroon. In that he was not alone. Advertisements for runaways at times mention *capoeiras* who had been sent to rural estates outside the city and escaped to return to Rio and their old lives as urban *capoeiras.* See *Diário do Rio de Janeiro,* July 7, 1849, 4.

291. ANRJ, IJ6-165, 1831–32, August 4, 1831, and Ij6-169, May 2, 1834.

292. Arago, *Narrative of a Voyage,* 90.

293. Cf. ANRJ, Ij6-194, 1839, September 6, 1839, and codex 323, vol. 15, February 9, 1839, for other examples of deportation to Angola.

294. According to Henderson, deportation to Angola was the common sentence for murderers who threw themselves at the mercy of the king. "No one had suffered the penalty of death for a long period before July 22, 1819, when a wretched criminal['s . . .] punishment would have been commuted for transportation to Africa, had he not imbrued his hands in the blood of a pregnant female, whom he stabbed mortally" (Henderson, *History of the Brazil,* 78). Given that assassins were often recruited among *capoeiras,* it is quite possible that some were sent back to Angola. Although he was not Angolan or formally deported, there is the *capoeira* Joaquim Inácio da Cunha, aka Orelha. He was given a large sum of money and guaranteed immunity to eliminate the romantic rival of Princess Carlota Joaquina. Although he would later return to Brazil under the protection of José Bonifácio, it appears that he spent many years in Angola. Deported *degregados* were sent in largest numbers to Luanda but also to Benguela, where they would have served as soldiers. For a detailed study on a similar practice of sending Martinican bondsmen to Senegal, see John Savage, "Unwanted Slaves: The Punishment of Transportation and the Making of Legal Subjects in Early Nineteenth-Century Martinique," *Citizenship Studies* 10 (February 2006): 35–53. See also Ribeiro, *Crônicas,* 39–43.

Chapter 6: Conclusion

1. It is important to note that these maritime connections may have linked martial traditions in the Atlantic and Indian Ocean worlds. There seem to be some fascinating similarities between the martial games of the Lesser Antilles and those of bondsmen in the Francophone Indian Ocean. See T. J. Desch-Obi, "Moring: Indigenous Boxing in East Africa and the African Archipelago," paper presented at the "Women, Gender, and Sport in Africa Symposium," Ohio University, Athens, February 24–25, 2006, and "Le Defi: Mascarene Pugilism and the African Diaspora," paper presented to the African Studies Association Conference, New York City, October 18–21, 2007.

2. Chinea, "Quest for Freedom," 51–87; Hall, "Maritime Maroons," 476–98.

3. Scott, "Common Wind," 94; Chinea, "Quest for Freedom."

4. Although the details of the transition are unclear, these various versions of stick-fighting *kalenda* are all linked to speakers of "French Creole" who migrated in the Circum-Caribbean as a result of the Haitian Revolution and other migrations already mentioned. In late nineteenth-century Trinidad *kalenda* was associated with the *negue jardin, malta*–like groups "whose main object was to forge a reputation for stick-fighting prowess or to defend one already established," particularly during Carnival. See Errol Hill, *The Trinidad Carnival: Mandate for a National Theatre* (Austin: University of Texas Press, 1972), 25–28; and Shane Bernard and Julia Girouard Bernard, "'Colinda': Mysterious Origins of a Cajun Folksong," *Journal of Folklore Research* 29 (1992): 37–52. From Trinidad it spread to the nearby Carriacou in the twentieth century. See Donald R. Hill, *The Impact of Migration on the Metropolitan and Fold Society of Carriacou, Grenada,* vol. 54, pt. 2 (New York: American Museum of Natural History, 1977), 322–24. On *kalenda* in Trinidad, see also Liverpool, *Rituals of Power,* 160–69; and Donald R. Hill, *Calypso, Calaloo* (Gainesville: University Press of Florida, 1993), 25–32.

5. Legal formalities that limited foreign shipping in Caribbean colonies were loosened in the eighteenth century and often ignored by locals who required trade with other islands for survival, particularly in times of war when trade with the metropole was extremely curtailed. As noted earlier, trade with Barbados was essential to the early prosperity of South Carolina, and in the eighteenth century trade relations were established between the thirteen colonies and the French Caribbean. By 1790 the value of the United States trade to Saint Domingue was more than that of the rest of the Americas combined (Scott, "Common Wind," 83–84).

6. Scott, "Common Wind," 43–46. On the role of rivers to bring goods to market in South Carolina, see Brown, "Crossing Kalunga," 67–76.

7. Lovejoy and Richardson suggest, however, that contrary to claims of earlier usage, the practice of European traders joining *ekpe* was most associated with the trade after 1807. See Paul E. Lovejoy and David Richardson, "Trust, Pawnship, and Atlantic History: The Institutional Foundations of the Old Calabar Slave Trade," *American Historical Review* 104 (April 1999): 349.

8. The spreading of ideas is dealt with in Scott, "Common Wind"; and in Paul Gilroy, *The Black Atlantic: Modernity and Double Consciousness* (Cambridge, Mass.: Harvard University Press, 1993).

9. Moreau de Saint-Méry et al., *Description,* 1:479–80; Scott, "Common Wind," 60–61.

10. For a detailed examination of the bondswomen who dominated the marketplace in South Carolina, see Olwell, "Loose, Idle and Disorderly," 97–110.

11. Luzerne and Auberteuil cited in Scott, "Common Wind," 66–67.

12. Even South Carolina's Negro Seaman's Act could not isolate free black sailors from interacting with bondsmen as they were often held in the same jails. These jails could be breeding grounds for martial arts practices. Note that the *ladja* master Georges Oranger perfected his skills while in prison with other masters. See Bolster, *Black Jacks,* 190–214; and Georges Oranger, taped interview, Saint Esprit, Martinique, July 17, 2002.

13. Note descriptions of combat arts and dances demonstrated for Smith in William Smith, *A New Voyage to Guinea* (London: Frank Cass & Co. Ltd., 1967), 22.

14. Thomas Melvil quoted in Emma Christopher, "Another Head of the Hydra?: Slave Trade Sailors and Militancy on the African Coast," *Atlantic Studies* 1 (October 2004): 148.

15. Antônio Vianna described a dramatic fight in Salvador that began with a brawl in Cais do Ouro. When the police arrived, everyone ran, but one *capoeira* was caught. Using trickery he ended up head butting numerous police into the water. Antônio Vianna, *Casos e Coisas Da Bahia* (Salvador: Museu do Estado, 1950), 133–35.

16. Girarldo Balthazar Silveira, *Bahia de Iaiá e de Ioiô,* cited in Abreu, *Capoeiras,* 108.

17. Vianna, *Casos e Coisas Da Bahia,* 153–54.

18. ANRJ, Ij6-202, November 21, 1844.

19. Soares, *A capoeira escrava,* 247–304.

20. Rediker suggests that on slave ships the death rate among sailors could rival that of enslaved Africans below deck; see Marcus Buford Rediker, *Between the Devil and the Deep Blue Sea: Merchant Seamen, Pirates, and the Anglo-American Maritime World, 1700–1750* (Cambridge: Cambridge University Press, 1987), 47.

21. On *grumetas*, see Christopher, "Another Head," 150–53.

22. Hall, "Maritime Maroons," 490–92.

23. Bolster, *Black Jacks*, 167.

24. Equiano, *Life*.

25. Peter Linebaugh and Marcus Buford Rediker, *The Many-Headed Hydra: Sailors, Slaves, Commoners, and the Hidden History of the Revolutionary Atlantic* (Boston: Beacon Press, 2000), 162–64.

26. Bolster, *Black Jacks;* Linebaugh and Rediker, *Many-Headed Hydra;* Zachary Ross Morgan, "Legacy of the Lash: Blacks and Corporal Punishment in the Brazilian Navy, 1860–1910" (Ph.D. diss., Brown University, 2001), 82. On Caribbean sailors, see Alan Cobley, "Black West Indian Seamen in the British Merchant Marine in the Mid-Nineteenth Century," *History Workshop Journal* 58 (January 2004): 259–74.

27. Bolster, *Black Jacks*, 2.

28. Although it was common for sailors of all backgrounds to fight together, people of African descent may have played a more prominent combat role among pirates, where blacks were highly represented among the vanguard and were considered "the most trusted and fearsome men who were designated to board prospective prizes." For example, more than half of the boarding party of the pirate captain Edward Condent's ship, the *Dragon*, were blacks. See Linebaugh and Rediker, *Many-Headed Hydra*, 165.

29. Equiano, *Life*, 65–66.

30. See T. J. Desch-Obi, "Fighting Sweet: African Combat Aesthetics and British Boxing," paper presented at the African Diaspora Interdisciplinary Conference, City University of New York, October 2004.

31. Bolster, *Black Jacks*, 110–19.

32. Nathaniel Hawthorne, *The Yarn of a Yankee Privateer* (New York: Funk & Wagnalls Company, 1926), 187.

33. It is interesting to consider whether or not variants of these head-butting and kicking arts spread rhizomatically across the Americas into new bonded communities via sailors or relocating bondsmen taken to new areas. These arts may have been carried to coastal cities in Africa, particularly given that at least a few *capoeiras* may have been sentenced to deportation back to Angola. It is clear, however, that this could not have been the origin of the Kunene *engolo*, considering linguistic data and the fact that no outsiders, including blacks in European-style dress or shoes, were allowed inside the heartland region.

34. Bolster has described the shared elements of physicality among black and white sailors but also a set of techniques unique to black sailors. See W. Jeffrey Bolster, "An Inner Diaspora: Black Sailors Making Selves," in *Through a Glass Darkly*, ed. Ronald Hoffman (Chapel Hill: University of North Carolina Press, 1997); and Bolster, *Black Jacks*, 102–30.

35. Richard Henry Dana, *Two Years before the Mast* (New York: Library of America, 1981), 430.

36. Butterworth, *3 Years Adventure*, 300–307.

37. Faux, *Memorable Days*, 10.

38. Not to be confused with the other French foot- and slap-boxing art of *savate*, which is often conflated with *chausson*. *Savate* emerged in the nineteenth century in Paris but would later also be promoted to the upper classes under the name *chausson* since the term *savate* carried negative associations with lower-class street toughs.

39. Philip Reed and Richard Muggeridge, *Boxe Française, Savate: Martial Art of France* (London: P. H. Crompton, 1975), 6. Of course, such kicks may have had local origins in cultural practices of Marseille, but there is no mention of such a legacy in the historical record. A popular myth ascribes the development of these kicks to the need for sailors to use their hands to keep balance while kicking high on a rocking boat. While the inverted position would help compensate for a ship's pitch, the real question is why these sailors would have been trying to kick so high when punching from a solid stance would have been much more practical in this context.

40. Jaques Komorn, personal communication, May 3, 2000. This hypothesis is certainly in keeping with the extensive cultural exchanges among black and white sailors and pirates. Such cultural exchanges were reflected in 1743 when some white sailors were court-martialed for defying their superiors by singing a "Negro song." See Linebaugh and Rediker, *Many-Headed Hydra,* 167.

41. Fryer, *Rhythms of Resistance,* 116–29.

42. Tinhorão, *Fado,* 49–67; Fryer, *Rhythms of Resistance,* 128–33.

43. Alberto Bessa, *A gíria portuguesa* (Lisboa: Gomes de Carvalho, 1901).

44. Pinto de Carvalho (Tinop), *História do fado* (Lisbon: Dom Quixote, 1982), 26; and Fryer, *Rhythms of Resistance,* 132, claim that "sailors' fado" was the only sung form prior to 1840.

45. Heinrich Friedrich Link, *Travels in Portugal, and through France and Spain: With a Dissertation on the Literature of Portugal, and the Spanish and Portugueze Languages,* trans. John Hinckley (London: T. N. Longman and O. Rees, 1801), 203–4.

46. ANRJ, IJ6-203, January 8, 1845; ANRJ, Ij6-166, June 9, 1833, "Extrato das partes."

47. ANRJ, IJ6-203, February 3, 1845.

48. OPJ, 1-9-593, March 28, 1836. Quoted in Soares, *A Capoeira Escrav,a* 299.

49. Between 1840 and 1888 only 3 percent of naval manpower was voluntary, and some may have been maritime maroons in the sense of using the navy as an escape from bondage; 85 to 90 percent of sailors were people of color. See Morgan, "Legacy of the Lash," 82.

50. OPJ, 1-9-606, April 5, 1848. For conscription of *capoeiras* in general, see Morgan, "Legacy of the Lash," 118–24.

51. José Machado Pais, *A prostituição e a Lisboa boémia do séc. XIX aos inícios eo séc. XX* (Lisbon: Querco, 1985), 45–50, 131–42.

52. For a detailed exploration of the *ginga* and its origins in the languages of Angola and its importance to Brazilian culture in general, see Tavares, "Gingando."

53. Bessa, *A gíria portuguesa.*

54. While kicking a wrap similarly represents the living extension of a wrestling tradition into North America, the Kunene unarmed martial arts with their wider dispersion will be used as a case study to consider the qualities of an African tradition in the diaspora.

55. Vansina, *Paths in the Rainforests,* 259–60.

56. One of the nice features of this concept of traditions is that the "scale" is flexible so that one can speak more specifically of a Baptist tradition unique to the American Southern Baptists without losing sight of its place in the larger Christian and Judeo-Christian traditions. As such, it may serve as a way to establish common ground between scholars who approach Africans in the Americas by emphasizing

their creative processes in situ with those who stand by the importance of understanding their African backgrounds as well.

57. Vansina, *Paths in the Rainforests,* 258.

58. Matthias Röhrig Assunção, *Capoeira: A History of an Afro-Brazilian Martial Art* (New York: Routledge, 2005).

59. The stances and knife blows utilized by the masters João Grande and João Pequeno in Jair Moura's film (70 mm) *Danca da guerra* reflect the blade being used as an extension of existing postures within the *jogo de capoeira* rather than any technical influence from the blade styles of Europe or Africa.

60. Moura, *A luta regional Bahiana,* 9.

61. This use of razors in the feet was paralleled in Martinique as well. See Cally-Lézin, *Musiques,* 60.

62. Vansina, *Paths in the Rainforests,* 258.

63. Burlamaqui, *Gymnastica nacional,* 30.

64. Edison Carneiro, *Capoeira* (Rio de Janeiro: Campanha de Defesa do Folclore Brasileiro, 1975), 7. Head butts that were most systematically integrated were the ones from the characteristic lunge positions already in the art form.

65. Oliveira, *Frevo,* 93.

66. An *engolo* practitioner who visited Brazil in the merchant marine noted that "the Brazilian *capoeira* is nothing other than our *engolo* done to different songs." While *ladja* represented a merger of forms, it was still firmly within the realm of mutual intelligibility with the other Bantu pugilistic traditions in the Americas. After having seen *capoeira,* the *ladja* group AM4 observed, "It is important to note that if the elders who had seen *capoeira* did not recognize themselves in the music, they certainly did in its style of execution." Conversely a Brazilian *capoeira* master remarked on the similarity of his art with the *ladja* he witnessed: "The Martinique athletes had a very different way of performing *negativa,* but they did go down defensively; they definitely had a kind of *ginga* [the buoyant dance step that comes between blows], but less developed. They put their hands on the ground and made full circle kicks like our *meia lua de compasso* [circular kick with hands supporting weight]; they made full spin-kicks from behind like our *armada de costa* [spin kick], and they had *au,* the cartwheel." Although these were all twentieth-century reactions, it is clear that in the nineteenth century, before the early twentieth-century stylization of *capoeiragem* that transformed the art's aesthetics and music and before the modern transformative revival of *ladja,* similarities between these styles would have been even more striking. See Gabriel Mangumbala, personal communication, August 23, 1997; AM4, *Asou chimen danmyé,* 21; and Mestre Jelom quoted in Robert F. Thompson, "Black Martial Arts of the Caribbean," *Latin American Literature and Arts Review* 37 (January 1987): 47.

67. ANRJ, codex 403, vol. 1, October 27, 1812.

68. Butterworth, *3 Years Adventures,* 304–7.

69. Joseph, *Warner Arundel,* 2. While fictional in some regards, much of the text was based on thinly disguised real characters and events, which caused a sensation when the book was published.

70. Ibid., 52–53.

71. Patterson, *Slavery and Social Death,* 77–101.

72. Ibid., 41–42.

73. Henson, "Josiah Henson," 32–33.

74. ANRJ, Tribunal de Relação, codex 24, book 10, July 25, 1789.

75. Labat, *Nouveau voyag,e* 4:189–95.

76. Patterson, *Slavery and Social Death,* 13, 78.

77. Julian Pitt-Rivers, "Honor," in *International Encyclopedia of the Social Sciences,* ed. David Sills (New York: Macmillan, 1968), 6:505.

78. Douglass, *My Bondage,* 247.

Select Bibliography

Archives

Chivilly-Larue, France
    Archives Generales Congregation du Saint-Esprit (AG)
Lisbon, Portugal
    Arquivo Nacional da Torre do Tombe, Lisbon (ANTT)
London, England
    Public Records Office (PRO)
Luanda, Angola
    Arquivo Historico (AHNL)
Namibia, Windhoek
    National Archives of (NA)
New York, United States of America
    A. Schomburg Negro Collection, New York Public Library (SNC)
Paris, France
    Archives Nacionales (AN)
    Collection Moreau de Saint-Méry Série F (microfilmed)
Rio de Janeiro, Brazil
    Arquivo Nacional (ANRJ)
    Arquivo Publico do Estado (AP)
St. Augustine, Trinidad
    West Indiana & Special Collections Dept., University of the West Indies (WIS)

Contemporary Newspapers

Correio Mercantil
Diário do Rio de Janeiro
Gazeta de Noticias
Independent Chronicle and Universal Advertiser
Journal do Commercio
Revista Popular

Unpublished Sources

Aufderheide, Patricia. "Order and Violence: Social Deviance and Social Control in Brazil 1780–1840." Ph.D. diss., University of Minnesota, 1976.

Brown, Ras Michael L. B. "Crossing Kalunga: West-Central Africans and Their Cultural Influence in the South Carolina–Georgia Lowcountry." Ph.D. diss., University of Georgia, 2004.

Chambers, Douglas Brent. "'He Gwine Sing He Country': Africans, Afro-Virginians, and the Development of Slave Culture in Virginia, 1690–1810." Ph.D. diss., University of Virginia, 1996.

Cowley, John Houlston. "Music and Migration: Aspects of Black Music in the British Caribbean, the United States, and Britain, before the Independence of Jamaica and Trinidad & Tobago." Ph.D. diss., University of Warwick, 1992.

Curto, José. "Alcohol and Slaves: The Luso Brazilian Alcohol Commerce at Mpinda, Luanda, and Benguela during the Atlantic Slave Trade c.1480–1830 and Its Impact on the Societies of West Central Africa." Ph.D. diss., University of California, Los Angeles, 1996.

Elder, Jacob Delworth. "Evolution of the Traditional Calypso of Trinidad and Tobago: A Socio-Historical Analysis of Song-Change." Ph.D. diss., University of Pennsylvania, 1966.

Fadahunsi, Olayinka. "Dahomey and 'The Real National Weapon' in the Shadow of Oyo and Egba, 1727–1890." Paper presented at "Perspectives on Yoruba History and Culture," University of Texas at Austin, March 26–28, 2004.

Ferreira, Roquinaldo Amaral. "Dos Sertões ao Atântico: Tráfico ilegal de Escravos e Comércio Lícito em Angola, 1830–1860." M.A. thesis, Universidade Federal do Rio de Janeiro, 1996.

———. "Transforming Atlantic Slaving: Trade, Warfare and Territorial Control in Angola, 1650–1800." Ph.D. dissertation, University of California, Los Angeles, 2003.

Gerstin, Julian Harris. "Traditional Music in a New Social Movement: The Renewal of Bèlè in Martinique." Ph.D. diss., University of California, Berkeley, 1996.

Gomes, Maria. "A autoridade da ombala nos Nyaneka-NKumbi: Estrutura, funcionamento, e influência na vida deste povo no passado e no presente." These de licenciatura, Agostinho Neto University, Lubango, 1993.

Heckscher, Jurretta Jordan. "All the Mazes of the Dance: Black Dancing, Culture, and Identity in the Greater Chesapeake World from the Early Eighteenth Century to the Civil War." Ph.D. diss., George Washington University, 2000.

Kampungu, Romanus. "Okavango Marriage Customs." Ph.D. diss., Pontifical University, Rome, 1965.

Karasch, Mary C. "The Brazilian Slavers and the Illegal Slave Trade, 1836–1851." M.A. thesis, University of Wisconsin, 1967.

Kouri, Christopher Henry. "The Search for Knocking and Kicking: Notes toward a Definition and Historical Understanding of the Old Time Slave Derived Martial Art and Related Fighting Techniques of the Gullah." B.A. thesis, Yale University, 1990.

Miller, Joseph C. "Struggling for Identity through Enslavement in Angola and under Slavery in Brazil." Paper presented at "Enslaving Connection: Africa and Brazil during the Era of the Slave Trade," York University, Toronto, Canada, October 15, 2000.

———. "Missione evangelica al regno del Congo, et altri circonvicini, siti nell Ethiopia interiore parte dell Africa meridionalae, fata dalla religione capuccina, con il racconto di varii successi seguiti." Unpublished manuscript, 1667, available at the University of California, Los Angeles.

Montreuil, Françoise. "Rites mortuaires et représentation collective de la mort à la Martinique." M.A. thesis, Université R. Descartes, 1973.

Morgan, Zachary Ross. "Legacy of the Lash: Blacks and Corporal Punishment in the Brazilian Navy, 1860–1910." Ph.D. diss., Brown University, 2001.

Moritz, Mark. "Honor Psychology and Pastoral Personality: An Ecocultural Analysis of Herding Routines and Socialization into the Honor among Nomadic Fulbe in West Africa." Unpublished article.

Pfouts, Anita. "Economy and Society in Northern Namibia 500 BCE to 1800 CE: A Linguistic Approach." Ph.D. diss., University of California, Los Angeles, 2003.

Raphael, Alison. "Samba and Social Control: Popular Culture and Racial Democracy in Rio de Janeiro." Ph.D. diss., Columbia University, 1980.

Salamone, Frank. "Persistence and Change in Ethnic and Religious Identity." Ph.D. diss., State University of New York, Buffalo, 1973.

Salockoski, Märta. "On the Dynamics of Pre-colonial Society in Northern Namibia." Unpublished paper in National Archives of Namibia, Windhoek, 1985.

———. "Symbolic Power of Kings in Pre-colonial Ambo Societies." These de licenciatura, University of Helsinki, Franzeninkatu, 1992.

Salvdori, Maria Angela Borgres. "Capoeiras e malandros: Pedaços de uma sonora tradição popular (1870–1980)." M.A. thesis, Universidade Estadual de Campinas, 1990.

Scott, Julius Sherrard. "The Common Wind: Currents of Afro-American Communication in the Era of the Haitian Revolution." Ph.D. diss., Duke University, 1986.

Siiskonen, Harry. "Ovamboland and Economic Change in Southwestern Africa." Paper presented at "Studying the Northern Namibia Past" Research Seminar in Tvarminne, December 1985.

Tavares, Julio Cesar de Souza. "Gingando and Cooling Out: The Embodied Philosophies of the African Diaspora." Ph.D. diss., University of Texas at Austin, 1998.

Tigges, Gabriela. "The History of *Capoeira* in Brazil." Ph.D. diss., Brigham Young University, 1990.

Vieira, Luís Renato. "Da vadiação à *Capoeira* regional: Uma interpretação da modedrnização cultural no Brasil." M.A. diss., Universidade de Brasília, 1990.

Willis, John Charles. "Behind 'Their Black Masks': Slave Honor in Antebellum Virginia." M.A. thesis, Baylor University, 1987.

Young, Jason Randolph. "Rituals of Resistance: The Making of an African-Atlantic Religious Complex in Kongo and along the Sea Islands of the Slave South." Ph.D. diss., University of California, Riverside, 2002.

Published Sources

Abrahams, Roger D. *The Man-of-Words in the West Indies: Performance and the Emergence of Creole Culture.* Baltimore: Johns Hopkins University Press, 1983.

———. *Singing the Master: The Emergence of African-American Culture in the Plantation South.* New York: Pantheon Books, 1992.

Abrahams, Roger D., and John F. Szwed, eds. *After Africa: Extracts from British Travel Accounts and Journals of the Seventeenth, Eighteenth and Nineteenth Centuries Concerning the Slaves, Their Manners and Customs in the British West Indies.* New Haven, Conn.: Yale University Press, 1983.

Abreu, Frederico José de. *Capoeiras: Bahia, Século XIX*. Salvador: Instituto Jair Moura, 2005.

Abreu, Plácido de. *Os capoeiras*. Rio de Janeiro: Tip. da Escola Serafim Alves de Brito, 1886.

Achebe, Chinua. *Things Fall Apart*. New York: Anchor Books, 1994.

Achebe, Nwando. *Farmers, Traders, Warriors, and Kings: Female Power and Authority in Northern Igboland, 1900–1960*. Portsmouth, N.H.: Heinemann, 2005.

Adams, John. *Sketches Taken during Ten Voyages to Africa, between the Years 1786 and 1800; Including Observations on the Country between Cape Palmas and the River Congo; and Cursory Remarks on the Physical and Moral Character of the Inhabitants: With an Appendix, Containing an Account of the European Trade with the West Coast of Africa*. 1822. Repr., New York: Johnson Reprint Corp., 1970.

Afigbo, A. E. *Ropes of Sand: Studies in Igbo History and Culture*. Ibadan: Published for University Press in association with Oxford University Press, 1981.

———. *The Warrant Chiefs: Indirect Rule in Southeastern Nigeria, 1891–1929*. London: Longman, 1972.

Ahye, Molly. *Golden Heritage*. Petit Valley, Trinidad and Tobago: Heritage Cultures, Ltd., 1978.

Algranti, Leila Mezan. *O feitor ausente: Estudo sobre a escravidão urbana no Rio de Janeiro*. Petrópolis: Vozes, 1988.

Allain, Émile. *Rio-de-Janeiro: Quelques données sur la capitale et sur l'administration du Brésil*. Paris: L. Frinzine, 1886.

Almeida, António, and Franca Camarate. "Recintos mulharados de Angola." *Estudos sobre a Pré-história do Ultramar Português* 16 (1960): 109–24.

AM4. (Association Mi Mes Manmay Matnik). *Asou chimen danmyé: Propositions sur le danmyé, art martial martiniquais*. Fort-de-France, 1992.

Anburey, Thomas. *Travels through the Interior Parts of America*. 2 vols. 1789. Repr., New York: New York Times, 1969.

Anyanwu, U. D. "Kinship and Warfare in Igbo Society." In *Warfare and Diplomacy in Precolonial Nigeria: Essays in Honor of Robert Smith*, ed. Robert Sydney Smith, Toyin Falola, and Robin Law. Madison: African Studies Program, University of Wisconsin at Madison, 1992.

Arago, Jacques. *Narrative of a Voyage round the World, in the Uraine and Physicienne Corvettes, Commanded by Captain Freycinet, during the Years 1817, 1818, 1819, and 1820*. London: Treuttel & Wurtz, Treuttal, jun. & Richter, 1823.

Araujo, Elysio de. *Estudo histórico sobre a polícia da capital federal, 1808–1831*. Rio de Janeiro: Imprensa Nacional, 1898.

Araujo, Oséas Morais de. *Notícias sobre a polícia militar da Bahia no século XIX*. Salvador: Claudiomar Gonçlaves, 1997.

Armstrong, O. K. *Old Massa's People: The Old Slaves Tell Their Story*. Indianapolis: Bobbs-Merrill, 1931.

Bailey, Cornelia, and Christena Bledsoe. *God, Dr. Buzzard, and the Bolito Man: A Saltwater Geechee Talks about Life on Sapelo Island*. New York: Anchor Books, a Division of Random House, 2001.

Baker, William, and James Mangen, eds. *Sport in Africa: Essays in Social History*. New York and London: Africana Publishing Co., 1987.

Ball, Charles. *Slavery in the United States: A Narrative of the Life and Adventures of Charles Ball, a Black Man.* 1837. Repr., Detroit: American Library, 1969.

Barnes, Sandra, ed. *Africa's Ogun.* Bloomington: Indiana University Press, 1989.

Beattie, Peter M. "Measures of Manhood: Honor, Enlisted Army Service, and Slavery's Decline in Brazil, 1850–1890." In *Changing Men and Masculinities in Latin America.* Ed. Matthew C. Gutmann, 233–55. Durham, N.C.: Duke University Press, 2003.

Beckwith, Martha Warren. *Black Roadways: A Study of Jamaican Folk Life.* New York: Negro Universities Press, 1969.

Berlin, Ira. *Many Thousands Gone: The First Two Centuries of Slavery in North America.* Cambridge, Mass.: Belknap Press of Harvard University Press, 1998.

Berlin, Ira, Marc Favreau, and Steven Miller, eds. *Remembering Slavery: African Americans Talk about Their Personal Experiences of Slavery and Freedom.* New York: New Press, 1998.

Berlin, Ira, and Phillip Morgan, eds. *Cultivation and Culture: Labor and the Shaping of Slave Life in the Americas.* Charlottesville: University Press of Virginia, 1993.

Bernard, Shane, and Julia Girouard Bernard. "'Colinda': Mysterious Origins of a Cajun Folksong." *Journal of Folklore Research* 29, no. 1 (1992): 27, 38–52.

Bessa, Alberto. *A Gíria Portuguesa.* Lisboa: Gomes de Carvalho, 1901.

Bettelheim, Judith. *Cuban Festivals: An Illustrated Anthology.* New York: Garland, 1993.

Bibb, Henry. "Narrative of the Life and Adventures of Henry Bibb, an American Slave." In *I Was Born a Slave: An Anthology of Classic Slave Narratives.* Ed. Yuval Taylor, 1–102. Edinburgh: Payback Press, 1999.

Blackburn, Robin. *The Making of New World Slavery: From the Baroque to the Modern, 1492–1800.* London/New York: Verso, 1997.

Blassingame, John. *The Slave Community.* New York: Oxford University Press, 1979.

———. *Slave Testimony: Two Centuries of Letters, Speeches, Interviews, and Autobiographies.* Baton Rouge: Louisiana State University Press, 1977.

Bolster, W. Jeffrey. *Black Jacks: African American Seamen in the Age of Sail.* Cambridge, Mass.: Harvard University Press, 1997.

Bontemps, Arna, ed. *Five Black Lives.* Middletown, Conn.: Wesleyan University Press, 1971.

Bösche, Eduard Theodor. *Quadros alternados: Impressões do Brasil de D. Pedro I.* São Paulo: Typ. da Casa Garraux, 1929.

Bosman, William. *A New and Accurate Description of the Coast of Guinea.* London/New York: Frank Cass/Barnes and Noble, 1967.

Brochado, José. "Descripção das terras do Humbe, Camba, Mulondo, Quanhamae, outras, contendo uma idéa da sua população, seus costumes, vestuarios, etc." *Annaes do Conselho Ultramarino,* unofficial part, 1st series (November 1855): 187–97.

———. "Notícia de alguns territórios, e dos povos que os habitam, situados na parte meridional da provincial de Angola." *Annaes do Conselho Ultramarino,* unoffical part, 1st series (December 1855): 203–9.

Brown, William Wells. *My Southern Home; or, the South and Its People.* 1880. Repr., Upper Saddle River, N.J.: Gregg Press, 1968.

Bruce, Henry Clay. *The New Man: Twenty-Nine Years a Slave, Twenty-Nine Years a Free Man; Recollections of H. C. Bruce.* 1985. Repr., Lincoln: University of Nebraska Press, 1996.

Bruce, Philip A. *The Plantation Negro as a Freeman: Observations on His Character, Condition, and Prospects in Virginia.* 1889. Repr., Williamstown, Mass.: Corner House, 1970.

Burlamaqui, Annabal. *Gymnastica nacional (capoeiragem): Methodisada e regrada.* Rio de Janeiro, 1928.

Burrows, D. "The Human Leopard Society of Sierra Leone." *Journal of the Royal African Society* 13 (January 1914): 143–51.

Butterfield, Fox. *All God's Children: The Bosket Family and the American Tradition of Violence.* New York: Alfred A. Knopf, 1995.

Butterworth, William [Henry Schroeder]. *3 Years Adventures of a Minor in England, Africa, the West Indies, South-Carolina, and Georgia.* 1823. Repr., Leeds: Thomas Inchbold, 1831.

Butt-Thompson, Frederick William. *West African Secret Societies: Their Organisations, Officials and Teaching.* London: H. F. & G. Witherby, 1929.

Cadornega, António de Oliveira de. *História geral das guerras angolanas.* 3 vols. Lisboa: Agência-Geral das Colónias, Divisão de Publicaçoes e Biblioteca, 1940–42.

Cally-Lézin, Sully. *Musiques et danses Afro-Caraîbes: Martinique.* Gros Morne: Sully-Cally/Lézin, 1990.

Caltanisetta, Luca da. *Diaire congolais, 1690–1701.* Ed. François Bontinck. Louvain: Éditions Nauwelaerts, 1970.

Campbell, Edward D. C., and Kym Rice. *Before Freedom Came: African-American Life in the Antebellum South.* Charlottesville: University Press of Virginia, 1991.

Carneiro, Edison. *Negros Bantus: Notas de ethnographia religiosa e de folk-lore.* Rio de Janeiro: Civilização brasileira s.a., 1937.

———. *A sabedoria popular.* Rio de Janeiro: Ministério da Educacão e Cultura Instituto Nacional do Livro, 1957.

Carney, Judith A. *Black Rice.* Cambridge, Mass.: Harvard University Press, 2001.

Carretta, Vincent. "Olaudah Equiano or Gustavua Vassa? New Light on an Eighteenth Century Question of Identity." *Slavery and Abolition* 20, no. 3 (1999): 96–104.

Cascudo, Luis da Camara. *Folclore do Brasil.* Rio de Janeiro: Editôra Fundo de Cultura, 1967.

Catterall, Hellen. *Judicial Cases Concerning American Slavery and the Negro.* 2 vols. New York: Octagon Books, 1968.

Cavazzi de Montecúccolo, Giovanni Antonio. *Descrição histórica dos três reinos do Congo, Matamba e Angola.* 2 vols. Ed. and trans. Graziano de Leguzzano. Lisboa: Junta de Investigações do Ultramar, 1965.

Chambers, Douglas Brent. "The Significance of Igbo in the Bight of Biafra Slave-Trade: A Rejoinder to Northrup's 'Myth Igbo.'" *Slavery & Abolition* 23 (April 2002): 101–20.

Chauleau, Liliane. *La vie quotidienne aux antilles françaises au temps de Victor Schoelcher: XIXe siècle.* Paris: Hachette littérature, 1979.

Childs, Gladwyn Murray. *Umbundu Kinship & Character: Being a Description of Social Structure and Individual Development of the Ovimbundu of Angola, with Observations*

Concerning the Bearing on the Enterprise of Christian Missions of Certain Phases of the Life and Culture Described. London: Published for the International African Institute by Oxford University Press, 1949.

Chinea, Jorge. "A Quest for Freedom: The Immigration of Maritime Maroons in Puerto Rico, 1656–1800." *Journal of Caribbean History* 31, nos. 1 & 2 (1997): 51–87.

Chireau, Yvonne Patricia. *Black Magic: Religion and the African American Conjuring Tradition.* Berkeley: University of California Press, 2003.

Christopher, Emma. "Another Head of the Hydra?: Slave Trade Sailors and Militancy on the African Coast." *Atlantic Studies* 1 (October 2004): 145–57.

Chvaicer, Maya Talmon. "The Criminalization of *Capoeira* in Nineteenth Century Brazil." *Hispanic American Historical Review* 82 (August 2002): 525–47.

Clarence-Smith, W. G. "Capitalist Penetration among the Nyaneka of Southern Angola, 1760s to 1920s." *African Studies* 37, no. 2 (1978): 163–76.

———. "Runaway Slaves and Social Bandits in Southern Angola, 1875–1913." In *Out of the House of Bondage: Runaways, Resistance and Maroonage in Africa and the New World.* Ed. Gad Heuman, 23–33. London: F. Cass, 1986.

———. *Slaves, Peasants, and Capitalists in Southern Angola, 1840–1926.* Cambridge: Cambridge University Press, 1979.

Cole, Herbert M. *Mbari, Art and Life among the Owerri Igbo.* Bloomington: Indiana University Press, 1982.

Collecção das Leis do Império do Brazil em 1831. Rio de Janeiro: Typ. Nacional, 1875.

Cosme, Leonel. "A expansão ultramarina Portuguesa no contexto do colonialísmo Europeu." *Boletim da Câmara Municipal de Sá de Bandeira* 38 (October 1974–March 1975).

Courlander, Harold. *The Drum and the Hoe: Life and Lore of the Haitian People.* Berkeley: University of California Press, 1960.

———. *A Treasury of American Folklore.* New York: Crown Publishers, 1976.

Coutinho, Daniel. *O ABC da capoeira de Angola: Os manuscritos do Mestre Noronha.* Brasília: Centro de Documentação e Informação Sobre a Capoeira, 1993.

Cowerly, John. *Carnival, Canboulay and Calypso Traditions in the Making.* Cambridge: Cambridge University Press, 1996.

Craft, William. *Running a Thousand Miles for Freedom: Or the Escape of William and Ellen Craft from Slavery.* London: William Tweedle, 1860.

Creel, Margaret Washington. *"A Peculiar People": Slave Religion and Community-Culture among the Gullahs.* New York: New York University Press, 1988.

Crow, Hugh. *Memoirs of the Late Captain Hugh Crow of Liverpool, Comprising a Narrative of His Life Together with Descriptive Sketches of the Western Coast of Africa, Particularly of Bonny, the Manners and Customs of the Inhabitants, the Production of the Soil and the Trade of the Country to Which Are Added Anecdotes and Observations Illustrative of the Negro Character.* 1830. Repr., [London:] F. Cass, 1970.

Cruls, Gastão. *Aparência do Rio de Janeiro.* 2 vols. Rio de Janeiro: J. Olympio, 1965.

Cyrille, Dominique. "Sa Ki Ta Nou (This Belongs to Us): Creole Dances of the French Caribbean." In *Caribbean Dance from Abakuá to Zouk: How Movement Shapes Identity.* Ed. Susanna Sloat. Gainesville: University Press of Florida, 2002.

David, Abbé Bernard. *Les origines de la population Martiniquaise au fil des ans 1635–1902.* Fort-de-France: Mémoires de la Société d'histoire de la Martinique, 1973.

Davis, Wade. *Passage of Darkness: The Ethnobiology of the Haitian Zombie*. Chapel Hill: University of North Carolina Press, 1988.

Dawie, Fourie. *Oshiwambo: Past, Present, and Future*. Windhoek: University of Namibia, 1992.

Dawson, C. Daniel. *Capoeira Angola and Mestre João Grande: The Saga of a Tradition; The Development of a Master.* New York, 1993.

De Almeida, Manuel Antônio. *Memórias de um sargento de milícias*. Rio de Janeiro: Livros Técnicos e Cientificos, 1978.

De Carvalho (Tinop), Pinto. *História do Fado*. Lisbon: Dom Quixote, 1982.

Debien, Gabriel. "Assemblées nocturnes d'esclaves á Saint-Domingue (La Marmelade, 1786)." *Annales Historiques de la Révolution* 44 (1972): 273–84.

———. *Les esclaves aux Antilles Françaises, xvIIe–xvIIIe siècles*. Basse-Terre: Société d'histoire de la Guadeloupe, 1974.

Debret, Jean-Baptiste. *Voyage pittoeresque et historique au Brésil, ou séjour d'un artiste francais au Brésil dépuis 1816 jusqu'en 1831 inclusivement*. Paris: Firmin Didot Frères, 1834.

Delgado, Ralph. *Ao sul do Cuanza: Ocupação e aproveitamento do antigo reino de Benguela*. Lisboa, 1944.

———. *História de Angola*. Benguela: Edição da Tip. do Jornal de Benguela, 1970.

Denbow, James. "Heart and Soul: Glimpses of Ideology and Cosmology in the Iconography of Tombstones from the Loango Coast of Central Africa." *Journal of American Folklore* 112, no. 445 (1999): 404–23.

Deren, Maya. *Divine Horsemen: The Living Gods of Haiti*. London and New York Thames and Hudson, 1953.

Dessalles, Pierre-François-Régis. *Annales du conseil souverain de la Martinique, ou tableau historique du gouvernement de cette colonie, depuis son premier établissement jusqu'à à nos jours*. 2 vols. 1786. Repr., Paris: A Bergerac, Chez J. B. Puynesge, 1977.

Dike, K. Onwuka, and Felicia Ifeoma Ekejiuba. *The Aro of South-Eastern Nigeria, 1650–1980: A Study of Socio-Economic Formation and Transformation in Nigeria*. Ibadan: University Press, 1990.

Djian, Tony, Jacques Sabatier, and Daniel Rouche, eds. *L'historial Antillais*. Pointe-'a-Pitre: Dajani éditions, 1981.

Douglass, Frederick. *My Bondage and My Freedom*. 1855. Repr., New York: Miller, Orton & Mulligan, 1994.

———. *The Life and Times of Frederick Douglass*. New York: Gramercy Books, 1993.

———. *Narrative of the Life of Frederick Douglass: An American Slave, Written by Himself*. Ed. David W. Blight. Boston: Bedford/St. Martin's, 1993.

Drew, Benjamin. *A North-Side View of Slavery: The Refugee; or, The Narratives of Fugitive Slaves in Canada Related by Themselves; With an Account of the History and Condition of the Colored Population of Upper Canada*. New York: Negro Universities Press, 1968.

Drouin, Bercy de. *De Saint-Domingue: De ses guerres, de ses révolutions, de ses resources, et de moyens a prendre pour y rétabilir la paix et l'industrie*. Paris: Chez Hocquet, 1814.

Du Bois, W. E. B. *Souls of Black Folk*. Ed. Natalie Zemon Davis, Ernest R. May, Lynn Hunt, and David W. Blight. Boston: Bedford/St. Martin's, 1997.

Dubois, Laurent. *Avengers of the New World*. Cambridge, Mass.: Harvard University Press, 2004.

———. *A Colony of Citizens: Revolution & Slave Emancipation in the French Caribbean, 1787–1804*. Chapel Hill: University of North Carolina Press, 2004.

Dubois, Silvia. "Silvia Dubois." In *Black Women in Nineteenth Century American Life*. Ed. Bert James Loewenburg and Ruth Bogin, 39–47. University Park: Pennsylvania State University Press, 1976.

Dugoujon, Abbé. *Lettres sur l'esclavage dans les colonies françaises*. Paris: Pagnerre, 1845.

Edwards, Bryan. *The History, Civil and Commercial, of the British West Indies; With a Continuation to the Present Time*. 5 vols. 1819. Repr., New York: AMS Press, 1966.

Eltis, David, Stephen D. Behrendt, David Richardson, and Herbert S. Klein. *The Trans-Atlantic Slave Trade: A Database on CD-ROM*. Cambridge: Cambridge University Press, 1999.

Epstein, Dena J. *Sinful Tunes and Spirituals: Black Folk Music to the Civil War*. Urbana: University of Illinois Press, 1977.

Equiano, Olaudah. *The Interesting Narrative of the Life of Olaudah Equiano*. Boston: Bedford Books of St. Martin's Press, 1995.

Estermann, Carlos. *The Ethnography of Southwestern Angola: The Non-Bantu Peoples; the Ambo Ethnic Group*. Ed. G. Gibson, vol. 1. New York: Africana Pub. Co., 1976.

———. "La fête de Puberté dans quelques tribus de L'Angola Méridionale." *Portugal in África: Revista de Cultura Missionária* 1 (November/December 1944): 340–55.

Estermann, Carlos. *The Ethnography of Southwestern Angola: The Nyaneka-Nkumbi Ethnic Group*. Ed. G. Gibson. Vol. 2. New York: Africana Pub. Co., 1979.

Falgayrettes-Leveau, Christiane, ed. *Le geste kôngo*. Paris: Musée Dapper, 2002.

Falola, Toyin, ed. *Igbo History and Society: The Essays of Adiele Afigbo*. Trenton, N.J.: Africa World Press, 2005.

Faux, W. *Memorable Days in America: Being a Journal of a Tour to the United States, Principally Undertaken to Ascertain, by Positive Evidence, the Condition and Probable Prospects of British Emigrants; Including Accounts of Mr. Birkbeck's Settlement in Illinois*. 1823. Repr., New York: AMS Press, 1969.

Fick, Carolyn E. *The Making of Haiti: The Saint Domingue Revolution from Below*. Knoxville: University of Tennessee Press, 1990.

Filho, Adolfo Morales de Los Reis. *O Rio de Janeiro imperial*. Rio de Janeiro: A. Noite, 1946.

Filho, Melo Moraes. *Festas e tradições populares do Brasil*. São Paulo: Editora da Universidade de São Paulo, 1979.

Flint, John E. *Nigeria and Ghana*. Englewood Cliffs, N.J.: Prentice-Hall, 1966.

Frevert, Ute. *Men of Honour: A Social and Cultural History of the Duel*. Cambridge, Mass.: Polity Press, 1995.

Fryer, Peter. *Rhythms of Resistance: African Musical Heritage in Brazil*. Middletown, Conn.: Wesleyan University Press, 2000.

G, A. P. D. *Sketches of Portuguese Life, Manners, Costume, and Character*. London: G. B. Whittaker, 1826.

Gadsden, Sam. *An Oral History of Edisto Island: Sam Gadsden Tells the Story*. Goshen, Ind.: Goshen College, 1975.

Gallant, Thomas W. "Honor, Masculinity, and Ritual Knife Fighting in Nineteenth-Century Greece." *American Historical Review* 105, no. 2 (2000): 359–82.

Gaspar, David Barry, and Darlene Clark Hine, eds. *More than Chattel: Black Women and Slavery in the Americas.* Bloomington: Indiana University Press, 1996.

Geggus, David P. "The French Slave Trade: An Overview." *William and Mary Quarterly* 58, no. 1 (2001): 119–38.

———. "Haitian Voodoo in the Eighteenth Century: Language, Culture, Resistance." *Jahrbuch für Geschichte von Staat, Wirtschaft, und Gesellschaft Lateinamerikas* 28 (1991): 21–51.

———. "Sugar and Coffee Cultivation in Saint Domingue and the Shaping of the Slave Labor Force," in *Cultivation and Culture: Labor and the Shaping of Slave Life in the Americas,* ed. Ira Berlin and Phillip Morgan, 79–90. Charlottesville: University Press of Virginia, 1993.

Genovese, Eugene. *Roll, Jordan, Roll: The World the Slaves Made.* New York: Pantheon Books, 1974.

George Tams, *Visit to the Portuguese Possessions in South-Western Africa.* 1845. Repr., New York: Negro University Press, 1969.

Georgia Writers Project. *Drums and Shadows: Survival Studies among the Georgia Coastal Negroes.* Athens: University of Georgia Press, 1940.

Gerstin, Julian. "Tangled Roots: Kalenda and Other Neo-African Dances in the Circum-Caribbean." *New West Indies Guide* 78, nos. 1 & 2 (2004): 5–41.

Gilroy, Paul. *The Black Atlantic: Modernity and Double Consciousness.* Cambridge, Mass.: Harvard University Press, 1993.

Gisler, Antoine. *L'Esclavage aux antilles françaises (17e–19e siècle): Contribution au problème de l'esclavage.* Fribourg: Éditions Universitaires, 1965.

Golding, Louis. *The Bare-Knuckle Breed.* New York: Barnes, 1954.

Gomez, Michael Angelo. *Exchanging Our Country Marks: The Transformation of African Identities in the Colonial and Antebellum South.* Chapel Hill: University of North Carolina Press, 1998.

Goodwine, Marquetta L., ed. *The Legacy of Ibo Landing.* Atlanta, Ga.: Clarity Press, 1998.

Gorn, Elliott J. "'Gouge and Bite, Pull Hair and Scratch': The Social Significance of Fighting in the Southern Backcountry." *American Historical Review* 90 (1985): 18–43.

———. "The Meaning of Prizefighting." In *The New American Sport History: Recent Approaches and Perspectives.* Ed. S. W. Pope, 225–50. Urbana: University of Illinois Press, 1997.

Gorn, Elliott J., and Warren Jay Goldstein. *A Brief History of American Sports.* Urbana: University of Illinois Press, 2004.

Graham, Richard. "Technology and Culture Change: The Development of the 'Berimbau' in Colonial Brazil." *Latin American Music Review* 12, no. 1 (1991): 1–20.

Graham, Sandra Lauderdale. "Honor among Slaves." In *The Faces of Honor: Sex, Shame, and Violence in Colonial Latin America.* Ed. Lyman L. Johnson and Sonya Lipsett-Rivera, 201–28. Albuquerque: University of New Mexico Press, 1998.

Grenada, Carriacou, Petit Martinique: Spice Island of the Caribbean. London: Hansib, 1994.

Gwaltney, John L. *Drylongso: A Self-Portrait of Black America.* New York: New Press, 1993.

Hahner, June E. *Poverty and Politics: The Urban Poor in Brazil, 1870–1920.* Albuquerque: University of New Mexico Press, 1986.

Hall, Douglas. *In Miserable Slavery: Thomas Thistlewood in Jamaica, 1750–86.* London: Macmillan, 1989.

Hall, Gwendolyn Midlo. *Africans in Colonial Louisiana: The Development of Afro-Creole Culture in the Eighteenth Century.* Baton Rouge: Louisiana State University Press, 1992.

———. *Slavery and African Ethnicities in the Americas: Restoring the Links.* Chapel Hill: University of North Carolina Press, 2005.

Hall, N. A. T. "Maritime Maroons: Grand Marronage from the Danish West Indies." *William and Mary Quarterly* 42 (October 1985): 476–98.

Hall, Neville A. T. *Slave Society in the Danish West Indies: St. Thomas, St. John and St. Croix.* Baltimore: Johns Hopkins University Press, 1992.

Harms, Robert W. *The Diligent: A Voyage through the Worlds of the Slave Trade.* New York: Basic Books, 2002.

Hartman, Saidiya V. *Scenes of Subjection: Terror, Slavery, and Self Making in the 19th Century America.* New York: Oxford University Press, 1997.

Hawthorne, Nathaniel. *The Yarn of a Yankee Privateer.* New York: Funk & Wagnalls Company, 1926.

Hearn, Lafcadio. *Two Years in the French West Indies.* New York: Harper & Brothers, 1923.

Henderson, James. *A History of the Brazil: Comprising Its Geography, Commerce, Colonization, Aboriginal Inhabitants, &c.* London: Longman, Hurst, Rees, Orme, and Brown, 1821.

Henderson, Richard. *King in Every Man.* New Haven, Conn.: Yale University Press, 1972.

Henson, Josiah. "Josiah Henson, 1789–1883." In *Slavery in the South: First-Hand Accounts of the Ante-Bellum American South from Northern and Southern Whites, Negroes, and Foreign Observers.* Ed. Harvey Wish, 23–37. New York: Noonday Press, 1968.

Herskovitz, Melville. *Rebel Destiny: Among the Bush Negroes of Dutch Guiana.* New York: McGraw-Hill and Company, Inc., 1934.

Heywood, Linda Marinda. "Portuguese into African: The Eighteenth-Century Central African Background to Atlantic Creole Cultures." In *Central Africans and Cultural Transformations in the American Diaspora.* Ed. Linda M. Heywood, 91–116. Cambridge: Cambridge University Press, 2002.

———, ed. *Central Africans and Cultural Transformations in the American Diaspora.* Cambridge: Cambridge University Press, 2002.

Hill, Donald R. *Calypso, Calaloo.* Gainesville: University Press of Florida, 1993.

———. *The Impact of Migration on the Metropolitan and Fold Society of Carriacou, Grenada.* Vol. 54, pt. 2. New York: American Museum of Natural History, 1977.

Hine, Darlene Clark, and Earnest Jenkins, eds. *A Question of Manhood: A Reader in US Black Men's History and Masculinity.* 3 vols. Bloomington: Indiana University Press, 1999–2001.

Holloway, Joseph E. *Africanisms in American Culture.* Bloomington: Indiana University Press, 1991.

Holloway, Thomas A. "'A Healthy Terror': Police Repression of *Capoeiras* in Nineteenth-Century Rio de Janeiro." *Hispanic American Historical Review* 69, no. 4 (1989): 637–76.

Holloway, Thomas H. *Policing Rio de Janeiro: Repression and Resistance in a 19th-Century City.* Stanford, Calif.: Stanford University Press, 1993.

Huang, Wenshan. *Fundamentals of Tai Chi Ch'uan: An Exposition of Its History, Philosophy, Technique, Practice, and Application.* Hong Kong: South Sky Book Co., 1973.

Isaac, Rhys. *The Transformation of Virginia, 1740–1790.* Chapel Hill: University of North Carolina Press, 1982.

Isichei, Elizabeth Allo. *A History of the Igbo People.* London: Macmillan, 1976.

———. *Igbo Worlds: An Anthology of Oral Histories and Historical Descriptions.* Philadelphia: Institute for the Study of Human Issues, 1978.

Itier, Jules. *Journal d'un voyage en Chine en 1843, 1844, 1845, 1846.* 3 vols. Paris: Dauvin et Fontaine, 1848–53.

Jacobson-Widding, Anita. *Red-White-Black as a Mode of Thought: A Study of Triadic Classification by Colours in the Ritual Symbolism and Cognitive Thought of the Peoples of the Lower Congo.* Stockholm: Uppsala, 1979.

Janzen, John M. *Lemba, 1650–1930: A Drum of Affliction in Africa and the New World.* New York: Garland, 1982.

Jeffreys, M. D. W. "Ibo Warfare." *Man* 56 (June 1956): 77–79.

Joseph, E. L. *Warner Arundel: The Adventures of a Creole.* London: Saunders and Otley, 1837.

Joyner, Charles. "The World of Plantation Slaves." In *Before Freedom Came: African-American Life in the Antebellum South.* Ed. Edward D. C. Campbell and Kym Rice, xv. Charlottesville: University Press of Virginia, 1991.

Kalm, Peter. *Peter Kalm's Travels in North America.* Trans John Forster. Barre, Mass.: Imprint Society, 1972.

Kaplan, Sidney. *The Black Presence in the Era of the American Revolution 1770–1800.* Washington, D.C.: Smithsonian Institution, 1973.

Karasch, Mary C. *Slave Life in Rio de Janeiro, 1808–1850.* Princeton, N.J.: Princeton University Press, 1987.

Kidder, Daniel P., James C. Fletcher, et al. *Brazil and the Brazilians Portrayed in Historical and Descriptive Sketches.* Philadelphia: Childs & Peterson, 1857.

King, Stewart R. *Blue Coat or Powdered Wig: Free People of Color in Pre-Revolutionary Saint Domingue.* Athens: University of Georgia Press, 2001.

Klein, Herbert S. *African Slavery in Latin America and the Caribbean.* New York: Oxford University Press, 1986.

Knight, Ian. *Brave Men's Blood: The Epic of the Zulu War, 1879.* London: Greenhill, 1990.

Kopytoff, Igor. *The African Frontier: The Reproduction of Traditional African Societies.* Bloomington: Indiana University Press, 1987.

Kraay, Hendrik. "Patriotic Mobilization in Brazil: The Zuavos and Other Black Companies." In *I Die with My Country: Perspectives on the Paraguayan War, 1864–1870.* Ed. Hendrik Kraay and Thomas Whigham, 61–80. Lincoln: University of Nebraska Press, 2004.

———. *Angolan Traits in Black Music, Games and Dances of Brazil: A Study of African Cultural Extensions Overseas.* Lisboa: Junta de Investigações Científicas do Ultramar, 1979.

———. "Drum Patterns in the 'Batuque' of Benedito Caxias." *Latin American Music Review* 11, no. 2 (1990): 115–81.

———. *Muziek van de Humbi en de Handa uit Angola.* Tervuren: Musée royal de l'Afrique centrale, 1973.

Kubik, Gerhard, and Moses Yotamu. *The Luchazi People: Their History & Chieftancy, Angola, Congo, Namibia, Zambia.* Lusaka: Central African Oral History Research Project, 1998.

Kuyk, Betty. "The African Derivation of Black Fraternal Orders in the United States." *Comparative Studies in Society and History* 25 (October 1983): 559–92.

———. *African Voices in the African American Heritage.* Bloomington: Indiana University Press, 2003.

Laband, John. *Fight Us in the Open: The Anglo-Zulu War through Zulu Eyes.* Pietermaritzburg: Shuter & Shooter, 1985.

Labat, Jean Baptiste. *Nouveau voyage aux isles de l'Amérique.* 6 vols. (Paris: T. Le Gras, 1722)

Lang, Alphonse, and Constant Tastevin. *La tribu des Va-nyaneka.* Corbeil: Impr. Crété, 1937.

Law, Robin. "Ethnicity and the Slave Trade: 'Lucumi' and 'Nago' as Ethnonyms in West Africa." *History in Africa* 24 (1997): 205–19.

Leti, Geneviève. *Sante et societe esclavagiste a la Martinique: 1802–1848.* Montreal: L'Harmattan, Inc., 1998.

Levine, Lawrence. *Black Culture and Black Consciousness: Afro-American Folk Thought from Slavery to Freedom.* New York: Oxford University Press, 1977.

Lewis, J. Lowell. *Ring of Liberation: Deceptive Discourse in Brazilian Capoeira.* Chicago: University of Chicago Press, 1992.

Lewis-Warner, Maureen. *Guinea's Other Suns: The African Dynamic in Trinidad Culture.* Dover, Mass.: Majority Press, 1991.

Ligon, Richard. *A true & exact history of the island of Barbados illustrated with a mapp of the island, as also the principall trees and plants there, set forth in their due proportions and shapes, drawne out by their severall and respective scales: Together with the ingenio that makes the sugar, with the plots of the severall houses, roomes, and other places that are used in the whole processe of sugar-making.* London: Humphrey Moseley, 1657.

Linebaugh, Peter, and Marcus Buford Rediker. *The Many-Headed Hydra: Sailors, Slaves, Commoners, and the Hidden History of the Revolutionary Atlantic.* Boston: Beacon Press, 2000.

Link, Heinrich Friedrich. *Travels in Portugal, and through France and Spain: With a Dissertation on the Literature of Portugal, and the Spanish and Portugueze Languages.* Trans J. Hinckley. London: T. N. Longman and O. Rees, 1801.

Littlefield, Daniel. *Rice and Slaves: Ethnicity and the Slave Trade in Colonial South Carolina.* Urbana: University of Illinois Press, 1981.

Liverpool, Hollis ("Chalkdust"). *Rituals of Power and Rebellion: The Carnival Tradition in Trinidad and Tobago, 1763–1962.* Chicago: Research Associates School Times Publications, 2001.

Loeb, Edwin M. *In Feudal Africa.* Bloomington: Indiana University Research Center in Anthropology Folklore and Linguistics, 1962.

Loguen, Jermain Wesley. *The Rev. J. W. Loguen as a Slave and as a Freedman.* Syracuse: J. G. K. Truair & Co., 1859.

Longin, Félix. *Voyage à la Guadeloupe.* Le Mans: Mannoyer, 1848.

Lovejoy, Paul E., and David Vincent Trotman. *Trans-Atlantic Dimensions of Ethnicity in the African Diaspora*. London and New York: Continuum, 2003.

Lucca, Lorenzo da. *Relations sur le Congo du père Laurent de Lucques, 1700–1717*. Ed. and trans. J. Cuvelier. Brussels: Institut Royal Colonial Belge, 1953.

MacGaffey, Wyatt. *Astonishment and Power.* Washington, D.C.: Published for the National Museum of African Art by the Smithsonian Institution Press, 1993.

———. *Kongo Political Culture: The Conceptual Challenge of the Particular.* Bloomington: Indiana University Press, 2000.

———. *Religion and Society in Central Africa: The Bakongo of Lower Zaire*. Chicago: University of Chicago Press, 1986.

Manfredi, Victor. "Philological Perspectives on the Southeastern Nigeria Diaspora." *Contours* 2, no. 2 (2004): 239–86.

McAlister, Elizabeth A. *Rara!: Vodou, Power, and Performance in Haiti and Its Diaspora*. Berkeley: University of California Press, 2002.

McCall, John C. *Dancing Histories: Heuristic Ethnography with the Ohafia Igbo*. Ann Arbor: University of Michigan Press, 2000.

Meek, C. K. *Law and Authority in a Nigerian Tribe*. New York: Barnes & Noble, 1970.

Mellon, James, ed. *Bullwhip Days: The Slaves Remember, an Oral History.* New York: Weidenfeld & Nicolson, 1988.

Mercier, Paul. *Les pêcheurs Lebou du Sénégal: Particularisme et evolution*. Amsterdam: Swets & Zeitlinger, 1970.

Métraux, Alfred. *Voodoo in Haiti*. Trans. Hugo Charteris. New York: Schocken Books, 1972.

Michalon, Josy. *Le Ladjia: Origine et pratiques*. Paris: Editions caribéennes, 1987.

Miers, Suzanne, and Igor Kopytoff, eds. *Slavery in Africa: Historical and Anthropological Perspectives*. Madison: University of Wisconsin Press, 1977.

Miller, Ivor L. "The Formation of African Identities in the Americas: Spiritual 'Ethnicity.'" *Contours* 2, no. 2 (2004): 193–202.

Miller, Joseph C. *Kings and Kinsmen: Early Mbundu States in Angola*. Oxford: Clarendon Press, 1976.

———. "Requiem for the Jaga." *Cahiers d' études Africaines* 13 (1973): 121–49.

———. "Retention, Re-Invention, and Remembering: Restoring Identities through Enslavement in Angola and under Slavery in Brazil." In *Enslaving Connections: Changing Cultures of Africa and Brazil during the Era of Slavery.* Ed. José C. Curto and Paul E. Lovejoy. Amherst, Mass.: Humanity Books, 2004.

———. *Way of Death: Merchant Capitalism and the Angolan Slave Trade, 1730–1830*. Madison: University of Wisconsin Press, 1988.

Moitt, Bernard. "In the Shadow of the Plantation: Women of Color and the *Libres de fait* of Martinique and Guadeloupe, 1685–1848." In *More than Chattel: Black Women and Slavery in the Americas*. Ed. David Barry Gaspar and Darlene Clark Hine, 37–59. Bloomington: Indiana University Press, 1996.

———. *Women and Slavery in the French Antilles, 1635–1848*. Bloomington: Indiana University Press, 2001.

Möller, Peter August. *Journey in Africa through Angola, Ovampoland and Damaraland.* Trans Ione and Jalmar Rudner. Cape Town: C. Struik, 1974.

Moreau de Saint-Méry, M. L. E. *De la Danse*. Parme: Bodoni, 1801.

Moreau de Saint-Méry, M. L. E., Blanche Maurel, and Etienne Taillemite, eds. *Description topographique, physique, civile, politique et historique de la partie française de l'isle Saint Domingue.* 3 vols. Paris: Société de l'histoire des colonies françaises, 1958.

Morgan, Philip D. *Slave Counterpoint: Black Culture in the Eighteenth-Century Chesapeake & Lowcountry.* Williamsburg: North Carolina Press, 1998.

Moultrie, William. *Memoirs of the American Revolution, so far as it related to the states of North and South Carolina, and Georgia compiled from the most authentic materials, the author's personal knowledge of the various events, and including an epistolary correspondence on public affairs, with civil and military officers, at that period.* 2. vols. New York: David Longworth, 1802.

Moura, Jair. *A luta regional Baiana.* Salvador: Divisão de Folclore, Departamento de Assuntos Culturais, Secretaria Municipal de Educação e Cultura, Prefeitura Municipal do Salvador, 1979.

Munford, Clarence J. *The Black Ordeal of Slavery and Slave Trading in the French West Indies, 1625–1715.* Vol. 3. Lewiston/Queenston/Lampeter: Edwin Mellon Press.

Murphy, Lawrence R. *The Slave Narratives of Texas.* Austin, Tex.: Encino Press, 1974.

Naipaul, Vidiadhar Surajprasad. *The Middle Passage: Impressions of Five Societies—British, French, and Dutch—in the West Indies and South America.* New York: Vintage Books, 1981.

Neves e Sousa, Albano. *Da Minha África e do Brasil que eu vi.* Luanda, n.d.

Nina Rodrigues, Raymundo, and Homero Pires. *Os africanos no Brasil.* São Paulo: Companhia Editora Nacional, 1945.

Nisbett, Richard E., and Dov Cohen. *Culture of Honor: The Psychology of Violence in the South.* Boulder, Colo.: Westview Press, 1996.

Nogueira, A. F. *A Raça Negra: Sob o ponto de vista da Civilisacão da Africa; Usos e costumes de alguns povos gentîlicos do interior de Mossamedes e as colonias portuguezas.* Lisbon: Typ. Nova Minerva, 1880.

Northrup, David. "Igbo and Myth Igbo: Culture and Ethnicity in the Atlantic World, 1600–1850." *Slavery and Abolition* 21, no. 3 (2000): 1–20.

———. *Trade without Rulers: Pre-Colonial Economic Development in South-Eastern Nigeria.* Oxford: Clarendon Press, 1978.

Nwabueze, Emeka. "The Masquerade as Hero in Igbo Traditional Society." *Frankfurter Afrikanistische Blätter* 1 (1989): 95–107.

Oliveira, Valdemar de. *Frevo, capoeira e "passo."* Recife: Companhia Editôra de Pernambuco, 1971.

Olmsted, Frederick Law. *A Journey in the Seaboard Slave States with Remarks on Their Economy.* New York: Dix & Edwards, 1856.

Olwell, Robert. "Loose, Idle and Disorderly: Slave Women in the Eighteenth Century Charleston Marketplace." In *More than Chattel: Black Women and Slavery in the Americas.* Ed. David B. Gaspar and Darlene Clark Hine, 97–110. Bloomington: Indiana University Press, 1996.

Onwuejeogwu, M. Angulu. *An Igbo Civilization: Nri Kingdom & Hegemony.* London: Ethnographica; Benin City, Nigeria: Ethiope, 1981.

Ortiz, Fernando. *Los instrumentos de la musica Afrocubana.* Vol. 4. Havana: Cardenas y Cia, 1954.

Osofsky, Gilbert, ed. *Puttin' On Ole Massa: The Slave Narratives of Henry Bibb, William Wells Brown and Solomon Northrup*. New York: Harper & Row, 1969.

Ott, Thomas O. *The Haitian Revolution, 1789–1804*. Knoxville: University of Tennessee Press, 1973.

Ottenberg, Simon. *Boyhood Rituals in an African Society: An Interpretation*. Seattle: University of Washington Press, 1989.

Owen, W. F., and Heaton Bowstead Robinson, eds. *Narrative of Voyages to Explore the Shores of Africa, Arabia, and Madagascar.* 2 vols. New York: J. & J. Harper, 1833.

Pais, José Machado. *A prostituição e a Lisboa boémia do séc. XIX aos inícios do séc. XX*. Lisbon: Querco, 1985.

Parish, Lydia. *Slave Songs of the Georgia Sea Islands*. Hatboro, Pa.: Folklore Associates, 1965.

Parkinson, Wenda. *This Gilded African: Toussaint L'Ouverture*. London and New York: Quartet Books, 1978.

Paton, Diana. "Punishment, Crime, and the Bodies of Slaves in Eighteenth-Century Jamaica." *Journal of Social History* 34, no. 4 (2001): 923–54.

Patterson, Orlando. *Freedom in the Making of Western Culture*. New York: Basic Books, 1991.

———. *Slavery and Social Death: A Comparative Study*. Cambridge, Mass.: Harvard University Press, 1982.

Pearson, Edward A. *Designs against Charleston: The Trial Record of the Denmark Vessey Slave Conspiracy of 1822*. Chapel Hill: University of North Carolina Press, 1999.

Perdue, Charles L. Jr., Thomas E. Barden, and Robert K. Phillips, eds. *Weevils in the Wheat: Interviews with Virginia Ex-Slaves*. Bloomington: Indiana University Press, 1980.

Peytraud, Lucien Pierre. *L'Esclavage aux antilles françaises avant 1789, d'après des documents inédits des Archives Coloniales*. Paris: Hachette et cie, 1897.

Piersen, William Dillon. *Black Legacy: America's Hidden Heritage*. Amherst: University of Massachusetts Press, 1993.

———. *Black Yankees: The Development of an Afro-American Subculture in Eighteenth-Century New England*. Amherst: University of Massachusetts Press, 1988.

Pigafetta, Filippo. *A Report of the Kingdom of Congo and of the Surrounding Countries: Drawn Out of the Writings and Discoveries of the Portuguese, Duarte Lopez*. Trans Margarite Hutchinson. London: F. Cass, 1969.

Portsmouth Public Library. *Readings in Black and White: Lower Tidewater Virginia*. Portsmouth,Va.: by the author, 1993.

Prado, Almeida. *Tomas Ender: Pintor austriáco na côrte de D. João V.I. no Rio de Janeiro, um episódio da formação da classe dirigente brasileira 1817/1818*. São Paulo: Companhia Editôra Nacional, 1955.

Price, Richard. *Maroon Societies: Rebel Slave Communities in the Americas*. 2nd ed. Baltimore: Johns Hopkins University Press, 1979.

Querino, Manuel Raymundo. *Bahia de Outrora: Vultos e factos populares*. Bahia: Livraria Economica, 1916.

———. *Costumes africanos no Brasil*. Rio de Janeiro: Civilização brasileira s.a., 1938.

Quevedo, Raymond (Atilla the Hun). *Atilla's Kaiso: A Short History of Trinidad Calypso*. St. Augustine: University of the West Indies, 1983.

Ramassamy, Diana. *Guide de la veillée mortuaire*. Petit-Bourg: Ibis Rouge, 2002.

Ravenstein, Ernest George. *The Strange Adventures of Andrew Battell, of Leigh, in Angola and the Adjoining Regions*. 1901. Repr., Nendeln: Liechtenstein Kraus Reprint, 1967.

Rawick, George P. *The American Slave: A Composite Autobiography*, 19 vols. Westport, Conn.: Greenwood Press, 1972.

Reed, Philip, and Richard Muggeridge. *Boxe Française, Savate: Martial Art of France*. London: P. H. Crompton, 1975.

Reefe, Thomas Q. *The Rainbow and the Kings: A History of the Luba Empire to 1891*. Berkeley: University of California Press, 1981.

Rego, Waldeloir. *Capoeira Angola Ensaio Sócio-Etnográfico*. Rio de Janeiro: Gráf. Lux, 1968.

Reis, João José. "Batuque: African Drumming and Dance between Repression and Concession, Bahia, 1808–1855." *Bulletin of Latin American Research* 24, no. 2 (2005): 201–14.

———. "'The Revolution of the Ganhadores': Urban Labour, Ethnicity and the African Strike of 1857 in Bahia, Brazil." *Journal of Latin American Studies* 29 (May 1997): 355–93.

———. *Slave Rebellion in Brazil: The Muslim Uprising of 1835 in Bahia*. Trans Arthur Brakel. Baltimore: Johns Hopkins University Press, 1993.

Ribeiro, Fernando Bastos. *Crônicas da polícia e da vida do Rio de Janeiro*. Rio de Janeiro: Departamento de Imprensa Nacional, 1958.

Ribeyrolles, Charles. *Brasil pitoresco: História, descrições-viagens-colonização instituições*. São Paulo: Livraria Martins, 1941.

Rio, João do. *A Alma Encantadora das Ruas*. Rio de Janeiro: H. Garnier, 1910.

Roberts, John Storm. *Black Music of Two Worlds*. New York: Praeger, 1972.

Ruel, Malcom. *Leopards and Leaders: Constitutional Politics among a Cross River People*. New York: Tavistock Publications, 1969.

Rufz, E. *Chronologie des maladies de la ville de Saint-Pierre (Martinique) depuis l'année 1837 jusqu'à l'année 1856*. Paris: Baillière, 1869.

———. *Recherches sur les empoisonnemens pratiqués par les nègres a la Martinique*. Paris: J.-B. Baillière, 1844.

Rugendas, Johann Moritz. *Viagem Pitoresca através do Brasil*. Trans Sérgio Milliet. São Paulo: Livraria Martins, 1940.

Russell-Wood, A. J. R. "Black and Mulatto Brotherhoods in Colonial Brazil: A Study in Collective Behavior." *Hispanic American Historical Review* 54 (1974): 567–602.

Salamone, Frank A. "Gungawa Wrestling as an Ethnic Boundary Marker." *Afrika und Übersee* 57, no. 3 (1973–74): 193–202.

Sanoja, Eduardo. *Juego de garrote larense: El método venezolano de defensa personal*. Caracas: Federación Nacional de la Cultura Popular, 1984.

Schneider, John T. *Dictionary of African Borrowings in Brazilian Portuguese*. Hamburg: Buske, 1991.

Schuler, Monica. *"Alas, Alas, Kongo": A Social History of Indentured African Immigration into Jamaica, 1841–1865*. Baltimore: Johns Hopkins University Press, 1980.

———. "Liberated Central Africans in Nineteenth-Century Guyana." In *Central Africans and Cultural Transformations*. Ed. L. Heywood, 319–52. Cambridge: Cambridge University Press, 2002.

Schwartz, Phillip J. *Twice Condemned: Slaves and the Criminal Laws of Virginia, 1705–1865*. Union, N.J.: Lawbook Exchange, 1988.

Schwartz, Stuart B. *Slaves, Peasants, and Rebels*. Urbana: University of Illinois Press, 1992.

Serpa Pinto, Alexandre Alberto da Rocha de. *How I Crossed Africa: From the Atlantic to the Indian Ocean, through Unknown Countries; Discovery of the Great Zambesi Affluents, &c.* 2 vols. London: Sampson Low, Marsten, Searle, & Rivington, 1881.

Shaw, Thurstan. *Igbo-Ukwu: An Account of Archaeological Discoveries in Eastern Nigeria*. Evanston, Ill.: Northwestern University Press, 1970.

Shepherd, Verene. *Slavery without Sugar: Diversity in Caribbean Economy and Society since the 17th century*. Gainesville: University Press of Florida, 2002.

Silva Porto, António Francisco Ferreira da. *Viagens e apontamentos de um portuense em África*. Lisboa: Divisão de Publicações e Biblioteca, Agência Geral das Colónias, 1942.

Simmel, Georg. *The Sociology of Georg Simmel*. Trans Kurt Wolff. Glencoe, Ill.: Free Press, 1950.

Slenes, Robert W. *"Malungu, Ngoma vem!" África encoberta e descoberta no Brasil*. Luanda: Ministério da Cultura, 1995.

Smith, Robert Sydney, Toyin Falola, and Robin Law, eds. *Warfare and Diplomacy in Pre-Colonial Nigeria: Essays in Honor of Robert Smith*. Madison: African Studies Program, University of Wisconsin at Madison, 1992.

Smith, William. *A New Voyage to Guinea*. London: Frank Cass & Co. Ltd., 1967.

Soares, Carlos Eugênio Líbano. *A capoeira escrava e outras tradições rebeldes no Rio de Janeiro, 1808–1850*. Campinas: Editora da UNICAMP CECULT, 2001.

———. *A Negregada Instituição: Os capoeiras no Rio de Janeiro*. Rio de Janeiro: Prefeitura da Cidade do Rio de Janeiro, Secretaria Municipal de Cultura, Departamento Geral de Documentação e Informação Cultural Divisão de Editoração, 1994.

———. *Zungú: Rumor de muitas vozes*. Rio de Janeiro: Arquivo Publico de Rio de Janeiro, 1998.

Spierenburg, Petrus Cornelis. *Men and Violence: Gender, Honor, and Rituals in Modern Europe and America*. Columbus: Ohio State University Press, 1998.

Stedman, John Gabriel. *Stedman's Surinam: Life in an Eighteenth-Century Slave Society*. Baltimore: Johns Hopkins University Press, 1992.

Austin Steward. *Twenty-Two Years a Slave and Forty Years a Freeman*. New York, 1968 [1857].

Stewart, Frank Henderson. *Honor*. Chicago: University of Chicago Press, 1994.

Stuckey, Sterling. *Slave Culture*. New York: Oxford University Press, 1987.

Sweet, James H. *Recreating Africa: Culture, Kinship, and Religion in the African-Portuguese World, 1441–1770*. Chapel Hill: University of North Carolina Press, 2003.

Talbot, Percy Amaury. *The Peoples of Southern Nigeria: A Sketch of Their History, Ethnology and Languages, with an Abstract of the 1921 Census*. London: F. Cass, 1969.

———. *Tribes of the Niger Delta*. London: Barnes & Noble, 1967.

Taylor, Yuval, ed. *I Was Born a Slave*. Edinburgh: Payback Press, 1999.

Thésee, Françoise. *Les Ibos de l'Amélie: Destinée d' une cargaison de la traite clandestine à la Martinique 1822–1838*. Paris: Editions Caribéenees, 1986.

Thompson, Robert Farris. *Flash of the Spirit: African and Afro-American Art and Philosophy*. New York: Random House, 1983.

Thornton, John K. "African Dimension of the Stono Rebellion." *American Historical Review* 96, no. 4 (1991): 1101–13.

———. "African Soldiers in the Haitian Revolution." *Journal of Caribbean History* 25, nos. 1 & 2 (1991): 58–80.

———. "The Art of War in Angola, 1575–1680." *Comparative Studies in Society and History* 30, no. 2 (1988): 360–78.

———. "Cannibals, Witches, and Slave Traders in the Atlantic World." *William and Mary Quarterly* 60, no. 2 (2003): 1–16.

———. "'I Am the Subject of the King of Congo': African Political Ideology and the Haitian Revolution." *Journal of World History* 4, no. 2 (1993): 181–214.

———. "Religious and Ceremonial Life in the Kongo and Mbundu Area, 1500–1700." In *Central Africans and Cultural Transformations*. Ed. L. Heywood, 71–90. Cambridge: Cambridge University Press, 2002.

———. *Warfare in Atlantic Africa, 1500–1800*. London: UCL Press, 1999.

Tinhorão, José Ramos. *Fado, dança do Brasil, cantar de Lisboa: O fim de um mito*. Lisboa: Editorial Caminho, 1994.

Tomich, Dale W. *Slavery in the Circuit of Sugar: Martinique and the Wold Economy, 1830–1848*. Baltimore: Johns Hopkins University Press, 1990.

Tonjes, Herman. *Ovamboland: Country, People, Mission*. Trans Peter Reiner. 1911. Repr., Windhoek: Namibia Scientific Society, 1996.

Torres, Manuel Júlio de Mendonça. *O distrito de Moçâmedes nas fases da origem e da primeira organização, 1485–1859*. Lisboa: Divisão de Publicações e Biblioteca, Agência Geral das Colónias, 1950.

Trochim, Michael R. "The Brazilian Black Guard: Racial Conflict in Post-Abolition Brazil." *Americas* 44, no. 3 (1988): 285–301.

Trotman, David Vincent. *Crime in Trinidad: Conflict and Control in a Plantation Society 1838–1900*. Knoxville: University of Tennessee Press, 1986.

Tyler, Ronnie C., and Lawrence R. Murphy. *The Slave Narratives of Texas*. Austin, Tex.: Encino Press, 1974.

Uchendu, Victor Chikezie. *The Igbo of Southeast Nigeria*. New York: Holt, Rinehart and Winston, 1965.

Umeasiegbu, Rems Nna. *The Way We Lived: Ibo Customs and Stories*. London: Heinemann Educational, 1969.

Uri, Alex and François. *Musiques & musiciens de la Guadeloupe: Le chant de Karukéra*. Paris: Con brio, 1991.

Urquhart, Alvin W. *Patterns of Settlement and Subsistence in Southwestern Angola*. Washington, D.C.: National Academy of Sciences–National Research Council, 1963.

Vanhee, Hein. "Central African Popular Christianity and the Making of Haitian Vodou Religion." In *Central Africans and Cultural Transformations in the American Diaspora*. Ed. L. Heywood, 243–64. Cambridge: Cambridge University Press, 2002.

Vansina, Jan. *How Societies Are Born: Governance in West Central Africa before 1600*. Charlottesville: University Press of Virginia, 2004.

———. *Paths in the Rainforests: Toward a History of Political Tradition in Equatorial Africa*. Madison: University of Wisconsin Press, 1990.

Vianna, Antônio. *Casos e coisas da Bahia*. Salvador: Museu do Estado, 1950.

Vlach, John Michael. *The Afro-American Tradition in Decorative Arts*. Athens: University of Georgia Press, 1990.

Washington Creel, Margaret. *"A Peculiar People": Slave Religion and Community-Culture among the Gullahs.* New York: New York University Press, 1988.

Watson, John F. *Annals of Philadelphia, being a collection of memoirs, anecdotes, & incidents of the city and its inhabitants, from the days of the Pilgrim founders: To which is added an appendix, containing olden time researches and reminiscences of New York City.* Philadelphia: E. L. Carey & A. Hart, 1830.

Wax, Darold D. "Preferences for Slaves in Colonial America." *Journal of Negro History* 58, no. 4 (1973): 371–401.

Weeks, John H. *Among the Primitive Bakongo: A Record of Thirty Years' Close Intercourse with the Bakongo and Other Tribes of Equatorial Africa.* London: Seeley, Service & Co., 1914.

Wetherell, James. *Brazil: Stray Notes from Bahai.* Liverpool: Webb and Hunt, 1860.

Wheeler, Everett L. "*Hoplomachia* and Greek Dances in Arms." *Greek, Roman and Byzantine Studies* 23 (1982): 223–33.

White, Shane, and Graham White. *Stylin': African American Expressive Culture from Its Beginnings to the Zoot Suit.* Ithaca, N.Y.: Cornell University Press, 1998.

Wiggins, David. "Leisure Time on the Southern Plantation: The Slaves' Respite from Constant Toil 1810–1860." In *Sport in America.* Ed. Donald Spivey, 25–50. Westport, Conn.: Greenwood Press, 1985.

Wilder, Craig Steven. *In the Company of Black Men: The African Influence on African American Culture in New York City.* New York and London: New York University Press, 2001.

Williams, Frieda Nela. *Precolonial Communities of Southwestern Africa: A History of Ovambo Kingdoms 1600–1920.* 1991. Repr., Windhoek: National Archives of Namibia, 1994.

Willis, John C. "From the Dictates of Pride to the Paths of Righteousness: Slave Honor and Christianity in Antebellum Virginia." In *The Edge of the South: Life in Nineteenth-Century Virginia.* Ed. Edward L. Ayers and John C. Willis, 37–55. Charlottesville: University Press of Virginia, 1991.

Wood, Peter H. *Black Majority: Negroes in Colonial South Carolina from 1670 through the Stono Rebellion.* New York: W. W. Norton & Company, 1975.

Wunenberger, Charles. "La mission et le royaume de Cunène sur les bords de Cunène." *Les Missions Catholiques* 20 (1888): 224–72.

Wyatt-Brown, Bertram. *Southern Honor: Ethics and Behavior in the Old South.* New York: Oxford University Press, 1982.

Young, Everild, and Kjeld Helweg-Larsen. *The Pirates' Priest: The Life of Père Labat in the West Indies, 1693–1705.* [London:] Jarrolds, 1965.

Zobel, Joseph. *Laghia de la mort: Nouvelles Antillaises.* Fort-de-France: Impr. A. Bezaudin, 1946.

Index

About the Author

T. J. Desch-Obi received his doctorate in African history from the University of California, Los Angeles. His research focuses on historical ethnography, which he explores through the lens of African and African diaspora martial arts. He is currently an assistant professor of African and African diaspora history at the City University of New York's Baruch College.